WA AND THE WALA

AFRICAN STUDIES SERIES 63

GENERAL EDITOR
J. M. Lonsdale, *Lecturer in History and Fellow of Trinity College, Cambridge*

ADVISORY EDITORS
J. D. Y. Peel, *Charles Booth Professor of Sociology, University of Liverpool*
John Sender, *Faculty of Economics and Fellow of Wolfson College, Cambridge*

Published in collaboration with
The African Studies Centre, Cambridge

A list of books in this series will be found at the end of the volume.

WA AND THE WALA

Islam and polity in northwestern Ghana

IVOR WILKS
Department of History
Northwestern University

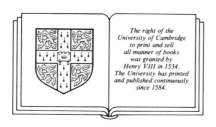

The right of the
University of Cambridge
to print and sell
all manner of books
was granted by
Henry VIII in 1534.
The University has printed
and published continuously
since 1584.

CAMBRIDGE UNIVERSITY PRESS
CAMBRIDGE
NEW YORK   NEW ROCHELLE   MELBOURNE   SYDNEY

Published by the Press Syndicate of the University of Cambridge
The Pitt Building, Trumpington Street, Cambridge CB2 1RP
32 East 57th Street, New York, NY 10022, USA
10 Stamford Road, Oakleigh, Melbourne 3166, Australia

First published 1989

Printed in Great Britain at the University Press, Cambridge

British Library cataloguing in publication data

Wilks, Ivor
Wa and the Wala: Islam and polity in North-western Ghana. – (African studies series,
ISSN 0065–406X; 63).
1. Ghana. Wala. Cultural processes
I. Title   II. Series
305.8′9667

Library of Congress cataloguing in publication data

Wilks, Ivor
Wa and the Wala: Islam and polity in North-western Ghana. – Ivor Wilks
        p.   cm. – (African studies series: 63)
Bibliography.
Includes index.
ISBN 0-521-36210-5
1. Wa (Ghana) – Politics and government.   2. Islam and state –
Ghana.   3. Wala – Ghana – Wa – Politics and government.   I. Title.
II. Series
DT512.9.W3W55 1989
966.7–dc19

ISBN 0 521 36210 5

US

To the Amanor-Wilks family

Contents

List of illustrations	*page* x	
List of tables	xii	
Preface	xiii	
List of abbreviations	xvi	

Preamble 1

1 Wa and the Wala

Introduction	5
The Wala polity	8
Who are the Wala?	13
Tendaanlun and *nalun* in Wala	17
The Wa Nam	21
The Muslim community	24

2 Wala origins: *Lasiri* and *Kubaru*

Introduction	29
Wala origins: a Tendaanba account	32
Wala origins: a Muslim account	35
Wala origins: a Nabihi account	36
Wala origins: ambiguities and contradictions	40

3 Wala origins: the 'alim as local historian

Introduction	47
The 'First Tribe' in Wala	49
The 'Second Tribe' in Wala	51
The 'Third Tribe' in Wala: the Old Muslims	53
The second group of Muslims: the scholars	59
The third group of Muslims: the Hausa	62

Contents

4   Wa chronology: an exercise in date-guessing

Introduction   64
The Limams of Wa: family reconstitution   64
The Wa limamate: rules of succession   69
Chronology of the Wa limamate: nineteenth and twentieth
centuries   74
Chronology of the Wa limamate before the nineteenth century   78
Wa chronology: the Wa Nam   80
Early Wala: the regional setting   85

5   *Tajdid* and *jihad*: the Muslim community in change

Introduction   91
Learning in Wa: *mujaddidun* and others   93
Wala and the Karantaw: the roots of faction   100
Wala and the Zabarima intrusion   103
Dondoli and Dzedzedeyiri: the politics of confrontation   108
Slaves and salvation: unbelievers as captives   112

6   Colonial intrusions: Wala in disarray

Introduction   116
New intruders: British, French and Samorians   118
The Samorian ascendancy in Wala   121
Sarankye Mori, the Dagaaba, and Babatu: a failure of policy   125
Confusion worse confounded: the British fiasco   128
A new French initiative: in again, out again   132
Factional responses to changing situations: a review   135

7   'Direct rule': Wala in the early twentieth century

Introduction   141
The imposition of the *Pax Britannica*   142
Ruling the Wala: the *'alim* as collaborator   148
Mahdi Musa in Wala: the Muslims in turmoil   152
A crisis averted: the Muslims under Na Dangana   157
Conflict unresolved: the Muslims under Na Pelpuo III   161

**8   Wala under 'indirect rule': power to
the Na and schism in the *umma***

Introduction   165
The Wala Constitution of 1933: perpetrating a fraud   167
Rotation between the gates: an exercise in futility   173

Turmoil in the Muslim community: the Ahmadiyya Movement 178
Changing fortunes: Ahmadiyya gains the Nam 183
New directions and old conflicts: Wala under Mumuni Koray 185
The durability of faction: Wala under Na Saidu and
Na Sidiki Bomi 190

9 Review: the peculiarities of Wala

Introduction 196
The Antinomy of the Impassable Gate 197
The Antinomy of the Landless Landowners 198
The Anomalies of Chieftaincy 199
The Anomalies of Islam 202
Whither Wa? 204

Notes 207
Bibliography 234
  Books, articles and dissertations 234
  Field notes 238
Index 240

Illustrations

Plates

1 The palace of the Wa Na, Ashura Festival, 1966   *page* 6
  SOURCE: author's photograph
2 Wa Central Mosque, early twentieth century   6
  SOURCE: A. E. Kitson, *The Geographical Journal*, November 1916,
  facing p. 389
3 The British fort at Wa, *c.* 1902   7
  SOURCE: M. Delafosse, *Les Frontières de la Côte d'Ivoire, de la Côte
  de l'Or et du Soudan*, Paris, 1908, p. 169
4 Sungma masked dancers in Wa, 1925   21
  SOURCE: H. H. Princess Marie Louise, *Letters from the Gold Coast*,
  London, 1925, facing p. 120
5 *Al-akhbar Saltanat Bilad Wa* (HSW/a, first part)   38
  SOURCE: Karamoko Siddiq b. Sa'id, see Wilks FN/145, 8 March
  1963; IASAR/151
6 *Al-akhbar Saltanat Bilad Wa* (HSW/b, first part)   39
  SOURCE: NAG Accra, No. 1427 of 1959
7 List of Wa Limams to 'Uthman Dun   65
  SOURCE: Wa Limam Al-Hajj Muhammad Bakuri, see Wilks
  FN/148, 3 May 1966; IASAR/386
8 Wa Friday Limam Siddiq b. 'Abd al-Mu'min (with staff) and
  'ulama', 1963   72
  SOURCE: author's photograph
9 *Ibtida' Din Wa fi 'Am 875 ila 'Am 1382*   94
  SOURCE: Wa Friday Limam Siddiq b. 'Abd al-Mu'min, see Wilks,
  FN/124, 6 March 1963; IASAR/18
10 Teaching chain, Dondoli school   96
  SOURCE: Limam Al-Hajj 'Abd al-Mu'min of Obuase, see Wilks,
  FN/157, 10 April 1966
11 *Al-akhbar Zabarima*   104
  SOURCE: NAG Accra, No. 1427 of 1959

12 Ishaq Dodu, once cook to Babatu, in 1964   117
    SOURCE: author's photograph
13 *Alhabari Samuri daga Mutanen Wa* (ASMW)   121
    SOURCE: NAG Accra, No. 1427 of 1959
14 Wa Na Saidu Takora (left) and notables, 1897   129
    SOURCE: F. B. Henderson, *The Idler*, 1898, p. 495
15 Wa Na Mumuni Koray, 1949–53   178
    SOURCE: Idris Mumuni Koray, Wa
16 Graves of Wa Nas Saidu II (right) and Mumuni Koray, 1966   193
    SOURCE: author's photograph

Maps

1 Wa in its regional setting   9
2 Principal Wala villages, by Division   12
3 Wa: The old town   27

Figures

1 Population of Wa town, *c.* 1885 to 1984   13
2 The origins of the Wa Nam: family reconstructions   42
3 Dzangbeyiri genealogy   63
4 The early Wa Limams   78
5 Family reconstitution, a segment of Busa gate   83
6 Distribution of limamates by house   110
7 The gate system, early twentieth century   170

Tables

1.1	Wa and its Divisions under the Native Authority system	*page* 11
1.2	Population, Wa and the fourteen Divisions	13
1.3	The structure of Wa town, 1948	26
4.1	The Wa Limams	66
4.2	Succession to the Wa limamate	68
4.3	Changing patterns of succession in the Wa limamate	71
4.4	Pre-eminence of the house of 'Abd al-Qadir	71
4.5	Wa Limams by generation and order of succession	75
4.6	The Wa Nas to Sidiki Bomi, died 1978	81
5.1	Tamarimuni and Dondoli teaching chains	97
5.2	Wa Limams by house and generation	109
6.1	Wala factions, second half of the nineteenth century	139
7.1	Livestock taxed, Wa and Bole Stations, 1902–5	145
7.2	Merchandise taxed, Kintampo, Wa and Bole Stations, 1902–5	146
7.3	Caravan tax 1902–5	147
8.1	Distribution of Wa Nas by gate and Divisional population	171
8.2	Succession of Wa Nas Pelpuo III, Sumaila and Saidu II from Busa gate	173
8.3	Succession of Wa Na Hamidu Bomi from Pirisi gate	173
8.4	Succession of Wa Na Mumuni Koray from Sing gate	174
8.5	Composition of the Wala District Council	186

Preface

This work is not a cultural, economic or social history. It is essentially a study of the roots of conflict and communal violence in Wala. It is, however, necessarily historical in approach, for those roots are deep and therefore ancient ones. They have to be understood in what Fernand Braudel has taught us to call the *longue durée*, which for the Wala spans some three centuries. This is, in a sense, an old-fashioned type of study; at least, I like to think that it is. I am concerned first and foremost with the content rather than the structure of the texts I use. I want them to inform me about what real people did in a real past. That I cannot ever *know* whether the information they convey is or is not in this sense veridical is a fact of life. That the information can be used to *make sense* of the Wala situation as it is now, in the late twentieth century, is all I require of it. I am concerned with the peculiarities of the Wala, for these are precisely what make them Wala. This study is accordingly minutiose in character. It is attentive to detail. It seeks neither to offer generalizations nor to make comparisons. If it is of use to the generalist or comparativist, all to the good. It is, however, directed more towards the policy maker and administrator whose practical involvement in Wala affairs can only be the more effective the more he or she understands how the Wala have become as they are.

In 1955 I was appointed Resident Tutor for the Northern Territories by the Institute of Extra-mural Studies, a department of what was then the University College of the Gold Coast. In the three years I held that post I had occasion frequently to visit Wa. In 1958 I became Resident Tutor for Asante, and became absorbed in its history. The Institute of African Studies was founded at the University of Ghana (as the University College had become) in 1961. I joined it. Among the priorities we set the new organization was research into Islam in Ghana. In 1962 I decided to focus my own activities primarily, though by no means exclusively, on Wa. Most of the fieldwork on which this study is based was carried out between 1962 and 1969. Thomas Hodgkin, who assumed the Directorship of the Institute, was highly supportive. More than that, he joined me in Wala on many occasions (sharing with me, by way of detail, the rent of a room in a building adjacent to the Central Mosque).

The results of my work in Wala have clearly been long in the gestation. Concerns with Asante, Welsh and Gonja history intervened to absorb my attention. In the meantime two important contributions to Wala studies have appeared in print, both based upon dissertations. Nehemia Levtzion worked in Wala in the first half of 1964, and there is a chapter on it in his *Muslims and Chiefs in West Africa* (Levtzion, 1968, ch. 8, based upon Levtzion, 1965). I introduced Mona Fikry to Wa in 1966. A summary of her work appeared in R. M. Dorson's *African Folklore* (Fikry-Atallah, 1972, pp. 237–53, based upon Fikry, 1970). I have found the writings of both scholars useful and complementary to my own, though their central concerns differ from mine.

I am indebted to numerous persons who in one way or another facilitated my work in Wala. First and foremost I must mention Al-Hajj 'Uthman b. Ishaq Boyo of Kintampo, a well-known figure in Muslim communities throughout Ghana. He accompanied me to Wa on many occasions, placed his extraordinary skills in languages at my disposal as translator, and was instrumental in obtaining the cooperation and indeed participation of the *'ulama'* in the inquiry. Seidu Awouri of the Wa Urban Council, and a chief of the gunmen of Bulenga, also assisted me with introductions and interpretation. Many informants generously shared their knowledge and ideas with me, and the list of interviews in the bibliography to this volume records the names of most, but not all, of them. At the risk of being invidious I may especially mention Ishaq Dodu of Wa Tagarayiri and Karamoko Fanta Sidiki of Wa Tamarimuni. The former may best be described as my patron, the latter as my senior tutor. It is sad to have to report that both are now dead. I may note that my decision not to record on tape the many conversations I had with informants had obvious disadvantages, but ones more than compensated for by the freedom with which they spoke and the warmth of the relationships that often developed. They were, nevertheless, as concerned as I was that their comments were fully and accurately recorded in writing for, as they frequently remarked, they wanted their children and grandchildren to know all they had said.

In the interests of economy it has been decided, with the exception of the 'ain and hamza, to use the standard English alphabet in transliterating from Arabic script. The assumption is that those who know Arabic will not be misled (and that those who do not will in any case be none the wiser). The Arabic and Hausa texts drawn upon in this study present many problems of exegesis. Some writers had a competent knowledge of the languages; some used what are virtually literary pidgins. I have received help from numerous colleagues who have translated, or assisted in translating, various of the items: Hamidu Bobboyi, Al-Hajj Dantani, Mona Fikry, Salah Ibrahim, Nehemia Levtzion, B. G. Martin, A. B. Moru, T. Mustapha and Al-Hajj 'Uthman Boyo. Many readings remain in doubt, however, and I have finally had to make my own decisions. While deeply grateful to those upon whose expertise I have drawn, I must therefore absolve them from responsibility for the errors that remain. Some apology is in order for my transliterations from Walii. No accepted orthography existed in the 1960s, subtle differences in dialect are involved, and I have failed to be entirely consistent. I have, for example, used the form 'Na Kpasa' rather than 'Na Kpaha' but 'Yerihi' rather than 'Yerisi'. I doubt that any confusion will result.

The detailed nature of this study makes it impossible to insert on any map the names of most of the villages mentioned in the text. The index has therefore been used to provide the reader with some guidance in this matter. Places shown on maps 1 and 2 are indexed accordingly. Wala villages which do not appear on either map are identified by Division in the index and may thus be approximately located by reference to map 2.

J. J. Holden, whose work on the Zabarima related closely at points to mine on the Wala, travelled with me many times to northern Ghana, Burkina Faso and as far as Niger. I gained much from innumerable discussions with him. My colleague J. O. Hunwick has also been a source of constant stimulation. Karen Aldenderfer made my rough maps look intelligible. I am grateful to the Institute of African Studies at the University of Ghana for the facilities and finances that made much of the work on Wala possible. My first attempts to write up the material were made in 1966–7, when I held a Senior Simon Fellowship in the Department of Social Anthropology and Sociology of the University of Manchester. I must acknowledge my debt to colleagues there – and particularly Paul Baxter and the late Max Gluckman – who so usefully commented on my provisional drafts. I am also grateful to the Division of Research Programs of the National Endowment for the Humanities; from its grant for the project on 'The Changing Role of the 'Ulama' in Africa' I was enabled to undertake work in Britain and Ghana during the period 1984–7 without which this study could not have been brought to completion. Finally, it is a pleasure to record my appreciation of the care with which Elizabeth Wetton, Wendy Guise, Jean Field and the staff at Cambridge University Press have seen this book through its production.

Abbreviations

Abbreviated references to texts cited

AS	*Al-akhbaru Samuru* (Hausa)
ASBW	*Al-akhbar Saltanat Bilad Wa* (Arabic)
ASMW	*Alhabari Samuri daga Mutanen Wa* (Hausa)
AWK	*Al-akhbari Wala Kasamu* (Hausa)
AZWS	*Alhabari Zabarimawa, Wala da Samuru* (Hausa)
HSW	*Al-habari Sarauta Wa* (Hausa) and *Al-akhbar Saltanat Bilad Wa* (Arabic)
KC	*The Konate Clan. Our Grandfathers, Their Names and Places They Settled in* (English)
ST	*Samori Taahuu* (Walii)
TATM	*Ta'rikh Ahl Tarawiri min Mandi* (Arabic)
TAW	*Ta'rikh Ahl Wala* (Arabic) and *Magana Wala* (Hausa)
TM	*Ta'rikh al-Muslimin* (Arabic) and *Magana Muslimi na Daurri* (Hausa)
TTI	*Ta'rikh Tadhkirat al-Imamiyyin fi Biladina Wa* (Arabic)

Other abbreviations

Wilks, FN	Field notes, Ivor Wilks. Copies of these notes are deposited in the archives of the Africana Library, Northwestern University, Evanston, Illinois
CO.879/	Colonial Office Confidential Print, Public Record Office, London
CO.96/	Colonial Office Original Correspondence, Public Record Office, London
IASAR/	Arabic Collection, Institute of African Studies, University of Ghana
NAG Accra	National Archives of Ghana, Accra
NAG Tamale	National Archives of Ghana, Tamale

Preamble

The first European writer to mention the Wala ('Oalla', 'Oala') appears to have been G. A. Robertson in 1819. His informant was Adu Gyese, an Asante 'in the habit of travelling into the interior for the purposes of trade'.[1] Thereafter Wala remained unnoticed for almost seventy years, escaping the attention even of the incomparable Henry Barth in the middle years of the century.[2] The first European to pass through Wa, capital of the Wala, seems to have been G. A. Krause in 1887. He merely noted its existence on his itinerary.[3] Two years later R. Austin Freeman visited Bonduku. There he learned that Wa was 'a town of considerable importance' and that its people 'appear to be exclusively Mahommedan'.[4]

In 1892 the Governor of the Gold Coast sent an agent, the Fante G. E. Ferguson, into what was ingenuously described as the 'Hinterland of the Gold Coast Colony'. It was, in fact, the hinterland of Asante, a kingdom that still retained its independence. Ferguson did not reach Wa on this occasion but he obtained a certain amount of information about it in the Gonja towns he visited. In December 1892 he reported to the Governor in Accra that he had met a caravan leader who knew both Wa and Accra and said that the former was the larger town.[5] The trader's information was somewhat outdated, for in 1887 Wa had been attacked by the forces of the Zabarima warlord, Babatu, and many of its people had fled. Before that catastrophe, however, Wa was believed to have had at least six thousand inhabitants.[6]

Today Accra, with a population approaching a million, is capital of the Republic of Ghana. Wa, some 360 miles distant from it, is capital of the Upper West Region and has a population of about 36,000. Ghana's two national newspapers, the *Daily Graphic* and the *Ghanaian Times*, are both published from Accra. They seldom carry reports from Wa other than when the town is periodically convulsed by crisis, as, for example, in 1978 and 1980.

In 1978 Wa was in the throes of sectarian crisis. The Ahmadiyya Movement had begun actively to proselytize there in the early 1930s. Serious clashes had occurred between its adherents and those who called themselves 'the orthodox' in 1934, 1939 to 1941, and 1951, the last involving rioting on a

1

scale such that the Wala refer to it as a civil war. Violence was never far below the surface over the succeeding decades. 'We war with the Ahmadiyya', I was told by a prominent leader of the orthodox in 1963,[7] though for a time the 'war' was marked by nothing more serious than the occasional fracas between elderly and venerable men wielding their umbrellas as weapons. On 25 August 1978, however, fighting broke out during the Friday prayers and only prompt action by the police averted more serious trouble. The *Ghanaian Times* for 30 August carried the headline, 'Moslems Now Need Permit To Worship at Wa Mosque'. The orthodox Muslims, it reported, must obtain police permits to attend Friday prayers and 'will also have to be searched by the police at various entry points to the mosque to ensure that no weapons or missiles are carried to the mosque'.

The police were unable to act so effectively in 1980. On 1 April the *Daily Graphic* reported that 'more than 26 people were shot dead and 42 others seriously injured in a three-day scuffle involving factions of the Wa chieftaincy dispute'. The Fongo section of Wa had been under a state of siege, and the true death toll was probably over forty. The destruction to property was estimated at 3m cedis.[8] The death of Wa Na Sidiki Bomi in 1978 had engendered the crisis. Two candidates, J. N. Momori and Yakubu Seidu, advanced claims to the vacant position, and the 'kingmakers' of Wa were deeply and bitterly divided. By the beginning of 1979 one faction had recognized J. N. Momori, one Yakubu Seidu, as new Na. The matter was taken to the Northern Region House of Chiefs, which decided in favour of the latter. It was then appealed to the National House of Chiefs, but fighting broke out before the case was heard. The momentum of events was such that the Wala had reverted to an older way of resolving succession disputes. It was one succinctly described in a relevant context by Muhammad Gado Bakwakwa in the middle of the nineteenth century: 'when a king dies, there is no regular successor, but a great many rivals for the kingdom spring up, and he who can achieve his object by power and strength, becomes the succeeding king, thus war settles the question'.[9]

In 1980 war could not be allowed to settle the question. President Hilla Limann of Ghana instructed his Inspector General of Police to restore order in Wa, but the prognosis was ominous. Within a week or two of the fighting one faction of the 'kingmakers' petitioned Limann, warning him 'that any attempt by anyone to impose Yakubu Seidu on them would be resisted'.[10] When the National House of Chiefs decided in favour of Yakubu Seidu on 10 April 1981 further violence was only contained by the looming presence of the police and military. Four years were to elapse before the crisis could be considered over. On the last day of 1981 Flight-Lieutenant J. J. Rawlings took over the Government of Ghana by coup. By a decree of 15 July 1982 the Provisional National Defence Council placed the palace in Wa, and all the property of the Wa Skin, under the control of its Officer-in-Charge there, and by a subsequent decree of 28 July 1982 banished both candidates from the Wala District.[11] The matter was finally heard in Accra before the Supreme

Court of Ghana in July 1985. With considerable sagacity the five appeal judges refrained from choosing between the two aspirant Wa Nas, but contented themselves with redefining the composition of the body of Wala 'kingmakers'.[12] On 29 August 1985 this body met in Wa and confirmed J. N. Momori in office, as Wa Na Momori Bondiri II.[13]

Policy makers, at whatever level of government, are under severe disadvantages in knowing how to manage, let alone resolve, the sort of crises that periodically engulf Wa and for that matter other of the old pre-colonial polities that together comprise the present Republic of Ghana. This is true of the succession of governments that have presided over Ghana's destiny since 1957 no less than of the preceding British colonial administration. Such crises are seldom the result of ephemeral factors that can be readily identified and corrected, though the overworked policy maker is almost inevitably obliged to treat them as such – and hope that the next crisis will be someone else's problem. The fact of the matter is that the recurrent crises are generated from within the deeper structures of society, and the compromise solutions that are the stock-in-trade of the policy maker as often as not aggravate rather than ameliorate the situation. However capable, the administrator rarely has access to data of a quality commensurate with the complexity of the problems to be addressed. A law professor in Ghana in the early 1960s could still remark of the northern third of the country which embraces Wala that

> detailed data on the organization and functioning of the indigenous societies of the area are fragmentary, and it is therefore difficult to assess adequately the degree of distortion and dislocation of traditional institutions effected after the advent of British administration in 1901.[14]

At present (1988) the state of knowledge of the region is somewhat, if only marginally, better.

The deeper structures of a society are ones that tend to be peculiar to it. They can only be investigated in specific local contexts. They are also, virtually by definition, ancient; that is, they have to be studied in appropriately extended time perspectives. Wala is not the only society in northern Ghana to be periodically engulfed in violence. Dagomba, for example, is another.[15] It requires no great insight to recognize that both societies are embroiled, *inter alia*, in 'chieftaincy disputes', but this is to do no more than attach a convenient label to a complex phenomenon. The deeper structures that generate conflict in Dagomba are in fact quite different from those that generate it in Wala. This, clearly, is not an observation welcome to the policy maker, whose task would be much lightened were it possible successfully to apply lessons learned from one society to others. Nor, of course, is it an observation congenial to scholars of a comparative and generalizing cast of mind who seek to extrapolate from better- to lesser-known societies.

Almost half a century ago W. M. Macmillan noted the contributions which anthropologists were beginning to make to the knowledge of 'native custom' in what is now Ghana. Perceptively, however, he commented that 'its professors have not so far fixed on the social chaos of tribes in the Gold Coast Colony as a favourable field for their studies'.[16] It is precisely this element of *chaos* that is so apparent in Wala. It will be argued that conflict and violence are not the result of the breakdown of 'traditional' social and political processes, although this is commonly assumed to be the case. They are the result of ambiguities and contradictions which are structural and indeed functional aspects of those very processes. Policy makers have sought and continue to seek for the rules and norms of Wala society. It is in many respects a chimerical pursuit. It is the anomalies and antinomies of Wala that have to be understood, the reasonable but nevertheless incompatible views of the nature of Wala society which the Wala themselves articulate. This study will therefore give little comfort to those who choose to think of societies as self-organizing systems tending innately to attain a state of fundamental equilibrium. Chaos rather than harmony is the problematic.

Ghana is presently poised on the brink of a major experiment in the decentralization of government. Barring unforeseen upheavals, in 1989 new District Assemblies will assume deliberative, legislative and executive functions, 'exercising state power as the people's local government' in such a way as to 'democratise state power and advance participatory democracy and collective decision-making at the grassroots'.[17] The concept is similar in some respects to that of the indirect rule essayed in the colonial era. The success of any such experiment will depend upon highly specific information on locality being available to the policy makers. This study addresses the 'peculiarities' of Wala.

1

Wa and the Wala

Introduction

Why is Wala? Nothing in its environment decrees that it should be. The climate is unreliable, the soils indifferent, and disease rife. There are, however, its people. Wala is, because people at some point in time decided that it should be and at other points in time took further decisions to ensure that it should continue to be. People made Wala, but, to use one of Karl Marx's memorable phrases, they did not make it under circumstances of their own choice. The very indifference of the environment meant that their strategies for survival were often more in the nature of gambles than of calculable expectations.

Wala is an antique land. Its agrarian base was created perhaps between three and four millennia ago. No one can say how often, over that span of time, older peoples have been displaced by newer, or have been overrun and assimilated without trace. Today, despite the seemingly inexorable forces that are impelling people to congregate in towns with or without any obvious means of support, the majority of the Wala remain rural. They live in family 'compounds', some with a hundred or more members, which are often grouped to form larger or smaller villages. In the less densely populated areas, fallows are long. In the more densely populated areas, particularly around the town of Wa, continuous cultivation has become usual. The soils in the more northern and western parts of the region favour cereal cultivation, and in the more southern, yam.[1] Livestock never quite flourishes, but the more northerly the location the better it does. Cattle are reared for local slaughter and for sale at more distant markets. They are also a mark of wealth. They are used for marriage payments and for procuring political support, and are sacrificed on festive occasions. Few herds number more than 200 head, and rustling is not uncommon. Vegetable gardening is everywhere a necessity; hunting is now little more than a gainful sport.

The town of Wa has long enjoyed the status of a central place. Until the end of the nineteenth century it was indeed the capital of the small but independent Wala polity. The first agent of the Government of the Gold Coast Colony to visit the town testified to its distinctive appearance. 'Wa is

Plate 1 The palace of the Wa Na, Ashura Festival, 1966

Plate 2 Wa Central Mosque, early twentieth century

not a walled city', wrote G. E. Ferguson in 1894, 'but the flat roofed buildings and date palms present it with an eastern appearance. It is the capital of Dagarti.'[2] It was quite apparent that the town was a seat of authority. 'At Wa, as in other towns in this part of the bend of the Niger', the first Frenchman to arrive there, Lieutenant Baud, wrote in 1895, 'there are

6

Plate 3 The British fort at Wa, *c*. 1902

three authorities: the king, the Iman, and the chief of the capital [*village-capitale*].'[3] He was acknowledging one of the basic features of Wala society, that is, the plurality of authority derived from access to the instruments of coercion (the 'king' or Wa Na), to Islam (the Imam), and to the Earth-god. In the last decade of the nineteenth century the most visible symbols of the three kinds of authority were the palace of the Wa Na, a somewhat undistinguished but rambling flat-roofed building,[4] subsequently rebuilt in a style more appropriate to the office (plate 1); the impressive mosque built in the Western Sudanese idiom (plate 2); and the Dzandzan Pool in which dwelt crocodiles sacred to the Earth-god. To these was to be added, in 1898, the British fort, symbol of the arrival of a new and overarching authority (plate 3).

French forces, from their bases on the Senegal, moved into the region of the Upper and Middle Niger in the early 1880s. In 1893 Jenne was occupied, and in early 1897 the Mossi kingdom of Wagadugu. From their bases on the Gold Coast the British carried out the occupation of Kumase at the beginning of 1896. Wa was, for a time, the object of intense interest to both powers, the key to control of that extensive tract of territory lying immediately east of the Black Volta which the French tended to describe as part of 'Gourounsi' and the British to distinguish as 'Dagarti'. On 4 May 1894 G. E. Ferguson had signed a Treaty of Friendship and Trade with Wa Na Saidu Takora, and the 'Country of Dagarti, otherwise known as Dagaba' was thereby regarded as within the British sphere of influence.[5] A year later, almost to the day, the same Wa Na signed a Treaty of Protection with Lieutenant Baud, representing the French government.[6] The British reasserted and strengthened their claims to the 'Country of Dagarti' by a Treaty of Friendship and Protection of 9 January 1897. The principals were Lieutenant F. B. Henderson and Na Saidu.[7] On 12 June 1897, however, Na

Saidu entered into yet another treaty with Captain Hugot, representing French interests.[8] After a flurry of diplomatic activity and military posturing such as to make an armed engagement between French and British troops seem inevitable at the end of 1897, the French finally abandoned their claims to Wa.[9] The town and its dependent villages became part of an ill-defined British military command known as the Northern Territories of the Gold Coast. These territories were formally constituted a Protectorate by an Order of Council of 26 September 1901, which placed them under the jurisdiction of the Governor of the Gold Coast Colony. The Wala had lost their independence.

The Wala polity

It is impossible to map the boundaries of the nineteenth-century Wa polity with precision, for they were not precisely defined. In 1894 Ferguson questioned Wa Na Saidu on the very topic. The Daboya Volta, the Na said, 'ran in the neighbourhood of Walembele. It is between this river and the one running past Tantama that his territory extended northward to Dasima, a week's journey from Wa'. The Daboya Volta is clearly the Kulpawn River, which joins the White Volta above Daboya. Tantama is on the Black Volta. In so far, then, as Ferguson accurately represented the Na's response, his jurisdiction was regarded as extending from the Black Volta in the west to the valley of the Kulpawn in the east, and from Dasima in the northeast to Tantama in the southwest. The situation, however, was a confused one. The Wa Na also informed Ferguson that a number of villages under his authority were currently in rebellion. These included Charipon ('Cherepaw'), Sampina ('Sawpawna'), Busie ('Busei') and Nandaw.[10] All were situated in the northern part of the area, across the country between the Black Volta and Dasima (map 1).

Three years later, in 1897, Henderson entered Wa territory from the south. He identified Kulmasa as 'the frontier town of Dagarti, of which Wa is the capital'.[11] He appears, however, to have made no further attempt to describe the extent of the 'Country of Dagarti' though this did not deter him from committing the British to its protection. In fact the Wa Na's authority had disintegrated further since the time of Ferguson's visit. The rebellions of 1894 had not only sustained their momentum but had spread into virtually all of the northern villages over which the Wa Nas had claimed authority. The situation was analysed in reports by Lieutenant-Colonel H. P. Northcott. At the very beginning of 1898 he found that all but one of the 'Dagarti' dependencies had repudiated the Wa connection for over a year. The exception was Mwankuri ('Makauri'), to the northwest of Busie. Referring to 'a declaration by the Dagartis of their independence', Northcott therefore felt it necessary to enter into new treaty arrangements with each of their major centres: with Kaleo on 10 December 1897, and with Issa (including Samanbaw), Busie (including Nandaw), Wogu and Nadawli between 9 and

8

Map 1 Wa in its regional setting

11 January 1898.[12] The rebellions, moreover, affected not only the northern villages but also the Dorimon district west of Wa. For good measure, a separate treaty was signed with it on 2 January 1898.[13]

The changed situation was described by Captain D. Mackworth in a military intelligence report of 6 June 1898. Acknowledging the fact of the rebellions, he felt obliged to draw a distinction between 'the country of Wa' and 'the country of Dagarti'. The former, he remarked, somewhat ingenuously

> comprises all the districts which acknowledge the King of Wa as their chief. It is bounded on the north by Dagarti, which country comes down to within four miles of the town of Wa; from Wa the line is roughly drawn in a northeast direction till it strikes the Kulpawn River, somewhere in the neighbourhood of Kajikewri [Kojopere], which is a Wa village. The eastern boundary is a line from the Kulpawn River, through Dusei [Ducie], Dusei and its small villages being the most east Wa district. On the south it is bounded by the country of Bole, boundary uncertain. On the west it is bounded by Lobi, the river Volta being the boundary.[14]

With little more than these few reports to inform their policy, in 1898 the British military administrators mapped out the region. The 'Country of Dagarti' of the treaties of 1894 and 1897 was divided into a Dagarti Sub-District to the north and a Wa Sub-District to the south, and both were included with the Bole and Gurunshi Sub-Districts in the Black Volta District.[15] Probably more out of ignorance than by design, the boundary between the Wa and Dagarti Sub-Districts was drawn with scant regard for the realities of the situation. Old Wala villages such as Nasa were placed within the latter, for example, while the former was extended southwards to embrace districts over which the Wa Nas had never claimed jurisdiction.

In 1907, civil administration was established throughout the Protectorate of the Northern Territories of the Gold Coast. The Dagarti and Wa Sub-Districts were combined to form the Wa District, the boundaries of which were revised to correspond more or less closely with those of the Wa polity before its decay in the late nineteenth century. In particular, the villages which had rebelled were for the most part reintegrated into the Wa District; only the northernmost were assigned to the Lawra District for reasons of administrative convenience. Not surprisingly, there was persistent opposition to this reconstitution of the older jurisdiction and as late as 1925 the Governor of the Gold Coast was obliged to clarify the situation by Order in Council:

> The Wa District shall comprise all the lands subject to the Chief of the Wala tribe, together with that portion of the lands occupied by the Dagati tribe lying South of the Izeri River and that portion of the land occupied by the Isala Grunshi tribe on the right bank of the Kulpawn River.[16]

By the Native Courts, Native Authority and Native Treasuries Ordinances of 1932 a system of indirect rule was introduced into the Protectorate of the

Table 1.1. *Wa and its Divisions under the
Native Authority system*

		Population	
Division	Category	1931	1948
Wa	Wala	13,025	15,827
Busa	Wala	4,498	4,629
Sing	Wala	1,818	2,363
Pirisi	Wala	2,351	3,139
Guli	Wala	[included in Pirisi]	
Dorimon	Wala	8,017	10,152
Wechiau	Wala	5,463	6,988
Kojopere	Wala	2,905	1,614
Funsi	Sisala	2,529	3,184
Kundungu	Sisala	2,923	2,267
Kaleo	Dagarti	12,055	16,760
Busie	Dagarti	3,079	4,579
Daffiama	Dagarti	2,158	2,544
Issa	Dagarti	2,593	3,398
Nadawli	Dagarti	8,702	8,035
Total		72,116	85,479

Northern Territories. In the following year the Wala Native Authority (frequently referred to as the 'Wala State' or even more anachronistically as the 'Kingdom of Wala') was set up. The colonial administrators were required carefully to ascertain the extent and nature of pre-colonial jurisdictions and in the case of Wa this was again interpreted to mean the jurisdiction prior to the rebellions of the 1890s. The boundaries of the existing Wa District were found to be acceptable approximations to those of the pre-colonial Wala polity (map 1).

The Wala Native Authority embraced 3,362 square miles of country. Under the overarching authority of the District Commissioner, the Wa Na presided over the affairs of Wa town with its villages, and over those of fourteen Divisions.[17] Seven of the Divisions were regarded as 'Wala', two as 'Sisala' and five as 'Dagarti'. The structure of the Native Authority, and its population according to the Gold Coast Censuses of 1931 and 1948,[18] is shown in table 1.1 and on map 2.

The population of the district embracing Wa and its Divisions has increased rapidly in the present century. A count carried out in 1921 is the earliest upon which some reliance may be placed, though there is little doubt that many smaller communities escaped attention.[19] Progressively more accurate were the Censuses of 1931, 1948, 1960, 1970 and 1984.[20] The returns are shown in table 1.2. Wa remains the only urban centre in the district, no other place having at present a population in excess of 5,000. With its palace,

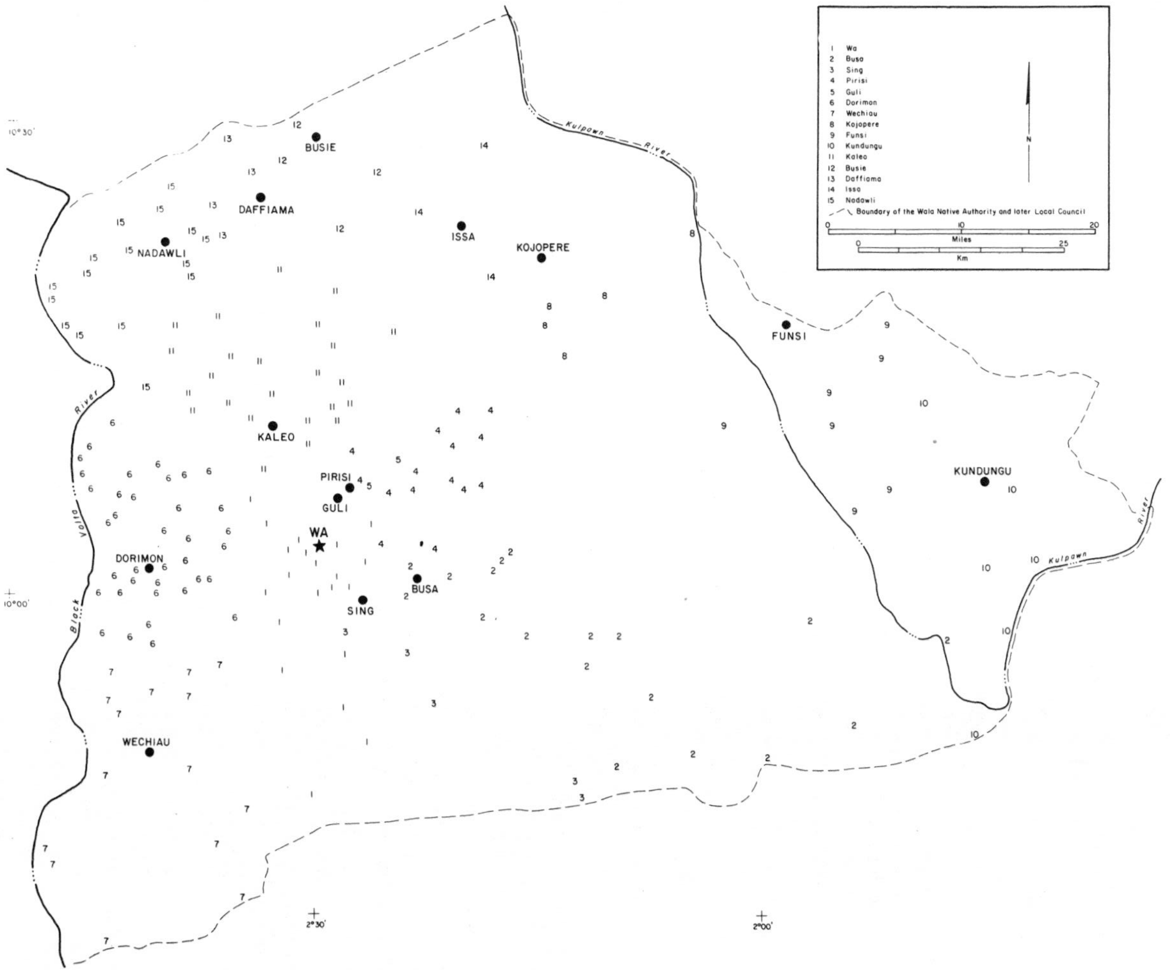

Map 2 Principal Wala villages, by Division

Table 1.2. *Population, Wa and the fourteen divisions*

Year	Population	Density per sq. mile	% of population in Wa Town
1921	43,168	12.8	6.5
1931	72,323	21.5	7.2
1948	85,479	25.5	6.0
1960	130,964	38.95	11.0
1970	153,909	45.78	13.9
1984	223,643	66.52	16.1

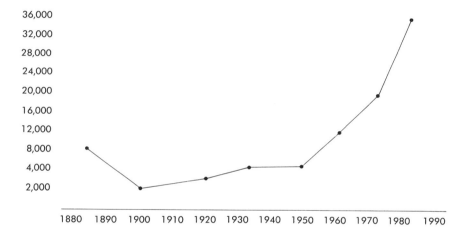

Figure 1 Population of Wa town, *c.* 1885 to 1984

mosques and schools, and its general cosmopolitan aspect, the town has long been a centre of culture, and the distinction between townsfolk and *fulfule*, peasants, is one deeply rooted in the mentality of its people.[21] Under the successive governments of the Gold Coast and Ghana it has remained a seat of regional administration. Change in its population can be reconstructed over the last hundred years, though the early figures are estimates rather than counts and at best crude approximations to the reality.[22] Figure 1 indicates, however, the long-term effects of the collapse of the Wala polity in the troubled decades of the late nineteenth century.

Who are the Wala?

The homespun Census of 1921 broke down the population of the Wa District by 'tribe'. The number of Wala counted was 16,905, of Dagarti 19,619, of Grunshi (or Sisala) 5,346, and of others described as Fulani, Hausa, Lobi,

13

etc., 1,298. The Wala were, then, not the largest 'tribe' in Wala. No such analysis was attempted in the 1931 Census. In 1948, however, the Census takers were again required to identify people by 'tribe', and for this purpose were supplied with a list of sixty-two 'tribal divisions' covering the whole of the Gold Coast. Unfortunately the returns were compiled for the Wa Administrative District and not, separately, for the three Native Authorities which then constituted it, namely, Wa as such, Tumu, and the Lawra Confederacy. Four 'tribes' numerically dominated the whole Administrative District, the Dagarti (106,349 people), the Sisala (37,246), the Lobi (30,673) and the Wala (22,299). It is impossible to establish the distribution of these groups within the three component Native Authorities. There were, however, 25,923 Wala in the whole of the Gold Coast, of whom 22,802 were resident in the Northern Territories. Of these latter, all but a few of the 22,299 in the Wa Administrative District were undoubtedly resident in the Wa Native Authority area. Since its total population in 1948 was 85,479, it follows that only about a quarter of its people were classified as Wala.[23]

The 1960 Census allows for more precision. The concept of ethnicity was much in vogue in scholarly circles in the 1950s and 1960s, and an enumeration by 'tribal divisions' was attempted, avowedly 'to give the research worker in the social sciences (especially the sociologist) a few basic data on population groups which are distinguished by certain characteristics and are generally referred to as tribes or tribal groupings'.[24] 47,200 Wala were enumerated throughout Ghana, of whom 37,320 were in the Northern Region (that is, the former Northern Territories). Of these 33,920 were resident in the Wala Local Council District, corresponding to the older Wala Native Authority area. They comprised, therefore, 26% of the population of 130,973 recorded for that District, much the same proportion as that indicated for 1948.

The overall profile of the Wala Local Council District by 'tribe' in 1960 was: Dagarti, 50%; Wala, 26%; Lobi, 13%; Sisala, 5%; and a miscellany of others, 6%.[25] These data are, however, too raw to be of much use until they are superimposed upon a matrix of historical, geographical and ethnographical materials. The problem in characterizing the four principal 'tribes' identified in the Census is that the labels 'Dagarti', 'Wala', 'Lobi' and 'Sisala' (or 'Grunshi') are not all semantically equivalent. Any discussion of this matter must proceed from J. R. Goody's painstaking and probably definitive analysis of the terms 'Dagarti' and 'Lobi' (and the many combinations and permutations of them), to which the reader is referred.[26]

The Lobi of the 1921 Census, together with the Fulani, Hausa and others with whom they were grouped, then constituted less than 3% of the population of the Wa District. In 1960 the Lobi alone constituted 13%. The most obvious explanation of their increase, that it was a result of migration into Wala, is the correct one. This migration was still too insignificant to be noticed in the 1910s, though it had probably commenced.[27] Goody identifies the newcomers in question as Birifor, DagaaWiili and, though fewer,

Lowilisi from west of the Black Volta, moving to escape the higher taxation and more repressive conditions in French administered territory. Significantly, perhaps, the traditions of many of the immigrants make reference to a time when their ancestors had been forced to cross the river in the opposite direction as a result of invasions.[28] The Lobi, the District Commissioner of Wa reported in 1955, 'continue to migrate from French Territory in considerable numbers and, though some of them move south to Gonja, a large number stay in this district'. He considered them by then a majority of the population along the left bank of the Black Volta in the Dorimon and Wechiau Divisions of Wala.[29]

In the 1921 census 5,346 Grunshi were counted in the Wa District, comprising 12.4% of the population. In 1960, when they are described as Sisala, they numbered 7,190, but constituted only 5% of the population. Their decline as a percentage of total population must largely reflect the demographic consequences of Lobi immigration. The Sisala villages of Wala lie in the broad but sparsely populated valley of the Kulpawn, almost all of them being east of that river. They are grouped around Funsi (population 1948: 1,193; 1960: 1,405) and Kundungu (population 1948: 584; 1960: 1,133). Their people speak Pasaala, one of the Sisala languages.[30] The clear implication of the 1948 Census of the Wa Administrative District, which enumerated 37,246 Sisala, is that considerably under a fifth of them were located specifically within the Wala Native Authority area.

The name 'Dagarti' appears to have been coined by the first Europeans to visit the region, from the vernacular root *dagaa*. Correctly, 'Dagari' is the name of the language, 'Dagaaba' or 'Dagara' that of the people, and 'Dagaw' or 'Dagawie' that of their land. In 1948, 106,349 Dagaaba were enumerated in the Wa Administrative District, when the *total* population of the Wala Native Authority area was only 85,479. Clearly, then, the majority of Dagaaba were not within the latter jurisdiction. Those that were lived, for the most part, in those Dagaaba villages over which the Wa Nas claimed authority in the nineteenth century, but whose people won a short-lived independence at the end of that century before the colonial administration restored the *status quo ante bellum*. The Dagaaba villages thus returned to Wala are grouped around a number of local centres, notably Busie (population 1948: 1,417; 1960: 1,556), Daffiama (population 1948: 1,162; 1960: 1,670), Issa (population 1948: 1,055; 1960: 1,364), Kaleo (population 1948: 1,127; 1960: 1,511), and Nadawli (population 1948: 713; 1960: 1,281). Of these, Kaleo was the most proximate (some eight miles) to Wa town, Busie the most distant (some thirty-two miles). In 1921 about 45.5% of the population of the Wa District was labelled 'Dagarti'. The count was 19,619 persons. By 1960, although the number enumerated had risen to 65,510, the percentage had not changed radically; Dagaaba comprised 50% of the total population. In these figures, the demographic effects of Lobi immigration are again apparent, tending to reduce the proportion of Dagaaba to total population. However, some migration of Dagaaba from parts of Dagawie never historically within Wala also occurred in the period of the censuses. It cannot be quantified, but showed for the most part in the growth of a number of Dagaaba settlements around Tanina, near the Gonja border due south of Wa.[31]

Of the four categories used by the Census takers, that of the Wala as such is the most difficult to define. The problem was recognized, though not resolved, by the anthropologist R. S. Rattray, half a century ago. 'Wala', he wrote, 'as the name of a tribe, is in reality nothing more than an arbitrary title derived from the name of the capital town, Wa, and applied to the heterogeneous peoples who have nominally come under the jurisdiction of the *Na* (Chief) of that place.'[32] Rattray was correct in seeing that the description 'Wala' denoted not a 'tribe' but 'heterogeneous peoples'. He was incorrect, however, in characterizing them as only nominally under the jurisdiction of the Wa Nas. The Wala were those who not only recognized the authority of the Wa Nas, but who identified themselves with the whole system of governance of which the Nas were themselves part. Cultural assimilation and not simply political domination is at issue.

The common language of the Wala is Walii, which is a dialect of Dagari little different from that spoken in Kaleo and the other Dagaaba villages of the district. For the vast majority of the Wala this is also their first language. The mass of the Wala are undoubtedly Dagaaba by origin. There is also a significant element that is of Mande or Mandeka background. This was recognized by L. G. Binger almost a century ago, when he described the basic population of Wala as 'Dagari' or 'Dagabakha' mixed with 'Mande-Dioula'.[33] The situation gives rise to the perplexing linguistic conventions current in Wa town and its environs. There are, for example, Wala Muslims who use a Malinke dialect (Juula) as their first language and identify themselves as Wala, but who refer to their unconverted Wala compatriots as Dagaaba, a term which in this context virtually takes on the meaning of 'pagan'. Those so described, however, invariably refer to themselves as Wala and firmly resist identification for any purposes, Census or otherwise, with the unassimilated Dagaaba of the northern belt of the Wala district. To compound the confusion, the chiefly class in Wala is neither Dagaaba nor Mande by origin, but Mamprusi. They identify themselves as Wala for most purposes, but in certain contexts as *Wala piene*, 'white Wala'.

The truth of the matter is that the concept of 'tribe' or even of 'ethnicity' is too crude to be of more than marginal value in investigating the nature of the Wala polity. People may identify themselves, or be identified by observers, in one context by reference to historical origins, in another to language and culture, and in yet another to traditional political affiliation. The Censuses not only fail to distinguish Wala of Dagaaba from those of Mande or Mamprusi origins, but do not even hint at the existence of two other peoples who either identified themselves, or were identified by the census enumerators, as 'Wala'. These are the Potuli and Chakalle. The Potuli villages are clustered around Kojopere (population 1948, 747; 1960, 1347), some twenty-eight miles northeast of Wa town. Their language, a Sisala one, is rapidly giving way to Walii, and the beginnings of their assimilation appears to date from the middle of the nineteenth century.[34] The Chakalle villages lie to the southeast of Wa. A number of them, clustering around Bulenga (population 1948: 657; 1960: 1,013), are now Walii-speaking, others around Ducie (population 1948: 350; 1960: 529) are bilingual in Walii and Chakalle.

To be Wala, it might be said, is an achieved rather than an ascribed status, though it is clearly not one which all those historically within the political ambit of Wa have sought. Some Dagaaba have aspired to become, and succeeded in becoming, Wala. Some – indeed, the majority – have successfully resisted assimilation. In question are processes of acculturation that can only be investigated in an appropriately extended framework of time. Key to any such inquiry is the three spheres of traditional authority to which reference has briefly been made. That based on access to the Earth-god is referred to in Walii as *tendaanlun*, and that based on control of the instruments of coercion as *nalun*. The third is Islam.

Tendaanlun and *nalun* in Wala

Through the exercise of *tendaanlun*, the community obtains the favour of the Earth-god and seeks to avert the disasters that occur when the Earth-god is offended. The Earth-god is omnipresent, but certain natural features – often rocks, trees, pools and the like – are designated its shrines, *tengani*. Each *tengani* has its priest, the *tendaana*. It is, then, the *tendaana* who has *tendaanlun*.

The most ancient units of organization for production in Wala are the *ten* (singular, *teng*), a word often translated by the English 'parish'.[35] Few if any of the *ten* survive in anything like their original form in Wala, newer structures of chieftaincy having been superimposed upon them. An agrarian history of the Wala region, tracing the boundaries of the *ten* and the circumstances of their creation, is not an impossibility. It would, however, require resources of time and money exceeding those available to scholars investigating comparable problems in much more favoured research environments; one thinks particularly of current work on the origins of English parishes.[36] In the absence of any such study the remarks that follow are necessarily tentative, impressionistic rather than firmly grounded in documented fieldwork.

The original *ten* were self-sustaining and self-reproducing communities. Their autonomy was defined not politically but ritually. Each was a tract of arable, fallow and waste land capable of sustaining the people, the Tendaanba, who lived on it. Each had a *tengani* or shrine through which its *tendaana* interceded with the Earth-god on behalf of the Tendaanba. It was the responsibility of the *tendaana* to ensure that the Tendaanba observed the norms of communal life. If they did so, the Earth-god would in turn ensure the harvest, on which the very survival of the community depended. If they

17

did not do so, then drought, crop diseases and a host of other afflictions might result. The *tendaana* was therefore the locus of authority, that is, of *tendaanlun*, in the *teng*, though he would act in consultation with the heads of the various lineages farming the land. Ultimately, however, whether in the allocation of land, the resolution of disputes, the punishment of those who violated social mores, the marketing of any surpluses, and so forth, it was the *tendaana* who was responsible for the well-being and indeed the very reproduction of the *teng* and its people.[37]

The *teng* was divided into farms, basically units of food-crop production. Each farm, *pwo*, had its occupant, the *pwosob*. Farming rights were regarded as essentially allodial, that is, as created by the first settler on the land in question, and as heritable by his descendants.[38] The position of *tendaana* was customarily held within the senior line of those descendants. Farming rights could, however, be extinguished by the *tendaana* in cases where the descendants put the wider community at risk by behaviour offensive to the Earth-god, or they could be transferred to others by descendants of the first settler with the approval of the *tendaana*. Farming rights could also be usurped. This is perceived to have happened on a massive scale in Wala. Specifically, the farming rights of the Tendaanba, the people of the land, are regarded as having been extensively expropriated by newcomers, the Nabihi. Over large areas *tendaanlun* gave way to *nalun*.

The Nabihi comprise a well-defined class within Wala society. Their status is an ascribed one which only the immediate descendants of previous Wa Nas and other incumbents of chiefly office can claim. Their apical ancestor in the male line is Saliya, one of the three warlords who founded the Wala polity. These matters are treated in texts that are the subject of chapters 2 and 3. Three sons of Saliya are said to have founded three towns, namely, Guli, Gbetore and Yaro. Their descendants in time extended their power over the countryside, bringing the Tendaanba under the authority of Nabihi chiefs each representing locally the authority or *nalun* of the Wa Na. It was in the course of this process that the Nabihi (and, we shall see, the '*ulama*') acquired farming rights previously held by Tendaanba.

In 1955 the District Commissioner of Wa, in a note on 'Land Tenure', remarked:

> There is no individual ownership of land in the area. The land is held in trust by the divisional chiefs for the Wa-Na, and is granted to those who require it by the chiefs on his behalf. The tendanas are the actual guardians of the land, and none may be apportioned without their prior consent. Provided a person makes good use of the land he may keep it as long as he wants it.[39]

This is not incorrect, but it does not fully represent the complexity of the situation. The Wala make a distinction between land as such (*ten*) and the farm (*pwob*) that is made on it.[40] Land is in a sense inalienable. It belongs to the Earth-god, to whom the *tendaanas* alone have access through the local *tengani* or shrines. This is the sphere of *tendaanlun*, of *tendaana*-authority. It is, therefore, not the ownership of land but the exercise of farming rights that has been extensively usurped by the Nabihi. Matters of customary land tenure, in other words, have been brought into the sphere of *nalun*, of chiefly authority. Yet in such matters the exercise of *tendaanlun* and *nalun* remain intricately linked. The wise chief does indeed consult the *tendaana* before allocating land for the use of individual farmers, and the prudent farmer, however he has acquired his farming rights, will provide the appropriate local *tendaana* with fowl, sheep, goats or money from time to time, in order to continue having sacrifices made to the Earth-god.

Nalun has not so much extinguished *tendaanlun*, but rather has formed a new tier of authority above it. Thus a local *tendaana*, or sometimes several, will almost invariably be found among the senior councillors of those holding Nabihi skins, from the Wa Na himself to a village chief.[41] No statistics exist that enable the proportion of land in Wala still farmed by Tendaanba, in the sense of descendants of first settlers, to be computed. Indeed, it is not clear how any such inquiry could be conducted. There are communities in the Wala heartlands, the sphere of preponderant *nalun*, that will identify themselves, with a sort of gloomy pride, as Tendaanba. They will usually do so, however, only in contexts in which claims to allodial rights over land are at issue. Otherwise they tend not to distinguish themselves from the amorphous mass of Wala commoners, which includes, *inter alios*, the numerous descendants of Nabihi who have lost that status by failing, over the generations, to secure chiefly office. In 1908 the Commissioner of the North-Western Province remarked that the 'original people' of Wa itself were only to be found at the small village of Kpaguri a mile and a half distant from the town.[42] There are, of course, other Tendaanba communities in or proximate to Wa, but it is significant that the Commissioner could believe otherwise.

The Tendaanba know that, in the context of Wala history, they have been the losers.[43] They are acutely aware of their decline in status, resulting from the erosion of their farming rights. Remarkably, nothing in tradition suggests that this was a violent process. The fact of the matter, it seems, is that the Nabihi (and the *'ulama'*) regularly recruited wives from the Tendaanba without reciprocating that service. The complaint is frequently and quite explicitly made by Tendaanba, that their communities have long been decaying because they have given away their daughters to Nabihi and Muslims but have been unable to obtain women from them in reciprocation. Unable adequately to reproduce their communities in terms of sheer number, the Tendaanba have been unable to reproduce their communities in terms of production. They have been obliged to transfer their farming rights to others, specifically to their Nabihi and Muslim sons-in-law. The expropriation of Tendaanba farming rights is to be seen, in other words, as a consequence of the expropriation of their daughters. Nabihi and Muslims acknowledge this when they observe, as they frequently do, that their 'grandmothers' were Tendaanba.

To the preceding generalizations a caveat has to be made. There were early Muslim settlers in the Wala area (the Yerihi or Old Muslims as distinct from the 'ulama') who, the texts have it, were able to establish a number of *ten* where snakes and the like had deterred others from settlement. They, too, created allodial rights to land and they, too, are landowners. Unlike the Tendaanba, however, they have not had their customary tenures eroded by newcomers. Their status allowed them to obtain daughters, reciprocally, from Nabihi and 'ulama' communities. In such places as Nasa, only fourteen miles northeast of Wa town, the intercession of Allah rather than of the Earth-god was from inception solicited to ensure the success of the harvests and the general well-being of the community. Indeed, in Nasa today the Yeri Na, a descendant of the putative 'first settler', sees himself as exercising *tendaanlun*. By a curious inversion of roles, Nasa Limam, though outranked by Yeri Na, is regarded as exercising the equivalent of *nalun*.[44]

In later chapters it will be seen that the Wala refer the development of their polity to three warlords. The Wala have a penchant for triads. The earliest was Sidi 'Umar, or in Walii Sanda Muru. His descendants are the Yeri Nas, chiefs of the Wala Yerihi. The next was Suri, whose successors are the Widanas, titular heads of the Wala Tendaanba. The last was Saliya, apical ancestor of the Wa Nabihi and therefore of the Wa Nas. The Wala render the terms Yerihi, Tendaanba and Nabihi into English as 'Muslims' (or better, for reasons that will become apparant, 'Old Muslims'), 'Landowners', and 'Princes' or 'Royals'. These translations are not entirely satisfactory, though no more felicitous equivalents come readily to mind.[45] There is a temptation to follow Goody's lead, in his analyses of Gonja society, and refer to these three categories as 'estates' (in the sense, of course, of the English 'estates of the realm').[46] The usage should probably be resisted in so far as it may suggest that all Wala can be sorted into one or other of the three categories. This is not the case. Different but overlapping spheres of authority are in question rather than social identification as such. Reference has already been made to the commoner masses, those for whom claims to ultimate Tendaanba, Yerihi or Nabihi origins have become for most purposes irrelevant since no longer conferring rights to office or land.

Each Wa Na, Wa Widana and Wa Yeri Na exercises a form of *nalun*, though of different origins and different natures. In matters of secular rule, all Wala recognize the authority of Wa Na (or, overarching that, the new levels of local and national government). In matters relating to Islam all Muslim Wala come technically under the authority of the Wa Yeri Na, as exercised through the limams. In matters relating to land ownership, the Widana retains a jurisdiction. As Friday Limam Al-Hajj Siddiq remarked in 1969, 'the royals, the Muslims and the tendambas [Tendaanba] combine to settle problems. Then they all go back to their own affairs. The law from the Government comes to the Na, who will then tell the Muslims. But matters pertaining to Islam come to the Limam, who will then tell the rest of the

Plate 4 Sungma masked dancers in Wa, 1925

town.'[47] Such aspects of the Wala situation defy succinct description. They will become more intelligible as we probe the deeper structures of society.

The Wa Nam

'Wa *nalun*' will refer to the authority of Wa Na as distinct from that of Wa Widana and Wa Yeri Na. Wa *nalun* is exercised by those who 'eat the *nam*'. The concept is a complex one. '*Nam*', however, appears to denote the whole bundle of privileges that come with the exercise of Wa *nalun* and therefore 'eating the *nam*' may contain an allusion to the appropriating nature of chieftaincy as such. Indeed, '*nam*' appears often to be used in a sense little different from that of the English word 'wealth'. It is commonly rendered in English as 'skin'. The allusion is to the animal skin upon which those exercising *nalun* quite literally sit. Thus to be made a chief is to be 'enskinned' and to be removed from office is to be 'deskinned'.

The Dzandzan Pool is regarded as a particularly potent point of access to the Earth-god, perhaps because the seat of the Wa Nas is within its ritual area.[48] The Sungma masks owned by the Tendaanba of Sing and Mengwe appear also to function as shrines, and command widespread respect and awe (plate 4).[49] Nevertheless, *tendaanlun* is essentially local and discrete in its exercise. The *tendaanas* or shrine priests do not fall within any hierarchical system of authority but each is responsible directly to the Earth-god. Wa *nalun*, by contrast, is centralized and essentially unitary. It may, however, be delegated, and those to whom it is delegated form a pyramidal system of

21

chiefs at the apex of which is the Wa Na. Wa *nalun* is delegated by the creation of subordinate skins. By custom, such skins are held by Nabihi, defined as the immediate descendants – usually sons or grandsons – of a Wa Na or other senior office holder. The occupants of Wa Nabihi skins share, then, in 'eating the *nam*'.

New skins can be created by the Wa Na and the decision to do so involves rational calculations of needs and returns. The Katua skin is a case in point. Soon after coming to office in 1920, Wa Na Pelpuo III decided to appoint a Nabihi chief over the Chakalle village of Katua some forty miles east of Wa, thereby bringing it the more securely within the sphere of *nalun*. He assigned the newly created skin to Hamidu Bomi of Pirisi, perhaps in acknowledgement of the support the latter had given him in his bid for Wa. Hamidu Bomi, however, did not want 'to eat Katua', having aspirations to the more senior Pirisi skin. He therefore sold Katua back to Wa Na Pelpuo, who paid £3 in cash for it and promised to support Hamidu Bomi's candidacy for Pirisi. Wa Na Pelpuo then traded the Katua skin for a yam farm owned by Bogsuo of Busa. Bogsuo thus became first Nabihi chief of Katua, and the village was incorporated into the Busa Division.[50]

The Wa Nabihi skins are located in Wa and the Wala Divisions of Busa, Guli, Pirisi and Sing. All claim the status of *dinorin*, 'gates', to the Wa Nam, that is, the right of promotion from the gate to Wa itself. Reference to Table 1.1 shows that Dorimon, Wechiau and Kojopere are also classed as Wala Divisions. None of the three skins is held by Wa Nabihi. Known as *namburi* skins, each is terminal; that is, no promotion to any higher skin is possible. Each has, however, its own subordinate skins. The Dorimon Nabihi, for example, hold skins within the Division from which promotion to Dorimon Na, but not to Wa Na, is possible. Dorimon, Wechiau and Kojopere thus have a certain measure of autonomy, and it has been noted that it was possible for Dorimon Na Meni to make a bid for independence in 1898.[51] Any such attempt at secession on the part of the divisional chiefs of Busa, Guli, Pirisi and Sing would be quite unthinkable in view of their status as gates to the Wa Nam.

Wa *nalun* is centralized and unitary, but it is not unchecked. The way in which the Wa *nam* is 'eaten' is supervised by a group of elders representing Tandaanba and Muslim interests. They comprise the Nalun Kpanbihi and are often referred to in English collectively as the Nalun Council. When indirect rule was introduced into Wala in 1933, this body was described as 'the Wala Judicial Council and Court of Appeal from the Divisions'.[52] The Nalun Kpanbihi themselves fixed its membership at eight in 1933, thereby satisfying the desire of the colonial administrators for neatness but departing from tradition. Customary practice appears to have been to vary the number of councillors according to the nature and importance of the business on hand. No less than sixteen functionaries, for example, were present when Wa Na Saidu entered into the treaty with the British in early 1897.[53] Three particular elders appear, however, always to have been the ranking members of the Nalun Kpanbihi. Wa Widana represents the Tendaanba and Wa Yeri Na the Muslims. The third is Foroko. He is head of a section of Wa town known as Tuomuni, 'under the baobab'. The tree in question is a *tengani*, an Earth shrine, and Foroko has the status of a *tendaana* even though he and his people have long been Muslims. Indeed, they claim origins from 'Mande'. They are either strangers who took over an existing *teng* or Tendaanba who have taken over traditions of origin not their own.[54] It may be that it is Foroko's anomalous position as Muslim *tendaana* that qualifies him to serve as spokesman for Wa Na and the Kpanbihi.

The role of the Wa Widana, Wa Yeri Na and Foroko was succinctly explained by Foroko Abu in 1964: 'When there is anything, the Chief informs Foroko, then Foroko informs the Yeri Na, and then Yeri Na asks Bellumi [Widana]: Haven't you heard what Foroko says the Na has said?'[55] The three assume a major role in the selection and enskinment of a Wa Na. The candidates are allowed adequate time to build up their constituencies, mustering support *inter alia* by distributing largesse in cash or kind in demonstration of their wealth. No one wants an impoverished, and so by implication incapable, Na. At an appropriate time the Widana, on behalf of the Tendaanba, visits various of the Earth shrines to seek guidance through the *tendaanas*, after which he informs the Yeri Na of his choice of candidate. The Yeri Na, in consultation with the limams and other of the *'ulama'*, must then approve the choice or request reconsideration of the matter. The choice made, the name of the successful candidate is announced and a day appointed for the enskinment. People from all the Divisions assemble in Wa and by convention accept the candidate. He is then seated upon a new animal skin. The Muslims and Tendaanba make prayers and sacrifices to, respectively, Allah and the Earth-god, whereupon Foroko enrobes the new Na in a white gown and hat.[56] The selection process did not, of course, always work smoothly, and constitutional procedures might give way to armed struggle. This happened most recently, we have seen, after the death of Wa Na Sidiki Bomi in 1978.

The primary responsibility of those entitled to 'eat the *nam*' was, traditionally, the defence of the country against not only human but also animal predators. As late as 1938, for example, the Wa Na marshalled his 'mighty hunters' to save farms from invading elephants.[57] There is virtually nothing in the nineteenth-century sources to indicate the nature of the demands which a Wa Na made upon the Wala populace in return for the protection he was expected to provide. With the introduction of the Native Authority system in the early 1930s, however, the colonial officers attempted to determine the nature and extent of such exactions. According to a report filed at this time, 'the Chief of Wa with his elders was the final authority over village Chiefs and Headmen and if he was strong enough collected fines, slaves and cattle as his dues: He would give orders for defence and attack and for the working of his farms'. Chiefs, the report continued, were entitled to five days' work annually on their farms from all able-bodied men. This was taken according to the farming cycle: one day clearing grass and scrub immediately after the rains, one day hoeing and mounding yam fields as soon as the soil was sufficiently dry, one day weeding when the crop was established, one day hilling the crops, and one day harvesting. Much of the income of the chiefly class thus derived from farm produce or from payments in cash or kind made by those who chose not to supply their labour. A chief, however, was also entitled to fees and fines accruing in his court; to a portion of the 'first fruits', that is, the harvest, rendered to the *tendaana* who then passed on a ('good') half; to presents made to him by those wishing to obtain favours; and to levies on traders. The hunter was also required to surrender part of his kill.[58]

There is no reason to doubt the basic information in the report, though some caution is called for. It is my impression that the demands a chief might make upon those under his jurisdiction with regard to labour on his farms and the provision of 'first fruits' depended upon the nature of their tenure. Customary tenures varied with the way farming rights had been acquired, whether by inheritance, grant or whatever. It is also my impression that the precise nature of the various forms of customary tenure became as uncertain over time for the Wala as they did for the copyholders on the manors of fifteenth- and sixteenth-century England. Whatever the case, the exactions of the Wala chiefs were apparently accepted with resignation. Such appears to be the implication of popular song texts collected by Fikry which are, she comments, 'fatalistic about the poor man's incapability of escaping his miseries'.[59]

The Muslim community

In 1921 the Muslim population of the Wa District was counted as 3,771, representing 8.7% of the total population of Wala, Dagarti, Grunshi and 'others'.[60] It is impossible even to guess at the accuracy of the figure, though it is perhaps more likely that Muslim households in the villages were miscounted as non-Muslim than the reverse. There is no doubt, however, that the major concentrations of Muslims were to be found in Wa town, and in a number of villages such as Nasa and Guropise which the colonial administrators had long recognized as exclusively or predominantly Muslim.[61] No count by religion was made in the censuses of 1931 and 1948 and the returns for 1960 cannot be broken down for Wala as such. Conversion has undoubtedly occurred on a quite massive scale over these decades. In the 1960s I found few villages of any size in the Wala and Sisala divisions that did not have a growing Muslim component. New mosques were being erected, limams (Walii, from Arabic *al-imam*) appointed to them, and Qur'anic schools opened. It is a widely received view in Wa that a considerable majority of those who regard themselves as 'Wala' are now Muslim. Certainly most of the Wa Nabihi are believers, and Tendaanba converts are numerous.

In 1960 the Ghana Census Office sampled data on education. Of those enumerated as 'Wala', 8.7% of the males and 0.9% of the females were found to have completed some type of formal education. Of the males, 76.6% had attended schools described as 'Arabic', and 40% of the females (though the figures for the latter are so small as to be of dubious statistical value). Of those Wala currently undergoing education in 1960, that is, 9.5% of the males and 2.6% of the females, 43.3% of the former and 29.6% of the latter were at 'Arabic' schools.[62] Although these figures testify to the current importance of Muslim education in Wala, they do not adequately represent the situation. In particular, the label 'Arabic schools' appears to refer only to those within the public school system – in point of fact those established by the Ahmadiyya Movement. Wala who had undergone or were undergoing instruction in the numerous traditional Qur'anic classes in Wa and in many of its villages appear to have escaped enumeration.

Historically, we shall see, the role of the Muslims in Wala society has been a culturally hegemonic one. Their influence has extended across the whole spectrum of Wala society and has manifest itself in, for example, the widespread adoption of Muslim names by unbelievers and, as in the case of Damba, the assimilation of older festivals to Muslim ones. Conversion, however, was not a primary instrument of hegemonization before the present century. The *'ulama'* of Wa have long been attached to the Suwarian tradition, one that I have characterized elsewhere as pacifistic in rejecting *jihad* as an instrument of political change; quietist in rejecting active proselytism, urging that true conversion must occur not in man's but in God's time; and accommodating in that it permitted the coexistence of believers and unbelievers in so far as the religious obligations of the former were not jeopardized.[63] This tradition continues to be supported by the more conservative *'ulama'* of Wa. The Ahmadis, in contrast, proselytize vigorously, and this is a source of much tension.

Although the Wa Nas have always had their seat in Wa town, most of the Nabihi are dispersed in the Divisions of Busa, Guli, Pirisi and Sing. The *tendaana* likewise attend their shrines in the villages. Islam, by contrast, requires the existence of a critical mass of scholars in one place. In Wa there are libraries which contain the works essential to the maintenance of the true path, and schools where not only the Qur'an is taught in the traditional manner but also a range of the Islamic sciences. Wa is quite apparently a Muslim town. It is difficult to offer any succinct description of its structure and even more difficult to assess the relative numerical strengths of its various component communities. In 1948 the Census enumerators, by quirk rather than fiat, produced an invaluable if flawed conspectus of the town. The relevant data, for present purposes, are reproduced in table 1.3.

The various sections of Wa listed in table 1.3 are in some cases wards of the town and in other cases what the Muslims call *kabilas* (Arabic *qabila*), that is, communities defined by reference to origins rather than necessarily by location on the ground. The Balum, or better, Balume, of the table are

Table 1.3. *The structure of Wa town, 1948*

| Section | Population | | | Number of houses | Number of | Persons per | |
	Total	Male	Female	or compounds	rooms	House	Room
Balum	141	57	84	10	64	14.1	2.2
Fongo	649	341	308	9	211	72.1	3.1
Kabanya	655	326	329	19	300	34.5	2.2
Limamyiri	1,098	395	703	17	384	64.6	2.9
Tagarayiri	343	171	172	22	196	15.6	1.8
Wa	1,820	943	877	155	1,018	10.9	1.7
Wa Nayiri	450	250	200	18	233	25.0	1.9
Total	5,156	2,483	2,673	250	2,406		

Tendaanba from two wards, Suriyiri and Sokpariyiri. There are other Tendaanba groups in Wa, most notably those in Tuomuni and Daanayiri. The former, long Muslim though (we have noted) still custodians of an Earth shrine, are probably subsumed under Tagarayiri. The latter, Daanayiri, are the owners of the market and are almost certainly included within Kabanya. Whatever the case, however, Tendaanba comprised a very small section of the town's population in 1948. Tagarayiri, Kabanya and Limamyiri are the three traditional Muslim *kabilas*. Tagarayiri is an Old Muslim community and seat of the Wa Yeri Na. The Dzangbeyiri people, descendants of nineteenth-century Hausa settlers whose head holds the title of Sambadana, must have been included within Tagarayiri in the prospectus. Kabanya is also an Old Muslim community. Limamyiri is not. It is the *kabila* of later Muslim immigrants and customarily provides the Wa Limam or *imam al-balad* and the Wa Friday Limam or *imam al-jum'a*. It is a community of *'ulama'*, and comprises several wards, including Limamyiri proper in the centre of the town and Dondoli on its outskirts.

Wa Nayiri is the ward in which the Wa Na, and those of the Nabihi who make their home in the capital to serve him, reside. Fongo is also technically a Wa Nabihi ward. It is headed by Tendaga Na who belongs to the Guli gate. The 649 people enumerated in Fongo in 1948 were, however, probably for the most part strangers including many from the south – from Asante and the Gold Coast – lured to Wa by the opportunities it offered for careers in Government service as teachers, clerks and the like. The 'Wa' of the 1948 prospectus must surely be the Zongo, the growth of which followed the incorporation of Wala into the Protectorate of the Northern Territories. It attracted immigrants from afar, Muslims for the most part, who sought to set up business there. It must be assumed to have included many of the 365 Southern Nigerians, 556 Wangara, 268 Hausa and at least some of the 1,405 Fulani enumerated within the Wala District in 1948. The Zongo (a term widely used in Ghana for such immigrant settlements and perhaps ultimately

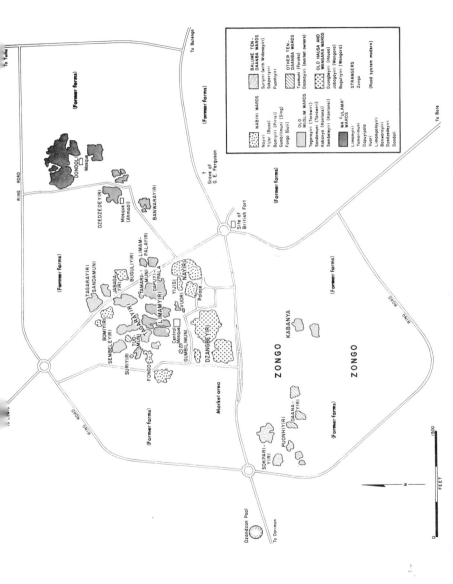

Map 3 Wa: the old town. Based on a survey by W. M. Hamilton, Town Planning Officer, Northern Territories, c. 1960

NABIHI WARDS
Nayiri (Busa)
Yijisi (Buso)
Bomiyiri (Piirisi)
Gumbilimuni (Sing)
Fongo (Gusi)

BALUME TEN-DAANBA WARDS
Suriyiri (with Widaoayiri)
Sokpariyiri
Puonhiyiri

OLD MUSLIM WARDS
Togoreyiri (Torawiri)
Sondomuni (Torawiri)
Kabanya (Kantonsi)
Senbelayiri (Kantonsi)

OTHER TEN-DAANBA WARDS
Tuomuni (Faroko)
Daanayiri (market owners)

WA ᶜULAMAᶜ WARDS
Limamyiri
Tamar-muni
Dapuyiplia
Vuori
Limamollayiri
Banwarayiri
Dzedzedeyiri
Dondoli

OLD HAUSA AND WANGARA WARDS
Dzangbeyiri (Wangoro)
Jabagayiri (Hausa)
Bugullyiri (Wangoro)

STRANGERS
Zongo

(Road system modern)

Dzendzon Pool
To Dorimon
To Lawra
RING ROAD
SOKPARI-YIRI
PUONHIYIRI
DAANA-YIRI
Market area
(Former farms)
SEMBELEYIRI
SURIYIRI
BOMIYIRI
TUO-MUNI
TAGARAYIRI
FONGO
GUMBILIMUNI
Central Mosque
DZANGBEYIRI
YUORI
YIJISI
NAYIRI
Police
IMAMYIRI
TAMAR-MUNI
DAPUYI-PLIA
LIMAM-PALAYIRI
BUGULIYIRI
JABAGA-YIRI
TAGARAYIRI
SANDAMUNI
(Former farms)
KABANYA
ZONGO
ZONGO
RING ROAD
To Bole
(Former farms)
(Former farms)
Site of British Fort
Grave of G. E. Ferguson
(Former farms)
BANWARAYIRI
Mosque (Ahmadi)
DZEDZEDEYIRI
DONDOLI
Mosque
(Former farms)
RING ROAD
To Bulenga
To Tumu

0 1500 FEET
N

derived from the Arabic *suq*, 'market') has continued to expand rapidly, and in the 1960s its head, the Sarkin Zongo or Zongo Na, was afforded recognition as a Wa Kpanbihi, an elder of Wa Na. Today the Zongo people constitute by far the largest component of the urban population, their numbers greatly augmented by the influx of refugees in the 1960s and 1970s from the more northerly drought-stricken neighbours of Ghana.

A Wa Urban Council was created in 1952. It comprised six traditional members, that is, Kpanbihi or their representatives nominated by Wa Na, and twelve elected members. These latter were distributed by *kabila* rather than ward. Tendaanba, Kabanya and Nayiri were each assigned two seats, Tagarayiri and Dzangbeyiri (included in Tagarayiri in the 1948 census) one each, and Limamyiri four.[64] The Zongo and Fongo were unrepresented, probably because their people were for the most part strangers and therefore ineligible to vote. The dominant position of the traditional Muslim *kabilas* in the town was thus perpetuated. Limamyiri, Tagarayiri, Kabanya and Dzangbeyiri together controlled eight of the twelve elective offices.

This brief introductory account of the complex entity that is Wala has paid little heed to its history, to the way in which communities of different origins came together within the one polity. This matter will be turned to next. For the most part Wala sources will be drawn upon, many of them transmitted orally over considerable periods of time before finally, in one circumstance or another, being committed to writing. It is not supposed that the analysis of these sources, however painstaking, will disclose how Wala 'really' originated. It will, however, reveal the ways in which the Wala have chosen and still choose to view their past, and these have their own sort of reality. It is the ambiguities and contradictions within them that chart the structure of conflict in Wala. As for the divergence between the past as the Wala construct it and the veridical past, that, as the Muslims say, Allah alone knows.

2

Wala origins: *lasiri* and *kubaru*

Introduction

The earliest attested dates in Wala history are two provided by a contemporary Gonja annalist. Under 1143 AH (1730/1) the *Kitab Ghanja* notes the death of 'Abdallah, 'king of Wa', and under 1151 AH (1738/9) reports that Wa was plundered by assailants who cannot definitively be identified.[1] No further dates can be considered firm until the first Europeans penetrated the region in the late nineteenth century. The archaeological record for Wa, moreover, is virtually non-existent.[2] It would in any case be unlikely to resolve many of the matters under consideration in this study. In one sense, then, the beginnings of the Wa polity are not only unknown but are likely to remain so. The Wala do, however, make constant reference to origins in their descriptions of the social and political order. This is the 'past' that the Wala choose to live with and in terms of which they construct reality as they see it. It is embodied in oral and written texts which are a key aspect of Wala culture. This constructed 'past' cannot all be veridical, for it contains numerous contradictions. Conversely, it must be presumed that it is not all invented. It is putatively historical in character precisely because it is partly, and perhaps even extensively, truly historical in character, drawing upon the remembrance of 'real' events. Whether veridical or not, however, it is a powerful determinant of social behaviour.

The Wala past, the constructed past, is not the preserve of any cadre of trained specialists such as the drummers of Dagomba, the *griots* of Mali or the *kwadwom* singers of Asante. Fikry, who worked in Wa in 1966–7, remarked that

> the Wala have no set historical narrative or *a* way of telling their history. I was once asked, 'Why didn't you let them talk and narrate their history?' The Wala do not conceive of their history in that manner ... History was told in a conversational manner, with questions and answers given, stressing the freedom of interpreting facts as desired by the narrator.[3]

This is partly but not entirely true. Much of my knowledge of the Wala past was indeed gained in the course of innumerable conversations. Some were so informal and unstructured that it was impossible to record them in any systematic way. Some, however, were so measured and carefully expressed that it was clear that their authors were drawing upon a store of collectively transmitted knowledge. On such occasions informants often insisted that every word be committed to paper. Quite obviously there were different ways in which the past could be discussed, and what was appropriate in one set of circumstances might not be deemed appropriate in another.

Baderi, Spider, is the classical West African trickster in his Wala guise. Baderi, the Wala relate, started life with a grain of corn given him by God. With his innate cunning, Baderi succeeded in exchanging the grain of corn for a cockerel, the cockerel for a ram, and the ram for a human corpse. He then exchanged the corpse for *nalun*, political authority over the Wala. The tale elicits exclamations of astonishment, amazement and amusement from the audience. But that is not its end of the tale. The rise from rags to riches is not the point of the story, for Baderi was *much* too clever to end up by ruling the Wala! He tricked a stranger, Saliya, into taking *nalun* from him, and Saliya's descendants have had to rule the Wala ever since.[4] Many other tales follow from this one. They recount various encounters between Baderi and Na, Spider and King. In them Baderi sometimes supports the Na, sometimes opposes him, but in either case generally emerges the better off.[5]

Such popular tales as those of Baderi and Na belong to the corpus of *sinsolo* (singular, *sinsolun*) or *silima* (singular, *silin*). They are told for entertainment by anyone who knows them and to anyone willing to listen: man, woman or child. They are, however, didactic in intent. Often sardonic and wry in tone, they are a satirical commentary on social and political reality. They are complementary to, but quite different in character from, those stories about Wala origins that are known as *lasiri*.

Lasiri is, strictly speaking, an activity. It is regarded with great respect, to be approached only with an appropriate seriousness of purpose. It is, by and large, a prerogative of the older men of the community. Stories told for entertainment are not part of the corpus of *lasiri*. The word itself is a borrowing. The Malinke root *siri* has the sense of 'binding together', of 'connecting', and *lasiri* is an act that binds together or connects people with people or people with their gods. Hence, in Malinke as in Walii, to recount stories of origins is *lasiri*, for such stories by their very nature tell how different peoples and their gods became bound together as a community. *Lasiri* is concerned with the usable past, and the use to which it is put is in the determination of status and jurisdiction, of customary rights to office, land, tributes and so forth.

A number of works are extant in Wa, written in Arabic script and in both Arabic and Hausa languages, which are quite apparently recensions of oral *lasiri*. They are referred to in Walii as *kubaru*, borrowed through Malinke from the Arabic *khabar*, 'information, news, a story'.[6] The *kubaru* to be considered in this chapter purport to narrate the circumstances in which the

Wala polity came into existence. They may be seen as intended to describe, on the basis of *lasiri*, the constitutional relationships between the various communities that comprise Wala. They are not, however, attempts to codify those relationships; they are more in the nature of evidence than of judgements.

It is not known when and in what circumstances the Muslim literati of Wa first became involved in the task of committing *lasiri* to writing, though at least one of the extant texts may derive from an early-nineteenth-century original. The documents are not regarded as in any sense esoteric. They are readily made available for consultation and discussion, and no one ever objected to my having either manuscript or photographic copies of them made. The whole oral corpus of *lasiri* is by now, I suspect, deeply influenced by the considerable sections of it that have been cast into literary form; that is, 'feedback' from written to oral texts has occurred.

In 1964, in the course of a conversation on Wala origins with leading *'ulama'* of the Dzedzedeyiri section of Limamyiri, Mu'min b. al-Hasan took command of the proceedings. He produced a manuscript and proceeded to read from it.[7] Two years later Fikry elicited from the same scholar his views on recording *lasiri* in writing:

> He says, when they tell him a story and he doesn't write it down, then he forgets. And so, he has been writing them down ... For the tradition, some of it is written down by the Muslims and there are others who narrate them. The stories they hear and what they read, there is a bit of conflict there. So if you want to hear about the history of the Wala, then he'll refer you to what is written.[8]

Clearly Mu'min b. al-Hasan regarded that which was written as thereby acquiring a certain authority. While acknowledging that 'the stories they hear and what they read' may conflict, however, he did not allow that 'what they read' is also often contradictory. Yet this is patently the case. Nothing like consensus emerges in the manuscript sources, and it is not to be expected that it should. It is of the very nature of *lasiri* in Wala, and therefore of the *kubaru* that are based on it, that the purpose is not the manufacture of consensus but the affirmation of positions. As recensions of *lasiri*, the writings reflect the partisan concerns of Tendaanba, Nabihi and Yerihi.

Wala traditions, whether in the oral form of *lasiri* or the written form of *kubaru*, do not present a continuous history. They are neither annals nor chronicles of the kind kept by the *'ulama'* of the neighbouring Gonja kingdom from the early eighteenth century.[9] *Lasiri* and *kubaru* are for the most part thematic rather than narrative in approach. They explore topics. One of their fundamental themes is the relationship between the three sources of authority in Wa, *tendaanlun, nalun* and Islam. It is signal of the non-annalistic character of both *lasiri* and *kubaru* that while events are ordered in time relative one to the other, virtually no attention is paid to chronology. Occasionally a Muslim redactor of *lasiri* might introduce into his text a date, but invariably it is one based upon his own computations rather than authority.

In the following sections, the substance of three *kubaru*, all specifically concerned with Wala origins, will be presented. In no case do we have access to the original work, but only to copies. There is reason to believe that some copies are faithful to their originals; others, however, have clearly been heavily edited and revised in the course of their transmission. Each *kubaru* tells a different story and at points the stories are incompatible. The areas of incompatibility in the texts, and the fierce and frequently violent conflicts which continue (as in 1980) to surround secular and religious affairs in Wa, are analogues. Both articulate, in theory and in practice as it were, the ambiguities and contradictions in the very structure of Wala society.

Wala origins: a Tendaanba account

Al-akhbari Wala Kasamu, 'The Story of Wala, Our Land', is known from two manuscripts. One, in five folios and nine pages, is accessioned as No. 1428 of 1959 in the National Archives of Ghana, and a photocopy is accessioned as IASAR/21 in the Arabic Collection, Institute of African Studies, University of Ghana. Malam Sulayman b. Ibrahim of Dzangbeyiri, Wa, produced another manuscript of the work, also in five folios and nine pages, a photocopy of which was deposited in the Institute's collection in 1962 and accessioned as IASAR/45. Both manuscripts are in Hausa language and Arabic script. In an interview in 1966 Malam Sulayman said that the original text was written by his father, a Borno settler in Wa, at the request and dictation of the Balume Tendaanba apparently around the turn of the nineteenth century.[10] The names of the Tendaanba informants are in fact listed at the end of the work, but cannot be read with any confidence.[11] The two manuscripts differ only in minor respects, the results of copyists' errors or of their attempts to improve the quality of the Hausa. Both are, therefore, probably close to the original. The work will be referred to as 'AWK'. A far-from-satisfactory translation of IASAR/45 into English has been made by S. Pilaszewicz.[12]

AWK tells how a warband left 'Niyirtiwu', a place that has not been identified,[13] and entered the Wa area. A mouse revealed a spring to the warriors; henceforth they tabooed eating that animal. They fought with the Lobi, capturing some and driving others across the river; presumably the Black Volta is meant. They then settled in Wa under their leader (Hausa, *sarki yaki*), referred to later in the text as 'Widana'. They took under their protection another settlement of people near Wa, whose leader was Zarma and whose centre was at Mango, now part of the western outskirts of Wa town. The implication of the text is that these two groups together constitute the Balume ('Baduri', 'Baluri') Tendaanba, and it may be inferred that

Widana and Zarma respectively represent the two wards of Wa now known as Suriyiri ('the house of Suri') and Sokpariyiri ('the house of Sokpari').

A further group of people arrived in Wa. They said that they had come from 'Ghu'; that they were not traders but had left their town as a result of quarrels; and that they wished to settle in Wala. Their leader was Gura. Widana informed Zarma of the arrival of the strangers, and asked him to provide them with lodgings at Mango. 'Ghu' probably refers to Gwo, an old village nine miles due west of Wa town. The text may be read to suggest that Gura's people originated from Gwo; otherwise, and more probably, it was the last place they passed through before arriving in Wa.

Gura's end was an ignominious one according to AWK. He fell into a pit latrine. The story is treated at some length and with a touch of black humour. 'One day the elder of the strangers, Gura, rose and went out to the latrine (*bayan gida*). He did not return.' People went to look for him, and found his stick, shoes, gown and hat lying on the ground. They called him. He answered from the ground. They summoned Zarma. He too heard Gura, and in turn summoned Widana. It was all to no avail. Gura remained in darkness; *ya zama dufu*. Mango became a 'dark place' for his people. They removed to Wa, to stay with Widana. There a son of Gura, not named in the text, married a daughter of Widana, Ashaytu (*dan Gura ya yi aure da dan Widana mata sunasi Shaytu*). A son was born, Kpasa.

In time Widana died. His sons who survived him were young. Kpasa, however, had grown up. He was therefore chosen to assume his maternal grandfather's authority (*Kpasa ya zamna sarauta*). The manner of Kpasa's succession is treated at some length:

Shi ne ya fara sarauta cikin muta- nen Gura. Dan Widana ya ba Sarki Kpasa sarauta don dan mace. Mutanen Gura Kpasa nan da mutanesa ba su saye ba sarauta nan ba su yi fada ba. Su karba sarauta nan wurin mutanen Widana don mi jumuta. Muka duba sunka ba Sarki Kpasa sarauta nan.	He was the first in the rule among the people of Gura. The son of Widana gave Na Kpasa the rule because of who his mother was. The people of Gura, Kpasa and his people, neither bought the rule nor did they seize it. They received the rule from the people of Widana because of kinship. We saw them give Na Kpasa the rule.

There are a number of highly obscure passages in the text of AWK. It appears, however, that to this point in the work the narrators of Balume tradition have sought to affirm three positions. First, *nalun* (translated by the Hausa *sarauta*) was brought to Wa by a warband led by Widana, *sarkin yaki* or warlord. Second, Widana acquired *tendaanlun* in the Wa region by his defeat of 'Lobi' peoples and his agreement with Zarma's community at Mango. And third, the sons of Widana fully consented to the transfer of *nalun* to their sister's son, Kpasa. *Tendaanlun* and *nalun* thus became separated.

In time Kpasa died. AWK gives the following account of the succession:

Alla ya dauka sa. Ya mutu. Kpasa kanesa 'ya'ya ubasu akwai su. Dan'ubasa shi ma ya roke sarauta nan. Don mi kaza roko dan baban Kpasa yaro Widana sunka ba shi kuma sarauta nan. Kane Kpasa ya zamna kuma sarauta nana. Yaro Widana suna aiki shi ma kaman suna aiki Sarki Kpasa na. Ba su rika shi ba kaman ba dankisu ba. Duka sun zama danki.	God took him. He died. Kpasa had a younger brother, they were sons of their father. His half-brother asked for the rule. Because of this begging by the son of Kpasa's father, the son of Widana gave him the rule again. The half-brother of Kpasa sat in the rule again. The son of Widana sent him [to rule] like he had sent Na Kpasa. They would not have continued this but for their relationship. All of them were related.

Kpasa's paternal half-brother is named Pelpuo ('Bilbu') later in the text. Descended from Widana in neither the male nor female line, his succession met with some opposition. A report reached Pelpuo that an animal had been slain by the Widana people, but none of the meat had been sent to him. The then head of Widanayiri, Widana's house, claimed to know nothing of the matter, but subsequently found out that his younger brother was the culprit. He had him flogged. Thereupon the brother fled into the bush, claiming that the Nam should have remained with the descendants of Widana. The head of Widanayiri, however, assured Na Pelpuo of his loyalty, saying: *mu ba ka sarauta nan da farin ciki kaman da muka ba yayaka Kpasa*, 'we gave you the rule happily, like we gave it to your elder brother, Kpasa'. This, the narrators remark, was the origin of the Wa Nam: *asli sarautan Wa haka ya zama*. The theme of AWK is, then, that in effect the people of Widanayiri willingly permitted *nalun* to pass the descendants of Gura.

It remained for the narrators to add one more story. Kajikpara arrived in Wa at the time of Na Kpasa. They were like brothers and did not want to fight each other. They arranged a meeting and exchanged salutations. Na Kpasa invited Kajikpara to stay with him for a few nights. Kajikpara did so, but fell ill and died. Na Kpasa buried him. He had a tomb built over the grave, and designated the sons of Widana its custodians. Everyone knows the place. The grandfather of Kajikpara's people was Sandamu. This story has to be contextualized from other sources. 'Sandamu' is known as Sanda Muru in Walii and as Sidi 'Umar in Arabic. He is regarded as apical ancestor of the Tagarayiri community in Wa and Nasa, that is, of the Yeri Na's people.[14] Kajikpara is less well remembered but must be the early Yeri Na, Konjekuri.[15] It is clear, then, that the story is intended to account for the third sphere of authority in Wa, that exercised by Yeri Na.

The whole work, AWK, ends with the Tendaanba informants making a resounding claim to veracity. That they should do so is not surprising. Their very status within the Wala community was at issue, and particularly their position *vis-à-vis* the Wa Nam. The text is difficult to read, but the following tentative rendering probably captures its sense.

Amana ni su yi masa ajayi. Maganaga da ya fadi ga gaskiyani. Zuru ruba munafucci kira wanda ya kira karya. Ni barawo ne.	Those who have put this down are to be trusted. This account is told with truth. Whoever [says it is] falsehood, boasting, hypocrisy, forgery, he is telling a lie. He is a thief.

Wala origins: a Muslim account

Al-akhbar Saltanat Bilad Wa, 'The Story of the Sultanate in the Land of Wa', is known in only one manuscript. I was shown the work by Al-Hajj Siddiq b. Sa'id ('Fanta Sidiki') in 1964, and allowed to photocopy it (accessioned as IASAR/298). It is a single folio, written on both sides in Arabic. According to Al-Hajj Siddiq, he and his father made the copy in the late 1920s from an older and deteriorating manuscript. Its author, he claimed, was his great-grandfather, Wa Limam Sa'id b. 'Abd al-Qadir.[16] If the ascription is correct, the work is probably an early-nineteenth-century one in origin, though since it exists only in a late copy it is difficult to know how heavily it has been edited. It will be referred to as 'ASBW'. In 1964, Al-Hajj Siddiq made an extensive verbal commentary on this work, which will be cited as 'ASBW/com'.[17] Its importance stems from the fact that Al-Hajj Siddiq was required to study ASBW with his grandfather, son of its putative author. 'My grandfather Ahmad b. Limam Sa'id', he said, 'made me learn it. He would call me to his house from time to time and ask me to repeat it. This happened more than thirty times. When I could not understand anything, my grandfather explained it.'

ASBW commences, after doxology and title, with the statement, *fi awwal zaman mulk yumalakun anfusahum*, 'in the first times they themselves possessed authority'. Then, the text continues, feuding (*khusuma*) occurred among them. This was in the time of their king (*malik*) Suri. Suri heard of a warband (*jaish*) that had arrived at Ghiraba, that is, Jirapa some thirty-eight miles north by northwest of Wa. He sent messengers there to solicit help, but they learned that the warriors had moved to Nalerigu (*Nadiriku Nayiri*, 'the Na's place, Nalerigu'). The messengers were told to follow them. They met with the Na of Mampurugu (*Malik Nadiriku*), who was favourable to Suri's request. The warriors agreed to return to the Wala country. The Na attached his son Saliya to them. Three of Saliya's junior brothers also brought their own men to join the march.

The warband reached some ruins (*talal*) east of Wa. The warriors were suffering from the heat. Saliya prayed and it rained. The band advanced on

35

Wa, fought there, and was victorious. Suri said that he had nothing to give those who had come to his help except his land. Retaining one-third for himself, he awarded one-third to Saliya and one-third to the leader of the original warband. Saliya settled at Mango. He married the eldest daughter of Suri, who gave birth to Gura. He took as second wife 'one of the Kanbali' (*ba'd Kanbali*), and Harun was born.[18] He took as third wife a virgin he had brought with him from Nalerigu. Juri was born.

ASBW does not treat the affairs of the Wa Nam further, but rather takes up the story of Juri and the Muslims. At this point the text becomes very difficult to follow without the exegesis in ASBW/com. Juri asked his father, Saliya, for permission to settle at the spot where he (Saliya) had prayed for rain. ASBW/com identifies it as Nasa. The Muslims were three, Sidi 'Umar, Yusuf and 'Umar Fitini (Malinke, 'Small 'Umar'). All were 'brothers', presumably in the sense that all (according to ASBW/com) used the patronym 'Tarawiri'. The senior of the three was Sidi 'Umar or Sanda Muru, and it is implicit in ASBW but explicit in ASBW/com that he was leader of the warband that had entered the region at Jirapa. His companions, the full brothers Yusuf and 'Umar Fitini, were not warriors but scholars according to ASBW. 'Umar Fitini left Nasa to found a school at Chegli ('Thakili', with an extra point under the *tha*'). Juri left to settle at Charingu ('Tharinghu'). Sidi 'Umar and Yusuf remained in Nasa.

The relatively extended treatment of these matters in ASBW shows that it was written with the primary purpose of explaining the origins of the Wala Muslim communities. Indeed, the Muslim provenance of ASBW is clearly indicated in its conclusion, in which the writer essayed even a date: 'this is the history (*ta'rikh*) of our forefathers of old in Wa and at that time there was no-one who called himself a Muslim until the year 717 of the Prophet [AD 1317/18]'.

Wala origins: a Nabihi account

A manuscript also having the title *Al-akhbar Saltanat Bilad Wa*, and one having the Hausa title *Al-habari Sarauta Wa*, 'The Story of the Rule in Wa', are closely related Arabic and Hausa versions of the same work. Their preservation results from the activities of Friday Limam Ishaq b. 'Uthman (commonly known as Malam Isaka), who died in 1931. He collected materials from an older generation of scholars,[19] and had them copied into a bound volume supplied him by the District Commissioner. The volume is inscribed, 'Dec. 1922 This book is given to Mallam Isaka on condition that he writes the History of the Walas in it in Hausa. P. J. Whittall D. C. Wa.'[20] It is now in the National Archives of Ghana, Accra, accessioned as No. 1427 of 1959 (and a photocopy is accessioned as IASAR/22 in the Arabic Collection, Institute of African Studies, University of Ghana). Each text is in two pages, the Arabic on pages 12 and 13 of the bound volume and the Hausa on pages 7 and 14. The two pages of the latter are in different hands, neither of which is that of the Arabic. Another text in Arabic having the same title is sufficiently closely related to these texts to be regarded as derivative from a common source. A copy of it was made in 1963 by Al-Hajj Siddiq b. Sa'id from an older manuscript in his possession.[21] It is in one page, and is accessioned as IASAR/151. To avoid confusion with ASBW, which has the same Arabic title, the work represented by these three manuscripts will be referred to as 'HSW', from the Hausa title.

All three version of HSW commence identically:

> The Story of the Sultanate of the Land of Wa. Their forefather was named Saliya. He left the country of Da[w]aba and arrived in the country of Wa. At that time the people of the land of Wa were not many in number. He sat with them, all together. And the name of the *harami* of Wala was Suri.

The *waw* in 'Da[w]aba' has two diacritical marks over it and must represent a vernacular 'gb'. The reading, then, is 'Dagbaba' for Dagbamba, more familiar in English as Dagomba. In one version of HSW (IASAR/151) *harami* is glossed: 'that is, *hadiman*'. I cannot explain the gloss. *Harami*, however, is clearly from the root *haram*, 'forbidden', 'sacred', and is perhaps used in the context to refer to Suri's exercise of *tendaanlun*.

At this point in the work the Arabic version copied in 1963 (which will be referred to as HSW/a) differs greatly from the Arabic and Hausa versions copied in 1922 or 1923 (HSW/b). On internal evidence it seems that HSW/a is generally but not invariably closer to the original work; HSW/b shows signs of extensive but imperfect editing. The texts read:

HSW/a	HSW/b
The offspring [*wuld*] of Saliya. His sons [*awlad*] were many and the senior of his sons was Ghura. He was the son of Suri's daughter. He became sultan after the death of his grandfather Suri. He sat immediately after him. When he died they all assembled and gave the sultanate to Harun. He was Pilpu. He had a long life.	The son [*walad*] of Saliya was named Pilpu and the sons [*awlad*] of Saliya were many. As for Pilpu, he was the senior of them. They all assembled and gave the sultanate to Pilpu. Pilpu had a long life. When he died he left many children. And as for Suri, his community is the people of Ghuli.

The texts continue to diverge. HSW/a has Pelpuo succeeded by his brother Juri. HSW/b shows signs of the editorial process in apparently returning to the story of Pelpuo and repeating itself:

When he [Harun] died his brother Juri sat and he had a long life. The sons of Harun were many, and of Juri too. The senior of the sons of Pilpu were Na Yijinsunu and Na Kunzayushi, and of the sons of	So they gathered and made him sultan. He also had a long life. He left many children and the senior of them was Janyusi. He was their sultan. He had a long life. Then he died. Then among them their

37

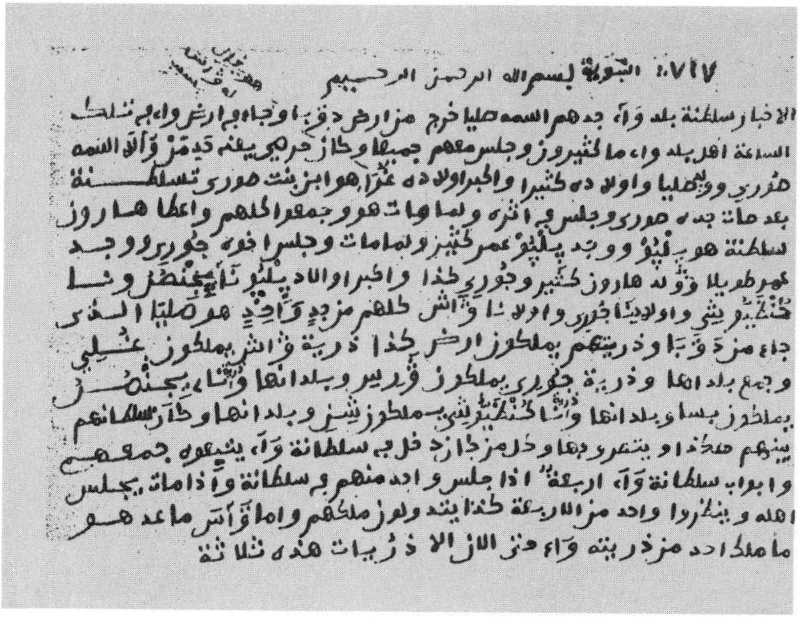

Plate 5 *Al-akhbar Saltanat Bilad Wa* (HSW/a, first part)

Juri the first was Na Kpasha. All of them were from one grandfather, Saliya, who came from Dagbaba. Their descendants [*dhurriyat*] possess the land.

senior was from the people of Pirisi. They made him sultan and he had a long life. He had many children. He died. There was a man named Ghuluki from the people of Chaghlu. He became sultan of Wala.

The basic theme of HSW/a is clear. After Pelpuo (or Harun) and Juri had held the Nam, it passed to their sons. It continued, in other words, to be held by the descendants of Saliya in the male line and did not revert to the descendants of Suri in Widanayiri. The theme of HSW/b is obscure, and its elucidation is possible only with reference to later sections of the text.

The redactor of the traditions set down in HSW turned next to the origins of the system of gates to the Nam. Again, extensive changes have been made in the course of the transmission of the work. Most worthy of note, the gates to the Wa Nam are four in number according to HSW/a and five according to HSW/b:

So the descendants of Kpasha possess Ghuli and all its villages. The descendants of Juri possess

The first Pilpu was from the people of Busa and all its villages. As for Kpasa, he was from the people

38

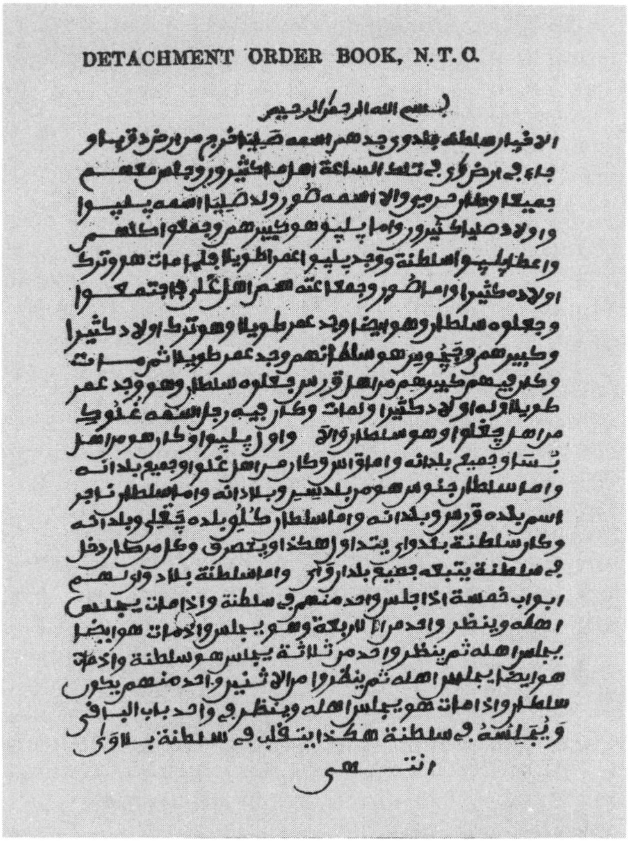
DETACHMENT ORDER BOOK, N.T.C.

بسم الله الرحمن الرحيم

Plate 6 *Al-akhbar Saltanat Bilad Wa* (HSW/b, first part)

Kpirisi and its villages. The descendants of Na Yijinsunu possess Busa and its villages. The descendants of Na Kunzayushi possess Shini and its villages.

of Ghuli and all its villages. As for Sultan Janusi, he was from the country of Sini and its villages. As for Sultan Najari, the name of his country is Pirisi and its villages. As for Sultan Kuluwi, his country is Chaghli and its villages.

The most remarkable feature of HSW/a is that Kpasa, who earlier in the text had been relegated to the status of son of Juri, appears as founder of the first gate, Guli. Equally remarkable, Kpasa appears as founder of the second gate in HSW/b, even though there is no previous reference to him in that text. In HSW/b Pelpuo is regarded as founder of Busa gate; in HSW/a this is attributed to his son Yijisi ('Yijinsunu'). Both texts attribute the foundation of the Sing gate to Pelpuo's son Djonyusi ('Kunzayushi', 'Janusi'), and that of the Pirisi gate ('Wirisi', with two diacritical marks over the *waw*) to Na Djare ('Juri', 'Najari'). HSW/b has a fifth gate, Chegli ('Jaghlu', 'Jaghli', with three diacritical marks under the *jim*), founded by Kunlugi ('Ghuluki', 'Kuluwi'). In this respect HSW/b may preserve an older tradition.[22] Be this as it may, the discrepancies between HSW/a and HSW/b with respect to the gates are reproduced in the account each gives of the mode of succession:

Their sultanate was between them. It functioned thus. The way of entering the sultanate of Wa, he succeeds from all of them. The gates [*abwab*] of the sultanate of Wa are four. When one among them sits in the sultanate and dies, his people sit and decide on one among four. Thus their kingship rotated. As for Kpasha, none of them are counted kings from the descendants [*dhurriyat*] of Wa. Until now the descendants [*dhuriyyat*] are three.

The sultanate of the country of Wa circulated. It functioned thus. The way of entering the sultanate, he succeeds from all of the countries of Wa. As for the sultanate of the country of Wa, it has five gates [*abwab*]. When one of them sits in the sultanate and dies, his people sit and decide on one among the four. He sits. If he dies, too, his people sit. Then they decide on one among the three. He sits in the sultanate. If he too dies, his people sit. Then they decide on one among the two. He becomes sultan. If he dies the people sit and decide on one in the remaining gate and he sits in the sultanate. In this way the sultanate of the country of Wa turns around.

HSW ends with a list of the Wa Nas. All three versions, in HSW/a and in the Arabic and Hausa texts of HSW/b, differ in the early sections but correspond from Na Danduni onwards. The matter of the early incumbents of the Wa Nam will be addressed further in chapter 4.

Wala origins: ambiguities and contradictions

The various authors of the *kubaru* clearly did not achieve agreement in their accounts of the origin of the Wala polity. That they did not do so was not a matter of incompetence or carelessness, but resulted from the very nature of the underlying *lasiri*. The scribes were not seeking to establish an authoritative version of Wala history nor were they attempting to codify Wala constitutional law. Their writings express the very ambiguities and contradictions in Wala society to which reference has already been made.

The *kubaru* concerned with Wala origins share a common problematic. All seek to describe, in historical or putatively historical terms, the three sources of authority in Wa: *tendaanlun, nalun* and Islam. The Wala incline strongly to construct their views of society in sets of triads. Thus one moves from the three sources of authority to the more specific issue of the three kinds of *nalun*, namely Widana Nalun, Yeri Nalun and Wa Nalun. This is the theme of the three *kubaru* summarized above.

AWK treats Widana as leader of a warband which entered the Wa region from the unidentified 'Niyirtiwu'. For reasons that will become apparent below (figure 2), he is to be identified with the Suri whose place of origin is not referred to in ASBW and HSW but who is described in the former work by the Arabic term *malik*, suggesting his exercise of *nalun*, and in the latter by the Arabic *harami*, suggesting perhaps his exercise of *tendaanlun*. There is ambiguity but not necessarily contradiction in these sources, since ASBW and HSW neither assert nor deny that Suri – or Widana – was an immigrant.

Both ASBW and AWK treat the origins of Yeri Nalun. ASBW refers to Sidi 'Umar or Sanda Muru as leader of a warband that entered the Wala region from the west. After thrusting eastwards into Mampurugu, Sidi 'Umar is said to have retraced his steps to settle at Nasa. AWK refers to Kajikpara (or better, Konjekuri), 'grandson' of Sidi 'Umar, entering Wa itself at what must be presumed to be a later date. HSW does not treat the matter. Again, there may be ambiguities but there are no contradictions in the sources.

The burden of the texts, then, is to present the *nalun* possessed by the Widanas and Yeri Nas as based upon the warlord status of Suri and Sidi 'Umar respectively. The matter of Wa Nalun is much more complex. HSW and ASBW identify the apical ancestor of the Wa Nas in the male line as Saliya. HSW has him leaving Dagomba to settle among Suri's people in Wa. No explanation of the move is offered. ASBW tells of Suri's appeal for help that resulted in Saliya, son of the Na of Mampurugu, arriving in Wala with three of his brothers. 'Dagomba' is often used in the Wa texts to refer both to Dagomba proper, with its capital at Yendi, and to the sister kingdom of Mampurugu, with its capital at Nalerigu. No contradiction is necessarily involved. HSW and ASBW agree broadly in treating Saliya as the third warlord and the third source of *nalun*. AWK, however, offers a quite different and incompatible account of the origins of Wa Nalun.

According to AWK the apical ancestor of the Wa Nas in the male line was not Saliya but Gura. Gura arrived in the Wa country from or through Gwo, and met his pitiful end at Mango. It was by virtue of the marriage of his son, by inference Saliya, though he is not named, to a daughter of Suri that the Widana people allowed *nalun* (but not *tendaanlun*) to pass to a son of that marriage, namely Kpasa. AWK is not unsupported in treating Saliya as son of Gura. District Commissioner Whittall entered a note on Gura in the Wa District General Information Book for 1924–5. The Wa chiefship, he wrote, was founded by Gura who came from Yendi or Gambaga (the town of the Mampurugu Limams) with three sons. The first son, Sorlia (that is, Saliya), established himself at Wa; the second, Denga, at Dorimon; and the third,

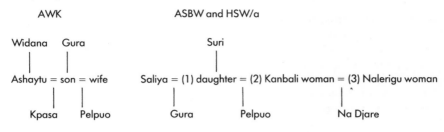

Figure 2 The origins of the Wa Nam: family reconstructions

Bunkani, at Buna.[23] The triad of the three sons of Gura was probably given to Whittall by Ishaq b. 'Uthman, who is known to have been his principal informant. The triad is isomorphic with that of the three brothers of Saliya which appears in ASBW, and this topic will be examined in chapter 3.

The nature of the contradiction between the tradition of HSW and ASBW on the one hand, and AWK on the other, is most clearly revealed in the treatment of the marriage of Suri's (or Widana's) daughter. Comparison of the two versions shown in figure 2 suggests certain equations. First, the Suri of ASBW and HSW/a is the same person as the Widana of AWK (and indeed to the present day the head of the Wa ward, Suriyiri, 'Suri's house', takes the title of Widana). Second, the unnamed daughter of Suri in ASBW and HSW/a is the Ashaytu of AWK, and conversely, the unnamed son of Gura in AWK is the Saliya of ASBW and HSW/a.

Granted this measure of agreement between the two traditions, there remains the major discrepancy with respect to Gura and Kpasa. AWK has *nalun* passing from Widana to Kpasa and then to Pelpuo. ASBW and HSW/a have it passing from Saliya to Gura and then to Pelpuo. The main text of HSW/b, though not the list of Nas with which it concludes, omits any reference to Gura, and has *nalun* passing directly from Saliya to Pelpuo. AWK and HSW/b are thus the most at variance of the texts under consideration. For convenience I shall refer to the version in AWK as the Na Kpasa tradition and to that in HSW/b as the Na Pelpuo tradition. I do so because it is key to the one that Na Kpasa, and to the other that Na Pelpuo, was the first 'true' Wa Na.

The Wala savants are well aware of the ambiguities and contradictions present in these accounts, and there is a constant effort to explore them. This, indeed, is characteristic of the activity known as *lasiri*. The traditions are constantly reworked in an attempt to remove ambiguities and resolve contradictions. The result is to produce innumerable variations on the theme of the Wa Nam. The *kubaru* ASBW contains, we have seen, the triad of the three wives of Saliya, namely, the daughter of Suri, the Kanbali woman, and the virgin from Nalerigu. If the original text of ASBW was indeed an early-nineteenth-century recension of *lasiri*, then the triad is an old one. It is compatible with both the Na Kpasa and Na Pelpuo traditions. It is supplemented in ASBW, logically enough, by the triad of the three sons of Saliya (by his three wives), namely, Gura, Pelpuo and Na Djare ('Juri'). This triad is a bridging one. It is entirely compatible neither with the Na Kpasa nor the Na Pelpuo tradition. It is incompatible with the former in making Gura son rather than father of Saliya, and Gura rather than Kpasa the senior son of Saliya. It is incompatible with the latter in making Pelpuo second rather than first son of Saliya. It is compromising, however, in making space for Gura to hold the Wa Nam after Saliya but before Pelpuo. In this respect it may be seen as underwriting the inclusion of Gura in all lists of Wa Nas (for which see chapter 4, table 4.6). The triad conforms more closely to the Na Pelpuo tradition, but introduces Gura into it. It conforms less closely to the Na Kpasa tradition in assigning Na Kpasa's space to Gura. In effect, then, ASBW is a recension of *lasiri* that may be located, on a continuum between the Na Kpasa and the Na Pelpuo traditions, nearer to the latter.

I was told a story in Wa in the 1960s, the full significance of which eluded me at the time.[24] Gura made his son Saliya the Na in Wa. Saliya died before Gura, and there were disputes about who should succeed him. Gura therefore said that he would take the Nam for himself. In this way Gura came to rule in Wa in succession to his own son, Saliya.[25] I have no way of knowing whether this story was invented for my benefit or whether it has a longer ancestry. It was, however, clearly an effort at reconciliation, intended to explain how Gura could be both the father of Saliya, as required by the Na Kpasa tradition, and the successor in office of Saliya as stipulated in the lists of Wa Nas. It was, in a sense, contrapuntal to the story in ASBW. It leaned towards the Na Kpasa tradition, yet remained incompatible with it in allowing that both Gura and Saliya held the Wa Nam.

It is quite impractical to attempt to record all the stories that lie somewhere on the continuum between the Na Kpasa and the Na Pelpuo traditions. The permutations and combinations of the basic elements are virtually limitless, given the imaginative fertility of the Wala savants and their deep concern with the Wala past. It is, however, in the matter of the gates to the Nam that the ambiguities and contradictions in *lasiri* and *kubaru* became of acute practical significance. Fundamental is the triad of the three towns of the three sons of the three wives of Saliya. The triad is very widely known and occurs, for example, in the *Ta'rikh Al-Muslimin* (a work which will be discussed in chapter 3). The three towns are Guli, Gbetore and Yaro, associated with Kpasa (or Gura), Pelpuo and Na Djare respectively.

Guli lies about four miles north by northeast of Wa. The Na Kpasa tradition has it founded by Na Kpasa, eldest son of Saliya and maternal grandson of Suri. He left it to become the first Na to make his seat in Wa, where he established the Fongo section of the town. The Na Pelpuo tradition has Guli founded by Gura, thus contradicting the Na Kpasa tradition (as in AWK) that Gura lived at Mango and disappeared there. It is noteworthy, however, that all versions of HSW refer to Guli as the Na Kpasa gate. HSW/a lists it first among the gates: 'the descendants of Kpasha possess

Ghuli and all its villages'. HSW/b lists it second: 'as for Kpasa, he was from the people of Ghuli and all its villages'. Significantly, however, HSW/b also has the remark, 'as for Suri, his community is the people of Ghuli'. Granted that HSW/b represents the Na Pelpuo tradition, the remark is perhaps intended to imply that Kpasa possessed Guli by virtue of his maternal rather than his paternal descent, thus distinguishing Guli from the other gates.

The matter of the second town, Gbetore, is complex. It was, according to the *Ta'rikh al-Muslimin*, the senior of the three towns (Hausa, *buban garinsu*). Its status as such is to be associated with the view that it was actually founded by Saliya rather than Pelpuo. ASBW has Saliya established at Mango,[26] and other accounts associate him with Degu, some three miles east of Wa.[27] There are, however, very strong traditions that name Gbetore as Saliya's principal seat and that have Pelpuo succeeding him as Gbetore Na.[28] When Pelpuo removed to Wa to take the Nam, he founded the section of the town that became known as Yijihi. Gbetore was abandoned.[29] Pelpuo's sons, however, subsequently settled in Busa, some eight miles southeast of Wa, which then became the Yijihi or Pelpuo gate to the Wa Nam. HSW/a treats Yijihi, idiosyncratically, as the eponymous founder of the gate, and lists it third: 'the descendants of Na Yijinsunu [Yijihi] possess Busa and its villages'. HSW/b lists the gate first: 'Pelpuo was from the people of Busa and all its villages'. With Pelpuo's assumption of the Wa Nam, the title of Gbetore Na became for long extinct. It was, however, apparently used by Yamusa of Busa before he was enskinned as Wa Na Pelpuo III in 1920. It was revived by Wa Na Mumuni Koray (1949–53) and awarded to Sumani, a son of the former Busa Na Bukari (1922–42).[30] Gbetore Na Sumani became Busa Na in 1969 but there was much controversy about the matter. It was argued that Gbetore Na outranked Busa Na and should therefore only seek promotion to Wa.[31]

Yaro lies eleven miles northeast of Wa. It is generally recognized as having been the town of the third son of Saliya (by his Nalerigu wife), namely, Na Djare. The story in ASBW, that Na Djare ('Juri') founded a town where his father Saliya had successfully prayed for rain, undoubtedly refers to Yaro. ASBW/com, however, has it as Nasa. The contradiction may be more apparent than real, for it will be seen in chapter 3 that Nasa, only three miles distant from Yaro, was in fact the town of Na Djare's Muslims. Be that as it may, when Na Djare became Wa Na he founded the Bomiyiri section of Wa town. His descendants subsequently removed from Yaro to Pirisi, which thus became the Na Djare gate. HSW/a lists it second of the gates: 'the descendants of Juri possess Kparisi and its villages'. HSW/b lists it fourth: 'as for Najari, the name of his country is Pirisi and its villages'.

To this point in tradition the triadic structure of analysis is observed: Guri is the Na Kpasa gate, Gbetore (or later, Busa) the Na Pelpuo gate, and Yaro (or later, Pirisi) the Na Djare gate. The symmetry, however, of the three sons of Saliya and the three gates to the Nam breaks down. There is a fourth gate that has to be accounted for. Pelpuo is said to have had a full brother named

44

Djonyusi. He also became Wa Na and founded the Gumbilimuni section of the town. His sons settled at Sing, six miles southeast of Wa, to create the Djonyusi or Sing gate to the Wa Nam.[32] HSW/a lists this fourth of the gates: 'The descendants of Na Kunzayushi possess Shini and its villages.' HSW/b lists it third: 'as for Sultan Junusi, he was from the country of Sini and its villages'.

HSW/b is to the best of my knowledge unique among the sources in recognizing a fifth gate to the Nam, that created at Chegli, presumably by the descendants of Na Kunjokun ('Kunlugi'). Chegli is less than a mile from Pirisi. This putative fifth gate will be disregarded. Not only is there no evidence that anyone from it ever became Wa Na after Na Kunjokun but, more to the point, there is no evidence that anyone from Chegli ever subsequently contested the Wa Nam.

The fundamental contradiction between the Na Kpasa and Na Pelpuo traditions may, then, now be clarified though certainly not resolved. According to the former tradition, Na Kpasa inherited *nalun* from his maternal grandfather Suri, and by virtue of the exercise of it became Wa Na. His father, Saliya, was irrelevant to his claims to the Nam. According to the Na Pelpuo tradition, Gbetore Na Saliya exercised *nalun* by virtue of his status as warlord, and his son Pelpuo in turn inherited this and took it to Wa on becoming Wa Na. In the Na Kpasa tradition Wa *nalun* originated from Widana, passed to Na Kpasa, and was voluntarily transferred to Na Kpasa's half-brothers. In the Na Pelpuo tradition Wa *nalun* originated from Saliya, and was inherited by Na Pelpuo and his paternal brothers.

In its most uncompromising form, the Na Pelpuo tradition cannot recognize Na Kpasa as a Wa Na. Although a son of Saliya, and even his eldest son, Na Kpasa chose to exercise Widana's *nalun*. Pelpuo was thus the first true Wa Na, the first to exercise Saliya's *nalun* derivative ultimately from the Mampurugu Nam. In *lasiri* attempts are made to mediate the extreme positions. Two examples must suffice. There is a story that has Saliya leaving Mampurugu not in response to Suri's request for help (as in ASBW), but as a result of a dispute over the Mampurugu skin. He settled in the Wa region. He was welcomed by Suri, who gave him a wife. At this time Suri held both *tendaanlun* and *nalun*. Suri said that since Saliya had been seeking *nalun* in Mampurugu but had failed to acquire it, he would transfer his *nalun* to him. Quite evidently, the purpose of this story is to explain how *nalun*, first owned by Suri as required by the Na Kpasa tradition, passed to Saliya as required by the Na Pelpuo tradition.[33] Another attempt at reconciliation makes Na Kpasa a grandson of Saliya. It is attested in HSW/a, which treats him as a son of Na Djare.[34] Quite incompatible with the Na Kpasa tradition, it nevertheless allows for the appearance of Na Kpasa on most lists of Nas though leaving his position as predecessor of Na Djare quite unexplained.

The various attempts to reconcile the Na Kpasa and Na Pelpuo traditions have had little impact in the sphere of practical skin politics. On the one hand is a faction that maintains the rights of the Na Kpasa or Guli gate to the Wa

Nam, on the other a faction that denies these. Both factions, however, agree on one matter: that other than Na Kpasa no one from Guli has ever succeeded to the Wa Nam. In the circumstances, this may be assumed to be veridical. It is, then, all the more surprising that the Na Kpasa gate is still able to advance its claims to the Nam vigorously albeit not successfully. In the contest of 1978–85, which we have seen erupted into violence and occasioned many deaths, the candidate Yakubu Seidu belonged to the Guli gate. More than the matter of the Wa Nam as such was and is at issue. The descendants of Na Kpasa in Guli gate, by virtue of their claims to have acquired *nalun* from Widana Suri, have a natural constituency among the Tendaanba. Their inability to secure the Nam reflects the weakness of that constituency. Conversely, the resolution with which the Guli gate continues to contest the Nam is a reflection of the strong sense of grievance of its Tendaanba constituents, that is, of those 'landowners' who have seen their customary tenures so extensively eroded. Matters of access to land, an increasingly scarce resource in Wala, subtly underlie matters of access to chiefly office.

3

Wala origins: the 'alim as local historian

Introduction

Each of the three *kubaru*, AWK, ASBW and HSW, is partial in approach, reflecting the interests of Landowners, Muslims and Princes respectively. The earliest known, and probably the earliest, attempt to use *lasiri* and *kubaru* to produce a unified account of the origins of the Wala polity as such dates from 1922. The work in question exists in both Arabic and Hausa versions. The author was conscious of his departure from the *kubaru* tradition, and signalled this by his use of the term *ta'rikh*, 'history', rather than *khabar* in the Arabic titles, and somewhat idiosyncratically, of *magana*, 'talk', rather than *labari* in the Hausa.

The work is known in a manuscript copy made for J. Goody in 1952 at the behest of Limam Salih b. al-Hasan. It is accessioned as IASAR/152 in the Arabic Collection, Institute of African Studies, University of Ghana. It comprises two parts. The first is entitled *Ta'rikh Ahl Wala*, 'History of the Wala People' and *Magana Wala*, 'Talk about Wala', in the Arabic and Hausa respectively. The second is entitled *Ta'rikh al-Muslimin*, 'History of the Muslims', and *Magana Muslimi Na Daurri*, 'Talk about the Old Muslims'. The first part will be referred to as 'TAW', the second as 'TM'. The manuscript is written on lined paper, measuring 18.5 by 23 cm. The Hausa version of TAW is on pages 1–5 and of TM on pages 6–9; the Arabic version of TAW is on pages 10–13, and of TM on pages 14–16. Each of the four texts is, however, paginated independently in Arabic.

Both versions of TAW are dated to 1922 and the presumption is that TM was written at the same time. All four texts underwent some modification when they were copied in 1952, in that the lists of Wa Nas and Wa Limams were updated to that year. The Arabic and Hausa texts are so alike that translation was clearly involved. It is difficult to be sure whether this was from Arabic to Hausa or vice versa. Both TAW and TM are divided into chapters (Arabic *fasl*, Hausa *fasali*). The Hausa has five such chapters in each part. The Arabic text is less neatly subdivided. It may be, then, that the Arabic text was written first, and that it was the translator into Hausa who took the opportunity to tidy up the structure of the texts.

The manuscript does not identify the author of the work. He was, we may be confident, the Friday Limam Ishaq b. 'Uthman (more generally known as Malam Isaka). Reference has been made earlier to the bound volume given to Limam Ishaq by District Commissioner Whittall in 1922, 'on condition that he writes the History of the Walas in it in Hausa'. Rather than do this, Limam Ishaq had scribes copy into it a number of items, *kubaru* (including HSW), office lists, letters and various miscellaneous notes in both Hausa and Arabic. These items must have been among the materials he had assembled for use in compiling his Wala history, which is clearly the work represented by TAW and TM. Indeed, in 1964 I spoke to a son of Limam Ishaq and several others of his family about this matter. They remembered Limam Ishaq collecting materials from an older generation of scholars then alive, especially, they said, 'from 'Uthman Daleri of Yeri Nayiri and Malam Abu, also of Yeri Nayiri'.[1] This puts the question of the authorship of TAW and TM virtually beyond doubt. A provisional English translation of the Arabic text of both TAW and TM was made by N. Levtzion in 1963, and an indifferent translation of the Hausa by S. Pilaszewicz in 1969.[2]

Limam Ishaq, of the Dzedzedeyiri section of Wa Limamyiri, was son of Friday Limam 'Uthman Dabila and grandson of Wa Limam Ya'qub. He was born probably in the 1860s, and died in 1931. No critical apparatus is present in his writings. He did not identify his sources, though some of them can be identified. He did not present conflicting evidence and argue for one interpretation rather than another, though we know that the evidence he worked with had many contradictions. He was concerned to synthesize Tendaanba, Nabihi and Muslim views of their own respective pasts in such a way as to produce a unified account of Wala origins. He went beyond the passive role of redactor and assumed the more active one of historian. He used the traditional predilection for triads to develop a schema in terms of which to order his materials. The rigour with which he followed this schema is only slightly obscured by the fact that he also attempted to separate out, in TAW and TM respectively, the history of the Wa Nam from the history of the Muslims.

Wala, as Limam Ishaq saw it, was the creation of three warrior 'tribes'. The word *qabila* is most commonly used in the Arabic, and *zuri'a* in the Hausa; in English only the much-scorned word 'tribe' has the vagueness necessary to convey the loose sense of the original. The first tribe, according to TAW, came from Yendi, the second from Nalerigu, and the third from Mande. The first tribe had three leaders. One settled in Wa, one in Gwo and one in Wechiau. The first tribe was troubled by three subject peoples and was obliged to seek help. In response, the second warrior tribe arrived. Its leader and his immediate followers established themselves in three towns near Wa, namely, Yaro, Guli and Gbetore. He also had three subordinate commanders. They established themselves at Funsi, Kojopere and Walembele. The third warrior tribe came from Mande. It consisted of three sections. The first (itself consisting of three sections) founded Palewogo, the second Visi, and the third Nasa.

In TM the perspective changes. The image of the Muslim rather than the warlord as such is the dominant one. The first Muslims to enter Wala were the warriors from Mande. The second were scholars, also from Mande. The third were traders, from Hausaland ('which is called Najiriyya', that is, Nigeria). These latter were also in three sections.

The *kubaru* discussed in chapter 2 were concerned principally with the origins of *nalun* in Wa and particularly with the matter of the *nalun* exercised by the Wa Nas. Limam Ishaq's perspectives are much wider ones. Indeed, he glosses over the contradictions and ambiguities present in the *kubaru* in a quite cursory manner. He is more concerned to set the early history of Wala in a regional context and thereby to explain the pluralistic nature of Wala society. In the following sections, Limam Ishaq's schematic presentation of Wala history will be followed. His access to earlier written *kubaru* and to oral *lasiri* of a generation now long vanished, and his native sense of the structures of Wala society, afford him an authority that no-one can ever approach again. Respect is therefore appropriate in attempting both to expound and critique his work.

The 'First Tribe' in Wala

In the *Ta'rikh Ahl Wala* (TAW) Limam Ishaq commences his account of the 'First Tribe' (*Qabila al-Awal*) with reference to the affairs of Gonja, the sprawling kingdom on the northwestern fringes of which the Wala country lies. The translation follows the Hausa text:

> So be it. The Tanpulinsi ['Tanbulinsi', with three points under the *ba*'] stayed here together with the Gonja people ['Ghunjawa']. The Tanpulinsi were more powerful than the people of Gonja. They troubled them, inflicting violence on them. The people of Gonja complained. They went to the king of Yendi [*Sarkin Yandi*]. [They asked him] to make war against their enemies. He agreed to make war against their enemies. He assisted them in war. He assisted them in this war against their enemies. So they came, they fought, they defeated them. They divided the land of Tanpulinsi into two. The land of Wala was given to the princes ['*yan sarakuna*] from Yendi. They settled. The Gonja people also settled in their land and the land of the Tanpulinsi.

Yendi, which Limam Ishaq describes as capital of part of the Dagomba, lies about 180 miles east by southeast of Wa. The Gonja divisional capital, Daboya, is about midway between the two. Limam Ishaq does not identify the 'Tanpulinsi'. They are clearly to be associated with the Tampolense who now occupy a broad belt of country extending from the southern boundaries of Wala to the White Volta in the Daboya area. The old road from Wa via Ducie to Daboya passed through their country.[3] The major Tampolense centre was Tampolima Yabum, lying some 20 miles beyond the easternmost tip of Wala.[4] Now a village of about 500 people, it was formerly much larger.[5] Its historic importance stemmed from its position on the old trade route from the Asante capital, Kumase, to the Middle Niger entrepôt, Jenne.[6]

Presently within the Gonja division of Wasipe, Tampolima Yabum is the seat of those with claims to the extinct Gonja divisional skin of Kandia. Kandia itself, whose people are both Gonja and Tampolense, now lies within the Busa division of Wala.[7] As late as 1923, however, the chief of Tampolima made claims to Kandia and its former subjects, namely, the Chakalle of the Busa division.[8] In both social structure and language the Chakalle and Tampolense show a close affinity.[9] The Pasaala-speaking communities of Kundungu and Gulunbele in the extreme east of Wala, moreover, claim to have migrated from Tampolima Yabum.[10] It may be, then, that Limam Ishaq used 'Tanpulinsi' to denote those speakers of Sisala dialects now found on both sides of the southern and eastern boundaries of Wala.

No *kubaru* has been found that has the story of the Gonja asking assistance from the Dagomba. Limam Ishaq was presumably drawing upon *lasiri*.[11] There is, however, an earlier trace of it in a brief note made by B. M. Read, Commissioner of the North-Western Province, in 1908. A certain Nasaje, he wrote, came to Wa from 'Yabum in Dagomba'.[12] There is no Yabum in Dagomba, but whether the reference is to the Gonja capital or to Tampolima Yabum is quite unclear. In any case the issue in TAW is not the Gonja but the Dagomba connection.

The warband from Dagomba, Limam Ishaq writes, was commanded by Widana, who was accompanied by two princes ('*yan sarakuna*). One was Dakpana ('Da(w)ana', with three points above the *waw*). The other is unnamed. Both were sons of Dariziogu ('Darziyaku'), son of a Ya Na (*dan Sarkin Yandi*). Widana established himself in Wa, and his people are those of Sokpariyiri ('Su[w]ariyiri', with three points over the *waw*) and Suriyiri. Dakpana settled in Gwo ('Ghu'), which Limam Ishaq locates in Dorimon ('Dalmur'). The second prince settled in Wechiau ('Wukkaw').[13] A son of Dakpana campaigned as far as Buna and defeated its people. He took a wife there and they had a son, Bunkani. The descendants of Bunkani rule in Buna. At this point the account of the 'First Tribe' ends.

It is clear that Limam Ishaq's treatment of the 'First Tribe' draws upon Tendaanba traditions not unlike those recorded in AWK. From the text, however, it does not seem that he was familiar with that work. Widana figures in both AWK and TAW as a warlord, but from the unidentified 'Niyirtiwu' in the former and quite specifically from Yendi in the latter. AWK lacks any account of the circumstances which brought the Widana to the Wa region, while TAW places it in the setting of the Gonja and Tampolense troubles. AWK is concerned primarily with the settlement of Widana in Wa; in TAW Limam Ishaq introduces the triad of Widana and his two commanders, and thereby touches also on the origins of the semi-autonomous Wala divisions of Gwo (or Dorimon) and Wechiau, and of the independent Buna polity.

The triad of Widana and his two commanders is clearly isomorphic (though incompatible) with that of the three sons of Gura recorded, as we have seen, by District Commissioner Whittall in the early 1920s. According to Whittall, one son of Gura, Saliya, established himself at or near Wa, and the other two, Denga (that is, Dakpana) and Bunkani, at Dorimon and Buna respectively. The triad of the three brothers of Saliya, which appears but is not developed in ASBW, is presumably another isomorph. Buna lies in the Kulango country west of the Black Volta. An independent account of the origins of its ruling house was published by Labouret in 1931. Bunkani was, according to his descendants in the seventh generation, son of a Dagari named Toroboussien whose family had left Yendi to settle in Dorimon.[14] The Buna tradition appears congruent with that reported in TAW.

A version of the story of the 'first tribe' was published in English in 1933. Its author, St J. Eyre-Smith, served in the colonial administration in Wa, Lawra and Tuma in the 1920s, and he was able to embellish whatever account of the matter he received in Wa with tales told him in Hiel and Zini in the Tumu district. 'Bands of marauders', he wrote,

> armed with Dane guns, consisting of Dagombas (as a result of a dispute over the Na-ship, a band of disaffected Dagombas had moved from the Dagomba Kingdom, under their leader Dozio [Dariziogu], and arrived in Daboya), Tampoulimas, and possibly Gonjas, set out from Daboya and overran the whole of the northwest of the Northern Territories, driving the Lobis and Dagatis from around Wa and the Janni [Dyan] people from what is now the Lawra District.[15]

This movement resulted in the foundation of the Wa Kingdom by 'the Yelia family'. It was, he thought, 'a Tampoulima family'. Elements in Eyre-Smith's account may well be derived from TAW. If so, they had become much distorted in their transmission.

The 'Second Tribe' in Wala

According to the Arabic version of TAW, the 'First Tribe' or, as Limam Ishaq sometimes has it, the 'First Branch' (shu'ab al-awwal), remained long in Wa. Then the time came when their commoner subjects (suqa) did to them what the Tempolense had done to the Gonja. The Hausa versions refers to the Wa landowners (masu kasan Wa) troubling the princes ('yan sarakuna). Both Arabic and Hausa versions of TAW identify the troublemakers as the 'Dagati', 'Wiili' and 'Birfu'. These, then, are the Tendaanba over whom the warlord Widana had established his authority. They are presumably to be identified as Dagaaba, Wiili and Birifor, all of whom speak dialects of Dagari.[16] The troubles are clearly the same as the feuding which, according to ASBW, threatened Suri.

Limam Ishaq appears to envisage a virtual uprising of the Tendaanba against Widana. In ASBW/com, Al-Hajj Siddiq b. Sa'id presented the matter somewhat differently. Suri's people, the Dagaaba, he said, had brothers called the Lobi. They were doing evil things on each other. The Lobi were over the Suri, they were head of the group. At one time the Lobi came and beat the Suri people, took all their children, and killed many of them.

The matter of the Tendaanba is complicated by the fact that the Wala, as we have seen, use 'Dagati' or 'Dagaaba' to refer both to non-Muslim Wala and to the unassimilated Dagari-speaking people to the north. They also refer to the more westerly Dagari-speakers such as the Wiili and Birifor as 'Lobi', so failing to distinguish them from true Lobi-speaking peoples such as the Dyan. In this usage they were followed by the British colonial officers.[17] Whether, then, Widana had the support of the Dagaaba against the 'Lobi', which seems to be the implication of ASBW/com, or faced the combined opposition of Dagaaba and 'Lobi' as suggested by TAW, remains unclear. To the point, however, is that Widana, or Suri, was in need of help.

The 'First Tribe', Limam Ishaq writes, solicited assistance from 'Naliriku', capital of 'another tribe of the Dagomba'. Nalerigu is the capital of Mampurugu. It lies some 160 miles east by northeast of Wa. A road, taken by G. E. Ferguson in 1894, linked the two capitals via Ducie, Bele (or Gulunbele), Yagaba and Walewale.[18] The route was an old one. It was known to the Asante trader Adu Gyese in the early nineteenth century, though Robertson reported (or perhaps misreported) him as placing both Bele ('Baree') and Walewale ('Wallewalee') four days nearly north of Wala.[19] In response to the request from the 'First Tribe' in Wala, the Na of Mampurugu sent troops (Arabic, *jaish*) to its assistance. They were led by his son, Saliya, and three other commanders. At this point Limam Ishaq appears to have been drawing, selectively, upon a text of the *kubaru* ASBW.

According to the Arabic text of TAW, the troops from Mampurugu fought 'them'; the Hausa identifies 'them' as the 'Dagatawa', the Dagati people (and not, it will be noted, as Lobi). Both texts report that some of the defeated fled across the Dalmu River, that is, the Dorimon River or Black Volta, and that others submitted. A recension of *lasiri* made in Walii in the mid 1950s refers to the *Willi Luobihi*, 'Wiili Lobi people', and reports that they were driven from Wa. They crossed the river to settle in 'Lagma and Tubogu', that is, Legmoin and Tobo, Wiili villages near the Black Volta, in what is now Burkina Faso.[20]

Following the military successes, the Hausa text of TAW has the Yendi princes (*'yan sarakuna Yandi*) in Wa giving the Nam (*sarauta*) to Saliya. The Arabic text has the old kings (*al-muluk al-qudama'*) conferring the Nam (*mulk*) upon Saliya. Saliya then ordered his three commanders to return home. At Issa they divided. Each conducted his own campaign in a different locality, Funsi, Kojopere ('Karikpiri') and Walembele ('Walinbaliyya'), where each founded his own chiefdom. Funsi and Kojopere were, we have seen, Sisala-speaking divisions of Wala lying west of the Kulpawn. Walembele is located east of that river, and although for that reason never securely under the political control of Wala, was within its cultural ambit.

Limam Ishaq thus explains Wa hegemony over Dorimon and Wechiau in the context of the story of Widana, and over Funsi, Kojopere and Walemebele in the context of that of Saliya. He then turns briefly to the matter of Saliya and the Wa Nam. He makes no reference to the marriage of Saliya and Widana's daughter although there can be little doubt that he knew of it from the *kubaru*. Indeed, he treats the early history of the Wa Nam in one bold but patently evasive passage. Saliya had many children (in the Hausa, *ya haife diya da yawa*), Limam Ishaq writes, and proceeds to assign seven early Nas to this category. He names them in a somewhat random order as Pelpuo, Gura, Kpasa, Djonyusi, Saka, Kunjokun ('Kunluki') and Na Djare. Quite apparently following some version of HSW, though neither HSW/a nor HSW/b, Limam Ishaq then lists the four gates to the Wa Nam as Busa, Sing, Pirisi and Guli, belonging respectively to the descendants of Pelpuo, Djonyusi ('Janyusi'), Na Djare ('Najari') and Kpasa. He next identifies each Wa Na (updated in the extant text of TAW to Mumuni Koray, in office in 1952) to a gate and finally, repetitiously, presents a list of the Nas which is clearly based on that in the Hausa version of HSW/b (for which see chapter 4). With that TAW concludes.

The 'Third Tribe' in Wala: the Old Muslims

The origins of Widana (from Dagomba) and of Saliya (from Mampurugu) having been explained, the logic of the schema dictates that Limam Ishaq next turns to the matter of the Yeri Nas. This he does not in TAW but in *Ta'rikh al-Muslimin*, TM. The reason is quite apparent. He wishes to use the third warband both to complete the triad of the three warlords and to open a further triad, that of the three Muslim communities of Wala. This is the subject of TM.

We have seen that ASBW contains an account of the Muslim warlord, Sidi 'Umar, and that the arrival in Wa of his grandson, Konjekuri ('Kajikpara') is briefly noted in AWK. In TM, Limam Ishaq characteristically takes a broader view of the topic. He refers to the Old Muslims (Arabic, *al-Muslimun al-qudama' fi ard Wala*; Hausa, *Muslimi na fariko a nan kasan Wa*) and states that they came from the Mande country (Arabic, *bilad Mandi*; Hausa, *kasan Mandi*). They fought and defeated the people of Kunduqi. The rendering of the name is identical in both Arabic and Hausa texts, and the reference must be to the subjection of the Sisala-speaking peoples of the Kundungu region.

Limam Ishaq develops the story by introducing the triad of the three Old Muslim settlements (Arabic, *masakin*). These were at Palewogo ('Walu'u Wuk', with three points over the initial *waw*), Visi ('Qisi', with three points over the *qaf*), and Nasa. Those who settled at Palewogo were of three tribes (Arabic, *qaba'il*; Hausa, *iri*), namely, Sienu ('Siyanu'), Dabo ('Dawu') and Zono ('Juna'). Those who settled at Visi were of one tribe, namely, Kunatay ('Kunati'), and at Nasa of one tribe, namely, Tarawiri ('Tariwari'). The history of the three tribes took different courses. The settlers at Palewogo and

Visi became locked in internecine struggles. They fought. As a result there was a mass exodus of people from both places. Some fled to the Kasena country to the north, but others took refuge in Wa town. There the Kunatay, Dabo and Zono created the Kabanya ward and the Sienu the ward known as Sembeleyiri. The Tarawiri of Nasa established a ward in Wa in different circumstances. They became involved in the affairs of the Mampurugu immigrants and provided the *wazir* to Gbetore Na Pelpuo. When Pelpuo moved from Gbetore to take the Nam in Wa, the *wazir* followed him. The section of Wa known as Tagarayiri (that is, 'house of the Tarawiri') was founded, and the office of *wazir* became that known in Walii as 'Yeri Na', chief of the Yerihi or Old Muslims. With that Limam Ishaq ends his account of the Old Muslims, having taken his reader from the origins of the three settlements of the Old Muslims to the origins of the three Old Muslim wards of Wa town.

Palewogo was located within the bend of the Kulpawn River, some fifteen miles or less south of Kundungu and about fifty miles east of Wa. The nearest inhabited place is the Sienu hamlet of Abuduyiri (population in 1960: 183).[21] The old road from Wa through Ducie and Gulunbele to Yagaba, Walewale and Nalerigu passed through Palewogo. Indeed, when G. E. Ferguson took that route in 1894 he mentioned 'Kpawkpawlawgu', which must be Palewogo, and located it rather conservatively 'a long day's march of 27 miles' from Yagaba.[22] It was totally abandoned only in the late nineteenth or early twentieth century.[23]

The Sienu, Dabo and Zono, identified by Limam Ishaq as the Mande settlers at Palewogo, are among those who call themselves the Kantonsi[24] and who are known in Walii as Samuni, 'the easterners'. The Juula refer to them as the Dagari-Juula, which calls attention to the fact that the first language of the Kantonsi has been, at least in recent centuries, a dialect of Dagari that differs little from Walii. Their settlement in Palewogo is universally believed to have long preceded the arrival of either the Dagomba or Mampurugu warbands in Wala. The topic is one treated in *lasiri*. After the foundation of the Wala polity there was conflict between the Wala and the Kantonsi. The Wa Limam and his people prayed. As a result dissension occurred among the Kantonsi and the great dispersion resulted.[25] There are also Kantonsi manuscripts that address the subject.

A *kubaru* of Wa Sembeleyiri provenance has it that the Kantonsi entered Buna and from there crossed the Black Volta. They moved eastwards into Mampurugu, but then retraced their steps to settle at Palewogo. There came a time when they quarrelled with the Yeri Na's people in Wa. A debt arising from the sale of a horse was the issue. The Wa Limam made prayers. Then 'things went badly' for the Kantonsi and they dispersed.[26] Another Kantonsi *kubaru*, perhaps also ultimately of Wa provenance, was in the possession of Al-Hajj 'Abd al-Rahman Sienu of Koho or Shukr li-'llahi, near Wahabu (some 130 miles north of Wa, in Burkina Faso). It exhibits the familiar triadic form, but the triad of the three settlements of the Old Muslims – Palewogo, Visi and Nasa – found in TM is replaced by that of the three Kantonsi settlements. The following section of it was recorded as it was translated from the Arabic of the original through Juula:[27]

> There were three people who came from Mali. The first was Sheku Barabara. The second was Yakina. The third was Jaligungu. Barabara stayed at Kanda and that is his *nisba* [patronymic]. Yakina stayed in Palewogo. Their *nisba* is Sienu. Jaligungu stayed at Visi, and their *nisba* is Kunatay ... The people stayed in different places, Palewogo, Visi and Kanda, because of their fear of war. Palewogo gave the chiefs, Visi gave the *karamokos* [Juula, 'scholars'], and Kanda gave the elders.

The Tarawiri of Nasa, although among the Old Muslims of Wa treated in TM, are not considered Kantonsi by themselves or others. Nasa thus does not appear as one of the three Kantonsi settlements. Kanda takes its place, but the reference is obscure. It may be Kandia, the former Gonja and presently Wala village which lies almost midway between Wa town and the abandoned Palewogo. I know of no Kantonsi, however, who now use 'Kanda' as a patronymic.

Visi is, like Palewogo, now deserted. It lay about eighteen miles northeast of Wa, near the present hamlet of Bugu.[28] Contrary to the evidence of TM, several informants spoke of the Dabo being Visi rather than Palewogo people; they were, it was said, 'children' of the Kunatay.[29] The Kunatay are the subject of a work in English entitled, 'The Konate Clan. Our Grand-fathers, their Names and Places they Settled In.' It was written by Al-Hajj Salifu of the Kabanya section of Wa in 1964. He claimed that it was based on an earlier work of his, in Arabic, which he had compiled 'from manuscripts in the possession of different Kunatay communities'. These 'communities' were, it seems, different families within Kabanya, whose elders he listed by name.[30] The work had, like TAW and TM, the character of *ta'rikh* rather than *kubaru*. I shall refer to it as 'KC'.

The ancestor of the Kunatay of the Voltaic region, according to KC, was Sharif Abu Bakr of Timbuktu, a descendant of the Prophet through his grandson Husayn. Sharif Abu Bakr waged 'religious wars'. He settled first in Kudugu in the Mossi country, then in To to its south, then in Tongo (the location is uncertain), and finally in Visi. In the course of his progress southwards he acquired six companions. Four, Harun, Muhammad, 'Ali and Dawud are named and described as 'grandfathers' respectively of the Sienu, Tarawiri, Kambara and Dabo. A daughter of Sharif Abu Bakr was married to Harun. Their son, Ibrahim, became the first chief of Visi. The last chief of Visi, Tawula Kunatay, was a descendant of Sharif Abu Bakr in the seventh generation ('our seventh grandfather at Visee': Tawula b. Yusuf b. Fathur b. 'Abd al-Qadir b. Siddiq b. Karim b. Sharif Abu Bakr). There was trouble over a debt arising from the sale of a woman. The injured party had prayers made to obtain redress. That, KC has it, 'was 730 years after the Holy

Prophet left Mecca for Medina [and] by then Visee was 313 houses large and there was fighting and disease so the people of Visee fled. Tawula fled with his 13 sons, 14 daughters towards Tongo and he died on the way.'

Yamusa and Nuhu, according to KC, arrived in Wa. They were, it seems, two of the '13 sons' of Tawula. They settled with the Daanayiri people, the owners of the market, on land that had been given Daanayiri by the Tendaanba of Sokpariyiri. This became the Kabanya ward of Wa. At the end of KC its compiler traces his own descent from Yamusa in what seems to be nine generations. 'Umar, he writes, 'is my father and I am Alhaji Salifu who is sending you to tell you that all Kabanya's are Konates and descendants of Yamusah and Nuhu'.

The Kantonsi, then, comprise two distinct elements, the one of warriors and the other of scholars. The Sienu dominate the former, the Kunatay the latter. The traditions have the warriors moving from west to east to settle at Palewogo, and the scholars from north to south to settle at Visi. The Palewogo people are often spoken of as having mixed Muslim and non-Muslim practices. Their wars were not holy ones.[31] The Kunatay settlers in Visi are commonly referred to as the *'ulama'* for the Kantonsi and their movement in to the Voltaic region is associated, at least in KC, with 'religious war', that is, *jihad*.

The dispersion of the Kantonsi from Palewogo and Visi appears to have followed the same lines in reverse, from east to west and from south to north respectively. The *kubaru* from Koho referred to above gives some account of the matter.

> When the war came, some went to Wa, some to Sanga, some to Sissili, some to Dabin, some to Gori, some to Sadon, some to Kusugu, some to To, some to Dalu, some returned to Wa, some to Wiaku, some to Tikura, some to Gaou, some to Napuni, some to Suka, some to Boromo, some to Nasa.

Appended to the manuscript was a list of twenty-two Kantonsi ('Dagari-Juula') communities founded as a result of the dispersion. They extend, spatially, from Mampurugu in the east to Buna in the west, and from the vicinity of the abandoned Palewogo in the south to Boromo in the north.[32] Although Limam Ishaq, in TM, makes mention only of the Kantonsi patronymics Kunatay, Sienu, Dabo and Zono current in the Kabanya and Sembeleyiri sections of Wa, others are in use in the wider diaspora, for example, Kulibali, Sissay and Turay.[33]

We have remarked that the Old Muslims of Nasa, who use the patronymic Tarawiri, are not regarded as Kantonsi. Nasa lies fourteen miles northeast of Wa town, on the old road to Kojopere. In 1931 it was a village of only 149 people. In 1948 the population had increased to 289, in 1960 had fallen to 136, and in 1970 had increased again to 216. In 1964, however, the centenarian Ishaq Dodu remembered Nasa from his youth as a large place, 'bigger than Wa'.[34] A mass exodus of its people occurred in fact in the dry season of 1887–8, when it was attacked by the Zabarima under Babatu.[35] The present village is surrounded by an area, perhaps half a mile or more square, marked by much occupation debris. Many low mounds are all that remain of the earlier dwellings. The site of the mosque destroyed by Babatu is still visible. It was clearly a much larger building than the present one, and was apparently constructed on the same plan and in the same style as the old central mosque in Wa (plate 2). The Nasa mosque is said to have been 'taken to Wa' after its destruction; that is, the Wa mosque was acknowledged as *the* Friday mosque for Wala.[36] Nasa presently consists of three old wards: Tagarayiri belonging to Nasa Yeri Na, Limamyiri to Nasa Limam, and Samuniyiri to the Kantonsi. There is also a newer ward, Dondoli, in which both Limamyiri people and Wa Nabihi reside.

The *kubaru* ASBW, we have seen, refers to Sidi 'Umar as the leader of a warband which entered the region through Jirapa, moved eastwards into Mampurugu, responded to Suri's plea for help in Wa, and ultimately settled in Nasa. Limam Ishaq, in TM, simply says, 'those [of the Old Muslims] who settled in Nasa were of one tribe and their name was Tariwari'. The implication is that the Nasa Kantonsi and Limamyiri people are later settlers. Sidi 'Umar consistently appears as apical ancestor, 'Sanda Muru who came from Mande', in Tagarayiri pedigrees.[37] The office of Nasa Yeri Na remains vested in his descendants. So, too, does that of the Wa Yeri Na.

The Wa Yeri Nam is an office of later creation than the Nasa Yeri Nam. Its origin is bound up with the creation of the Wa Nam. The relationship of the Wa Yeri Na to the Wa Na is one that Limam Ishaq chose to describe in terms of the former being *wazir* to the latter. This may not be an entirely felicitous description. The authority he exercises is regarded as ultimately derivative not from the Wa Nam but from the Nasa Yeri Nam; in other words, from the *nalun* of the warlord Sidi 'Umar. Not surprisingly, however, the Na Kpasa and the Na Pelpuo traditions give differing accounts of the creation of the Wa Yeri Nam. We have seen that the *kubaru* AWK, written in the Na Kpasa tradition, has Konjekuri ('Kajikpara'), putative grandson of Sidi 'Umar, arriving in Wa at the time of Na Kpasa, first Wa Na according to that tradition. In TM Limam Ishaq adheres more to the Na Pelpuo tradition; someone came from Nasa to become *wazir* to Pelpuo, the first Wa Na in that tradition. The name of this first *wazir* is not given in TM, but the Hausa text has a space clearly intended for its insertion. *Lasiri* recorded by Dougah supply the name:

> Among Pelpuo's people was a Mohammedan friend called Bunsalibile. Bunsa-libile made his settlement in Tagirayiri, a ward in Wa. When Pelpuo came to power and controlled the whole town, he made Bunsalibile his Yeri Na (chief of the Mohammedans).[38]

The Wa Yeri Na (strictly, acting Yeri Na) in the 1960s regarded himself as forty-second in office.[39] No systematic list of the incumbents is extant, but both Konjekuri and Bunsalibile are remembered as among the early ones.[40] The implication of the traditions, then, may be that Wa Na Kpasa (who claimed *nalun* in succession to Widana), and Wa Na Pelpuo (who claimed it in succession to Saliya), each recruited his own *wazir* or Yeri Na from Nasa. It may be, furthermore, that this is reflected in the complex present structure of the Tagariyiri section of Wa. It comprises two quite distinct houses, Terinmu and Konukumba. Both are gates to the Wa Yeri Nam. There is also a third house, Sungumi, whose members are referred to as 'sons' of the Yeri Nas and excluded from the succession. Unfortunately my data does not allow clear correlations between structure and traditions to be made in this context.[41] Certainly, however, in the contest for the Wa Nam after the death of Sidiki Bomi II in 1978, one faction of Tagarayiri headed by acting Yeri Na Asheku came out strongly in support of the Na Kpasa candidate, Yakubu Seidu. When Yakubu Seidu's bid for the Nam finally failed, the Yeri Nam was given to one of those who had opposed him, Muhammad Kulendi.[42]

The *kubaru* ASBW has the ancestors of the Old Muslim Tarawiri entering the Wala country via Jirapa. This is common knowledge in Wala, for there are families in Jirapa who still use the patronymic Tagara (that is, Tarawiri) and who are considered to be descended from those of the immigrants who chose to remain there rather than continue the march. They apostasized.[43] Nevertheless, the Limams of Wa still extend their offices to the Jirapa Tagara. Indeed, Limam Ishaq himself visited there in 1916 ('to pay respect to friends long dead'), and the Jirapa chief came to Wa for his funeral in 1931.[44] It is therefore somewhat surprising that TM makes no reference to the Jirapa connection. Both TAW and TM, however, contain remarkably little detail. It may be that they should be seen as essentially Limam Ishaq's first drafts, in which he was concerned to develop an overarching schema (in triads) for a projected longer work. It is noteworthy, for example, that in TM Limam Ishaq was content merely to note of the Old Muslims, that they came 'from the Mande country'. He knew, however, much more than that.

An account of the migration of Sidi 'Umar is contained in the work, *Ta'rikh Ahl Tariwari min Mandi* (henceforth TATM), 'History of the Tarawiri People from the Mande'.[45] A copy of TATM, in two pages, was made for me by a son of Limam Ishaq, Al-Hajj Malik, in 1964. The manuscript from which he copied had been written by his father, who had collected materials for it from older men. The work has features which suggest that Limam Ishaq tapped very old traditions indeed, for it appears to have more affinity with Malian accounts of the dispersion of the Mandeka than with Wala accounts of the origins of their polity.[46] The relevant part of the work reads as follows:

> The origin of the Tarawiri people is from a town [*madina*] in Mande called Qaba. In the town of Qaba there is a part called Balunba and in it there is an idol [*sanam*]. Each year all the people of the town of Qaba assembled there, and the people of the villages and towns around, to serve it as was their custom. Mande is the name of the land [*qutr*] known to all. When the Tarawiri people left it, they settled in a town [*bilad*] called Kumayma and from the town of

Kumayma to the town of Langhfiyala, and from the town of Langhfiyala to the town of Busi, and from the town of Busi to the town of Durra. The Tarawiri people came to the lands [*diyar*] of Wala from these places.

'Qaba' is Kaba or Kangaba, lying on the Niger in the heartland of the Mandeka country between Bamako and Siguiri. It remains a most important centre of pre-Islamic religious observances. Indeed, the 'Balunba' of TATM may contain the element *bolo* or *blo*, and thus refer to the famous shrine, Mande Blo, in Kaba Koro.[47] It is possible to trace the putative route taken by the Tarawiri from Kaba to Wa. Kumayma has not been identified but Lanfiera ('Langhfiyala') and Busse ('Busi') are both in Burkina Faso, the former about 220 miles and the latter about 160 miles north by northwest of Wa on the same line.[48] Busse was near Safane, described in an early-nineteenth-century route book as a large town with a Muslim community (*al-jami'*).[49]

The tradition of TATM reports, then, the passage of a warband from Kangaba eastwards to the upper reaches of the Black Volta, and thence southwards along the line of that river to Jirapa and the Wa region. That Limam Ishaq knew the story but chose not to refer to it in TM may suggest that both TAW and TM were indeed in the nature of first drafts. It may be, however, that the story was too recondite for inclusion. In their attempt to construct a past of contemporary relevance, the Wala savants have no need to range so distantly in space and time. All that is commonly known and commonly needs to be known is that Sidi 'Umar 'came from Mande'. That is part of Wala popular culture. The story in TATM is both erudite and esoteric.

The second group of Muslims: the scholars

TM tells of the arrival of the second group (Arabic, *firqa*, Hausa, *iri*) of Muslims in Wala. Its ancestor, Ya'muru, was also from the people of Mande. He brought Islamic teaching to Wa. He settled first with the Old Muslims in Nasa. At that time the three towns of the Wa 'kings' were Yaro, Guli and Gbetore. The people of the three towns assembled and made Ya'muru their limam. When Pelpuo moved from Gbetore to Wa to take the Nam, Ya'muru accompanied him. Ya'muru had many children, and his descendants are the people of Wa Limamyiri. They hold the Wa limamate. Limam Ishaq's account of the origins of the *'ulama'* class is thus remarkably brief. Otherwise he offers only a list of the limams, twenty-two in the Arabic text and twenty-three in the Hausa, a matter to be considered in chapter 4.

Limam Ishaq knew, once again, much more than he recorded in TM. He elaborated on the theme in TATM:

> The Tarawiri ('Tariwari') people in the lands [*diyar*] of Wala are different, one of them Tarawiri Yeri Na and the other Tarawiri Limamyiri. The first of the people of Tarawiri Limamyiri to come to the lands of Wala was a man named Yusuf Langhfiyala and his brother 'Umar. They stayed with the king of Wala

59

called Na Djare ('Na Jari') in their town known as Yaro ('Yaru'). At that time the town of Gbetore ('Butari') was ruled by the other king of the people called Yijisi. They did not have among them any men of learning. So they went to the town of Yaro, to Yusuf Langhfiyala, to ask him for an imam. Yusuf told them, 'My brother, he is a man of learning.' He pointed to 'Umar. 'You may take him to be your imam for all your affairs.' They took him and returned with him to Gbetore. So they had an imam who was a man of learning.

The owner of TATM, Limam Ishaq's son, commented that Yusuf was known as 'Langhfiyala' because he was born there.[50] The reference must again be to Lanfiera on the upper reaches of the Black Volta.

Limam Ishaq's account in TATM is clearly closely related to that in the *kubaru* ASBW, which brings together Sidi 'Umar, Yusuf and 'Umar Fitini at the time of Na Djare ('Juri') to create, at the expense of chronology, a triad of the three ancestors of the Wa Tarawiri. The tradition represented in TM, TATM and ASBW is widely known in Wa. Most members of Wa Limamyiri are able to give their descent from Ya'muru (that is, the 'Umar of TATM and 'Umar Fitini of ASBW), first Wa Limam, or in some cases from Yusuf Lanfiera, first Nasa Limam. None, of course, claims descent from Sidi 'Umar, who is apical ancestor for Tagarayiri and not Limamyiri. So much is all part of popular culture. Again, however, there is a more recondite level of knowledge.

The late Al-Hajj Siddiq b. Sa'id (Fanta Sidiki) of Wa Limamyiri, born about 1897, was widely considered one of the most knowledgeable about the past in his generation. In January 1963, when he was living in the Asante gold-mining town of Obuase, he spoke of a 'book' in his possession. It was, he said, a chain (*silsila*) for Ya'muru through the town of Ja' to the destruction of Mande (*kharab Mandi*). The Tarawiri, he claimed, were Arabs, the descendants of Sidi 'Abbas, and the one who came to Mande was Muhammad Jatiyyu.[51] A few months later, at the request of Wa Limam Sa'id, Al-Hajj Siddiq made available a work entitled *Ta'rikh Tadhkirat al-Imamiyyin fi Biladina Wa*, 'History in Remembrance of the Imams in our Town of Wa'. It will be referred to as TTI. It is on one side of the folio accessioned as IASAR/151 in the Institute of African Studies, University of Ghana; the other side is the *kubaru* HSW discussed in chapter 2.[52] It is unclear whether Al-Hajj Siddiq had compiled the work at that time or whether he copied an existing text. Whichever the case, traditions are reported that appear (as in the case of TATM) to be ultimately of Mandeka provenance.

TTI contains a list of the Wa Limams, to be considered in chapter 4. To it is prefaced an account of Ya'muru's ancestry:

This is History in Remembrance of the Imams in our Town of Wa in early times concerning the time 717 of the Hijra of the Prophet [AD 1317/8]. As for the great Imam, he who took up residence in Wa, the Imam Ya'muru Tarwiriyyu, he was from the town of Ja, *'ajam* [i.e., vernacular], and he was Ya'muru b. Al-Hajj Alfa Mahmud b. 'Uthman b. Bakari Biriyyu b. Muhammad

Sunsu Jara, *'ajam*, al-Madaniyya Tarawiri. He was the one who left Mandi and Allah knows.

'Ja' is Dya (or Dia), an old centre of the Tarawiri in the southwestern region of the Middle Niger flood-plains.[53] The present town may or may not occupy the site of the 'Zagha' which Ibn Battuta mentioned in the middle of the fourteenth century, when it was well known for its Muslim learning.[54]

In conversations with Al-Hajj Siddiq in mid 1964 I asked him further about Tarawiri Limamyiri origins. He repeated the story that all Tarawiri were descendants of Sidi 'Abbas, an Arab; added that they therefore call themselves 'Abbasiyya; and said that Muhammad Sunsu Jara died in Mande. In the course of these conversations he consulted a short note in Arabic which he agreed to copy. It is accessioned as IASAR/297 in the Institute of African Studies, University of Ghana.[55] The text reads:

> The name of our forefather [*jadd*] who sired seven sons was Jata. 1, the eldest of the sons was Musa who was called Jiki. 2, Inkunduka. 3, Suyata. 4, Mali Biri. 5, Mali Kinani. 6, Bukari Biri. 7, Bukari Nikini. Jiki and Inkunduka and Suyata stayed in Mandi in a town called Kaba. The descendants [*dhurriya*] of Bukari Biri are in Ja'a [Dya] and Jani [Jenne] and Waya [Wa]. The descendants of Bubikar Kini are in Sikasu [Sikasso] and Kun [Kong, in the present Côte d'Ivoire]. Those who came to Wa in time, his name was Al-Hajj Mahmud b. 'Uthman. The descendants of Mali Biri and Mali Kinani, their descendants are in Jabarima [the Zabarima country]. The name of the son of Mali Biri was Dusu. Those whose forefathers are in Jabarima, their names are first Ghunbi[?], second Mawuri, and third Saja.

The reverse of the folio has the one line: 'And 'Uthman, he was the one who sired Alfa Mahmud.'

At the core of the texts given by Al-Hajj Siddiq is a version of the tradition of Mandeka dispersion and specifically of the dispersion of the Tarawiri. The apical figure is Muhammad Sunsu Jara (or, according to dialect, Jata, 'the lion'). In 1969 I asked Al-Hajj Siddiq about his authority for the story. 'I learned about this when I was young', he said, 'from the big men. I never mixed with children of my own age. I met people from Mande who knew about Alfa Mahmud and his ancestors. Muhammad Zakiyu of Mande had twelve sons. These were told to me, and I wrote the names of seven down, but the others I did not get.'[56] The provenance of the story of the dispersion, then, is apparently Mandeka. Less certain is the authority of the descent of the first Wa Limam, Ya'muru, from Alfa Mahmud, 'Uthman and Bukari Biri.

Bukari, or Abu Bakr, Biri (perhaps Juula *biri* from Arabic *barr*, 'righteous, pious') is probably to be identified with the Bukari Tarawiri whose name appears on a charm very popular among Muslims in the Voltaic region. The charm names twelve famous *'ulama'* of the past, and its owner acquires merit and protection by making prayers in the name of each. The first of the twelve is invariably Al-Hajj Salim Suwari, but there is considerable variation in the remaining names. The charms are, as it were, customized to include locally favoured figures. In 1962 I obtained two copies from Wa, both entitled

Fa'dat Ism al-Auliya' Allah, 'Sacrifice in the name of the Holy Men of God', and both having in the fifth position the name 'Al-Hajj Bukari Tarawali Jaraba', that is, Al-Hajj Bukari Tarawiri of Great Dya.[57] Forty years earlier, Marty recorded another version of the charm from the Côte d'Ivoire. The sixth name was that of Al-Hajj Bukari Tarawiri, but described as of Segu rather than Dya.[58] Yet another version from Namasa (Ghana, south of Banda) lacked any mention of Bukari.[59]

There is a well-documented Bukari Tarawiri who is indeed associated with the region of Dya and Jenne. The *Ta'rikh al-Sudan*, written in Timbuktu in the middle of the seventeenth century, lists the *qadis* of Jenne. The tenth, Ahmad b. 'Umar, left on pilgrimage and entrusted his duties to Bukari Tarawiri. The *floruit* of Bukari Tarawiri is to be placed in the 1570s or 1580s, for his successor was in office at the time of the Moroccan invasion of 1591.[60] The source makes it clear that Bukari Tarawiri was not a native of Jenne but of the province of Kala, which probably embraced Dya.

It is likely, though not demonstrable, that the Al-Hajj Bukari Tarawiri of the charms is indeed the Qadi Bukari Tarawiri of Jenne. At least one other *qadi* of Jenne, Mahmud Baghayughu, and his celebrated father, Muhammad Baghayughu, are also named in the charms.[61] It is impossible to determine whether the Wa tradition of Limam Ya'muru's descent from Bukari Tarawiri is a veridical one, or whether the well-known *'alim* was at some point in time adopted into that tradition for reasons of prestige. That the Limamyiri Tarawiri of Wa were, however, kin of the Tarawiri of the Dya and Jenne region seems not unlikely. In particular, the references to the birth of Ya'muru's brother, Yusuf, at Lanfiera seem to attest to the passage southwards of the Tarawiri at least from the direction of the Middle Niger.

Although there are texts which refer to the apical ancestors of Tagarayiri and Limamyiri people as 'brothers', this appears to be no more than an acknowledgement that both use the same patronymic. In fact the origins of the two communities are, as we have seen, treated quite differently in Wala traditions. The settlement of the Mande warriors at Nasa is regarded as long preceding the arrival of the scholars, and I know of no source that suggests that the ancestors of the Limamyiri people arrived in Wala in the capacity of *'ulama'* to the Tagarayiri people, or that, in other words, Ya'muru was limam to Sidi 'Umar. The origin of Sidi 'Umar is referred to Mande Kaba, that of Ya'muru to Dya.

The third group of Muslims: the Hausa

The third and last group of Muslims treated in the *Ta'rikh al-Muslimin* (TM) are those who 'came from the land of Hausa'. They were traders. Readers will not be surprised by now to learn that Limam Ishaq has them entering Wa in three groups. The ancestor of the first group was Muhammad, and the Hausa but not the Arabic text of TM names two of his sons as Muru Sa'id and Salih Tiyani. The ancestor of the second group was Jinba, and of the

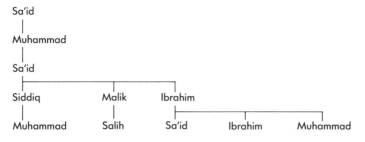

Figure 3 Dzangbeyiri genealogy

third Ibrahim. The descendants of the three comprise the section of Wa known as Dzangbeyiri ('Jan[w]ayiri', with three points over the *waw*).

Conversations in 1966 with the nonagenarian head of Dzangbeyiri, Malam Mahama, and various of his elders added to the brief account in TM. There was general agreement that the ancestors of the Dzangbeyiri Hausa were of Katsina origin, but they were said to have been settled in Dagomba prior to their arrival in Wa. Five informants gave their descent from Sa'id (figure 3).[62] The persons in the lowest generation ranged in age in 1966 from their nineties (Muhammad b. Siddiq, that is, Malam Mahama) to their forties (Muhammad b. Ibrahim). The Muhammad b. Sa'id of figure 3 is probably to be identified with the Muhammad of the account in TM, and the Sa'id b. Muhammad with the Muru Sa'id.

Dzangbeyiri informants were confident in their view that Sa'id arrived in Wa at the time of Wa Na Gangume and married Makansa, a sister of Yeri Na Konukumba. It will be seen in chapter 4 that the *floruit* of Wa Na Gangume was in the 1860s. The implication must surely be, then, that it was the apical ancestor of the genealogies who left Katsina but his grandson, Sa'id b. Muhammad or Muru Sa'id, who settled in Wa.[63] The Hausa immigrants are said to have lived first in Tagarayiri but then, as their numbers grew, to have been given the land by Yeri Na on which to found Dzangbeyiri. The increase in population was not entirely a result of natural growth. Wa Na Gangume asked the Dafin limams of Safane to send him a *karamoko*, a scholar. Ahmad Sansankori arrived. He married into the Hausa of Dzangbeyiri and his children joined that section. Other Dafin (or 'Wangara') joined them there.[64] The Dzangbeyiri section of Wa is in need of further study. Clearly, however, its people have no part in the early history of the Wala polity.

4

Wa chronology: an exercise in date-guessing

Introduction

The orally transmitted materials about the Wala past lack any system of absolute chronology, and the occasional dates that appear in the literary recensions of tradition are improvisations by the scribes. Events are, however, carefully ordered relative to each other in time, and nowhere is this principle more rigorously observed than in the lists of those who have successively held the offices of Wa Na and Wa Limam. It is these lists that provide the historian with the opportunity of 'date-guessing', which is a pleasingly modest term for what I have described elsewhere as 'geneametry' and 'regno-chronology'.[1]

The present Wa Na (1988) is probably to be reckoned the twenty-ninth, counting both Na Pelpuo and Na Kpasa as incumbents of the office. The present Wa Limam is seemingly the thirty-third in office. Only crude and virtually worthless chronological inferences can, however, be made from office lists as such. The time span of a specific list is not a simple function of the number of names on it, but will vary according to the system of succession and the demographic constraints within which that system works. For positions such as those of Wa Na and Wa Limam, which are (in a sense to be described) hereditary, a crucial variable is generation, or more specifically, the matter of how long an office is held in one generation before it is allowed to pass to the next. For the limamate this variable can be determined reasonably satisfactorily, for the Nam less satisfactorily so.

The Limams of Wa: family reconstitution

The '*ulama*' of Wa keep manuscript lists of the successive occupants of the limamate, that is, of the position of *imam al-balad*. I have been able to examine twelve such lists (table 4.1, lists A to L), and a thirteenth (list M) was obtained by Fikry in 1966–7.[2] The lists are written in Arabic script and Arabic language with the exception of lists D and G, which are in Hausa. They are read out from time to time in the mosques, when short prayers – incorporated into lists C, E, H, J and K – are made in the name of each

Plate 7 List of Wa Limams to 'Uthman Dun

incumbent. It is impossible to say how long this has been the practice in Wa, but the two oldest lists I have seen (A and B) date from the time when 'Uthman Dun, who died in or about 1887, was still in office. They are written in the same hand on both sides of a single watermarked sheet of paper probably made in Italy for the Muslim market.[3] The next oldest list (C) was written during the incumbency of the Salih who held office around 1910. It is on both sides of a single folio of coarse, non-watermarked paper. It will be apparent from table 4.1 that the list obtained by Fikry (M) is the most recent. The last limam on it, Al-Hajj Muhammad (known as Bakuri), died in 1971. He has been succeeded by Muhammad Kankanya, Al-Hajj Nuhu and, presently, Limam Al-Hajj Ya'qub.

Two principles have been observed in tabulating the data. First, all names have been entered in their Arabic rather than their vernacular forms, even

65

Table 4.1. *The Wa Limams*

	Name	A	B	C	D	E	F	G	H	I	J	K	L	M
1	Ya'muru	x	x	x	x	x	x	x	x	x	x	x	x	x
2	Muhammad al-Aswad	x	x	x	x	x	x	x	x	x	x	x	x	x
3	Mu'adh			x	x	x	x	x	x	x	x	x	x	x
4	Muhammad al-Ahmar	x	x	x	x		x	x	x	x	x	x	x	x
5	Idris	x	x	x	x	x	x	x	x	x	x	x	x	x
6	'Abd al-Qadir	x	x	x	x		x	x	x	x	x	x	x	x
[3]	Mu'adh	x	x											
7	Muhammad Faraqu	x	x											
8	Ishaq	x	x											
9	Musa	x	x	x	x	x	x	x	x	x	x	x	x	x
10	Muhammad	x	x	x	x	x	x	x	x	x	x	x	x	x
11	Sa'id	x	x	x	x	x	x	x	x	x	x	x	x	x
12	Ya'qub	x	x	x	x	x	x	x	x	x	x	x	x	x
13	Ya'muru	x	x	x	x	x	x	x	x	x	x	x	x	x
14	Idris	x	x	x	x	x	x	x	x	x	x	x	x	x
15	Ibrahim	x	x	x	x	x	x	x	x	x	x	x	x	x
16	Al-Siddiq	x	x	x	x	x	x	x	x	x	x	x	x	x
17	Sa'id	x	x	x	x	x			x	x	x	x	x	
18	'Uthman Dun	x	x	x	x	x		x	x	x	x	x	x	
19	Musa			x	x	x	x	x	x	x	x	x	x	x
20	Ibrahim			x	x		x	x	x	x	x	x	x	x
21	Salih			x	x	x	x	x	x	x	x	x	x	x
22	Ya'qub			x	x	x	x	x	x	x	x	x	x	x
23	Al-Hajj Muhammad				x	x	x	x	x	x	x	x	x	x
24	Al-Hajj Malik			x	x	x	x	x	x	x	x	x	x	x
25	Muhammad Saghir				x	x	x	x	x	x	x	x	x	x
26a	Al-Hajj Salih					x	x							x
26b	Al-Hajj Sa'id Soribo								x	x	x	x	x	
27	Yusuf									x	x	x	x	
28	Idris									x	x	x	x	x
[27]	Yusuf													x
29	Sa'id									x	x	x	x	x
30	Al-Hajj Muhammad													x
31	Muhammad Kankanya													
32	Al-Hajj Nuhu													
33	Al-Hajj Ya'qub													

Key: A – IASAR/383(i); Wilks FN/148. B – IASAR/383(ii); FN/148. C – IASAR/17; FN/263. D – IASAR/22; NAG Accra, Acc. N. 1427 of 1959. E – IASAR/447; FN/144. F – IASAR/152(i). G – IASAR/152(ii). H – IASAR/61; FN/125. I – IASAR/151; FN/145. J – IASAR/296; FN/52. K – IASAR/46; FN/265. L – FN/263. M – Fikry, 1970, vol. I, p. 68.

though some manuscripts have 'Mahama' for 'Muhammad', 'Saydu' for 'Sa'id', and the like. Second, the fullest and most descriptive form of a name is given, though it may not appear as such in all manuscripts. Thus

Muhammad al-Aswad ('the Black') also appears as Muhammad al-Awwal ('the First') or simply as Muhammad. There are also two variants in the lists which do not appear in table 4.1. First, list L has Al-Hajj Sa'id where all other lists have Al-Hajj Muhammad (No. 23). Al-Hajj Muhammad is in fact often referred to as Al-Hajj Muhammad Sa'id, where the Arabic *sa'id*, 'fortunate', translates the Walii *kulendi* (from Juula *kunandi*) which has the same sense. Second, list D notes that the limamate was vacant for a time between Ya'qub (22) and Al-Hajj Muhammad (23), and in list K the names of those who officiated in a temporary capacity during that period are inserted.[4] These have been omitted in table 4.1.

A number of the variants in the lists are clearly copyists' errors, for example, the omission of Muhammad al-Ahmar (4) and 'Abd al-Qadir (6) in List E, and the reversal of Yusuf (27) and Idris (28) in list M. In a different category is the discrepancy with respect to Al-Hajj Salih (26a) and Al-Hajj Sa'id (26b). There were, in fact, two rival limams in this period, the 1950s. Al-Hajj Salih was recognized by the Ahmadis of Wa and Al-Hajj Sa'id by those who described themselves as the orthodox, and it is significant that lists F, G and M are from Ahmadiyya sources. Why these three lists also omit the earlier Limam Sa'id (17) is unclear. The presumption is, perhaps, that his name was dropped in an examplar of all three in the mistaken belief that it was he who was the rival of Al-Hajj Salih, and the error was never rectified. List J shows signs of having been altered, to substitute the name of Al-Hajj Sa'id for that of Al-Hajj Salih. It does, however, list the earlier Sa'id (17).

There remain, then, the major discrepancies between lists A and B on the one hand, and lists C to M on the other. In the former, Mu'adh is treated as sixth rather than third limam, and we shall suggest that this was a result of error or confusion. On lists A and B, however, the additional names of Muhammad Faraqu and Ishaq appear as seventh and eighth limams. Clearly more than the errors or confusions of scribes are involved at this point.

The descendants of the first limam, Ya'muru, constitute the Wa Limamyiri community. Many, of course, are no longer resident in the original Limam-yiri, literally 'the house of the Limam'. Not surprisingly, Limamyiri people evince a strong concern with pedigree. A claim to patrilineal descent from Ya'muru is at one and the same time a claim to membership of that prestigious community. With the exception of a few senile or otherwise disadvantaged persons, I encountered no one in Limamyiri who was unable to narrate his (or, through the father, her) descent from Ya'muru. It is this feature of the Wa situation that permits reconstruction of the pattern of succession to the limamate.

Table 4.2 is based upon interviews with individuals, the lists of limams – particularly H (IASAR/61) and J (IASAR/296) – and a few gravestones. It plots lateral spread (columns a to r) against generation (lines I to VII). Tabulation of the data follows one, and only one, rule: an entrant is the son of the entrant in the same column in the line above or, if that position is empty, of the entrant in the next filled position to the left in the line above.

Table 4.2 *Succession to the Wa limamate*

	a	b	c	d	e	f	g	h	i	j	k	l	m	n	o	p	q	r
I	1																	
II	2															3		4
III	5	6														7		8
IV	X	10				11	12		13			X		X	X	9	X	
V	15	18		20	X	X	14	X	19	22	X	17	X	21	X	16	X	
VI		23	X	25	X	24		X		28		X		X		26b		X
VII			32	29				26a			30		31				27	

Key: 1–32: Wa Limams, by number following table 4.1. IV/a: 'Umar Dhakidi. IV/1: Yusuf. IV/n: Yahya. IV/o: Adam. IV/q: Sulayman. V/e: 'Umar. V/f: 'Uthman. V/h: Muhammad. V/k: Al-Hasan. V/m: Ya'qub. V/o: Al-Siddiq. V/q: Yusuf. VI/c: Adam. VI/e: Hamid. VI/h: Al-Hasan. VI/k: Harun. VI/m: Ibrahim. VI/q: Adam.

Thus, for example, Limam 10 in line IV, column b, is the son of Limam 6 in line III, column b, as are also Limams 11, 12 and 13 in columns f, g and i and the three entrants in columns 1, n and o, none of whom held the limamate. For the reader's convenience in following the subsequent analysis, the three sets of Ya'muru's descendants through his three putative sons, Limams 2, 3 and 4, have been separately boxed.

Some descendants of Limam 'Abd al-Qadir (6) tended to shorten their pedigrees by omitting Muhammad al-Aswad (2), thus affording 'Abd al-Qadir an undue pre-eminence in the Limamyiri genealogies. Challenged, they invariably admitted the inaccuracy. This matter will be returned to below. Otherwise the reconstruction of the lines of descent from Limam Ya'muru (1) through Limam Muhammad al-Aswad (2) is uncontroversial. Either it is veridical or, implausibly, the numerous individual pedigrees upon which it is based have been systematically distorted. Any mistakes that remain are more likely to be those of the investigator than of the informants.

The reconstruction of the lines of descent from Limam Ya'muru (1) through Limam Mu'adh (3) is somewhat tentative. There are gaps, and some conflicts, in the evidence. The descendants of Mu'adh comprise a group known in Walii as Manzuyiri, literally, 'the House of Mu'adh'. I know of no source in which Limam Mu'adh is given as other than a son of Limam Ya'muru.[5] I have therefore had little hesitation in accepting lists C to M (see table 4.1) which name Mu'adh as third limam, and in rejecting lists A and B, which, quite improbably on the available evidence, name him as the seventh. Lists A and B, however, are undoubtedly correct in naming Muhammad Faraqu (7) as a limam. His descendants live in that part of Manzuyiri founded by his son, Banwara, and thus known as Banwarayiri, 'the House of Banwara'.[6] I have preferred to follow sources which give Muhammad Faraqu as a son of Mu'adh rather than of Ya'muru.[7] I believe that the latter witness the tendency, noted above with reference to Muhammad al-Aswad, to shorten pedigrees by the elimination of names in Generation II. Another problem arises with respect to Limam Musa (9). The omission of Muhammad Faraqu from lists C to M of the limams is reflected in sources which give Musa as a son of Mu'adh,[8] and in one case seemingly of Limam Ya'muru.[9] I have chosen to follow a fuller pedigree which give Musa as the son of Limam Muhammad Faraqu.[10]

The treatment of Limam Ishaq (8) in table 4.2 is speculative. He is remembered as founder of a section of Limamyiri known as Vuori,[11] but he appears in none of the pedigrees I have recorded. His insertion in the table as son of Muhammad al-Ahmar, who likewise appears in none of the pedigrees, rests upon an assumption that both belonged to a line that is either extinct or has long been eliminated from the succession. The argument is, in other words, one *faute de mieux*, but the result has a certain rationality. It gains plausibility, perhaps from the fact that Ishaq has been dropped in all lists of the limams with the exception of the two oldest, lists A and B.

The Wa limamate: rules of succession

With the death of Limam Al-Hajj Nuhu (32) in 1984 the office passed to a descendent generation. From tables 4.1 and 4.2 certain inferences may be made about the rules or preferences which are exercised in the selection of a limam. These inferences are set out below, where they are matched against the views of prominent members of the Muslim community.

The Wa Limam, said Muhammad Bakuri – the later Limam Muhammad (30) – 'is always chosen from the descendants of the first imam, Limam Ya'muru'.[12] 'If', said Karamoko Sa'id b. 'Uthman Tiaro, 'there is an argument about your birth, then you cannot be an imam.'[13] 'Unless', remarked Al-Hajj Siddiq b. Sa'id (having just detailed his pedigree over seven generations), 'you can give your descent like this, then according to the Qur'an you cannot talk history.'[14] The Rule of Patrilineal Descent from Limam Ya'muru, clearly illustrated by table 4.2, is a fundamental principle which to the best of my knowledge has never been challenged. Maternal descent as such is of little relevance to the succession. The son of a slave wife could, for example, obtain the limamate, though not, it is true, the son of a prostitute.[15]

Informants in the 1960s enunciated a Rule of Seniority. In deciding the succession, Muhammad Bakuri remarked, 'they always look for someone who is senior in age.'[16] Al-Hajj Tamimu, a son of Limam Al-Hajj Muhammad (23), made the same point. 'The limamate goes by age', he affirmed; 'age is very important. Other things being equal, we prefer an older man to a younger.'[17] There is an ambiguity in these remarks to which Al-Hajj al-Hasan b. Mu'min drew attention when he observed that a person's seniority could be reckoned 'in terms of age and in terms of his descent'.[18] My understanding of the matter is that there is indeed a preference for the older man over the younger, the former being presumed the wiser and more experienced. The overriding preference, however, is for a man from a higher rather than a lower generation, for the *baraka*, or spiritual authority, transmitted from the first limam to his descendants is regarded as becoming weaker as each generation passes.

This interpretation is borne out by the data of table 4.2, which shows that the succession seldom alternated between generations, although some members of a lower generation must commonly have outranked in age some members of the ascendant generation. The two exceptions to this observation are Al-Hajj Salih (26a) and Yusuf (27) in Generation VII, both of whom apparently held office before Idris (28) of Generation VI. The cases are, however, special ones. The appointment of Al-Hajj Salih, who was the first member of Limamyiri to become an Ahmadi, was forced through by the Ahmadiyya faction in Wa; no acceptable candidate of that sect could be produced from the higher generation. It was, moreover, precisely the bitterness of the dispute between Al-Hajj Salih and Al-Hajj Sa'id (26b), both descendants of Limam 'Abd al-Qadir (6), that led the electors to seek the next limam from among the less factionalized descendants of Limam Mu'adh (3). As it happened, no candidate from that group was available from Generation VI.

The Rule of Seniority is qualified by a subordinate Rule of Personal Suitability. A viable candidate should have shown himself an able and industrious member of the community. Piety is presently somewhat more highly regarded than learning, though this may not always have been so (a matter which will be returned to later). Certain physical defects rule out candidacy, most notably (since so common) blindness. Al-Hajj Tamimu illustrated the point with reference to the election of Muhammad Bakuri as limam in 1965. 'When Limam Bakuri became limam', he said, 'it is true that there were two men older than him and we did not take them. But this was because both of them were blind, and so we couldn't make them imams: a blind man cannot lead the community.'[19] In the 1960s many people expected Al-Hajj Tamimu himself to become limam at some future date, but he too became blind and thus disqualified.[20]

In the 1960s informants attached great importance to a further rule applied in selecting a limam. 'What we do not like', said Al-Hajj Tamimu, 'is for a brother to follow a brother in the Limamate, or a son to follow his father. We don't like one small group to have it all the time. But a brother can follow his brother as long as other people come between and a son can similarly follow his father.'[21] Limam Muhammad Bakuri stated the matter in slightly different terms. 'We never take anyone from the same section [of Limamyiri] twice running', he said; the electors 'will look for a family that has not given a limam for a long time'.[22] Table 4.3, based upon the data of table 4.2, illustrates the development of what may be termed the Rule of Oscillation. It will be apparent from it that the prohibition upon a son immediately following his father in the limamate was established early in the history of the institution. Indeed, the sole exception to the rule in the case of

Table 4.3 *Changing patterns of succession in the Wa limamate*

Genera- tion	Number of limams	Number whose father was limam	Son immediately succeeding father	Brother immediately succeeding brother
I	1	—	—	—
II	3	3	1	2
III	4	4	0	1
IV	5	5	0	3
V	9	6	0	0
VI	5	3	0	0
VII	6	0	0	0
Total	33[a]	21	1	6

Note: a Includes both Limam Al-Hajj Salih and Limam Al-Hajj Sa'id

Table 4.4. *Pre-eminence of the House of 'Abd al-Qadir*

Genera- tion	Limams descended from:			
	Limam Idris (5)	Limam 'Abd al-Qadir (6)	Limam Muhammad Faraqu (7)	Limam Ishaq (8)
IV	0	4	1	0
V	1	7	1	0
VI	0	5	0	0
VII	0	5[a]	1	0
Totals	1	21	3	0

Note: a Includes both Limam Al-Hajj Salih and Limam Al-Hajj Sa'id.

Muhammad al-Aswad (2) was an unavoidable consequence of the overriding Rule of Patrilineal Descent.

By way of contrast, it is also apparent from table 4.3 that the prohibition on brother immediately succeeding brother in the limamate had taken full effect only by Generation V. Reference to table 4.2 will suggest the reason for the introduction of the prohibition. The sequential incumbencies in Generation IV of four sons (10, 11, 12, 13) of Limam 'Abd al-Qadir, immediately followed in Generation V by a son of one of the four (14), was presumably viewed by those not descended from 'Abd al-Qadir as an unseemly engrossment of the office by those that were. Selection of the next two limams appears to signal the introduction of the extended Rule of Oscillation: Limam Ibrahim (15) and Limam Al-Siddiq (16) were chosen from lines other than that of 'Abd al-Qadir.

Reference once more to table 4.3 shows that in Generations II to IV inclusive it was unknown for a limam to be chosen who was not himself the

Plate 8 Wa Friday Limam Siddiq b. 'Abd al-Mu'min (with staff) and *'ulama'*,
1963

son of a limam; that a strong preference to this effect continued to be
exercised in Generations V and VI; but that in Generation VII the preference
was no longer apparent. Informants in the 1960s maintained that being the
son of a former limam no longer gave a candidate any particular advantage
over one lacking that qualification. With reference to earlier practices,
however, several informants remarked that in the past people did not like
'seeing a son rise higher than his father' (or words to that effect). This may,
then, have been the form that the rule took. Although now discarded, the
rule has clearly had a strong impact upon the pattern of succession. Precisely
because four of the five limams in Generation IV were sons of 'Abd al-Qadir,
in Generations V and VI the continuing pursuit of candidates who were sons
of former limams inevitably favoured those from what was, in effect, the
House of 'Abd al-Qadir. The preference thus functioned in opposition to the
Rule of Oscillation in tending to confine the succession to that House. The
result is apparent from table 4.4. It will be seen that in Generation VI
none other than descendants of 'Abd al-Qadir held the limamate, and in
Generation VII only one.

In the 1960s the *de facto* exclusion of virtually all but the descendants of
'Abd al-Qadir from the limamate was in process of being made *de jure*. The
tendency in pedigrees for Limam Muhammad al-Aswad (2) to be omitted,
thus treating 'Abd al-Qadir as a son of Limam Ya'muru (1), has already been
noted. Nowhere is this basic step in the revisionist process more clearly set

out than in the short work, *Ibtida' Din Wa fi 'Am 875 ila 'Am 1382*, 'The Beginning of Religion in Wa in the Year 875 (1470/1 A.D.) to the Year 1382 (1962/3)'. It was written, at least in its present form, in 1963 by Friday Limam Siddiq b. 'Abd al-Mu'min, himself a descendant of 'Abd al-Qadir.[23] Religion began in Wa, it reads,

> with our grandfather named 'Umar [i.e., Ya'muru], the respected. It was he who came from Mandi to Wa with the religion of Islam. A son was born named Shaykh 'Abd al-Qadir, and to the son 'Abd al-Qadir twelve sons were born.[24]

I was not able to obtain a list of the twelve putative sons of 'Abd al-Qadir, and indeed the attribution of twelve sons to apical ancestors seems to have been something of a convention among the Juula. From table 4.2, however, it will be seen that seven sons of 'Abd al-Qadir figure in the pedigrees which serve to link the Wa Limams genealogically. Four were themselves limams, two (Yusuf and Yahya) appear as fathers of limams, and one (Adam) as grandfather of a limam.

Many informants in the 1960s, in much the same vein as the writer of the *Ibtida'*, spoke of Limamyiri as if it was coextensive with the House of 'Abd al-Qadir, and in effect re-stated the Rule of Patrilineal Descent from Limam Ya'muru as a Rule of Patrilineal Descent from Limam 'Abd al-Qadir. There was something approaching consensus that the House of 'Abd al-Qadir comprised four segments of major importance in the selection of a limam. *Prima facie*, it might be assumed that the four segments correspond to the four sets of descendants of the four sons of 'Abd al-Qadir who held the limamate. On this matter, however, consensus was lacking. Some informants did indeed identify the four segments as Dondoli, Tamarimuni, Dzedzedeyiri and Dapuyipala, comprising the descendants of Limams Muhammad (10), Sa'id (11), Ya'qub (12) and Ya'muru (13) respectively.[25] Others, however, omitted Tamarimuni and substituted Limampalayiri, comprising the descendants of Yusuf b. 'Abd al-Qadir. Compounding the problem, knowledgeable informants referred to 'Limam' Yusuf, although he does not appear as such on any known list.[26]

The lack of consensus extends even further. Some informants maintained that the four (whichever four) segments of the House of 'Abd al-Qadir had exclusive rights to the limamate.[27] Others asserted that the four had prime claims but that the electors might turn to other sections of Limamyiri if they were dissatisfied with all the candidates before them. They could, for example, elect a limam from among the descendants of Limam Mu'adh (3) in Manzuyiri and Banwarayiri or of Limam Idris (5) in Karanbileyiri.[28] The *de facto* pre-eminence of the House of 'Abd al-Qadir (to which the present limam also belongs) might make this seem an unlikely eventuality. In fact the descendants of Limam Mu'adh in particular continue to contest the limamate from time to time.[29] They have not succeeded in acquiring it for well over a century, but they do control a lesser though not unimportant position: that of a 'limam' who is responsible for naming the princes.[30]

Having chosen a limam-designate, the Limamyiri people are obliged to present him for the approval of the Yeri Na as titular head of the Wala Muslim community. The Yeri Na has, technically, the right to reject the choice, though I know of no occasion when a veto has been exercised. The Yeri Na has then to present the candidate to the Wa Na. There are conflicting opinions about whether the Wa Na also has a right of rejection.[31] The matter was put to the test in 1951 with somewhat inconclusive results. Limam Muhammad Saghir (25) died in that year. Al-Hajj Sa'id Soribo (26b) was chosen as successor and presented to Wa Na Mumuni Koray. The Na, however, was an Ahmadi. He rejected the candidate, and recognized the Ahmadiyya Limam, Al-Hajj Salih (26a), as Wa Limam. Neither side was prepared to give way. There were in effect two Wa Limams. The orthodox members of the community argued, as Dougah puts it, 'that since there can be two Imams in a town, there can also be two chiefs'.[32] They initiated steps to enskin a second, and orthodox, Wa Na. Sectarian violence threatened to engulf the town. The colonial administration moved rapidly to control the situation and thereby (happily, it must be admitted) denied the historian the results of what would have been an interesting but probably sanguinary trial of strength.

Chronology of the Wa limamate: nineteenth and twentieth centuries

The last member of Generation VII to hold the Wa limamate, Al-Hajj Nuhu (32), died in 1984. For the twentieth century, accurate dates are available for most incumbents. For the greater part of the nineteenth century, and for the eighteenth, this is not the case. It becomes necessary to 'date-guess' on the basis of the family reconstitution, the rules of succession, and the occasional hint to be gleaned from the traditions. We can do no more than aspire to informed rather than uninformed guesswork. Table 4.5 presents no new data, but for ease of reference depicts in a somewhat different way the distribution of limams by generation and order of succession. The numbers assigned to each incumbent in table 4.1 are retained.

The earliest dates that can be firmly established are ones in the middle of Generation V. Limam 'Uthman Dun (18) died in or about 1887, at the time of the battle between the Wala and Zabarima at Nasa.[33] His successor, Limam Musa (19), was a signatory to the treaty with the English of May 1894 and to that with the French of May 1895. He was dead by September 1898.[34] The last limam to be drawn from Generation V, Ya'qub (22), was in office in the late 1910s and in the first year or two of the 1920s.[35] On his death Friday Limam Ishaq, son of Friday Limam 'Uthman Dabila and grandson of Limam Ya'qub (12), made a bid for the office. The electors, however, preferred Al-Hajj Muhammad, a son of Limam 'Uthman Dun (18). Al-Hajj Muhammad decided to depart on pilgrimage to Mecca, but so strong was his support that the limamate was held open until his return.[36] He became limam in November 1926, the first from Generation VI.[37]

Table 4.5 *Wa Limams by generation and order of succession*

				14		
				15		
L				16		
I				17		26a
M			9	18	23	27
A		5	10	19	24	29
M	2	6	11	20	25	30
S	3	7	12	21	26b	31
	4	8	13	22	28	32
I	II	III	IV	V	VI	VII
		GENERATIONS				

Key: 1: Ya'muru. 2: Muhammad al-Aswad. 3: Mu'adh. 4: Muhammad al-Ahmar. 5: Idris. 6: 'Abd al-Qadir. 7: Muhammad Faraqu. 8: Ishaq. 9: Musa. 10: Muhammad. 11: Sa'id. 12: Ya'qub. 13: Ya'muru. 14: Idris. 15: Ibrahim. 16: Al-Siddiq. 17: Sa'id. 18: 'Uthman. 19: Musa. 20: Ibrahim. 21: Salih. 22: Ya'qub. 23: Al-Hajj Muhammad. 24: Al-Hajj Malik. 25: Muhammad Saghir. 26a: Al-Hajj Salih. 26b: Al-Hajj Sa'id. 27: Yusuf. 28: Idris. 29: Sa'id. 30: Al-Hajj Muhammad. 31: Muhammad Kankanya. 32: Al-Hajj Nuhu.

The incumbencies of the last four limams in Generation V, Musa (19), Ibrahim (20), Salih (21) and Ya'qub (22), thus extended over some thirty-five years, from c.1887 to c.1922, and the average of their tenures was a little under nine years. If the figure of nine years is generalized for the whole of Generation V, *notional* dates are obtained for the limamates of Idris (14), 1842–51; of Ibrahim (15), 1851–60; of Al-Siddiq (16), 1860–9; of Sa'id (17), 1869–78; and of 'Uthman Dun (18), 1878–87. There is one point at which this notional dating may be tested. Limam Al-Siddiq is reported on good authority to have been in office when the Zabarima under Alfa Hano arrived in the Grunshi country east of Wa.[38] In careful reviews of the evidence, Holden and Levtzion both suggest a date of about 1870 for the intrusion.[39] The notional dates for the limamate of Al-Siddiq appear, then, to approximate to the real; that is, he was indeed a figure of the 1860s.

If the notional date of 1842 for the beginning of the incumbency of Limam Idris (14) is accepted, then the limamate was held within Generation V for a full eight decades. The date may, however, be a little too early. In Generation IV, the most helpful synchronisms relate to the third limam, Ya'qub (12). In 1930 five elderly and leading members of the Wa Muslim community were asked by the District Commissioner to review relations between Wa and Gonja in the pre-colonial period. The panellists commenced with a description of the struggle between Bolewura and Tuluwewura for the Gonja paramountcy in which first the Buna, then the Wala, then the Gyaman and finally the Asante became involved.[40] At the time, they noted, 'Yakuba grandfather of Mallam Issaka was Limam.' Mallam Issaka, that is, Friday Limam Ishaq, was himself one of the panellists and was indeed a grandson of Limam Ya'qub (12). Fortunately, the events in question can be accurately dated. The return of the Asante army to Kumase in June 1844 was witnessed by the missionary, G. Chapman.[41] Granted, then, the reliability of the panellists' recollections (and at least one of them, Yeri Na 'Uthman Daleri, was a child at the time of the troubles), a *floruit* in the 1840s is indicated for Limam Ya'qub. One further limam, Ya'muru (13), succeeded Ya'qub in Generation IV. The transition from Generation IV to Generation V of the limamate, then, should probably be placed a little later than the notional dating suggests, and most likely in the early 1850s.

Three limams in Generation IV held office prior to Ya'qub, namely, Musa (9), Muhammad (10) and Sa'id (11). Limam Sa'id has a special place in the remembrance of the Wa Muslims. 'He was', to follow the *Ibtida' Din Wa* again, 'the one who went to the town of Pan [Kong, in Côte d'Ivoire] to look for knowledge.'[42] A fuller account of the matter was given me in 1964 by his descendant, Al-Hajj Siddiq b. Sa'id. 'After Ya'muru settled in Wa with the Qur'an', he said,

> all the old men of knowledge [*karamokos*] died. Men of knowledge became few. This continued up to the time of Imam Muhammad b. 'Abd al-Qadir. Then Imam Sa'id, my father's grandfather, went to Kong. He was not then imam, but was sent there. He spent twelve years in Kong. The teacher was Karamoko 'Abbas Saghanughu. Sa'id came back from Kong to Wa. He was a *mujaddid*, a reviver of Islam in Wa. Later he was made imam.[43]

Karamoko 'Abbas Saghanughu is to be identified with the renowned teacher, 'Abbas b. Muhammad al-Mustafa Saghanughu, who moved from Boron to Kong and became first Saghanughu limam of that town.[44] *Al-Jawahir wa 'l-Yawaqit fi Dukhul al-Islam fi 'l-Magharib ma'a 'l-Tauqit*, 'Jewels and Rubies on the Beginnings of Islam in the West, with Dates', is a recension of Saghanughu tradition put together by Al-Hajj Muhammad Marhaba Saghanughu in 1963. In it the role of Karamoko 'Abbas in the diffusion of learning, *inter alia* to the Wala, is described:

> Al-'Abbas brought his brothers also to settle there [Kong]. The *'ulama'* of that place gathered around him to have some of his knowledge. Thus his fame spread to other lands. The people of Buntuqu [Bonduku] and Wala and the lands of Ghayagha[?] and Ghiriha[?] and Banda and others came to acquire learning there.[45]

Limam 'Abbas died in Kong in 1215 AH, AD 1801.[46] It is likely, then, that the sojourn of Sa'id b. 'Abd al-Qadir in Kong fell within, or principally within, the 1790s. We have seen that the incumbency of Sa'id's successor in the limamate, Ya'qub (12), may be dated to the 1840s. Sa'id's limamate is therefore probably to be placed in the 1830s, a date perfectly compatible with his having studied in Kong in the 1790s.

There remain, then, the first and second limams to hold office in Generation IV, Musa (9) and Muhammad (10). The latter is an exceptionally highly revered figure in Wa and is often referred to by the honorific, Madani Tarawiri (Arabic *madani*, 'the civilized, refined, polished, urbane').[47] The data on him unfortunately do not provide any useful synchronisms. The data on Limam Musa do. Al-Hajj Siddiq b. Sa'id claimed that in early times prayers were made in an area marked off for the purpose by stones. It was in front of the Wa Na's house. The first true mosque was built in Limamyiri by Limam Musa, and Limam Sa'id was buried at it. I incline to accept this tradition as veridical. Prayers are still made in the names of those who founded mosques, and their graves are regularly visited and care is taken not to disturb the sites. Al-Hajj Siddiq added the detail that the Limamyiri mosque was built before his great-grandfather went to study in Kong.[48] There is some independent evidence that it was built not so much before Sa'id left Wa but perhaps while he was in Kong. In *Al-Jawahir wa 'l-Yawaqit*, Al-Hajj Muhammad Marhaba Saghanughu refers to a phase of mosque building which, beginning in Kong itself in 1200 AH (1785/6), spread to Buna in 1210 (1795/6), to Bonduku in 1212 (1797/8) and to Wa in 1216 (1801/2).[49] The authority for these dates is not known. If they are accepted, then the limamate of Musa would seem to belong to the end of the eighteenth century and the beginning of the nineteenth, which is also therefore the period of the transition from incumbents of Generation III to those of Generation IV.

The burden of the evidence, then, suggests that Generation IV extended over a period of perhaps five decades, from the late eighteenth century to the middle of the nineteenth century, and that five limams held office, with an average tenure of somewhat over ten years. Generation V extended over some seven decades, from the middle of the nineteenth century to the early 1920s, and nine limams held office with an average tenure of about eight years. In both generations the rules of succession appear to have remained constant. The presumption is that the trend towards more limams per generation, and a lower average tenure in office, is a reflection of the growth of the Limamyiri community. Quite simply, more candidates were available in Generation V than in Generation IV. The trend did not, however, continue. Generations VI and VII together extended over only some six decades, from the early 1920s to 1984, and ten limams held office in the period (counting Al-Hajj Salih and Al-Hajj Sa'id as one for this purpose). Two relevant factors may be identified. First, the length of time the limamate was held in Generation V presumably reduced the number of available candidates in Generation VI, many of them having predeceased their peers in the senior generation. Second, the defection of sections of Limamyiri to the Ahmadiyya Movement reduced the choice still further, particularly in Generation VII. That the average tenure of office over the two generations

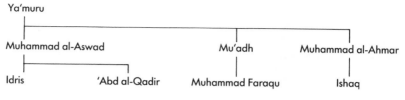

Figure 4 The early Wa Limams

fell to as low as six years attests, moreover, to the advanced age of many of the candidates chosen.

Chronology of the Wa limamate before the nineteenth century

The transition from Generation III to Generation IV of the Wa limamate has been assigned to the end of the eighteenth or beginning of the nineteenth century. The data are of different kinds, some soft, some hard, but their very coherence permits a reasonable degree of confidence in the dating. The chronology of the limamate in the eighteenth century is far more a matter of speculation. It is assumed, for reasons already considered, that the pedigrees are accurate. The problem thus reduces itself to one of guessing as shrewdly as possible the approximate dates of the transitions from Generation I to II and from Generation II to III.

The relevant genealogy is shown in figure 4. For purposes of date-guessing the death of Ishaq may be assigned to year x. In a large sample, the average separation in years between the death of a person and the death of his father should approximate to the average separation in years between the birth of that person and the birth of his father. This actuarial principle will be applied *faute de mieux*. The age of Muhammad al-Ahmar at the time of Ishaq's birth is unlikely to fall outside the range twenty to sixty years. The death of Muhammad al-Ahmar (and the end of Generation II of the limamate) might, then, be assigned to year $x-40$ ($+/-20$), that is, anything from twenty to sixty years before that of his son. If it fell outside this range, then the incumbency of Idris would start correspondingly earlier or later. The computation can, however, be refined.

The Rule of Seniority will, at this point, repay further consideration. Reference has been made earlier to its cultural aspect, that is, to the belief that the *baraka* of the founder of the limamate is transmitted to his descendants, but becomes progressively weaker from generation to generation. This is a belief that may be Islamic as such. It is certainly common to the Juula of the wider Voltaic region, and therefore must antedate the foundation of the Wa limamate. There is a presumption, then, that at the time of his death Limam Ishaq was the last surviving son of his father who could be regarded as qualified for office. The age of Muhammad al-Ahmar at Ishaq's birth is thus likely to have been in the upper rather than lower part of the range twenty to sixty, and the computed date of Muhammad al-Ahmar's death may reasonably be revised from year $x-40$ $(+/-20)$ to $x-50$ $(+/-10)$. An application of precisely the same actuarial and other arguments suggests that Ya'muru's death (and the end of Generation I of the limamate) may be guessed as year $x-100$ $(+/-20)$. Converted into absolute chronology, the thrust of the argument is that Generation III of the limamate ended in the late eighteenth or early nineteenth century, Generation II in the middle of the eighteenth century, and Generation I (that is, Ya'muru's limamate) in the later seventeenth or earlier eighteenth century.

Those who require rigorous standards of proof in the study of the past will probably already be alarmed at the speculative nature of the reconstruction. Those, however, who believe that the historian has an obligation to venture into uncharted seas (even though, like the early navigators, it becomes less and less sure just where one is) will perhaps bear with this inquiry. The chronological reconstruction indicates, on relatively hard evidence, that Generation V of the limamate extended over about seven decades and Generation IV over about five, and by controlled guesswork that Generations III and II each likewise extended over about five decades.

The implication of these arguments is, that by virtue of the Rule of Seniority, the limamate tended to pass to younger brothers rather than elder sons, so producing long generations. Since, moreover, younger brothers in one generation may often have been older than elder sons in the next, the cumulative tendency was towards the elimination of elder sons from the succession: that is, they were likely to be either dead or disabled by age before their candidacy could be advanced. It is not difficult to find a correlate of this tendency in the material base of Wala society.

The relative marginality of the Wala environment dictated that elder sons engaged themselves in productive activities that ensured the survival of the community; that is, they had to farm, manufacture (for example, cloth), or trade. Granted that the reproduction of the community was indeed ensured, then it was younger sons who might be released for less materially productive activities. They might study under scholars in other towns, make the pilgrimage to Mecca, and in time become teachers and in some cases limams. The community was voluntarily depriving itself of primary productive labour in order to nurture an intelligentsia. Elder brothers who were farmers, craftsmen and traders supported younger brothers who constituted the *'ulama'* class in society.

The thesis, that it was younger sons who were enabled to acquire the skills necessary for the assumption of specifically 'clerical' roles in society, is amenable to testing in the Wa context. It is generally recognized in Limamyiri that of all the surviving lines of descent from Limam Ya'muru, the 'strongest' is that through Limam Muhammad al-Aswad (2), Limam 'Abd al-Qadir (6), Limam Muhammad (10), Limam 'Uthman Dun (18), Limam Al-Hajj Muhammad (23), and Limam Al-Hajj Nuhu (32); 'strength' has reference to the transmission of the *baraka* of the founder. It is genealogically senior to all lines shown in table 4.2, other than that stemming from Limam Idris (5), which has long since ceased to provide limams and is, in that sense at least, extinct. Nevertheless, the 'strong' line is clearly not a line of elder sons. The death of Limam Muhammad (10) must have occurred around 1820, and the deaths of Limam 'Uthman Dun (18), Limam Al-Hajj Muhammad (23) and Limam Al-Hajj Nuhu (32) are datable to *c*. 1887, 1936 and 1984 respectively. The intervals between their deaths are such as to imply that, notwithstanding the seniority of the line, younger rather than older sons were attaining the office of limam.

A Wa Limamyiri tradition referred to in chapter 3 has the first Wa limam Ya'muru as a son of Alfa Mahmud, grandson of 'Uthman, and great-grandson of Bukari (or Abu Bakr) Biri. We have suggested that Bukari Biri may be the Bukari Tarawiri who was *qadi* of Jenne in the 1570s to 1580s. Clearly a late-seventeenth- to early-eighteenth-century *floruit* for Ya'muru is entirely compatible with his putative descent in the third generation from Qadi Bukari Tarawiri. This comment addresses itself, of course, to the plausibility rather than the veracity of the tradition.

Wa chronology: the Wa Nam

All three texts of HSW, we have noted, conclude with lists of the Wa Nas. These are shown in table 4.6. A fourth list is added from TAW. A fifth was recorded by District Commissioner Whittall in 1923.[50] Unlike HSW, both TAW and Whittall identify the Nas by gate. The spelling of the names of the Nas has been standardized. Although no lists are identical, all are probably derived from a common source. Those of the Hausa version of HSW/b and TAW differ only in the reversal of Bachigme and Dibayiyege, and this may be no more than a scribal error in the latter. Whittall's list is almost certainly derived from the Hausa version of HSW/b, the sole discrepancy being the description of Dibayiyege under a Muslim name, Saliya. The Arabic and Hausa version of HSW/b differ only in that the former lacks the names of both Djonyusi and Kunjokun; it is difficult to know whether the omissions are of significance or resulted from careless copying. HSW/a is clearly related to the Arabic version of HSW/b, for the names of Djonyusi and Kunjokun are also omitted. It also has features, however, that set it apart from the other lists. First, Suri is substituted for Saliya at the head of the list, which makes a political statement. Second, Kpasa is dropped from the list, which either makes a second (but incompatible) political statement, or may be no more than a copyist's error. Third, Yijisi is added to the list, seemingly treating the name of the Busa gate as an eponym. The two lists in HSW/b and those in TAW and Whittall all date, in their extant forms, from the early 1920s. The list in HSW/a is a copy made in 1963. Unless older manuscripts can be located, it is impossible to decide whether the split in the tradition predates or antedates the early 1920s.

No dates are present in any list other than Whittall's. He assigns the

Table 4.6. *The Wa Nas to Sidiki Bomi, died 1978*

WA NA	HSW/a	HSW/b Arabic	HSW/b Hausa	TAW	Whittall	Gate, from TAW	Gate, from Whittall
Suri	X						
Saliya		X	X	X	X		
Gura	X	X	X	X	X	Guli	Busa
Pelpuo	X	X	X	X	X		Busa
Kpasa		X	X	X	X	Guli	Guli
Na Djare	X	X	X	X	X	Pirisi	Pirisi
Yijisi	X						
Djonyusi			X	X	X	Sing	Sing
Saka	X	X	X	X	X	Busa	Busa
Kunjokun			X	X	X	Pirisi	Pirisi
Danduni	X	X	X	X	X	Pirisi	Pirisi
Fijolina	X	X	X	X	X	Busa	Busa
Buntigsu	X	X	X	X	X	Busa	Busa
Sadja	X	X	X	X	X	Pirisi	Busa
Pelpuo II	X	X	X	X	X	Busa	Busa
Jinsun	X	X	X	X	X	Pirisi	Busa
Sobuun	X	X	X	X	X	Busa	Busa
Bondiri	X	X	X	X	X	Sing	Sing
Gangume	X	X	X	X	X	Busa	Busa
Bachigme	X	X	X		X		Pirisi
Dibayiyege	X	X	X	X		Busa	
[Bachigme]			X			Pirisi	
Saliya					X		Busa
Balannoya	X	X	X	X	X	Sing	Sing
Mahama Fua	X	X	X	X	X	Busa	Busa
Saidu Takora	X	X	X	X	X	Pirisi	Pirisi
Momori Tangile	X	X	X	X	X	Busa	Busa
Dangana	X	X	X	X	X	Sing	Sing
Pelpuo III	X	X	X	X	X	Busa	Busa
Hamidu Bomi	X	end	end	X	end	Pirisi	
Sumaila	X			X		Busa	
Mumuni Koray	X			X		Sing	
Saidu II	X			end			
Sidiki Bomi	X						

beginnings of the incumbencies of Bondiri to 1841, Gangume to 1845, Bachigme to 1875, Dibayiyege (Saliya) to 1880, Balannoya to 1880, Mahama Fua to 1889, Saidu Takora to 1896, Momori Tangile to 1904, Dangana to 1908, and Pelpuo III to 1919. It is presumed that Whittall arrived at these dates in consultation with Limam Ishaq and, no doubt, other elderly members of Limamyiri, drawing upon their recollections of the lengths of successive incumbencies. Bondiri represented the limits of memory in the early 1920s.

The chronology of the recent Wa Nas is fully documented in the reports of the colonial administrators, and it is unnecessary to do more than summarize the data. Sidiki Bomi held the Nam from 1961 to 1978; Saidu II from 1953 to 1961; Mumuni Koray from 1949 to 1953; Sumaila from 1943 to 1949; Hamidu Bomi from 1936 to 1943; Pelpuo III from 1920 to 1935; Dangana from 1908 to 1920, and Momori Tangile from 1898 to 1908. Saidu Takora was removed from office by the British in 1898, having shown a marked lack of enthusiasm for their cause.[51] He was in office at least by 1894, when he treated with G. E. Ferguson. His predecessor, Mahama Fua, was active in the 1880s. After the Wala defeat by Babatu in 1887 he lost the confidence of his people. He is said to have committed suicide by poison, probably in 1887 or 1888.[52] No firm dates for the chronology of the Nam in the earlier nineteenth century exist. There are, however, a number of synchronisms which are useful in establishing *floruits*.

Some confidence may be placed in *Al-Akhbar Zabarima*, a short work preserved in the corpus of documents put together by Friday Limam Ishaq in 1922 or 1923.[53] According to its author, who appears to have written from direct memory, Wa Na Gangume was in office when the Zabarima under Alfa Hano arrived in the Grunshi country. Siddiq was Limam of Wa at the time. We have seen, in the discussion of the chronology of the limamate, that the events in question may be dated to the late 1860s.

In 1930 the panellists from whom the District Commissioner of Wa obtained a statement about nineteenth-century relations between Gonja and Wa included, *inter alios*, Yeri Na 'Uthman Daleri and Friday Limam Ishaq.[54] It contains two further synchronisms of relevance. The first has reference to a time when Bondiri was Wa Na, Idris was Limam, and Bruma (that is, Ibrahim) was Yeri Na. Idris is described as 'father' of Limam Ishaq, and Bruma as 'father' of Yeri Na 'Uthman Daleri. The latter relationship cannot be verified, but Limam Idris was in fact the senior brother (that is, in Walii, 'senior father') of Limam Ishaq's real father. Limam Idris (14) was the first to hold office in Generation V of the limamate, and a *floruit* in the early 1850s has been suggested for him. Wa Na Bondiri should, then, be located in this period. Yeri Na 'Uthman Daleri remarked that he was about ten years old at the time, and Limam Ishaq about five. The former died in 1932 and the latter in 1931. Both were very advanced in age, and would indeed have been, on this reckoning, in their early and mid eighties respectively.[55]

The second synchronism is contained in the same document: 'The present Chief of Wa's grandfather was the Chief of Wa; Yakuba grandfather of Mallam Issaka was Limam, Abudu Wala's grandfather was Yarona.' The Wa Na in 1930 was Pelpuo III, son of Wa Na Momori Tangile and grandson of Wa Na Pelpuo II.[56] Limam Ya'qub (12) was indeed the grandfather of Friday Limam Ishaq ('Mallam Issaka'). The Yeri Na ('Yarona') in question cannot be identified. The synchronism is presented in the context of the cycle of wars in which Asante became involved, from which the *floruit* of Limam Ya'qub – and hence of Wa Na Pelpuo II – has been dated to the early 1840s.

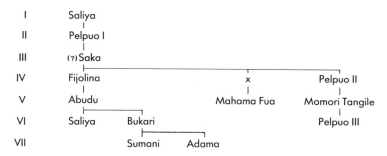

Figure 5 Family reconstitution, a segment of Busa gate

The synchronisms, then, indicate a *floruit* for Wa Na Pelpuo II in the early 1840s, for Wa Na Bondiri in the early 1860s, and for Wa Na Gangume in the late 1860s. These dates appear eminently acceptable when matched against the lists of Nas, but suggest that Whittall's reconstruction from (we have assumed) recollected reign lengths erred, though not grievously.

The Wa Nabihi appear not to preserve pedigrees with that degree of care shown by the Limamyiri people. It may be that this reflects no more than the scholarly (and Islamic) concern with chains of transmission (*isnad, silsila*) on the part of the latter. I am able to reconstruct only one pedigree extending from Saliya to members of the present generation (figure 5). It is for one segment of the Yijisi or Busa gate to the Nam and, excluding Saliya, locates genealogically seven Wa Nas.[57] Saka is the only member of the Busa gate to have held the Wa Nam between Pelpuo I and Fijolina. Although all available sources refer to members of Generation IV simply as grandsons of Pelpuo I, the assumption has been made that Saka is the link between Generations II and IV of the Nam; that – less likely perhaps – a brother of Saka may have been the link does not affect the argument.

Fijolina is said to have spent some years in exile 'in Mali' before returning to Wa to seize the Nam after having had Na Danduni assassinated.[58] Since two Nas held office between Fijolina and his brother Pelpuo II, whose *floruit* has been placed in the early 1840s, the former belongs in all probability to the 1810s or 1820s. His grandson Saliya was Busa Na from 1912 to his death in 1922, and his grandson Bukari from 1922 to his death in 1942. The latter made a strong bid for the Wa Nam on the death of Pelpuo III in 1935. His candidacy was ruled out of order by the District Commissioner on the grounds that he was from the same gate as the deceased Na, whereupon he pressed the claims of the Na Kpasa gate against those of the successful candidate, Hamidu Bomi from Pirisi.[59] Busa Na Bukari's son, Sumani ('Uthman), became Busa Na in 1969 and another son, Adama, better known as B. K. Adama, played and continues to play an important role in Ghana national politics. None of Wa Na Fijolina's descendants has, then, to date succeeded to the Wa Nam; one of his brothers, two of his nephews, and a son of one of his nephews have.

By contrast to succession to the Wa limamate, succession to the Nam was less a matter of rules, more one of power plays. It is, accordingly, difficult to make any chronological moves from the later to the earlier generations shown in figure 5. It is none the less clear that the generations of Nas, that is, the spans of time the Nam was held in one generation, were also relatively long ones. This is a result of the way the gate system operated. We have seen that the traditions, *lasiri* and *kubaru*, identify the three original towns of the Wa Nabihi as Guli, Gbetore and Yaro. From these arose the three gates of Guli, Busa, and Pirisi held by three sons of Saliya (by different mothers): Na Kpasa, Pelpuo and Na Djare respectively. A fourth gate, that of Sing, was created by a *full* brother of Pelpuo, namely, Djonyusi. The event appears to have involved the Nabihi in internecine struggle. The traditions referring to this vary in detail.[60] Their thrust, however, is that conflict resulted from the irreconcilable interests in the Nam of Pelpuo's full brother on the one hand, and Pelpuo's sons on the other. On the death of Na Djare, in other words, the succession was contested by both Djonyusi and a son of Pelpuo. The parties took to arms, Djonyusi emerged successful, took the Nam, seceded from the Yijisi gate, and founded Sing as another gate to the Nam. The struggles may not have escaped the attention of a contemporary annalist.

The *Kitab Ghanja*, 'Book of Gonja', contains a set of annals extending from 1122 AH (1710/11) to 1178 AH (1764). An entry for 1150 AH (1737/8) reports that 'the SN' people plundered Wa'. This is the reading in all but one late manuscript, which has 'Manghu' for SN'.[61] Accepting the better attested of the variants, it is difficult to suggest any context for the entry other than the conflict attending the successful secession of Sing from the parent Busa (or Gbetore) gate. If this is correct, then the *floruit* of Djonyusi was in the 1730s and 1740s.

The *Kitab Ghanja* has an earlier entry relating to Wa. In the year 1143 AH (1730/1) 'Abdallah died; he was 'the king of Wa'.[62] It is impossible to be sure to which Wa Na this refers. Pelpuo's Muslim name is given in the *kubaru* ASBW and HSW/a as Harun, and this must be given due weight. Na Kpasa's Muslim name is given in one late source as Osman, that is, 'Uthman.[63] These sources cannot be followed with such confidence as completely to rule out the identification of either Pelpuo I or Na Kpasa with the 'Abdallah of the *Kitab Ghanja*. It is, however, perhaps more likely that the reference is to Na Djare, whose death ushered in the period of strife terminated only by the accession of Djonyusi to the Nam. It will be recollected that the *kubaru* ASBW and TATM both identify Na Djare of Yaro, before he took the Wa Nam, as first patron of the immigrant Tarawiri who were to found the limamates of Nasa and Wa. In 1969 the aged and knowledgeable Al-Hajj Abu b. 'Abdallah expanded on this theme. Ya'muru and his followers, he said, came to Wala:

There they met the princes, the Najeri [Na Djare] people. The Najeri princes were the most powerful and, unlike the other princes, had the Qur'an. Ya'muru went to the Najeri people and saw the Qur'an. Then the Najeri princes said to Ya'muru, 'Do you want our Qur'an, or do you want our daughter?' But they gave him both. They still pray. It was the Yeri Na who took our grandfather Ya'muru to the Najeri princes.[64]

It may be that Na Djare's Muslim associations explain why his death, uniquely among the early Wa Nas, should have been noticed in the *Kitab Ghanja*.

These admittedly tentative readings of the Gonja annals suggest, then, *floruits* in the first half of the eighteenth century for the putative sons of Saliya, namely, Na Kpasa, Pelpuo, Na Djare and Djonyusi. This is chronologically compatible with the family reconstitution shown in figure 5. It is also compatible with the *floruit* assigned to Limam Ya'muru. Although the ambiguities and contradictions that surround the early history of the Wa Nam in *lasiri* and *kubaru* are incapable of resolution, it is nevertheless possible to have a reasonable degree of confidence in the chronological setting of that early history. The Wala polity did originate in some determinate period. The evidence points to the period in question being the late seventeenth and early eighteenth centuries.

Early Wala: the regional setting

Wala has the character of a palimpsest. There are peoples who must be considered, to all intents and purposes, autochthonous to the area: Dagaaba, Wiili and Birifor in the west, and Tampolense, Chakalle, Potuli and Pasaala in the east. Into the lands they occupied there moved, first, settlers from the west whose descendants still claim to be Mande by origin. They established themselves at Nasa, Visi and Palewogo. Later, settlers arrived from the east. Those whose descendants claim Dagomba origins established themselves at Wa, Wechiau, Dorimon and Buna, and those whose descendants claim Mampurugu origins at Gbetore, Guli, Yaro, Funsi, Kojopere and Walembele. The traditions which treat these movements universally make use of the image of the warlord and his warband; at issue are the small-scale invasions of warrior groups rather than the mass migrations of whole peoples. But the traditions also employ a second image, that of immigrant scholars. The Kunatay and Tarawiri *'ulama'* are thus added to the admixture of communities out of which the Wala polity, with its different layers of authority, arose.

The movement into the Wala area of warbands putatively of Mande origins – Tarawiri, Sienu, Dabo and Zono – must surely be seen as part of a more general phenomenon. The political empire that was Mali flourished in the thirteenth and fourteenth centuries and then, as is the wont of empires, slowly decayed. Regionally, its hegemony was challenged by the rising power of Songhay.[65] Globally, its decline became irreversible as the primacy of the

Mediterranean economy, of which it had long been part, gave way to that of the new and rising Atlantic economy, to which it was marginal.[66] Yet, paradoxically, as metropolitan Mali collapsed in on itself and the authority of the emperors disintegrated, new and autonomous Mande polities began to take shape beyond the peripheries of the old empire. Nowhere is this development more apparent than in the Voltaic region. The Gonja kingdom is an early and relatively well-documented instance. It was founded in the middle of the sixteenth century by the commander of an expedition sent from Mali to occupy the important trading town of Bighu south of the southern bend of the Black Volta. He defected and with his followers established a local jurisdiction over the autochthonous peoples of the grasslands between the Black and White Voltas. In this he had the collaboration of scholars from Bighu, who founded the Gonja limamates.[67]

It is in this general context that the settlement of Nasa, Visi and Palewogo (only in fact some sixty or so miles north and northwest of the early Gonja centres) should be seen. In TM, it will be recollected, Limam Ishaq referred to the people of Kundungu ('Kunduqi') being defeated by the Mande immigrants. Recent discoveries in the district immediately east of Kundungu, on the north bank of the Kulpawn between Palewogo and Yagaba, are of relevance. A large number of stone-circle burial mounds have been located there. The closest parallels known in West Africa are from Senegal and Mali. Artefacts show many signs of exogenous influences, most notably perhaps in the terracotta sculptures of camels and their riders.[68] It is difficult not to see in such material evidence of the intrusion of the 'Old Muslims ... from the Mande country' into the area, that is, of the early Kantonsi settlers. Radio-carbon dates from the sites are not yet available. Thermoluminescent dating of terracottas, however, yields dates of $1505 +/- 80$ and $1579 +/- 135$, and it may be that these provide some confirmation of Wala traditions that the movement of the 'Old Muslims' into the area east of the Black Volta long preceded that of the Dagomba and Mampurugu.

We have noted the tradition that associates the Kantonsi of Palewogo with Buna. 'Before they were in Buna it is not known where they were', I was told. 'From Buna they moved to Mankurago ... From Mankurago they moved to Palewogo; this can be regarded as their capital town.'[69] The importance of Buna in the history of the region has never been fully appreciated. I have suggested elsewhere that Buna may have been the town of the 'ulama' of Bighu, the great trading centre lying a hundred miles to its south on the Akan frontier.[70] If so, it was also in its own right an important mart in the gold trade, situated near workings along the Black Volta.[71] Its wealth apparently led to its sack in the middle of the sixteenth century by the Malian warband that occupied Bighu and subsequently founded the Gonja kingdom.[72] Abu Bakr al-Siddiq of Timbuktu and Jenne has left some account of the town in the late eighteenth century. Both his father and uncle had been active in its gold trade and Abu Bakr himself studied there under teachers from as far distant as Futa Toro and Futa Jallon.[73] In the middle of the nineteenth century, Henry Barth knew of it as 'a place of great celebrity for its learning and its schools'.[74] It may have been Buna that lured into the Voltaic region those who went on to found Palewogo, as Bighu did those who went on to found Gonja.

Buna also figures prominently in Dagomba and Mampurugu traditions of expeditions to the west. The *kubaru* AWK has the first Wa Widana as an immigrant from the unidentified 'Niyirtiwu'. In TAW Limam Ishaq treats him as leader of a Dagomba warband. He was accompanied by two sons of Dariziogu ('son of a Ya Na'). The first son settled in Wechiau, the second in Gwo (Dorimon). A son of the second overran Buna, married there, and fathered Bunkani, from whom the rulers of Buna descend. There are Dagomba traditions that are clearly related to those of Wa. In the 1910s E. F. Tamakloe recorded Dagomba accounts of an attack on Buna. The Ya Na, Dalgudamda ('Darigudiemda'), married a Buna woman, and Bunkani was born.[75] Tamakloe says that the Dagomba Namo Na ('Chief Drummer') checked his account. The authority of the Namo Na, as senior custodian of the Dagomba 'past', cannot lightly be queried, but Tamakloe's report of the matter appears to be in some error. In particular, the campaign against Buna seems to belong not to the reign of Ya Na Dalgudamda but to the much later one of Ya Na Zokuli.

David Tait obtained an account of Ya Na Zokuli's expedition to the west from Dagomba drummers in the 1950s.[76] It is in general agreement with the version meticulously recorded in the 1970s by John Chernoff from the elder drummer, Al-Hajj Ibrahim M'ba Lunga:[77]

> We praise them [the Wala] with Naa Zokuli's name. And so you see the Walas and the Dagartis: they are Naa Zokuli's people, because he left here to look for gold there, and he remained there. He was in a river, and there was gold, and he turned and became a crocodile, and one part of him remained a human being. That river is at the town of the Dagartis, and we call the town Gbono [Buna], and it is now on the French side [that is, in Côte d'Ivoire]. And so it was Naa Zokuli who went and remained, and he had towns there.

The implication is, presumably, that Na Zokuli was drowned in the Black Volta between Wa and Buna. It is well known that he had no descendants who became Nas of Dagomba.

Na Zokuli was a junior brother of the father of Ya Na Muhammad Zanjina, the end of whose reign can be dated with some confidence to 1714/15.[78] Between Na Zokuli and Na Muhammad Zanjina one reign intervened, that of Na Gungobli. P. Ferguson has argued that Na Zokuli held the Dagomba Nam in the 1680s and 1690s.[79] She cannot be far off the mark. There is, then, an apparently satisfying synchrony between the Wala and Dagomba traditions. If the first Widana, Suri, established himself in Wala in the context of Na Zokuli's expedition in the 1680s or 1690s, then a key item in Wala tradition is chronologically acceptable, that Suri's daughter married the later Mampurugu immigrant, Saliya, for whose sons we have argued a *floruit* in the first half of the eighteenth century. Acceptable, too, is the story of TAW, that Suri was accompanied by two sons of Dariziogu. Dariziogu was the first Ya Na in the generation of Na Zokuli to reign.[80] The synchrony between Wala and Dagomba traditions may, however, be more apparent than real. As Chernoff notes, the Wala do not have their own drum recitals, and on festive occasions, such as Damba, drummers from Dagomba go there to praise the Wala with Ya Na Zokuli's names. There is, therefore, at least a possibility that Limam Ishaq, in the *kubaru* TAW, based his account of the Dagomba connection upon Dagomba drum recitals rather than Wala *lasiri*. If so, the evidential value of the account in TAW is reduced. The attempt to establish a chronology for Widana Suri would rest upon Dagomba tradition alone rather than upon its convergence with that of Wala.

Saliya, ancestor of the Wa Nas in the male line, is a figure of the late seventeenth or early eighteenth century; such must be the implication of an argument that assigns an early eighteenth century *floruit* to his putative sons. We have seen that Wala traditions, exemplified for example in ASBW, refer to the response of Saliya (and his three junior brothers) to appeals the Wala addressed to Mampurugu for help. We have seen that there are other Wala traditions that have Saliya an exile from Mampurugu, having left there as a result of a skin dispute.[81] There is material of relevance to these matters in the corpus of Mampurugu tradition.

In the late 1960s or early 1970s, A. A. Iliasu recorded stories of a seven-year expedition conducted by the Na of Mampurugu, Atabia. The campaigns extended as far west as (yet again) Buna and contact was made with the Mango on the Komoé river. According to one account (from Wungu near Walewale), Na Atabia 'appointed [chiefs to] places through which he passed and the descendants of those chiefs are to be found in the Grunshi, Sisala and Wala areas'.[82] In the early 1930s, both G. F. Mackay and R. S. Rattray recorded similar accounts of Na Atabia's expedition.[83] Earlier, in 1924, J. Withers-Gill published a translation of a manuscript in Hausa from the library of what was then the School of Oriental Studies, London University.[84] In it there is reference to the same campaign, though Na Atabia is not named. 'The men of Ganbaga', it commented, 'ruled over the Lobi and as far as the country of the Kolansawa', that is, the Kulango or Nkoran of the Buna region. The original work was written in the late nineteenth or early twentieth century by Malam Al-Hasan b. 'Umar of Kpabia, later to become Friday Limam of Salaga and to die in 1933.[85] Its genesis can, moreover, be traced further. Malam Al-Hasan noted that he obtained his material from Malam Salifu, a Mamprusi. The informant is almost certainly to be identified as the Salifu (of Dagomba origin) who served Na Bariga of Mampurugu as *lunse* or court drummer in the late nineteenth century.[86]

The Mampurugu tradition of Na Atabia's expedition to the west appears, then, to be a respectable one, in so far as it is witnessed a century ago. It is fortunate that the reign of Na Atabia can be dated. Under 1154 AH (1741/2) the *Kitab Ghanja* has the entry, 'In that year Atabya, the king of GhBGh [Gambaga], died. It is said that he reigned for fifty odd years.'[87] There is, then, a chronological fit between the *floruit* assigned to Saliya and the known dates for Atabia. It is difficult to avoid the conclusion that Saliya's settlement in the Wala country occurred in the context of Na Atabia's expedition to the west.

The nature of the Mampurugu expedition is not well explained in the various recensions of tradition. None of them presents the campaigns as particularly sanguinary ones. No great battles are apparently recalled, no glorious military victories. In this respect there is agreement with Wala traditions, in which the settlement of Saliya in Wa is not represented as an act of conquest, nor is that of his three commanders in (to follow the text of TAW) Funsi, Kojopere and Walembele. The Mampurugu may have sought to maintain political hegemony through the chiefs who established local jurisdictions in the west. If so, Wala traditions are silent on the matter. Indeed, to the contrary, Saliya is used to define not Wala subservience but Wala autonomy; he is apical ancestor of Nas who presided over the affairs of an independent Wala polity. In this may be found some clue to the nature of the ambiguities and contradictions in the accounts of the early history of the Wa Nam.

At the core of the matter of the origins of the Wa Nam is the contradiction between the Na Pelpuo tradition, that *nalun* was brought to Wa by Saliya from Mampurugu, and the Na Kpasa tradition, that *nalun* was transferred by the Widana people to Na Kpasa and the other sons of Saliya. The first tradition thus recognizes Saliya as a Wa Na; the second does not. If the truth of the Mampurugu accounts of Na Atabia's expedition, and of the implantation in Wala of a Mampurugu group under its warlord, Saliya, is accepted, then the thrust of the Na Kpasa tradition might seem to be twofold. First, the Widana people did not recognize the authority – the *nalun* – of Saliya. Second, the Widana people did subsequently acknowledge the authority of Saliya's sons, but only in the sense that they saw themselves as having voluntarily conferred that very authority upon first Na Kpasa and then his half-brothers. The corollary of this position is that the Wa Nam is held by the Wa Nabihi only by favour of the Widana and the Tendaanba. Conversely, the thrust of the Na Pelpuo tradition is that *nalun* was brought from Mampurugu to Wa by Saliya and became vested absolutely in his descendants. The corollary of this position is that since the descendants of Na Kpasa base their claims to the Nam on *nalun* derived from another source, these claims are without substance.

On the death of Wa Na Sidiki Bomi in 1978, J. N. Momori of Sing gate and Yakubu Seidu of Na Kpasa gate contended for the succession. Yakubu Seidu, we have seen, had himself made Na by the Tendaanba, maintaining that the Widana was the *only* 'kingmaker' in Wa.[88] This is to be seen as an assertion, in the sphere of practical politics, of the Na Kpasa tradition in its most uncompromising form: that Wa *nalun* derived from the first Widana and the Tendaanba, and had not been introduced by the immigrants from Mampurugu. That Wa erupted into violence testifies to the gravity of the issue.

5

Tajdid and *jihad*: the Muslim community in change

Introduction

In 1889 R. Austin Freeman, then in Bonduku, was led to believe that the people of Wa were 'exclusively Mahommedan'.[1] Three years later G. E. Ferguson learned in Gonja that Wa was 'a very large Dagari town with a Mussulman population'.[2] In 1898 the officer commanding the British forces in Wala, D. Mackworth, noted that 'the Wa people, or Wallas as they are called, are Mahomedans for the most part'.[3] Such reports much exaggerated the numerical strength of the Muslim population, not only in Wala generally but even in the town of Wa. They did, however, accurately attest to the influence which the Muslims had in Wala affairs. B. M. Read came closer to the mark when, in 1908, he reported that 'at the present time all the Wala chiefs and men of any standing at all in the country follow Mohammadanism, while the poorer classes remain pagan'.[4] Particularly among the chiefly class, however, many of those regarded as Muslims by Read were probably quite unversed in the Qur'an and untutored in their observance of the pillars of the faith. But that they were none the less Muslims is, the *'ulama'* of Wa constantly reminded me, a matter for God and not man to decide.

The authority of the Wa Yeri Nam is derived ultimately from the *nalun* exercised by the Old Muslim warlord, Sidi 'Umar Tarawiri. The Wa Yeri Nam is an offshoot of the Nasa Yeri Nam. The early Wa Yeri Nas Konjekuri and Bunsalibile came, we have seen, to Wa from Nasa, the former perhaps to join Wa Na Kpasa and the latter Wa Na Pelpuo. As Wa developed as a centre of power regionally, so the *de facto* authority of Nasa Yeri Na declined relative to that of Wa Yeri Na. Indeed, as Wa Tagarayiri grew in size it became increasingly common for Wa Yeri Nas to be selected from within it. It is, nevertheless, still the case that candidates may be chosen from Nasa Tagarayiri. Descent from Sidi 'Umar remains a prerequisite of office, and generational seniority is important. Thus in the early 1950s the Wa Yeri Nam was offered to Dogo, son of the former Nasa Yeri Na Muhammad Saburi. Dogo declined it, reluctant to leave Nasa for the 'big town'. It was then accepted by his brother, 'Uthman.[5]

A Yeri Na is a chief, and specifically an Old Muslim or Yerihi chief. Within the framework of the Wa polity, however, the Wa Yeri Na assumed a second role. He came to exercise authority over all Wala Muslims as such, whether Old Muslims, *'ulama'*, Nabihi and Tendaanba converts, or such settlers as the Hausa of Dzangbeyiri. The titles given to the Wa Yeri Na in languages other than Walii testify to both roles. On the one hand he is Shaykh al-Wangara (or Shehu Wangara) in Arabic, Sarkin Wangara in Hausa and Juula Massa in Juula, all with the sense of 'head of the Wangara or Juula', that is, of the Old Muslims from Mande. On the other hand he is also referred to as Amir al-Muslimin in Arabic and Sarkin Musulmi in Hausa, with the sense of 'head of the Muslims'.

There was, *prima facie*, a potential for conflict between Wa Na and Wa Yeri Na. Both exercised independent forms of *nalun*, but with respect to the Wala Muslims their jurisdictions overlapped. Relations between the two were mediated by a Nayiri or 'palace' Yeri Na. This functionary was appointed by the Wa Yeri Na to maintain regular contact with the Wa Na. He served as liaison between the two, thus minimizing the occasions on which they had physically to meet. The office appears to be of relatively little importance now, and may never have been so.[6] Much more important in this context was the institution of the Wa limamate.

The Wa limamate dates, we have seen, from the beginnings of the polity in its historic form; that is, from the time of the earliest Wa Nas. The authority of the limams is not a form of *nalun*. It is based upon their access to the Qur'an, the Traditions of the Prophet (*hadith*), and the Law (*fiqh*). The *'ulama'*, from whose ranks the limams are drawn, recognize the secular authority of the Wa Yeri Na. The Wa Limam, however, is not limam to the Wa Yeri Na. He is limam to the Wa Na. He is required to use his office for the well-being of the Wala polity as such. Hence he is known in Arabic as *imam al-balad*, 'imam for the country'.

The authority of the Wa Na, Wa Widana and Wa Yeri Na was self-sustaining. In so far as the Wala polity was autonomous, *nalun* could not be renewed. This had nothing to do with the origins of *nalun*. The Wa Nas from the Busa, Pirisi and Sing gates, for example, claimed that the *nalun* they exercised derived from that of Mampurugu. To solicit the intervention of the Nas of Mampurugu on their behalf in Wala affairs, however, would have been in a sense to renew their *nalun*, but only at the expense of Wala autonomy. There is no evidence that this ever occurred. The authority of the Wa Limams, in contrast, was not only renewable but by its very nature had constantly to be renewed. Like their counterparts in other towns of the Voltaic region, the *'ulama'* of Wa were acutely aware that their geographical isolation on the fringes of the Muslim world posed a constant threat to their very existence as a class. Regression through *ihmal*, non-observance or backsliding, to ultimate *kufr* or unbelief, was not unknown in the region.[7] Contact with scholars in other Muslim communities had therefore to be maintained in order to counteract such tendencies. Students had to be sent from Wa to work under renowned teachers elsewhere, and some of the '*ulama*' might make their way to Mecca. Books had to be procured, new styles of mosque building learned and emulated. The '*ulama*' of Wa use the Arabic term for renewal, *tajdid*, in referring to such matters.

Learning in Wa: *mujaddidun* and others

The idea of the *mujaddid*, the renewer of Islam sent by God in each century, was already current in the third century AH. It has been argued by J. Hunwick that the dissemination of the idea in West Africa was, in part at least, a result of the influence of the jurist Muhammad b. 'Abd al-Karim al-Maghili (died *c*.1505). Hunwick further traces the genesis of the view that there could be a plurality of *mujaddidun* in each century, and the logical development of this, that each locality might have its own. This latter position was apparently adopted by the Timbuktu jurist, Ahmad Baba (died 1036 AH, AD 1627) who identified his own teacher, Muhammad Baghayughu (died 1002/1593), as the tenth-century renewer of the faith in that town.[8] At some point in time the notion of the local renewer was transmitted to Wa.

The *Ibtida' Din Wa fi 'Am 875 ila 'Am 1382*, 'The Beginning of Religion in Wa in the Year 875 (1470/1) to the Year 1382 (1962/3)', was written in its present form, we have seen, by Friday Limam Siddiq b. 'Abd al-Mu'min in 1963.[9] The work builds (in a triadic mode yet again) on the theme of the three renewers of Islam in Wa. The first was 'Umar al-Muhtaram, the Respected, who 'came from Mande to Wa with the religion of Islam'. The second was Sa'id b. 'Abd al-Qadir, who went to Kong to acquire knowledge and returned with 'a renewed religion of Islam [*mujaddad din al-Islam*]'. The third was Al-Hajj Ibrahim. He also went to Kong and 'returned with knowledge to our town with renewed Islam [*mujaddad al-islam*]'. 'Umar al-Muhtaram is Ya'muru, first Limam of Wa, whose *floruit* we have placed in the late seventeenth or early eighteenth century. Sa'id b. 'Abd al-Qadir was, we have suggested, in Kong in the late eighteenth century and held the Wa limamate in the 1830s. Al-Hajj Ibrahim was son of Wa Limam 'Uthman Dun. He was apparently in Kong in the 1880s, and died in Mecca early in the next decade. 1100 AH corresponds to AD 1688/9, 1200 AH to AD 1785/6, and 1300 AH to AD 1882/3. The intervals between the arrival of Ya'muru in Wa, the return of Sa'id b. 'Abd al-Qadir to Wa from Kong, and of Ibrahim b. 'Uthman Dun to Wa also from Kong, were obviously regarded as approximating to the requisite hundred years between *mujaddidun*.

1400 AH corresponds to AD 1980/1 and the fourth Wa renewer is due. It might seem that Friday Limam Siddiq had this matter in mind when he penned the *Ibtida' Din Wa*. He reviewed a list of those who seemed to have claims for consideration. Wa Limam Al-Hajj Muhammad b. 'Uthman Dun of Dondoli, and Friday Limam Muhammad Zayd b. 'Uthman Kunduri of Tamarimuni, were two of them. Each, according to Limam Siddiq, spread the knowledge given to him by God so that people from distant places (*ahl al-*

Plate 9 *Ibtida' Din Wa fi 'Am 875 ila 'Am 1382*

afaq) came to him to renew their faith. Neither, however, was chronologically appropriate to be considered the fourth *mujaddid*. The *Ibtida' Din Wa* incorporates a short prayer for them. Of those alive in 1963, five are named. Three belonged to a senior generation, namely, Al-Hajj Muhammad b. Harun of Dapuyipala (who became Wa Limam in 1966 and died in 1971); Al-Hajj Tamimu b. Limam Al-Hajj Muhammad of Dondoli (who became blind in the 1970s and was passed over for the limamate); and Friday Limam Siddiq himself, of Tamarimuni (who was still in office in 1986, a nonagenarian). The two in the junior generation were men both highly respected for their work in the educational field: both 'opened schools in the towns and opened the towns with schools'. One was Sa'id b. 'Abd al-Rahman (of Dapuyipala, I believe, who was teaching in his father's school in Kumase in the 1960s), and the other Friday Limam Siddiq's own son, 'Uthman (who

94

died in a car accident in 1986). The identity of the fourth *mujaddid* remains, to the best of my knowledge, an unresolved matter.

The opening of schools, rather than simply teaching, appears to be central to the Wa concept of renewal. Of the many schools in Wa, two are regarded as pre-eminent. One is in the Tamarimuni section of the town, the other in Dondoli. The Tamarimuni school was founded by the second *mujaddid*, Sa'id b. 'Abd al-Qadir, upon his return from Kong. It was taken over on his death by his sons 'Uthman Kunduri and Ahmad Abi 'l-'Abbas, then successively by Friday Limam Muhammad Zayd b. 'Uthman Kunduri, 'Abd al-Mu'min b. Muhammad Zayd, and Friday Limam Siddiq b. 'Abd al-Mu'min. Pressure of space in Tamarimuni led Friday Limam Siddiq's son, Al-Hajj 'Uthman, to establish a branch of the school in new premises in the Fongo section of Wa. In 1967 there were ten teachers in the Fongo Arabic school. All had made the pilgrimage. They ran a four-year course in the Qur'an, having 218 boys and 80 girls in nine classes. At the Tamarimuni premises, Friday Limam Siddiq continued to instruct some twenty older, and in some cases elderly, students in advanced studies of the *Tafsir al-Jalalayn* of al-Mahalli and al-Suyuti, the *Muwatta'* of Malik b. Anas, and *Al-Shifa'* of 'Iyad b. Musa.[10] Ibrahim b. 'Uthman Dun, the third *mujaddid*, is said to have been a student at the Tamarimuni school before leaving for Kong. On his return to Wa, however, he founded the Dondoli school. After his death in Mecca it was taken over by his brother, Al-Hajj Muhammad, and on his death in 1936 by his son, Al-Hajj Tamimu. In 1966 there were about 150 pupils studying the Qur'an in the Dondoli school, and some thirty advanced students of *Tafsir, Muwatta'* and *Al-Shifa'*.[11]

Of much importance to the scholars of Wa are the *asanid* (singular, *isnad*) or *salasil* (singular, *silsila*), the written chains of authority for the study of *Tafsir, Muwatta'* and *Al-Shifa'* which are licences to teach.[12] *Prima facie*, the Wa chains should witness transmissions of learning from the first *mujaddid*, Limam Ya'muru. They do not. Nor have I found any chains that witness transmissions from the second, Sa'id b. 'Abd al-Qadir of Tamarimuni. It is said that the chains from Sa'id b. 'Abd al-Qadir 'were all spoiled when the Zabarimas came to Wa', that is, in or about 1887.[13] This I doubt. It appears to be the case that older chains however 'strong' are usually discarded in favour of newer ones, and the very preservation of the copies of them becomes a matter of chance. There are in fact two extant chains that are thought particularly prestigious. One is associated with the Tamarimuni school and the other with the Dondoli school. Both converge on the figures of Yahya and 'Abbas b. Muhammad al-Mustafa Saghanughu of Kong. An example of each chain, for the transmission of *Tafsir*, is shown in table 5.1.

The Tamarimuni chain will be seen to regress from Friday Limam Siddiq, through his father 'Abd al-Mu'min and his grandfather Friday Limam Muhammad Zayd, to his great-grandfather 'Uthman Kunduri. The Dondoli chain exemplifies the reluctance to refer directly by name to recent and revered ancestors. It regresses from Ya'qub b. Al-Hajj Sa'id through Al-Hajj

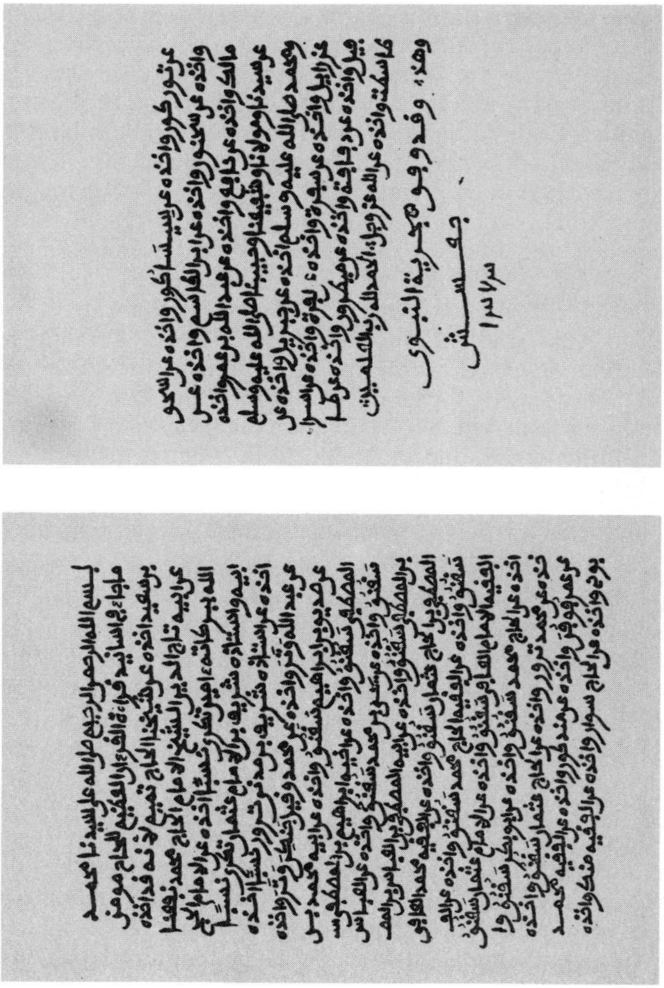

Plate 10 Teaching chain, Dondoli school

Table 5.1 *Tamarimuni and Dondoli teaching chains*

Tamarimuni *isnad*[a]	Dondoli *isnad*[b]
Abu Bakr al-Siddiq b. Mu'min Takari (i.e. Tarawiri), from his father	Ya'qub b. Al-Hajj Sa'id, from
Mu'min b. Muhammad b. 'Uthman b. Sa'id Takari b. 'Abd al-Qadir Takari, from his father	Imam Al-Hajj Tamimu b. Imam Al-Hajj Takari, from his father
Muhammad b. 'Uthman, from his father	Imam Al-Hajj Sharif b. Imam 'Uthman Takari, from
'Uthman, from	Sharif b. Madani Tarawiri, from
Muhammad Timiti b. Kunadi Timiti, from	'Abdallah Watara, from
Ishaq b. Sulayman b. Abu Bakr Sakanu (i.e. Saghanughu), from	Muhammad known as Jankira Watara, from
Al-Hajj 'Uthman b. Muhammad al-Aswad, from his brother	Siddiq b. Ibrahim Saghanu, from his father
Al-'Abbas Sakanu, from	Muhammad b. al-Mustafa Saghanu, from from his brother
Sa'id b. al-Mustafa Saghanu, from	Ibrahim b. al-Mustafa Saghanu, from
Yahya Saghanu, from	Yahya b. Muhammad Saghanu, from
'Abbas b. al-Mustafa Saghanu ...	'Abbas b. al-Mustafa Saghanu ...

Notes: [a] Wilks, FN/208, 17 July 1967

[b] Wilks, FN/69, 4 May 1966. Chains for two other students of Al-Hajj Tamimu are in Wilks, FN/157, 10 April 1966 (Al-Hajj Mu'min b. Sa'id, Limam of Obuase, Ghana) – the chain has one entry repeated in error – and FN/191, 14 May 1966 (Ahmad b. Siddiq Saghanughu, Limam of Wahabu, Burkina Faso).

Tamimu and his father Wa Limam Al-Hajj Muhammad ('Imam Al-Hajj Sharif') to his grandfather Wa Limam 'Uthman Dun ('Sharif b. Madani Tarawiri').[14] 'Uthman Kunduri and 'Uthman Dun of the Tamarimuni and Dondoli chains respectively were, it may be noted, cousins; the former was son of Wa Limam Sa'id b. 'Abd al-Qadir, and the latter son of Wa Limam Muhammad b. 'Abd al-Qadir. The cousins had, however, been educated in different schools, neither in Wa.

'Uthman Kunduri studied *Tafsir* presumably in Bonduku, where the Timitay ('Timiti') have held the limamate for well over two centuries. Indeed, Kunadi Timitay, father of 'Uthman Kunduri's teacher, is probably – Arabic *sa'id* and Malinke *kunadi* being equivalents – the fifth Bonduku limam, Sa'id b. Muhammad. He held office in the middle of the nineteenth century and appears in many other teaching chains from the region.[15] 'Abdallah Watara, teacher of 'Uthman Dun, is so far not known from any other chains. His teacher, however, is the Muhammad b. Ibrahim Watara who does appear in other chains.[16] He is presumably the Muhammad Watara known to be teaching in Buna at the turn of the eighteenth century.[17]

'Uthman Kunduri of Wa Tamarimuni had, then, pursued advanced studies under the Timitay of Bonduku, and 'Uthman Dun of Wa Dondoli under the Watara of (in all probability) Buna. The Timitay and Watara *'ulama'* had, in turn, acquired their learning from the Saghanughu scholars of Kong though not necessarily in Kong. The Sa'id b. al-Mustafa of the Tamarimuni chain was, for example, the first Saghanughu Limam of Bobo-Dioulasso (Burkina Faso), and the Ibrahim b. al-Mustafa of the Dondoli chain, whose death may credibly if not definitely be assigned to 1241 AH, AD 1825/6, was his successor in that limamate. Both were brothers of the Yahya on whom both chains converge, who taught in Kong. All three, Sa'id, Ibrahim and Yahya, were moreover younger brothers, as well as students, of 'Abbas b. Muhammad al-Mustafa, first Saghanughu Limam of Kong, whose death occurred in 1801.

Limam 'Abbas Saghanughu was, we have seen, reputedly the teacher of the second Wa *mujaddid*, Sa'id b. 'Abd al-Qadir.[18] The significant point is that the Tamarimuni and Dondoli chains from Limam 'Abbas through his brothers in Kong and Bobo-Dioulasso, and through their Timitay and Watara students, were regarded in Wa as superseding – renewing – the direct chain from Limam 'Abbas which Sa'id b. 'Abd-Qadir had taken to Wa in the early nineteenth century. Such is the very nature of *tajdid*, renewal. It follows that still newer chains are replacing the ones that regress through 'Uthman Kunduri and 'Uthman Dun. Friday Limam Siddiq b. Sa'id of Tamarimuni, for example, studied under Al-Amin b. Muhammad al-Abyad Kulibali of Kong and obtained from him an *isnad* which extends in eight stages through a succession of Saghanughu teachers to, once again, Limam 'Abbas Saghanughu of Kong.[19] Limam Siddiq regards this chain as 'stronger' than any he might have from his great-grandfather, the *mujaddid* Sa'id b. 'Abd-Qadir, or from his grandfather's brother, 'Uthman Kunduri.

Almost all of the *asanid* owned by the Muslim scholars of Ghana, Côte d'Ivoire and Burkina Faso converge on the highly revered figure of Kong Limam 'Abbas. His own and well-known chain regresses in twelve 'teaching generations' to Al-Hajj Salim Suwari.[20] Al-Hajj Salim is well known in Muslim (and indeed non-Muslim) tradition throughout a vast region of West Africa extending from Ghana and Burkina Faso in the east to Senegal and Gambia in the west. The Suwarian tradition in the West African Islam has still to receive the attention it merits, notwithstanding the excellent recent studies by T. C. Hunter and L. O. Sanneh.[21]

There are major problems in dating Al-Hajj Salim Suwari. I have inclined to assign him a late fifteenth-century *floruit* and in this Hunter concurs. Sanneh prefers a date some three centuries earlier. Whatever the case, Al-Hajj Salim's teachings were nurtured by his followers in the towns of the headwaters of the Niger and Senegal rivers and those of the Middle Niger. It was from both regions that scholars in the Suwarian tradition made their way into the Voltaic region in the course of the sixteenth and seventeenth centuries, when imperial Mali was in the late stages of its decline.

Sanneh has described one of the imperatives of the Suwarians as 'travel or mobility (*al-safar*)', involving 'the penetration of distant lands for religious purposes'.[22] I have suggested that it was such peripatetic scholars from the west who established themselves in the old trading centre of Bighu near the southern bend of the Black Volta.[23] From there, in the second half of the sixteenth century, the *'alim* Isma'il Kamaghatay and his son Muhammad al-Abyad laid the foundations of the Gonja limamates.[24] The next century witnessed the arrival in the Voltaic region of scholars from the north, that is, from the Middle Niger. In the Wala area Ya'muru and Yusuf Tarawiri, founders of the Wala limamates, came reputedly from Dya, and Sharif Abu Bakr Kunatay, founder of the Kantonsi limamates, from Timbuktu. In Dagomba a comparable figure is Sulayman b. 'Abdallah Baghayughu, also from Timbuktu.[25] These are the earliest Suwarians to penetrate the Voltaic region. Their patronymics – Kamaghatay, Tarawiri, Kunatay and Baghayughu – are in fact precisely those distinctive Malinke (or Wangara) ones appearing in the popular charms from the region which list the putative disciples of Al-Hajj Salim Suwari. An example of these from Wa, the *Fa'dat Ism al-Auliya' Allah*, has been discussed in chapter 3.

Meanwhile the eastwards movement of the Saghanughu *'ulama'* can also be tracked, from Manfara (near Kaba, in metropolitan Mali) through Koro and Kani to Boron (Côte d'Ivoire). From there, in the eighteenth century, they created the limamates of Kong and its dependencies west of the Black Volta.[26] They and their students inspired the great renewal of Suwarian learning in the Voltaic region and beyond in the late eighteenth and nineteenth centuries, to which the *asanid* are witness.

The Suwarian tradition has already briefly been characterized as pacifistic and quietist in content. Sanneh refers to Al-Hajj Salim's 'scrupulous principled disavowal of *jihad* as an instrument of religious and political change'.[27] I have suggested elsewhere that

> the Suwarians articulated at an ideological level, without straying from orthodoxy, the 'peculiarities' of the situation in which Muslims found themselves in the period following the collapse of imperial Mali. They created a praxis to enable Muslims to function within essentially non-Muslim societies, accommodating their interests to those of the wider society while at the same time combatting erosion of the distinctive Muslim identity. It was an ideology of pluralism, a delicate balancing of priorities such as to allow the faithful access to the material resources of this world without foregoing salvation in the next. The alternative was the ideology of *hijra* and *jihad*.[28]

Kufr, 'unbelief', the Wa *'ulama'* say, is *jahl*, 'ignorance'. It is the will of God that some people remain in ignorance when others have become enlightened. Only when the unbelievers threaten the very existence of the Muslim community is a call for *jihad* justified. Otherwise Muslims may settle among the unbelievers, thereby setting before them the example of the way of the Prophet. They should not seek to convert the unbelievers against their will, for true conversion comes in God's time. Then and only then will the unbelievers approach the Muslims, and ask to be converted.

I pursued such matters in innumerable conversations with scholars not only in Wa but more generally in the region, and found something approaching consensus. They were comfortable in acknowledging, for example, that they make prayers for the success of the harvest on behalf of believers and non-believers alike, and that they place their services at the disposal of the ruler, whether Muslim or not. In such circumstances, they said, the power of God and his Messenger was demonstrated. They were uncomfortable with the idea that they had any mission to proselytize other than by example. Such remain, by and large, the views of the orthodox *'ulama'* of Wa. They are not those of the Ahmadi *'ulama'*, who do actively proselytize. This departure from the Suwarian tradition has its roots, we shall see, in events that long preceded the introduction of Ahmadiyya teachings into Wala in the 1930s.

Wala and the Karantaw: the roots of faction

In the third decade of the nineteenth century, Gonja became embroiled in a struggle for the skin of Yagbon, the paramountcy, between the Bolewura Safo and the Tuluwewura Kali.[29] The *'ulama'* of Buna agreed to mediate the dispute but apparently betrayed their trust, enabling the partisans of Tuluwe to entrap and massacre many of the Bole. Safo committed suicide. Several of his sons and their followers took refuge in Wa. Tuluwewura Kali became Yagbonwura, but lived for only seven months. He was succeeded on the Yagbon skin by Kongwura Saidu. Saidu sent to Wa to demand the surrender of the Bole refugees. The Wala rejected the demand. Yagbonwura Saidu moved his forces into Wala country through Loggo to Boli. Pelpuo II was apparently Wa Na and Ya'qub b. 'Abd al-Qadir Wa Limam. The Wala forces took up positions at Sing. A battle resulted in a Wala victory. Yagbonwura Saidu then sought help from the Gyaman Ankobeahene, Kwasi Date. A second battle was again decided in favour of the Wala. The Gonja forces pulled back to Daboya. The Wala sent part of their booty to Asantehene Kwaku Dua Panin, requesting his intervention. An army under Kumase Nsumankwaahene Domfe Ketewa, subsequently reinforced by Kumase Anantahene Asamoa Nkwanta, linked up with the Wala. Yagbonwura Saidu was driven from Daboya and pursued through Walembele to Chiana (near Navrongo). There he was slain. Such is the sequence of events recorded in 1930 from the remembrances of five elderly Wa Muslims, among them Friday Limam Ishaq and Yeri Na 'Uthman Daleri.[30]

The Asante army re-entered Kumase in June 1844.[31] Wa and Bole were left under an obligation to pay what was known as 'the Asante debt', that is, an indemnity in slaves to offset the costs of the campaign to Asante. To procure captives, raids were made on the Dagaaba towns. Those directed against Issa (at the time of Wa Na Bondiri, Limam Idris and Yeri Na Ibrahim) embroiled the Wala in yet another series of wars with the Gonja.[32] It may be that these events were critical in inclining sections of the Wala Muslim community in this period towards a view of *jihad* that was incompatible with the prevailing Suwarian tradition.

A Marka scholar, Muhammad Karantaw, left Sarro (near Jenne) to settle at Douroula, in the Dafin country some thirty-five miles north of Safane. His son, Mahmud Karantaw, was born there.[33] Teaching chains show that Muhammad Karantaw had studied under a Muhammad al-Abyad b. Abi Bakr, himself a student of the Sa'id b. Muhammad al-Mustafa Saghanughu, first Limam of Bobo-Dioulasso, who appears in the ninth position in the Wa Tamarimuni *isnad* (table 5.1).[34] The chains also show that Muhammad Karantaw taught his son, Mahmud. There is a short work about Mahmud Karantaw, entitled *Ma'sala 'inda 'l-Rajalayn*, 'A Question put by Two Men'. It appears to date from the early part of this century.[35] A distantly related text, edited by Al-Hajj Muhammad Saghanughu of Bobo-Dioulasso from an older manuscript in 1963, will be referred to as *Ikhtilaf Rijalat*, 'A Dispute between Two Men'.[36] The *Ikhtilaf* has additional material on the education of Mahmud Karantaw. It names a succession of teachers under whom he studied, presumably after leaving his father's school. These included Shaykh Taslima Saghanughu of Taslima, which seems to refer to the Kantonsi town of Nabon to the southeast of Boromo,[37] and Karamoko Yara, 'the blind *wali* of God' famous for his glorious deeds (*al-manaqib*). Karamoko Yara (or Jara) is independently known as an early follower of Tijaniyya in the Safane area.[38]

Mahmud Karantaw became close friends with 'Ali b. Salih Tarawiri from Wa Tagarayiri, who had settled at Taslima. Indeed, a son of 'Ali Tarawiri, Sa'id, accompanied Mahmud Karantaw to study under Karamoko Yara. Such is the account given me in 1966 by a grandson of Sa'id b. 'Ali, namely, Al-Hajj Sa'id b. Abi Bakr of Wahabu.[39] Karamoko Yara, he said, taught at Douroula. Mahmud Karantaw then decided to make the pilgrimage. His point of departure was Taslima, where he stayed with 'Ali Tarawiri. When he returned from Mecca he made a call for *jihad* and 'Ali Tarawiri joined him.

The 'Question' or 'Dispute' (*Ma'sala* or *Ikhtilaf*) about Al-Hajj Mahmud Karantaw is why he, a scholar steeped by training in the Suwarian tradition, should have come to launch *jihad* in the region of the Black Volta. There is general agreement in the sources that his adoption of a militant ideology was a result of his pilgrimage. The *Ikhtilaf Rijalat* has the most specific account of the matter. In Syria Mahmud Karantaw came under the influence of 'Abd al-Rahim, a descendant of 'Abd al-Qadir al-Jilani. He took the Qadiriyya *wird* from him (having perhaps earlier become a Tijani while studying with Karamoko Yara), and promised that upon his return home he would conquer his country and build a mosque in every town.

According to an account of the *jihad* that Tauxier read in 1910, Al-Hajj Mahmud returned from the pilgrimage to Dourala to find that his father had died. After spending some years there he moved some sixty-five miles south to Doumakoro in the vicinity of Boromo, opened a school, claimed that the pagan Ko of the region wished to drive him away, and accordingly called for war.[40] The *Ikhtilaf Rijalat* has a somewhat different account of the matter. On his return from the pilgrimage, Al-Hajj Mahmud, it reports,

> came back to Wa whose people followed him and vowed to open [conquer] the countries. They followed him till they came to the town that lies behind the river where he sat under a *rimi* tree, I mean the town of Banda. He put up his tents and the people did not like that and there was a dispute between them. The first to pay allegiance to him were the Daghati Juala and the people of Wa from his students, Sinu, Kunatay and Tarawiri. His scribe Idris is the one who allowed me to look at their library. They helped the Shaykh against the unbelievers. He took them prisoner and his power was felt in the other towns. He then went to Boromo and took it.[41]

Banda has not been identified; it is clearly not the town of that name near the southern loop of the Black Volta. The reference to the 'Daghati Juala' is not, however, in doubt; it is to the Kantonsi. The burden of the story is that the first to join the *jihad* of Mahmud Karantaw were Old Muslims of Wala: Kantonsi Sienu ('Sinu') presumably of Palewogo, Kantonsi Kunatay presumably of Visi, and Tarawiri presumably of Nasa. In this light the oral testimony of Al-Hajj Sa'id of Wahabu becomes of added significance. He claimed that his great-grandfather, 'Ali b. Salih Tarawiri, was able to provide 300 men at a time when Al-Hajj Mahmud himself had only thirty-six.[42]

In 1888 Binger received accounts of the *jihad* that showed that it did not win universal support from the Muslims of the region. Few of the Dafin supported Al-Hajj Mahmud, he noted, for they had long enjoyed good relations with the unbelievers and preferred not to take part in the campaigns.[43] Indeed, Binger took a somewhat cynical view of the support that Al-Hajj Mahmud did muster. 'After some success bought easily in capturing the people of many small neighbouring Nieniegue villages', he commented, 'some fervent Muslims of Yatenga and Mossi, some Mande from Dagomba and some Hausa grouped themselves around the pilgrim, in the double hope of gaining many captives and paradise for eternity.' It is probable that the participation of Wala Old Muslims, with their military tradition, was connected with the matter of 'the Asante debt'; that is, that the captives were applied to its settlement.

There is reason to believe the *jihad* was supported by at least some of the Wa *'ulama'*. The *Ikhtilaf Rijalat* refers to Al-Hajj Mahmud's promise to build mosques, and therefore to appoint limams, in all the towns he conquered. The first Limam in Koho, renamed Shukr li-'llahi, was Ya'qub b. 'Abd al-Qadir of Wa Limamyiri. This account was given to me by Shukr li-'llahi Limam Al-Hasan Kunatay and Al-Hajj 'Abd al-Rahman Sienu, both Kantonsi, in 1966.[44] Wa Limam Sa'id b. 'Abd al-Qadir, they said, gave his daughter in marriage to Malik b. 'Ali b. 'Umar Kunatay. Malik Kunatay joined the *jihad* and was one of those who chose to settle in Shukr li-'llahi. Ya'qub was the brother of Limam Sa'id. He came from Wa to Shukr li-'llahi to visit his brother's daughter. The *jihad* was still in progress. Al-Hajj

Mahmud asked Ya'qub to take the limamate of Shukr li-'llahi. He accepted it, and did not return to Wa. When Ya'qub died, the limamate passed to the Kunatay, that is, to the children of Malik b. 'Ali by his marriage to the daughter of Wa Limam Sa'id. Limam Al-Hasan Kunatay, one of the informants, is their grandson.

It is difficult to see how Ya'qub b. 'Abd al-Qadir, first Limam of Shukr li-'llahi and brother of Wa Limam Sa'id, can be other than Ya'qub b. 'Abd al-Qadir, twelfth Limam of Wa. His *floruit* as Wa Limam has been assigned to the 1840s. In 1892 Binger referred to the *jihad* as having occurred about fifty years earlier, and recent scholars are in agreement in assigning it to the middle of the nineteenth century.[45] There is thus no chronological obstacle to the identification of Wa Limam Ya'qub with the Shukr li-'llahi Limam of the same name. The implication of the evidence is that Wa Limam Ya'qub accepted appointment as a limam for the *jihad* and thereby set his seal of approval on the action of the Wala Old Muslims who had cast in their lot with Al-Hajj Mahmud Karantaw.

In the middle of the nineteenth century, then, there are signs of division within the Wala Muslims, not only between Old Muslims and the *'ulama'* of Limamyiri but within the *'ulama'* class itself. The mass of the scholars undoubtedly remained conservatively loyal to the older Suwarian tradition. The attitude of some, however, began radically to change. Implicit in their support for the *jihad*, it may be thought, was the view that Wala was indeed *dar al-harb*, a 'land of war', and that it was incumbent upon them to fight the unbelievers, seize their property, and enslave their persons. A more informed opinion on such matters will become possible as subsequent developments in Wala affairs are reviewed.

Wala and the Zabarima intrusion

Alfa Hano was an *'alim* from the Zabarima country east of the Niger Bend (in what is now the Republic of Niger). He settled in the trading town of Salaga in eastern Gonja, where he is said to have devoted himself to religious studies. While he was there, a band of his countrymen, perhaps horse traders, arrived in Dagomba. They were persuaded to assist their hosts in obtaining captives to pay tributes which the Dagomba owed to the Asantehene. They began raiding westwards into the Grunshi country (and we shall retain the vague term 'Grunshi', since it is used in all the sources, local and otherwise).[46] The band soon severed its links with Dagomba, and began to establish its own bases in the Grunshi country. Alfa Hano joined it. He afforded the Zabarima a certain religious legitimacy, though whether their campaigns against the Grunshi were ever perceived as *jihad* is quite unclear. The move into Grunshi country can be dated to around 1870.[47]

Wa Limam Siddiq b. Musa took immediate steps to open communications with the Zabarima. An account of the matter is contained in a work in Hausa, *Al-Akhbar Zabarima*, 'The Story of the Zabarima', a copy of which is

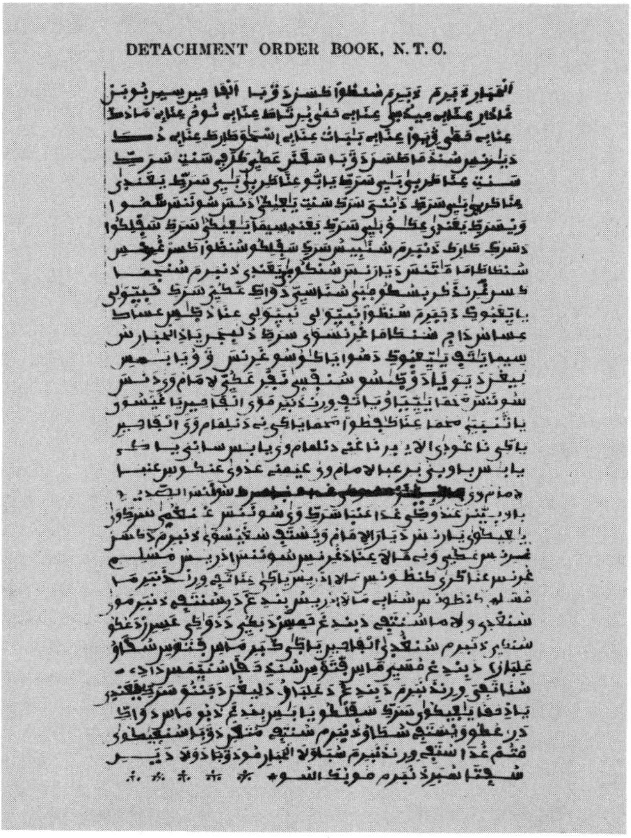

Plate 11 *Al-akhbar Zabarima*

included in the corpus of manuscripts put together by Friday Limam Ishaq in 1922 or 1923.[48]

Akwai Limamu Wa dansa sunansa Mahama ya yi yawo. Ya tafi wajin Zabarmawa. Alfa Hini ya gaisuwa. Ya tanbayi: Mahama, ina ka fito. Mahama ya ce: ni dan Limamin Wa. Alfa Hini ya ki: Na gode Allah ya bari na gani dan Limamin Wa. Ya bashi saniya. Ya ki ya bashi bawa biyu bari aba Limamin Wa yayi mani addu'a. An kawo shi an ba Lima-

Mahama, a son of Wa Limam, made a journey. He went to the Zabarima. Alfa Hini greeted him. He asked: Mahama, from where have you come? Mahama said: I am son of Wa Limam. Alfa Hini said: I thank God he has let me see the son of Wa Limam. He gave him a cow. He said he would give two slaves so that Wa Limam would make prayers for

104

min Wa sunansa Siddiqi. Bawa
biyun nan an dauki guda an ba
Sarkin Wa sunansa Gangume.

him. They were brought and given
to Wa Limam Siddiq. One of
these two slaves was taken and
given to Wa Na Gangume.

By this time the Zabarima had already extended their influence far into
Grunshi country, the Dolbizan and Nabiewale west of the Sissili river having
asked for their assistance in settling local feuds. At the same time the forces
of Al-Hajj Mahmud Karantaw were also thrusting deep into Grunshi
country from the northwest.[49]

According to *Al-Akhbar Zabarima*, Mahama returned to Wa after his
meeting with Alfa Hano and on the basis of his report Wa Na Gangume and
Wa Limam Siddiq opted for cooperation with the Zabarima:

Sarkin Wa ya aiko yaransa da
yaran Imamu wai su tafi suyi gai-
sawan Zabarima da kasan Gurunshi. Akwai wani malam yina da
Gurunshi sunansa Idrisu. Musulmin Gurunshi ana kira Kandaw-
ansi. Malam Idrisu ya ki: Ina tafe
wurin Zabarima. Musulmin Kan-
dawansi suna bin Malam Idrisu
bindiga dari. Sun tafi Zabarmawa. Sun gode. Wa ma sun tafi
da bindiga hamsin da bakwai da
dawaki 'ashirin da uku. Sun kai.
Zabarima sun gode.

The Wa Na sent his boys and the
boys of the Limam to go and greet
the Zabarima in the Grunshi
country. There was a certain
malam with the Grunshi named
Idris. The Grunshi Muslims are
called Kantonsi. Malam Idris
said: I am going to the Zabarima.
The Kantonsi Muslims followed
Malam Idris with a hundred guns.
They went to the Zabarima. [The
Zabarima] thanked them. The Wa
went with fifty-seven guns and
twenty-three horses. They
arrived. The Zabarima thanked
them.

Palewogo was, of course, in the Sisala (or Grunshi) districts of Wala, and the
hundred Kantonsi gunmen who followed Malam Idris must have been drawn
from that same Old Muslim constituency that had responded to Al-Hajj
Mahmud Karantaw's call for *jihad* two decades or so earlier. Malam Idris (or
Idi) is in fact remembered in Wa as having been the best Qur'anic reader of
his time, locally. He was most probably from the Visi Kunatay. He is said to
have incurred the envy of the *'ulama'* in Wa who used magic to induce him to
leave. It worked. He joined the Zabarima on their campaigns.[50] The fifty-
seven gunmen and twenty-three horsemen were, presumably, supplied by the
Wa Na. Binger, whose evidence on this matter may not be very reliable,
reported that Wa and Buna were the principal sources of recruits to the
Zabarima ranks in the period.[51]

Alfa Hano (or 'Hini' as the Hausa has it) died in or about 1870. His
successor in the Zabarima leadership, Alfa Gazare, made his headquarters at
Kassana, some fifteen miles northeast of Tumu. He held command for less

than ten years, dying in February 1878.[52] There are imprecisions in the chronology that make it difficult to reconstruct the course of Wala affairs in the decade, and I know of no evidence that enables the fortunes of the Wala contingents in the Zabarima forces to be followed. In the south, Wa continued to be embroiled in the affairs of Gonja. Indeed, it must have been in this period that the forces of the Gonja division of Kong massed at Jayiri, on the borders of Wa. The Wa Na assembled an army and won a resounding victory. Jayiri, it is said, was incorporated into Wala and the Bolewura also agreed to the transfer of a number of Chakalle villages.[53] In the north of Wala the Dagaaba apparently rebelled against a Nam that had not only ceased to afford them protection but had become involved in raiding them. No contemporary account of the upheaval exists, but in 1897 those described as 'Dagarti chiefs' stated: 'Twenty years ago Wa and Dagarti were one country, but then they separated after a great quarrel.'[54]

All these matters are poorly documented. Fortunately the sources became incomparably richer for the period when the Zabarima were led by Alfa Gazare's successor, Babatu. A number of accounts by those who took part in the campaigns of the last quarter of the nineteenth century are available. Most impressive of these is the lengthy series of anecdotes written in Hausa in or about 1914 by a certain Malam Abu, whose precise identity remains a mystery.[55]

Babatu appears to have exercised a much more ruthless style of leadership than Alfa Gazare. Malam Abu's anecdotes sometimes follow a chronological sequence and sometimes a thematic one, which confuses the chronology. It is clear from his work, however, that shortly after assuming command Babatu was active on the northeastern borders of Wala. He obtained the peaceful submission of, first, Walembele (dominated by Dafin Muslims)[56], and second, Dasima. He then put together an army that received the submission of Funsi, took Kojopere, and proceeded to ravage the Dagaaba villages along the road through Issa, Wogu, Busie, Sabuli and Mwankuri. Babatu then approached Wa town, taking Narung ('Nuru') and Baayiri ('Bayayiri') respectively only twenty miles north and sixteen miles northeast of Wa town. Amir Babatu became, as Malam Abu has it, not only 'king of the Grunshi' but also 'king of the Dagati'.

A Walii text entitled *Babatu Daga Paalun Pigubu*, 'The Invasion of the Dagaaba Country by Babatu', puts a rather different gloss on these events. The Wala attacked the Dagaaba town of Issa but were repulsed with heavy losses. Bajuri, a prince of the Busa gate, approached Babatu for help. The Zabarima leader demanded 100 cattle, 100 horses, 100 sheep and 100 slaves in return. He defeated the Dagaaba. The Wala, however, refused to pay their debt.[57] Another account was set down by E. F. Tamakloe, who spoke with many participants in the events in question. Babatu, he reported, fought the Dagaaba at the instigation of Bajuri. In the course of the campaign Babatu and Bajuri quarrelled and 'opprobious epithets were used'. Many of the Narung people fled to Wa. Babatu demanded their surrender but Bajuri refused.[58] Whatever the precise details, it is almost certainly correct that the Wala solicited Babatu's assistance but then refused to meet his demands. Notes on the sequence of events were made by Captain D. Mackworth only a decade later:

> King of Wa asks Barbattu to come and help him reduce the Dagartis to order, promises him a lot of slaves ... Barbattu then asks King of Wa for the slaves he promised. King of Wa expostulates. Barbattu replies that the agreement was that he was to be paid if he came to help. Barbattu then attacks Wa.[59]

A flurry of negotiations preceded the attack on Wa. Babatu sent an envoy. 'Ali b. 'Umar, to the town. Tamakloe says that seven of his entourage were taken captive and three killed.[60] Dougah says that Bajuri insulted the messengers, but that slaves, donkeys and cowries were indeed handed over to them. This served to make Babatu envious of the wealth of Wa.[61] Malam Abu reports that the Muslims of Wa said that they 'heard' Babatu's message, and then sent their own envoys to his camp to negotiate the dispute. Babatu accused them of deceiving him. He said he knew that Bajuri, with the support of the Muslims, was preparing to fight him. Babatu's information was correct. Wa Limam 'Uthman Dun of Dondoli was certainly actively assisting Bajuri.

As the Wala recount it, there had long been current in Dondoli a prophecy that one day war would come to Wala; there would be much fighting and many people would be enslaved; but finally white people would come and peace would return.[62] Upon learning that the Zabarima had entered Grunshi country, Limam 'Uthman Dun said that they would bring war to Wa in accordance with the old prophecy. He announced that he would die in the course of the struggles, but that he would first prepare a charmed gunpowder to guarantee the victory of the Wala. He did this, and gave Bajuri the gunpowder to distribute to his troops.[63]

The first engagement occurred near Baayiri. Bajuri's forces were defeated with great slaughter. Eight elders of Limamyiri hid in the abandoned town of Visi. They were found and killed. Bajuri fell back on Yaro, and then took up positions in Nasa.[64] Babatu entered Nasa. After fierce fighting, Wa resistance collapsed. Reports have it that Bajuri himself took flight.[65] One participant maintained that the Tagarayiri contingent in the Wala army was led by one of its own captives, a Sisala man. Seeing his brother in the Zabarima ranks, he defected to them with a quantity of Limam 'Uthman Dun's charmed gunpowder and 'thus ruined the war for the Wala'.[66] Babatu ordered that the Nasa mosque be destroyed.[67]

Babatu next marched on Wa. Mackworth noted: 'Barbattu then attacks Wa and burns it, is fired on by a lot of people who are occupying the mosque. The mosque is burnt.'[68] An eyewitness to the event reported that about a hundred Muslims had taken refuge in the central mosque, and that Babatu had them put to death and the mosque destroyed.[69] Wa Na Mahama Fua committed suicide.[70] Wa Limam 'Uthman Dun died at the same time, in circumstances that are unclear.[71] Wa was abandoned by those of the townsfolk who had escaped death or capture.

In 1894 Ferguson said that Babatu's attack on Wa had occurred six or seven years earlier, that is, in 1887 or 1888.[72] Writing in 1898, Mackworth put it ten or twelve years earlier, that is, between 1886 and 1888, and Henderson, also in 1898, put it eleven years earlier, that is, in 1887.[73] Krause passed through Wa on 24 February 1887, and says that it was attacked soon after.[74] The event may be assigned with confidence to 1887.

Dondoli and Dzedzedeyiri: the politics of confrontation

The Zabarima came, Holden has pointed out, 'from a region where militant Islam was a live issue and where a ready recourse to the gun had become common'.[75] In the first half of the nineteenth century the Zabarima had, by and large, fiercely resisted attempts to bring their country under the authority of the Sokoto caliphate. Some communities anciently Muslim, however, supported the Sokoto armies which, time and time again, tried without success to force the Zabarima to submit. It is widely held that the Zabarima who intruded into the Voltaic region came from precisely such communities.[76] Granted this background, the ruthlessness with which they devastated the Grunshi country is no cause for surprise. Whether or not Alfa Hano, Alfa Gazare and Babatu thought of themselves as *mujahidun*, leaders of *jihad*, they operated within a militant Muslim idiom. Unbelievers were to be captured and their property seized. Mukhtar Karantaw, successor of Al-Hajj Mahmud, found nothing inappropriate in conducting a number of joint campaigns with the Zabarima.[77] Babatu's attack on Wa, however, raised issues of a complex kind.

Babatu himself may have viewed his attack as sufficiently warranted by the failure of the Wala to satisfy the terms of the agreement by which he had assisted them against the Dagaaba. Among the *'ulama'* of the Zabarima bands, however, there must have been those who held the then modish view, that Muslims who befriended unbelievers and chose voluntarily to live in *dar al-harb* were themselves to be adjudged unbelievers.[78] Babatu's destruction of the mosques in Nasa and Wa, and his massacre of Wa Muslims, may thus have been seen by some as religiously justified. However this may be, Babatu's actions nevertheless met with much condemnation. The destruction of the mosque, Mackworth reported, 'gives Barbattu a bad name with many Mahomedans in the Hinterland'.[79] Even Malam Abu, who clearly admired the Zabarima leader, commented, 'When Amir Babatu defeated Wa his strength was spoiled; Amir Babatu, he who is ruler of the world, he who spoils the world; Amir Babatu who ruins the Muslims; Amir Babatu, ruler with two personalities.' There was a certain irony in the situation, for changes had in fact been occurring in Wa such as to strengthen the authority of Islam *vis-à-vis* that of the Nam.

Table 5.2 *Wa Limams by house and generation*

Generation	Number of limams by house				
	Dondoli	Tamarimuni	Dzedzedeyiri	Dapuyipala	Other
V	2	0	1	2	4
VI	2	1	0	1	1
VII	2	0	0	1	2
Total	6	1	1	4	7

Of the various houses which comprise Wa Limamyiri, we have seen that four originated with sons of Limam 'Abd al-Qadir who were incumbents of the Wa limamate in the first half of the nineteenth century. These were Limam Muhammad of Dondoli, Limam Sa'id of Tamarimuni, Limam Ya'qub of Dzedzedeyiri and Limam Ya'muru II of Dapuyipala. Reference to table 5.2 (which omits the Ahmadi claimant to the limamate, Al-Hajj Salih) shows that only one member of Dzedzedeyiri, Idris b. Limam Ya'qub, held the Wa limamate in Generation V, and none of Tamarimuni; that only one member of Tamarimuni, Al-Hajj Malik b. 'Uthman, held it in Generation VI and none of Dzedzedeyiri; and that no one from either house held it in Generation VII. Although the Rule of Oscillation was in force over the three generations (see table 4.3), clearly neither Tamarimuni nor Dzedzedeyiri were equitably represented in the actual succession. There is a presumption that either they were successfully excluded from it for the most part, or that they ceased vigorously to contest it. The latter is almost certainly the case. They came to hold, instead, a new limamate, that of *imam al-jum'a* or Friday Limam. Its creation attests to the development of faction within the *'ulama'* class. Key figures in the events to be described are shown in figure 6.

Three students were sent from Wa to Kong to improve their learning. Two were great-grandsons of Wa Limam 'Abd al-Qadir, namely, Ibrahim b. 'Uthman Dun of Dondoli and Yahya b. 'Uthman Dabila of Dzedzedeyiri. The third was 'Uthman of Tagarayiri, that is, the later Yeri Na 'Uthman Daleri.[80] They arranged in Kong for a well-known mosque builder to return with them to Wa. He is referred to as Karamoko Siddiq in some sources,[81] as Numaba (a nickname) in others,[82] and as 'Abdallah Watara in one.[83] He built a new mosque in Wa capable of accommodating its growing Muslim population for the Friday prayer.[84] The weight of the evidence is that the mosque builder was in fact recruited by Yahya of Dzedzedeyiri on behalf of his father, 'Uthman Dabila. By one report Dzedzedeyiri rewarded him with two slaves, 2,000 cowries and a gown. The Wa Limam and the Wa Yeri Na added five more slaves.[85] Another report has it that the Wa Na, the Wa Yeri Na, the Wa Limam and 'all the big men' contributed five slaves and 100,000 cowries.[86] The Dondoli people apparently commissioned the mosque builder to put up

DONDOLI

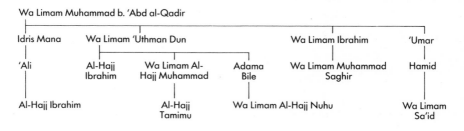

DZEDZEDEYIRI

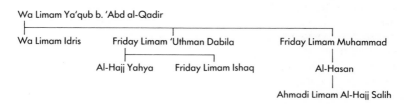

TAMARIMUNI

Figure 6 Distribution of limamates by house

another nearby, a structurally somewhat daring albeit small mosque which has in fact stood the test of time; it is known as the 'Qubba Mosque' from its mud-built dome.[87]

'Uthman Dabila of Dzedzedeyiri became limam of the new Friday mosque, that is, *imam al-jum'a*. Idris Mana of Dondoli removed his people from their section of Limamyiri to a new site about a quarter of a mile away, the present Dondoli. Factional differences were being expressed spatially. Two sons of 'Uthman Dun gave the new Dondoli community its institutional shape. Ibrahim, one of the three students sent to Kong (and later reckoned the third *mujaddid* of Wa), opened a school there to which reference has

already been made. His brother, Muhammad (later to hold the Wa limamate), supervised the building of the Dondoli mosque.[88]

The construction of the new Friday mosque occurred in 1885. This is the
date given by Dougah, though his authority is unknown.[89] An eyewitness
referred to its being built in four months, and said it was 'in the second year'
that Babatu destroyed it, which was in 1887.[90] The sojourn of the three Wa
students in Kong should, then, probably be dated to the first half of the 1880s
when, judging from what is known of their family histories, they must have
been in their twenties or thirties. The chronology seems reasonably clear.
There is, however, some reason to think that the Friday mosque of 1885
replaced an older building.

Dougah was apparently told that the mosque of 1885 was built in the time
of Wa Limam Ibrahim ('Jonguna Ibrahima I'). This could not have been so,
for Ibrahim I held office in the 1850s or 1860s. Dougah may not have been
simply in error, for in 1964 Levtzion obtained information that led him to
believe that a mosque had indeed been built in the early 1860s.[91] The
informant who saw the Friday mosque being built two years prior to
Babatu's occupation of Wa could also speak of it as many years old (he said,
in fact, forty-five years) when Babatu came. The matter is clearly of
importance to the history of the Friday limamate. Was 'Uthman Dabila
made Friday Limam only after the mosque of 1885 was built, or was it in his
capacity as Friday Limam of an earlier mosque that he commissioned his
son, Yahya, to bring a builder back from Kong to construct a (presumably)
larger and more imposing edifice? I have no source that enables this matter to
be resolved. Certainly, however, 'Uthman Dabila could have held the Friday
limamate as early as the 1860s, for he was by then probably already in his
forties.

Figure 6 shows clearly the privileged access to the Wa limamate enjoyed by
Dondoli *vis-à-vis* Dzedzedeyiri and Tamarimuni and, conversely, the privileged access to the Friday limamate enjoyed by Dzedzedeyiri and Tamarimuni *vis-à-vis* Dondoli. There is an ideological dimension to this. The Wa
limamate originated with the Wala polity and we have seen that its
incumbents exercised their office on behalf of the entire populace, believers
and unbelievers alike. They made prayers for the success of the Wa Na's
armies because those armies defended a polity of which the Muslims were
part. They made prayers for the success of the crops, and for freedom from
disease in both the human and animal population, because drought and
affliction did not differentiate between believers and non-believers. The
Suwarian tradition to which they belonged religiously permitted them to do
these things. The Friday limamate was instituted a century and a half or
more later. The Friday Limam was responsible solely to the *umma* of Wa,
and the affairs of the wider Wala polity were no concern of his office. The Wa
Limam, it was put to me in 1963, 'is for all the town, for the chiefs and the
Muslims' but the Friday Limam 'is for the Muslims, not for the Wa Na'.[92]

The creation of the Friday limamate represented a significant break with the past. It affected in a quite radical way the position of the Muslims within the polity. The Dzedzedeyiri section of Limamyiri provided the first Friday Limam, 'Uthman Dabila b. Wa Limam Ya'qub; the second, Muhammad b. Wa Limam Ya'qub; and the fourth, Ishaq b. 'Uthman Dabila. It is unlikely to be a coincidence that it was the founder of Dzedzedeyiri, Wa Limam Ya'qub, who appears to have broken with the Suwarian tradition by joining the *jihad* of Al-Hajj Mahmud Karantaw in the middle of the nineteenth century. The third Friday Limam, Muhammad Zayd, came from Tamarimuni. The founder of the section was Wa Limam Sa'id, whose daughter married a Kunatay partisan of Al-Hajj Mahmud Karantaw. The argument is that incompatible Islamic ideologies coexisted in Wa in the second half of the nineteenth century. The older and conservative one was the Suwarian. The newer one was much influenced by the currents of revolutionary change that had already swept over much of the Western and Central Sudans. The older one was represented primarily by the Dondoli faction, which came to dominate the Wa limamate. The newer one was represented primarily by the Dzedzedeyiri faction, which came to dominate the Friday limamate. We shall see that the opposition between the two factions remains to the present a major factor in Wa affairs.

Slaves and salvation: unbelievers as captives

Wa was apparently of little commercial importance until the second half of the nineteenth century. Eighteenth-century French cartographers, Delisle in 1722 and D'Anville in 1749, knew of Gonja ('Gonge') and could locate more or less accurately several of its towns: Gbuipe ('Goaffy'), Tuluwe ('Teloue') and Kafaba ('Caffaba').[93] Of Wa they knew nothing. It was an Asante in the early nineteenth century who was responsible for the first appearance of Wala on any map.[94] The Muslim traders in Kumase in that same period, however, owned route-books written for the use of travellers. One detailed the course of a major road that ran northwards from the Asante capital through Nkoransa, Gbuipe and Daboya to the large market of Yagaba, whence it veered to the northwest to pass through Kanjarga, Poura, Safane and Nouna to the ancient town of Jenne in the delta of the Middle Niger.[95] The road ran no closer to Wa than some seventy miles, and if any of the Muslim traders ever visited the town they did not see fit to mention it in their itineraries. In the middle of the century, Henry Barth assiduously collected information on routes he was unable to follow. He heard, for example, of the road that passed through Sansanne Mango, Yendi, Kpabia and Salaga; of another that ran from Kong through Lanfiera and Safane; and of an east–west road that linked Salaga with Kong via Bonduku. Of Wa he knew nothing.[96]

Germane in this context is Sanneh's description of 'the fundamental triad of clerical life' in the Suwarian tradition of the Jakhanke: 'diligence in learning (Ar. *al-qira'ah*), farming (*al-harth*), and travel or mobility (*al-*

safar)'.[97] Sanneh remarks that *al-safar* was less a matter of trade for the Jakhanke, more a matter of travel for educational and other broadly religious purposes. The triad appears highly relevant to the situation of the Wala Muslims prior to the second half of the nineteenth century; agriculture was the basis of their existence, as it was of the Wala generally, and trade was seemingly no more than local.

By the later nineteenth century all this had changed. Binger was never within a hundred or more miles of Wa, and knew nothing of Babatu's attack on it. Traders he met, however, constantly referred to the town. Late in 1888 he learned from caravan leaders in Kintampo that an all but straight road led from Accra through Kumase, Nkoransa and Kintampo to Bole. There it divided, one branch passing westwards through Buna and the Lobi country to [Bobo] Dioulasso and Jenne, the other eastwards through Wa, Walembele, Sati, Wagadugu, Mani, Douentza and beyond. These were, he wrote, 'the two great arteries by which kola reaches Timbuktu and, with the kola, European goods'.[98] Traders on the eastern road in 1888 were, he added, greatly involved in buying slaves and provisioning the Zabarima armies.[99]

Whatever benefits the Wala merchants obtained from the through-trade, they were clearly also functioning as brokers in a more local context. Wa itself lay at the centre of a network of lesser roads. In 1893 it was known to the Director of Military Intelligence in the War Office, London, as 'an important trading centre and junction of roads'.[100] Drawing upon Ferguson's reports, he named those from Lokosso, Buna, Bole and Daboya, respectively west, southwest, south and southeast of Wa. Binger saw many Grunshi in Salaga in October 1888 and learned that they came from 'Bole and particularly Wa, where many captives are found, by origin those taken by Babatu's bands'.[101] Binger also noted that gunpowder for the Zabarima was reaching Wa apparently from Accra on the Gold Coast via Kintampo, and guns from Krinjabo on the Côte d'Ivoire via Bonduku.[102]

Wa had apparently risen to a position of commercial importance over a few decades. It is evident that the transformation had to do with new patterns of supply (of slaves) and demand (for guns and gunpowder) created by the militant Muslim movements of the period: by the campaigns in the Voltaic region of Al-Hajj Mahmud and his successor, Mukhtar Karantaw, and of Alfa Hano and his successors, Alfa Gazare and Babatu. A glimpse of the change that occurred was provided by Muhammad b. 'Abbas, who was born in the Zabarima base at Kassana on the very day that Alfa Gazare died, 16 Safar 1296, 9 February 1878. His father, 'Abbas b. Ibrahim, and his father's elder brother, Muhammad, were from Kano. They settled in Wa, importing cloth from Kano and sending kola back. Then, said the informant,

> Alfa Hanno called for *jihad*. He had with him a *malam*, Malam Ladan from Katsina. Malam Ladan heard about my father, 'Abbas, in Wa and sent for him... Malam Ladan, like my father, had come to trade, but then joined the Zabarimas to make prayers for them. Even Alfa Hanno originally came to trade, and only later called for *jihad*... Then Malam Ladan sent to my father,

113

asking him to assist him. So my father joined him... I had all of this story from my father.

In or about 1883, 'Abbas b. Ibrahim and his brother left the Grunshi country and settled in Kintampo. There they continued, it may safely be assumed, to facilitate the flow of slaves to the south and of guns and gunpowder to the north.[103]

Many of the slaves that reached Wa were destined for sale into the virtually limitless labour market in the forest country to the south. Significant numbers, however, were absorbed into the local economy. My experience, like that of Fikry, is that the Wala are extremely reluctant to talk about such matters. Citizens of slave descent have been assimilated into free society and are indeed free. Reference to their origins is viewed as an highly antisocial activity. I encountered, and incline to accept, the almost universal belief in Wa that the use of slave labour was an innovation of the period of the Karantaws and Zabarima. Fikry encountered the same belief but inclined to discount it as based 'in pride and religious sentiment'.[104] It is clear, however, that the number of slaves (Walii, *dzemihi*, sing. *dzemi*[105]) owned by the Wala rose sharply in the period. The Zabarima armies required a constant supply of foodstuffs and fodder, and Wala entrepreneurs moved into the provisioning business. Large tracts of land were brought into cultivation with the use of unfree labour. They are known in Juula as *dyonso*.

Holden has described the *dyonso* in a wider regional setting, commenting that they 'may have been large enough and with production so geared to the market, as to be categorised as plantations'.[106] They involved a new departure in agricultural production. The slave was used not to supplement family labour in a subsistence system (which may well have been the case in earlier times), but specifically to produce commodities for a determinate market in which profits could be realized. The Wala plantations were established in the eastern and southern districts, shielded from Dagaaba depredations. There was a concentration of them around Guropise, where Mackworth in 1898 commented on the 'extensive cultivation', and around Bulenga, where he noted 'plenty of cultivation'.[107] The owners of the plantations were principally if not exclusively Wala Muslims. They often took up residence locally, and built small mosques to provide for their needs.[108] It is impossible even to guess how many captives were absorbed into plantation production in Wala. Much of the labour, however, was probably female. Mackworth reported that the Wala 'appear to have been good farmers, and to be fond of owning horses and cattle. The women are all slaves, and do nearly all the work.'

The first Europeans to enter the Voltaic region did so at the time of the upheavals caused by the Zabarima. They were not unaware, however, of the older Juula tradition of peaceful coexistence between Muslims and unbelievers. Binger wrote of the Juula (of Kong) as having 'an instinctive horror of war, which they consider as disgraceful when it is not a matter of defending territorial integrity'.[109] A few years later, Lieutenant Chanoine could remark more generally on the low level of proselytization; Juula settled among the unbelievers, he wrote, 'bringing with them Muslim civilization, and building mosques; but living among themselves, and recruiting few adepts from among the people very attached to their ancient beliefs'.[110] Among the 'ulama' of Wa these attitudes seem no longer to have commanded universal support. Changes in the material base of society were mirrored in changes in ideology. Hitherto unchallenged views about what was religiously permitted and religiously enjoined were being rejected. A fundamental issue was that of the correct attitude of Muslims towards unbelievers. Were the Dagaaba and Sisala of Wala free (albeit 'ignorant') cultivators of the land, or were they potentially 'captives' whose persons and properties could permissibly be seized? The period of the Zabarima intrusions into the Voltaic region was one that brought the Wala an unprecedented commercial prosperity. It was also one that thereby subjected the traditional body politic to stresses of an unprecedented kind. The development of Muslim factionalism was an aspect of the changes that were in progress.

6

Colonial intrusions:
Wala in disarray

Introduction

Before 1887, the Zabarima had made their headquarters first at Kassana and then at nearby Sati (the former to the southeast of Leo, in present-day Ghana, and the latter northwest of Leo, in Burkina Faso).[1] Wa was more advantageously situated with respect to long-distance trade than either of these earlier centres, and Babatu decided to make it his new capital. He took up residence in the Vuori section of Limamyiri.[2] Many of the townsfolk had fled, seeking refuge in Kintampo, Buna, Bole, Salaga, Bonduku, Kong and elsewhere.[3] There were, however, some who remained and collaborated, whether voluntarily or otherwise, with the Zabarima. Ishaq Dodu of Tagarayiri, then in his twenties, was one of these. He served as cook to Babatu,[4] and, living until 1972, became an important source of information on the period.

Many of Babatu's troops remained encamped at Baayiri, where there was good grazing land for the horses. Owners of the plantation-type farms in eastern Wala continued, it seems, to find profit in provisioning the occupying forces. As successor to the authority of the Wa Na, Babatu required the submission of the Dagaaba towns. The people of Sankana, only twelve miles northwest of Wa, took oaths to resist him. Babatu attacked them and suffered one of his rare defeats. The defenders were able to make use of the extraordinary rocky terrain to render the Zabarima attacks totally ineffective.[5] Malam Abu, whose cycle of stories about the Zabarima has been drawn upon earlier, reported that Babatu's 'ulama' had advised him against the enterprise but he had not heeded them. The defeat was seen as divine retribution for *alhakin Wala*, 'the Wala crimes', that is, the massacre of the Wa Muslims. Babatu was sufficiently convinced of this to abandon Wa. He moved his headquarters back to Sati. There, according to Malam Abu, he assembled his 'ulama', informed them that he was repentant, and asked them to obtain God's forgiveness for him.[6] This was probably in 1889, for there is agreement that the Zabarima occupation of Wa lasted only about a year.[7]

With the departure of Babatu's forces from Wa the refugees began to return. They may have anticipated the rapid reconstruction of the Wala

Plate 12 Ishaq Dodu, once cook to Babatu, in 1964

polity in its traditional form. Authority, however, was weak. Wa Yeri Na Saidu Mogona had apparently survived in office,[8] and Musa b. Ya'muru of Dapuyipala had been chosen to succeed 'Uthman Dun as Wa Limam. Nothing is known of the fate of the Wa Widana in the period. Significantly, however, no Wa Na had been chosen since the suicide of Mahama Fua. Wa was without that functionary responsible first and foremost for its defence. The Dagaaba of Kaleo found little to deter them from raiding the town with impunity. 'They used to kill Wa women and children when they went to their farms', said Ishaq Dodu.[9] Kaleo informants were more specific. 'The Kaleo people', they said,

> used to raid Dondoli a lot. There was a road from Kaleo through Jan to Dondoli, and you could get very near to Dondoli because there were so many rocks around and you could creep right up to it. They would kill or wound the men, and take away the boys and girls. The beautiful girls they would marry. The ugly ones they would sell.[10]

117

Compounding such problems, a serious rinderpest epidemic occurred in 1891–2.[11]

New intruders: British, French and Samorians

Having re-established his capital at Sati, Babatu imposed new taxes on Grunshi towns and villages which had long accepted his authority. A number of his leading Grunshi collaborators rebelled.[12] The centenarian Al-Hajj Muhammad Shifa of Wa recollected the occasion:[13]

> The Grunshis then fought and tried to defeat Babatu. They came to inform the people of Wa that they had not wanted to fight the Wala [that is, in the ranks of Babatu in 1887] but that the Wala were defeated because they had been unwilling to help themselves. Along with this message, they also sent as a token of peace a very fine horse and nine slaves to Ya Musa, the Imam of Wa, because there was no Wa Na. In return, the Wala agreed to fight with the Grunshis.

The Wala, however, were clearly in no position actively to assist the Grunshi though it is likely enough that Limam Musa would regard any alliance with Babatu's enemies as eminently politic.

G. E. Ferguson, representing the British Crown, entered into a treaty of friendship and trade with the Bole on 13 June 1892. He was unable to proceed north to Wa. He maintained, however, that the treaty included the Wala since they had been tributary to Bole since the time of the Zabarima occupation. 'The people of Wa themselves', he reported the Bolewura to have claimed, 'asked us to become their protectors.' Ferguson, whether as a result of excessive zeal or of misunderstanding, was clearly in error in regarding Wa as a dependency of Bole. He was rightly queried on the matter by the Director of Military Intelligence in London.

Defending his position, Ferguson pointed out that many Wala had been present at the signing of the treaty.[14] The Wala in question can only have been those who had taken refuge in Bole after Babatu's attack on Wa and who were, in that sense, under the Bolewura's protection. Among them was one described by Ferguson as 'a priest of Wa'.[15] It is probable that this was Friday Limam 'Uthman Dabila, who is remembered to have taken refuge there.[16] It is possible that he was pursuing a policy of his own, intended to involve Bole and Wa in some sort of mutual security pact. Whatever the case, two years later Ferguson acknowledged that he was in error in believing Bole to have had authority over Wa.[17]

In the middle of 1892 it was Ferguson's understanding that there was then a Wa Na. Saidu Takora had in fact been enskinned, probably in 1891.[18] He was previously Pirisi Na, from the Na Djare gate. His bid for the Wa Nam was contested by a candidate from the Busa or Yijisi gate. The two parties took to arms. Saidu Takora turned for support to the Dagaaba town of Kaleo where Dumba, son of Kaleo Na Gbani, is said to have been his friend.

The Yijisi forces were defeated.[19] The circumstances of Saidu Takora's accession were not likely to have received the approval of the Wa Muslims in general and of those of Dondoli in particular, who had been so harassed by Kaleo marauders. Nevertheless, the Wala polity appeared to be re-emerging, after its disastrous collapse, in something like its historic form.

G. E. Ferguson, on a second mission from the Gold Coast to the 'interior', entered Wa on 3 May 1894. The following day he signed, on behalf of the Crown, a treaty with the Wala authorities, namely, 'Seidu, surnamed Batakatiesa King of Dagaba' (Wa Na Saidu Takora); 'Alimami Gamusa Chief Priest' (Wa Limam Musa); 'Yenaa Chief of Wa' (Wa Yeri Na); 'Jembrugu Chief Dagaba' (Wa Widana); 'Kobitigi Chief of Wa' (unidentified); 'Kumblunaa Chief of Wa' (unidentified); 'Adama Linguist' (presumably Foroko, of Tuomuni); and 'Yengbeiri Prince' (presumably Sambadana, of Dzangbeyiri).[20] It will be remarked that Friday Limam 'Uthman Dabila was not a signatory; he was probably still in Bole.

The treaty of 4 May was one of 'friendship and freedom of trade' and not of protection as such. British officialdom, however, took a more generous view of it. A document which reached the Secretary of State for the Colonies in London read: 'by the circumstance that the country having been invaded by Gardiari [Gazare, meaning Babatu] the people desired alliance with the whiteman who conquered Ashanti [in order to] obtain munitions of war from the Coast or to obtain direct protection from the English'.[21] Ferguson was later to endorse this interpretation, remarking that 'to the native mind the friendly alliance of a powerful country with a weaker tribe implied a protection of some kind or other to be given by the former to the latter'.[22] It created, he added, 'an expectation of our alliance with them in defence of their territories'.

Whatever the British view of the treaty, the fact of the matter was that their resources in 1894 were concentrated on the Gold Coast far to the south of Wa, and the still independent power of Asante straddled the roads between. The realities of the situation must have been well known to the Wala, whose traders regularly visited the northern Asante markets and no doubt Kumase itself. It is scarcely surprising, then, that the Wala did not regard themselves as in any way exclusively committed to British interests by the treaty of 1894.

Lieutenant Baud of the French *infanterie de marine*, seasoned by months of campaigning in Borgu and Gurma, marched through Sansanne Mango, Gambaga and Walewale, and entered Wa on 1 May 1895. He commanded a small force of some fifty *tirailleurs* and fifty carriers. He met Wa Na Saidu Takora and his account of the proceedings is summarized in a contemporary report:[23]

> At his first interview the king handed him a paper that M. Ferguson had given him, asking what it meant and expressing the conviction that it was a certificate of *bonne hospitalité*. He was amazed to learn that it was a treaty of trade and friendship, by the terms of which he was forbidden to deal with any other

European power without the consent of the governor of the Gold Coast. M. Ferguson had delivered this treaty, which consisted of a printed form, with various farewell presents and without providing the least explanation.

Baud commented, somewhat ingenuously, that although the chiefs of Wa knew Arabic, Ferguson had obtained their thumbprints rather than their signatures. The treaty of 4 May 1894 was, he concluded, a sham.

The agreement that Baud made with the Wala was, he believed, *un traité loyal*, a fair treaty. The attestants whose signatures in Arabic were affixed to it were in fact the first four to have subscribed to Ferguson's treaty, namely, Wa Na Saidu Takora ('Seydou Drezogou', that is, Dariziogu); Wa Widana ('Diambourougou Massa, Chief of the town of Wa'); Limam Musa ('Moussa, Imaum of Wa'); and Wa Yeri Na Saidu Mogona ('Seydou Abdoulaye, Notable').[24] The French thought the Baud treaty one of 'une importance capitale', regarding the position of Wa as crucial in linking their possessions in Dahomey to the east with those in Côte d'Ivoire to the west.

In world historical terms, Wala had become part of the so-called 'Scramble for Africa'. The Wala, however, could scarcely have taken a global view of the matter. Ferguson had spent six days in Wa, and Baud five, leaving little but two papers and flags to witness their respective passages. Nevertheless, Wala had functioned as a polity once again. The Wa Na, Wa Yeri Na, Wa Widana and Wa Limam had together dealt civilly with strangers and had seen them off without incident. The semblance of unity was, however, to prove short-lived. Factional interests were to prevail as the Wala confronted a new situation created by the emergence on the regional scene of the Almami Samori Turay.

In the middle of 1892 Samori Turay, as a result of French military pressure, commenced the evacuation of his home territory in Wasulu (spanning the frontiers of present-day Guinée and Mali). In 1894 he was rebuilding his power some 350 miles to the east, in the Jimini country beyond the Komoé river in what is now Côte d'Ivoire. After protracted negotiations, Samori Turay finally obtained the unambiguous support of the Watara of Kong in April 1895. By this time he was already contemplating the extension of his influence to the markets of the Black Volta region. He turned his attention to Bonduku, the principal market town of the Gyaman. The Gyaman, however, rejected his calls for an alliance. Throughout May and June there was fighting between them and the redoubtable *sofas*, as the Samorian troops were known.[25] Resistance had collapsed by the end of June. The Juula of Bonduku had abandoned the town in anticipation of its fall. Samori Turay patiently negotiated their support, stressing his devotion to Islam and his wish for peace. They accepted his assurances, and returned to surrender Bonduku to him on 10 July 1895.[26]

Samori Turay moved back to Jimini at the end of 1895. He left the conduct of affairs in the Black Volta region in the hands of his son, Sarankye Mori. Sarankye Mori, in turn, entrusted the invasion of western Gonja to his

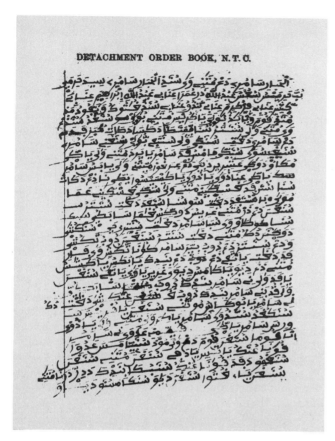

Plate 13 *Alhabari Samuri daga Mutanen Wa* (ASMW)

subordinate, Fanyinama of Korhogo.[27] Gonja accounts of the matter have it that Jamani, ruler of the Gonja Division of Kong, had asked for Samori's support in his bid for the Gonja paramountcy, and that it was in response that Sarankye Mori decided to establish a forward base at Bole.[28] Bole resistance rapidly crumbled and the town was occupied. A Samorian presence had been established less than seventy miles south of Wa.

The Samorian ascendancy in Wala

Malam Abu's anecdotal history of the Zabarima breaks, and takes up the story of Almami Samori Turay from its beginnings. His account of the Samorian intrusion into Wala is usefully supplemented by Wala sources. *Al-akhbaru Samuru* (henceforth AS), 'The Story of Samori', is an Hausa work in

121

seventeen pages.[29] It was written by Ibrahim, a Borno *'alim* in Wa, apparently before 1906.[30] Two other items are included in the corpus of manuscripts compiled by Friday Limam Ishaq b. 'Uthman in 1922 or 1923. The anonymous *Alhabari Samuri daga Mutanen Wa* (ASMW), 'The Story of Samori and the People of Wa', is in one page, and *Alhabari Zabarimawa, Wala da Samuru* (AZWS), 'The Story of the Zabarima, Wala and Samori', by Ishaq b. 'Uthman himself, is in two.[31] A Walii text entitled *Samori Taahuu* (ST), 'Samori's Invasion', is also of considerable interest. It was recorded apparently in the mid 1950s, but by whom and from whom is unfortunately unknown.[32] These various works are not *kubaru* in the sense of being recensions of oral *lasiri*. They are all apparently direct reports of events in which the writers (or their informants) participated. They are older, but of the same character, as the texts of interviews with survivors of the period conducted in the 1960s and 1970s, which also contribute much to an understanding of the period.

ST reports that the Wala sent gifts of cowries, horses, cattle and sheep to Sarankye Mori's commander in Bole, Fanyinama, in order to obtain his help against the Dagaaba. According to Dougah the approach was initiated by one 'Insah', a notable of Dondoli whose wife had been kidnapped by the Kaleo.[33] One such kidnapping is remembered as a *cause célèbre* of the period. The wife of Adama Bile, a leading *'alim* of Dondoli and son of no less than Limam 'Uthman Dun, was seized. All attempts to procure her release failed.[34] It may be that the 'Insah' of Dougah's account was in fact Adama Bile.[35] Whatever the case, the story suggests that the Muslims of Dondoli were instrumental in soliciting Samorian help against the Dagaaba. Ishaq Dodu of Wa Tagarayiri commented, 'before Samori arrived here, there was war between Wa and Dagari, that is why I helped Samori when he came'.[36]

When, according to Malam Abu, Sarankye Mori arrived in Bole from Bonduku he immediately sent two envoys to Wa Na Saidu Takora to inform him of his presence there. The Wa Na (who, it will be recalled, owed his skin to the support of the Dagaaba of Kaleo) was 'very frightened'. He took counsel. He was advised to be calm and to reciprocate by sending envoys to Sarankye Mori. He called an *'alim* who had recently returned from Mecca, namely 'Mahama the son of a *wali*,' and asked him to conduct negotiations. The 'Mahama' of Malam Abu's account is Muhammad, son of Limam 'Uthman Dun of Dondoli and brother of Adama Bile (see page 110). He is known to have left Wa on pilgrimage in or about 1905.[37] Assuming that Malam Abu is correct, this must have been his second pilgrimage. We have seen that his elder brother, Al-Hajj Ibrahim, died in Mecca, probably in the early 1890s, and it is not unlikely that the two had undertaken the journey together.

In 1963 Muhammad's son, Al-Hajj Tamimu, gave the following account of the mission to Sarankye Mori:[38]

> My father was in Wa when the news came that Samori [in fact, Sarankye Mori] was in Bole. The news came that Samori was spoiling Bole. My father, Al-Hajj Muhammad, went there to beg Samori not to bring war to Wa. There was an

old prediction. My father had been told by his grandfathers that one day war would threaten Wa, and that when that happened he, my father, should go and meet the people on the way and so avert the trouble. So my father went and met Samori.

Al-Hajj Muhammad Shifa was able to recall the full composition of the embassy. Other than Muhammad b. 'Uthman Dun it comprised Ibrahim Banwara, the informant's father; Abu Tarawiri; Adama Nabiri, of Dzangbeyiri; Gberi Na Konkoradori, from Wa Nayiri; Bukari, from Wa Nayiri; and Karamoko Yusuf Zorozoro.[39] The Hausa text, AS, states that 'Dakati' and 'Ghurusi' were asked to accompany the envoys; this must mean representatives of the Dagaaba and Sisala towns historically part of Wala. Predictably, perhaps, the former declined but the latter accepted the invitation.

The envoys had a purpose beyond that of saving Wa from attack. Following, perhaps, an earlier Dondoli initiative, they solicited Sarankye Mori's assistance against the Dagaaba. There is general agreement in the sources that Sarankye Mori required further payment from the Wala. According to AS the Wala produced thirty-two horses and 250 rams, and the Grunshi seventeen horses; according to ASMW the Wala produced twenty-two horses and 200 rams.[40] Sarankye Mori then announced that he would fight the Dagaaba. 'I cannot stay with pagans', Al-Hajj Muhammad Shifa reports him as saying; 'I will come and kill them.'[41] He entered Wa probably on 8 May 1896, a Friday.[42] Two days later he took the field against the Dagaaba.

Only two of the seven members of the embassy to Sarankye Mori were from the Nabihi, the Wala 'princes', and there was apparently no representative of the Widana. It seems that Wala policy was being dictated by the Muslims. There is, however, no reference in the sources to Friday Limam 'Uthman Dabila taking any part in the proceedings. Whether or not he had yet returned to Wa is unclear, but the authority of the Friday limamate appears to have been in eclipse. It may be that Wa Limam 'Uthman Dun's opposition to the Zabarima, and his death at the time of their occupation of Wa, had conferred something of an aura of martyrdom on him. For Malam Abu he was a *wali*, one beloved of God. In the teaching chains we have seen that he is referred to reverently as Sharif b. Madani Tarawiri. Perhaps the posthumous veneration of Wa Limam 'Uthman Dun grew at the expense of the current reputation of Friday Limam 'Uthman Dabila. Whatever the case, Malam Abu certainly regarded 'Uthman Dun's son, Al-Hajj Muhammad of Dondoli, as the moving force in Wala affairs in the critical period of the Samorian intrusion, and stressed the great respect accorded him by Sarankye Mori. One of Malam Abu's anecdotes has Sarankye Mori so pleased with the outcome of the embassy to Bole that he had Al-Hajj Muhammad tell the Wa Na to give him (and whether the 'him' refers to Muhammad or Sarankye Mori is unfortunately ambiguous) 150 pieces of cloth and 400 goats.

Malam Abu's text and those of AS and ASMW are in broad agreement on the invasion of the Kaleo country. The Dagaaba took up positions at Jan and Sankana, respectively about ten miles north and twelve miles northwest of

Wa. Those at Jan were put to flight. Those at Sankana, repeating their success against Babatu seven or eight years earlier, inflicted heavy losses on the Samorian *sofas*, who fell back on Wa. Sarankye Mori had a number of his commanders who had retreated flogged for cowardice. As a result Fanyinama defected to Babatu. Fanyinama's son recollected the episode in 1966. Sarankye Mori, he said,

> ordered a hundred lashes to be given to those who had fled. Mangursi was among them, and he bled from the mouth. My father did not like that, and he said that he could no longer follow someone who whipped his own people. So then my father called together his own warriors and he went to join Babatu. Four people came to him. They were sent by Samori to say that Samori was sorry about what had happened and that my father should come back. But my father said that he had followed Samori faithfully for three years and that then Samori had flogged some of his people. So my father stayed with Babatu.[43]

Fanyinama's defection notwithstanding, Sarankye Mori announced that he would resume the attack on Sankana immediately. Muhammad b. 'Uthman Dun counselled patience, saying that he would muster further men for the campaign. They were presumably the Wala led, according to the Walii text ST, by Adama Nabiri of Dzangbeyiri. Sarankye Mori took the field again 'two days after the new moon'; on the interpretation already given to the dating in AS, this should mean 2 Dhu 'l-Hijja or 15 May 1896. Setting fire to the bush, the *sofas* forced the Dagaaba to abandon their positions in the rocks and so were able to put them to flight. The Wala notables appeared at Sankana to congratulate Sarankye Mori who, Malam Abu reports, gave Muhammad b. 'Uthman many presents.

The first steps towards the incorporation of the Wala into the Samorian state were taken at this time. The separation of military and civil powers was a key aspect of Samori Turay's administrative policy. Sarankye Mori thus chose to establish his army headquarters at Sankana and not at Wa. He appointed, however, a civil functionary to supervise Wa affairs. This was a certain 'Ali Wangara, who is described in the translation of a letter by Samori Turay as a 'slave' of Sarankye Mori.[44] In 1963 Ishaq Dodu of Wa Tagarayiri reminisced about him:

> When Samori came he helped the Wa. He appointed a man to be his deputy [*khalifa*] in Wa. This was Ali, a Wangara man, one of Samori's people... He gave us Ali Wangara, who helped the Wa people... Ali stayed in Wa for several months, nine or ten, before the English came... He had many people in Wa. There were about sixty people with him. They were sofas. They had sofa wives with them. They had many guns, and they had their own blacksmiths, numu.[45]

Since 'the English came' in January 1897, Ishaq Dodu's testimony suggests that 'Ali Wangara was appointed shortly after the Sankana campaign. The Hausa work AS also refers to 'Ali Wangara and reports that twelve horsemen and thirty-five gunners were seconded to him when he was put in charge of Wa. The text of AS and the evidence of Ishaq Dodu are in agreement that

'Ali Wangara lodged in Dondoli. The implication, again, is that Muhammad b. 'Uthman Dun, and the Dondoli Muslims more generally, were the leading protagonists of the Samorian cause in Wa.

Sarankye Mori, the Dagaaba, and Babatu: a failure of policy

After his victory at Sankana, following the text of AS, Sarankye Mori sent one of his commanders with a large force of 3,000 guns in pursuit of the Dagaaba. He reached Lawra, almost forty miles to the northwest. He returned to Sankana with much booty, including 2,000 cows, ninety-nine adult male captives, and many women and children. Soon after, emissaries from various of the Dagaaba villages arrived in Wa. Appalled by their losses, they asked the Wala to intercede with Sarankye Mori on their behalf. Sarankye Mori agreed to grant them peace providing they supplied him with cattle and goats. They accepted the condition. Sarankye Mori then proceeded to make arrangements for their more complete pacification.

Saranke Mori assembled a number of the Wala fighting men, issued them with guns, and charged them with garrisoning the Dagaaba country. According to AS, 300 men were posted to each of the Dagaaba villages Busie, Nandaw, and Sabuli with Burbor; 200 men each to Narung, Wogu, Issa, Karni, Jirapa and Ulu; and 100 each to Kojopere, Lambussie and Nadawli. The policy was not only bold but novel in its conception, for no Wa Na is known to have attempted to establish a permanent presence in the Dagaaba towns over which he claimed authority. The northernmost of the garrisons, moreover, were assigned to Dagaaba villages never considered within Wala jurisdiction.

The Dagaaba, according to AS, asked the Wala whether it was intended that the men of the garrisons should kill them. The Wala replied that Sarankye Mori had promised the Dagaaba peace, but that such matters were in the hands of God. It was not in fact Samori Turay's way to kill those who had submitted to him. His policy was exploitative rather than genocidal. Its principal thrust was to reorganize agricultural production so as to generate surpluses that could be applied to the support of his military and civil administrations.[46] Indeed, in this period Samori Turay appears to have delegated the command of military operations to his sons and others, devoting himself primarily to economic matters. F. B. Henderson, who appeared before Samori Turay in Jimini in early 1897, remarked that the Almami 'appeared to be leading a quiet and settled existence after his somewhat stormy career ... to all appearances he was quietly cultivating the ground ... he cultivates the country round his capital with great success, while his sons do the plundering'.[47] The creation of the garrisons has to be seen as the first stage in the incorporation of the Dagaaba country into the Samorian system. The process required time and, as it turned out, time was precisely what Samori Turay did not have.

In the middle of 1896, with the Wala apparently dependable and the pacification of the Dagaaba in progress, Sarankye Mori turned his attention to the Sisala or Grunshi country. There Babatu remained locked in combat with his former collaborators led by the redoubtable Grunshi combatant, Amariya.[48] The opposed forces were encamped in the vicinity of Nwandawno, some sixty miles northeast of Wa. Malam Abu reported that Amariya was assisted by two Walas, Al-Hajj Nuhu and Al-Hajj Abu. Unfortunately neither has been identified. There is evidence that Sarankye Mori treated with Babatu and Amariya. He required both to lay down their arms and take to trade or farming, and the latter to supply him with 100 horses. Babatu refused the terms; Amariya may have seemed to comply. Shortly afterwards, alarmed by the activities of a French column in the Mosi country to the north, Samori Turay issued new orders to his son. Sarankye Mori was required to incorporate Babatu's forces into his own.[49]

Sarankye Mori summoned Babatu to Sankana. The Zabarima leader took the road in full fighting array. Sarankye Mori arranged for his commanders consecutively to greet Babatu on his way to Sankana, and then to block his lines of retreat. The texts of both Malam Abu and AS agree that Babutu realized he had been tricked. He was, however, well received at Sankana, which he reached in September 1896.[50] Malam Abu reported that Sarankye Mori resisted Wala pressures to put Babatu to death.

A French column led by Lieutenants Voulet and Chanoine marched swiftly south from Wagadugu to profit from the situation created by Babatu's move to Sankana. On 19 September, at Sati, the two officers signed a Treaty of Protection with Amariya, quite inaccurately described as 'roi du Gourounsi'. The column then moved forward through Dasima to the Kulpawn River before retiring northwards.[51] Learning of its presence on the Wala borders, Sarankye Mori's suspicions were aroused. He summoned the Wala (according to AS) and accused them of complicity with the French. The Wala denied the charge. By the time Sarankye Mori's envoys reached Dasima to investigate the situation, the French column had left. Whether there was any basis for the suspicions entertained by Sarankye Mori must remain an open question.

From Sati, in September, Voulet sent a letter to Samori Turay informing him of French claims to a protectorate over the Grunshi country and requesting him not to allow the *sofas* to operate there. The reply was received on 2 October. Samori Turay said that he did not want war, and that Sarankye Mori had already been ordered to withdraw from Sankana and his *sofas* to quit the Grunshi country.[52] It is probable enough that Samori Turay was disinclined to become involved in further hostilities with the French in a region so distant from his centres in Jimini. Sarankye Mori's withdrawal from Sankana was, however, a different matter.

Samori Turay had decided to transfer Sarankye Mori's headquarters to Buna, west of the Black Volta, before he was in receipt of Voulet's letter.[53] The reasons must have been primarily tactical. Samori Turay presumably disliked having his largest army positioned beyond a river unfordable for many months in the year. He may also have become doubtful about the prospects for truly pacifying the Dagaaba country. This may have been the substance of a rumour picked up by Henderson early in 1897, that 'of late' Samori Turay had become displeased with what he regarded as Sarankye Mori's inaction, and had expressed his dissatisfaction in a message threatening to 'give him a hoe', that is, remove him from his command.[54] Both Malam Abu and AS make it clear that Sarankye Mori was summoned to Jimini by his father, perhaps to be admonished, and that he was required to have Babatu accompany him.

The unfortunate Dagaaba, who had submitted to Sarankye Mori in order to obtain peace, now found that he no longer required their submission and therefore felt no obligation to afford them peace. They were no longer unbelievers enjoying the protection of a Muslim ruler; they were once again in *dar al-harb*, the sphere of war. Before leaving Sankana, Saranke Mori unleashed all the forces at his disposal against them. Those in the vicinity of Sankana and Kaleo, apparently accused of conspiring to kill the Samorian commander, were among the first to suffer the effects of the change in policy. Sarankye Mori's attack on them is dated in AS to 17 Jumada II, that is, 23 November 1896.

At the same point in time Sarankye Mori learned of the movement northwards through Asante, which had been occupied by the British at the beginning of 1896, of a column under Lieutenant F. B. Henderson. He assembled the Wa notables and accused them, this time, of having sent messages to Cape Coast to solicit British intervention. As if to test the loyalty of his allies, he then ordered a joint *sofa*, Zabarima and Wala attack on the Dagaaba of Burbor ('Bobowa'), near Busie. Both Malam Abu and the author of AS mention it. Many captives were taken, the Zabarima putting the *sofas* to shame by the zeal they displayed. The Kaleo and Sankana fugitives were next hunted down, and many women and children seized. AS reports that Sarankye Mori had all the prisoners brought before him, and the men separated out and counted. They numbered 120. The villages along the road to Charia, only eleven miles northwest of Wa, were then raided. Sarankye Mori was, it seems, concerned to replenish his finances before leaving Sankana. The number of captives, mainly women and children, reaching markets as distant as Krakye, over 200 miles southeast of Wa, was the subject of much comment at the time.[55]

Sarankye Mori again assembled the Wala authorities. According to AS, he announced his intention of commencing the withdrawal from Sankana on 7 Rajab, that is, 12 December, saying that he would pass through Wa. There was great consternation. The Wa asked him to leave them in peace. He agreed, on condition that they supplied him with foodstuffs for the march. The Wa Na and many of his people were unconvinced. They proposed abandoning the town. Wa Limam, however, opposed that course of action. He urged that Sarankye Mori be trusted, and called on the *'ulama'* to make prayers for the safety of the town. Unfortunately the text of AS does not name the limam.

In the event, it was not until 22 Rajab, 27 December, that Sarankye Mori struck camp. Only at that juncture did Babatu make it known that he had no intention of accompanying Sarankye Mori to Jimini. He informed the Wala, moreover, that he would defend them if they were attacked. Sarankye Mori entered Wa with his troops, and took up positions in the main market. He asked the limam to summon the Wa Na. Saidu Takora assumed that he was to be executed and said that he would rather be killed in his house. AS reports that it was 'Malam Isaka' who finally persuaded the Wa Na to put his trust in God and to obey Sarankye Mori's summons. This was the son of Friday Limam 'Uthman Dabila, later himself to become Friday Limam. His appearance signals the re-emergence of the Dzedzedeyiri faction in Wala politics.

The Wa Na, Wa Limam and Wa Yeri Na went to the market with a hundred guns. Their fears had been exaggerated. Sarankye Mori informed them that he was departing for Bole and that he wanted the hundred Wa gunmen to accompany him there. Malam Abu stressed that Sarankye Mori specifically called for Muhammad b. 'Uthman Dun in order to say goodbye to him: 'may God let us benefit from Alhaji Mahama', he piously added. It became clear that Wa itself was not to be deserted by the Samorians; 'Ali Wangara would remain there to represent their interests.

It was reckoned a journey of at least six days from Wa to Bole. In the course of it, according to AS, the men of the Wa contingent deserted and returned to join Babatu.[56] Only two, Adama Nabiri of Dzangbeyiri and an unidentified 'Uthman, reached Bole. They were sent back to Wa, to inform the Wa Na and the Wa Limam that Sarankye Mori intended to visit them again from his new base in Buna. The Walas understandably read a threat into the message. The Walii text, ST, reads, *Wala an dzaahi a ba sun Samori ni ka bila ihi u suuri un yeli ka u na dogehi la Wala yaga ba dzaahibu ni dzun*: Samori was so angered by the conduct of the Wala that he planned to punish them severely. There was talk once more of abandoning the town.

Confusion worse confounded: the British fiasco

Sarankye Mori's *sofas* were in the process of moving out of Bole on their way to Buna when the British mission under Henderson's command arrived there from Asante. Henderson was accompanied by Assistant Inspector Irvine in charge of 100 men of the Hausa constabulary, Dr Part and a small medical staff, G. E. Ferguson (on his second visit to Wa), and 300 carriers. In despatches dated 1 and 2 January 1897, Henderson estimated that there were between ten and twelve thousand *sofas* encamped near the town and reported that another large force was at the crossing of the Black Volta.[57] Neither the Samorian nor the British commander had reason, or authority, to engage in hostilities: the former because it was Samori Turay's policy to establish friendly relations with the British, the latter because his commission was to assert, *vis-à-vis* the French, British claims to Wa and Buna. Henderson entered Wa on 8 January without incident.

Plate 14 Wa Na Saidu Takora (left) and notables, 1897

The British mission was received by Wa Na Saidu Takora who, Henderson claimed, said that 'he was much in need of a strong friend, as his enemies were closing in upon him'.[58] Henderson (who took the reference to be to Babatu, though the much-feared return of Sarankye Mori was probably meant) thought that 'central authority' in Wala had been greatly weakened since the Zabarima attack, and that the 'King's writ' ran with little success.[59] On 9 January the notables of Wala assembled and a new treaty, this time of 'friendship *and protection*', was entered into. Seventeen representatives of the Wala subscribed to it.[60] Saidu Takora appeared on the document as 'King of Dagarti'. The Yeri Na was 'Umar Kulendi ('Kunadi Yenaa Chief of Wa'), who had succeeded Saidu Mogona from a different house in Tagarayiri.[61] Jumburugu ('Jembrugu Na Chief of Dagaba') was still Widana. 'Uthman Dabila signed as 'Almamy'; he had, then, certainly returned to Wa by this time. Among the other attestants Foroko Adama ('Adama Chief Linguist'), Sambadana Adama Nabiri of Dzangbeyiri ('Yengbeira Adama Prince'), Qasim, head of Kabanya ('Kasimu Kabanya Chief'), and Nakori Na Idris ('Idi Nakawraw-Na') may all be identified with confidence.

Conspicuously missing from the attestants to the treaty was the Wa Limam. Limam Musa died sometime between May 1895, when he signed the Baud treaty, and September 1898.[62] The Dondoli had been unable to replace Limam 'Uthman Dun with another of the descendants of Limam Muhammad b. 'Abd al-Qadir because of the Rule of Oscillation. On Limam Musa's death, however, they secured the limamate again to the exclusion of the other houses of Limamyiri. Ibrahim, a brother of 'Uthman Dun, was elected. It is possible that Limam Musa may just have died when Henderson entered Wa and that Ibrahim had not yet been elected. In that case there should have been an acting limam present at the gathering of notables, to represent the vacant office and signal approval of the proceedings. Of the unidentified attestants to the treaty, however, none appears to have been from Limamyiri.[63] The more obvious explanation is that the Wa Limam, whether Musa b. Ya'muru or Ibrahim b. Muhammad, felt that his commitment to the Samorian connection did not permit him to subscribe to a treaty with Christians.

Henderson, with the full cooperation of Wa Na, commenced construction of a fort in Wa. The situation appeared so settled that he even felt able to undertake a journey deep into the Sisala country, reaching Leo.[64] Doubtless aware of Samori Turay's desire for peace with the British, 'Ali Wangara permitted his *sofas* to provision the newcomers.[65] Not all was as it seemed, however. A communication from Wa reached Sarankye Mori in Buna, to the effect that the British were not wanted there, but that they were building a fort. The complaint was supposed to have come from the Wa Na, which in the circumstances seems highly improbable. The Wa Limam appears a more likely source.[66] However that may be, Wa was thrown into turmoil once again by the appearance of refugees from Buna. They carried news of Sarankye Mori's slaughter of Muslims there.[67] It was not such as to inspire the Wala with confidence in their own safety should Sarankye Mori revisit them. In AZWS Friday Limam Ishaq provides an interesting detail. Asked by the *sofas* in Wa to bring the Buna refugees to them, the Wa Na begged that they first be allowed to rest, since it was Ramadan (3 February to 4 March). The *sofas* agreed. It may have been the *sofa* demand that decided Henderson to expel them from Wa.

The Hausa texts AS and AZWS say that it was one night in Ramadan that 'Ali Wangara was told by Henderson to leave Wa, because 'two strong men cannot live in the same town': *masu karfi biyu ba su zamna gari guda.*[68] Despite 'Ali Wangara's protest that he had fasted all day and that the evening was when he could eat and drink, he was not allowed to stay till morning. He travelled to Bole, killing a number of Wala travellers on the road at the border village of Kulmasa. Henderson sent a force in pursuit and was able to rescue a further thirteen Wala.[69] The expulsion of the *sofas* from Wa occurred on 22 February.[70] Samori Turay himself gave the Governor of the Gold Coast an account of the matter: '[the English] went to Wa and stayed in it. They said to a slave of the son of the "Imam": get out of Wa for it is our country, and this slave, who was called Ali, went to Ghelmes [Kulmasa] after they had driven him away.'[71]

Henderson's action was an unwise one. Not only was it British policy at the time to avoid conflict with Samori Turay, but Henderson's own commission was to proceed to Bole in order to 'show the flag', not to Sarankye Mori but to the French. Holden has suggested that Henderson acted in direct contravention of his orders.[72] Henderson's next move showed even less appreciation of the realities of the situation. He was expecting Captains

Cramer and Haslewood to reinforce his column with fifty men and artillery. Without awaiting their arrival, however, he led a detachment of the Hausa constabulary out of Wa on 2 March. He crossed the Black Volta and set up camp at Dokita, some thirty miles southwest of Wa. It had become the principal camp of refugees from Buna.[73] Henderson had thus in effect invaded Sarankye Mori's territory. Two weeks or so later the *sofas* took up positions near Dokita. Sarankye Mori sent a message to Henderson, that he should abandon Dokita or be killed. Henderson says that he ignored it. Malam Abu says that Henderson replied that if Sarankye Mori came to Dokita he would not live out the day. By 29 March Dokita was under seige. Two days later Sarankye Mori sent a further communication. According to Henderson it was to the effect that he, Sarankye Mori, 'did not wish the English to die of hunger and thirst; that his quarrel was not with them, but with the Bonas and Lobis; and we had better go away across the water', that is, retire east of the Black Volta. On 1 April Henderson withdrew from Dokita under cover of darkness, but the wounded – including Ferguson – slowed the retreat. The *sofas* were close in pursuit. Henderson reached Wa on the morning of 3 April.[74]

The Hausa text, AS, reports that the Wa heard the sound of gunfire from nearby Chansa and began to flee the town. Henderson found Wa Na Saidu Takora still there and asked him to supply horsemen as scouts. There were none. The Wa Na then disappeared; he fled, in fact, to Dasima.[75] Sarankye Mori set up camp on the outskirts of Wa. By this time the British reinforcements under Cramer and Haslewood had arrived. They engaged the *sofas* but were hopelessly outnumbered. Henderson decided to visit the *sofa* camp. Sarankye Mori demanded the surrender of the British force. Henderson refused and was permitted to communicate his decision to the garrison in Wa. By a prior arrangement with Henderson, Cramer and Haslewood commenced the withdrawal from the town.[76] Dagaaba guides had to lead them.[77]

The evacuation was clearly an ignominious affair, and the British may have been allowed to pass through the *sofa* lines only after laying down their weapons.[78] The Wala gave some account of the matter to Lieutenant-Colonel H. P. Northcott some months later. At the appropriate point, he noted, 'there was an eloquent pause, during which it was understood that the story of our disaster was better left untold'.[79] Malam Abu also glossed over the episode, noting merely that the Wa Na fled, his people fled, and the English fled. Captain Hugot, then in Boromo, heard the news and affords us a French reaction: 'This Sarankye Mori – no less! – has done an excellent job for us ... The unfortunate ones were stripped of everything; Sarankye took from them two cannons, ammunition, their provisions and their baggage.'[80] Samori Turay took a grander view of the matter. When Henderson was at Dokita, the Almami wrote, Sarankye Mori addressed his troops, saying:[81]

'Be patient, for God is with those who are patient, until I have written a letter, saying there is friendship between us. Let us inform them [the British], and then, if otherwise (they will not listen), then, war to the knife.' We had patience, and then we advanced, and God be praised for that! – and we made them flee to Wa. God gave victory to the army of the Moslems, and we took Henderson – God be praised for that!

Sarankye Mori entered Wa town in person on 7 April. He had Henderson with him, a captive. On 9 April both departed for Buna, whence Henderson was sent under escort to Samori Turay in Jimini.[82]

A new French initiative: in again, out again

Sarankye Mori's withdrawal from Sankana on 27 December 1896 left Babatu free to pursue his own policies. Early in January he was raiding the Dagaaba once more. Henderson sent Ferguson to protest. Babatu struck camp and moved back into the Grunshi country.[83] It seems that he went with assurances of British support for a renewed campaign against Amariya, now a firm supporter of the French.[84] On 14 March Amariya, reinforced by French *tirailleurs* under Lieutenant Chanoine, attacked and drove Babatu south to the Kulpawn River at Yagaba. This market lay on the road from Wa to Gambaga, a vital line of communication for the French colonies in Côte d'Ivoire and Dahomey. Chanoine accordingly marched to the Kulpawn upriver from Yagaba and on 20 March made a treaty of protection with Sibu Napona, whom he called 'the king of Asseydou'. The identity of the 'king' is unclear, but Chanoine was near the old Palewogo in country that would have been considered, in earlier and more settled times, within the jurisdiction of the Wa Nas. Chanoine also obtained an agreement in Funsi – likewise within Wala jurisdiction – that its people would follow Amariya.[85]

Over the course of the next few weeks it became official British policy (though stemming from the Resident in Kumase rather than the Colonial Office) to recognize Babatu as the legitimate ruler of the Grunshi country, and to encourage him to regard himself as under British protection. The French continued to claim that same country by virtue of their treaty with Amariya. By an agreement of 22 April between the British Resident in Kumase and the French Resident in Leo, a provisional line of demarcation between their spheres of interest was drawn. It used the confluence of the Kulpawn and the White Volta to confine the British (and Babatu) south and west of that point, and the French north and east.[86] Shortly after, under the British flag, Babatu moved from Yagaba (on the British side of the line) through Sibu Napona's country (on the French side), and so into the Chakalle districts of Wala. The countryside was devastated.[87] Babatu may have thought that the British would see his action as in their interests. They did not, and under French pressure agreed to pay reparations to the affected villagers. Some idea of the scale of the depredations is conveyed by the claims made by Ducie, a Chakalle town in the Busa division of Wala. The loss of 509 men (both free and slave), of 124 cows, and 100 sheep was reported. The British and French adjudicators admitted 400 men valued at 40,000 francs,

100 cows at 5,000 francs, and 80 sheep at 400 francs. Including sundry other items, the total claim of 54,605 francs was allowed.[88]

The Zabarima occupation of Ducie occurred probably early in May 1897. The French Resident in Leo, Hugot, received a letter (which has not been found) from those he described as 'the Almamys of the country of Wa'. They asked for French protection. Hugot replied on 22 May to the effect that the 'Almamys of Wa' are said to have recognized the English as their masters; if this was not so, they should inform both the English and French of the fact. Hugot, however, was encouraged to advance towards Wa, knowing that the British had been forced to evacuate it. The response to his letter, of which a French translation of the Arabic is extant, reached him at Funsi. It came from Wa Na Saidu Takora. It was dated 28 Dhu 'l-Hijja, that is, 30 May, but unfortunately lacks the name of the writer. In it the Wa Na is styled both *sultan* and *amir*. He complained that his country was surrounded by many enemies; 'the soldiers of Samori are before me, those of Babatu behind. I am immobile.' He asked that the French defend him against all his enemies and recover his territory from their hands. It was, he said, a lie that he was under the British; indeed, Samori (that is, Sarankye Mori) had taken away both the British flag and treaty and he only had the French one now.

On 3 June Hugot sent a letter from Funsi to the Commandant of the Niger-Volta region, saying that he considered Wa under French protection with immediate effect.[89] Wa Na Saidu Takora had apparently not yet returned to his capital; his own testimony indicated that he had recently moved from Dasima to the divisional town of Busa.[90] The identity of the 'Almamys' who must have been with him will be left unresolved for the present. One of them, to judge from the translation of the Wa Na's letter, had a very respectable command of Arabic.

On 6 June Hugot drove Babatu out of Ducie, and on 12 June he signed a treaty of protection with Wa Na Saidu Takora at Busa.[91] He clearly found pleasure in keeping the British, still discomposed by the retreat from Wa, informed of his progress.[92] Displaying political acumen, Hugot decided that the Wa Na should be obliged to return to his capital. He was escorted there by two *tirailleurs*, who took up residence with him in the palace.[93] The size of the French 'garrison' testifies eloquently to the fact that Wa had become, for the Europeans involved in the scramble for empire, a token. Abandoned by most of its inhabitants, it was certainly no longer that thriving town whose commodity traders could profit the local economy by managing the demands of an occupying power – whether Zabarima, Samorian, British or French.

On 15 September 1897 Governor Maxwell of the Gold Coast ordered a British force to reoccupy Wa. On 19 October Captain D. Mackworth entered the town; he was accompanied by Assistant Inspector Leland, a surgeon, an African officer, fifty soldiers and ten Grunshi recruits. The column had one maxim gun and one rocket trough, but only £4 in cash, the remainder having been stolen.[94] On 29 November reinforcements under Major C. Jenkinson arrived. At this time the French garrison had also been augmented, and the

Wa Na was living in his palace with two of its corporals and four of its privates.[95]

Jenkinson met with the Wala authorities. He reported that they agreed, not surprisingly, 'to try as soon as possible to restore Wa to its former position of a great central market for traders from the 4 points of the compass'. He decided that the first step in accomplishing this grand design was to remove the Wa Na from French supervision. Saidu Takora was virtually kidnapped and taken into the British fort. The French protested, arguing that an international Court of Arbitration had the status of Wa under review, and the Wa Na (whom they sometimes called the 'Almamy of Wa') should be released pending its findings.[96] Such matters of high politics appear to have been of little concern to Lieutenant-Colonel H. P. Northcott, British Commissioner and Commandant of the Northern Territories, who arrived in Wa in December.

Northcott peremptorily had the French garrison escorted out of Wa. The French higher command moved into Wa a larger force, consisting of an officer and 30 *tirailleurs*. Northcott requested permission from the Governor of the Gold Coast to drive them out. It was refused, since the status of Wa was still *sub judice*. Northcott reluctantly informed the French garrison commander that he might stay in Wa but without prejudice to the 'absolute rights of sovereignty' of the British. These events occurred between December 1897 and February 1898. As Kanya-Forstner remarked, 'an armed clash seemed almost inevitable'.[97] Northcott's belligerent posture towards the French, however, was but one aspect of his policy; he was also actively consolidating British influence over the Wala authorities.

On 29 December 1897 Northcott held a meeting with Friday Limam 'Uthman Dabila and Yeri Na 'Umar Kulendi ('Asumana and Kulendi, the two chief priests') and the incumbents of thirteen skins ('the principal Chiefs'), of whom Busa Na was the senior. Neither the Wa Na nor the Wa Limam was present. The fifteen notables assured Northcott of their loyalty to the British treaty and claimed that 'whatever the King and the people of Wa did for the French was done out of fear of them, as they were killing people all round'. The next day the same body reassembled, though this time Wa Na Saidu Takora was also present. Northcott accused the Na of treason for 'having intrigued with Samory, and the French'; informed him that the penalty for treason was death; and commuted the punishment to a fine of £200 ('in cash or in kind') payable within two weeks, under threat of banishment.[98] On 31 December, somewhat inconsistently, Northcott obliged Saidu Takora to make a statement, sworn on the Qur'an, that he had never invited the French to Wa, that he had signed no treaty with them, and that he had been brought from Busa to Wa as a prisoner of the French. The statement was witnessed by Northcott, Leland and a Limam, clearly 'Uthman Dabila.[99]

By the beginning of 1898 the Dondoli faction of Limamyiri appears to have had little influence on a new style of Wala politics aligned towards collaboration with the British. Wa Na Saidu Takora had also lost any authority he might have retained during the last tumultuous year. In June 1898 it was reported that he 'is hated by his people... [who] look upon him as the cause of all their troubles'. The Busa Na was popularly favoured for the Nam.[100] The end of the crisis was in sight. By the Anglo-French Convention of 14 June 1898 the British secured Wala.[101] In September Northcott ordered Major H. S. Walker, commanding the Black Volta military district, to remove Wa Na Saidu Takora from office for having failed to pay the fine imposed on him six months earlier. The Busa Na Momori Tangile, a son of Wa Na Pelpuo II, was chosen as successor and formally installed on 28 September 1898. The British approved the choice and presented him with a velvet cloth and a Dane gun. They laid on, moreover, 'an official programme of sports and entertainment'.[102] Truly a new era had dawned in the affairs of Wa.

Factional responses to changing situations: a review

Any attempt to understand Wala responses to the succession of later-nineteenth-century intruders – Zabarima, Samorians, British and French – must avoid the use of hindsight. In the mid 1890s there was little reason for the Wala to think that the British would ultimately emerge as the sovereign power. Indeed, throughout most of 1896 and in early 1897 the future of Wala must have appeared to lie in its association with the Samorian state. Yet the last of the Samorian *sofas* left Wa no later than May 1897. After being driven from Ducie the next month, the Zabarima moved eastwards and their involvement in Wala affairs was at an end. The French finally relinquished their interest in Wa in June 1898. The British were not to relinquish theirs until 1957.

Within the Samorian state, the authority of Sarankye Mori was second only to that of Samori Turay himself. He commanded the largest of the Almami's armies. His occupation of Wa in May 1896 was part of a grander design: that of extending the Samorian system into lands east of the Black Volta. When Sarankye Mori established his military headquarters at Sankana it seemed that Wa was to become not so much an outpost of the Samorian state but rather the civil capital of its trans-Volta territories. The plan to garrison the Dagaaba country pointed the way ahead.

There is no hint in the sources that Sarankye Mori met with opposition when he entered Wa. It was undoubtedly known that Samori Turay enjoyed the support of the prestigious *'ulama'* of Kong, who had used the network of their students to press other communities to cooperate with the Almami.[103] The Wa Na had cause for apprehension, granted the circumstances in which he had gained the skin. He was, however, a Muslim, though certainly not one of learning. Wisely, he left the conduct of negotiations with Sarankye Mori to those better versed in the appropriate procedures. The mission to Bole was led by Muhammad b. 'Uthman Dun of Dondoli, who became a leading supporter of the Samorian regime. So, too, did another member of the mission, Adama Nabiri, head of the Dzangbeyiri section of Wa. We have seen that the Friday Limam, 'Uthman Dabila, is noticeably absent from the record in this period.

Wala responses to the Samorian intrusion were presumably dictated by the expectations that different constituencies had about how they would fare within the new system. What these were is now a matter of speculation. The old polity, it may be thought, would probably have survived as a relatively autonomous unit under the overarching authority of the Almami, but the pluralistic system of traditional authority could scarcely have remained undisturbed. Of the three possessors of *nalun* the Yeri Na, as head of the Muslims, might well have enjoyed an increase in status *vis-à-vis* the Wa Na and the Wa Widana. *Nalun*, however, was secular authority, and there can be little doubt that those who possessed a relevant spiritual authority – that is, the limams – would have emerged as effective leaders of the polity. Conversion on a major scale, and a massive expansion of Muslim education, must surely have occurred. In the event, such changes were not to be put to the test. By late 1896 Samori Turay had recognized that the drive to expand east of the Black Volta could not be sustained in the face of French and British activities in the region. The military occupation of Asante by the British had, moreover, precluded the possibility of an alliance in that quarter. The Almami was obliged by political realities to attempt to consolidate his position in Jimini at the expense of his expansionist ambitions. At best Wa might, in such changed circumstances, have remained a distant outpost of empire.

The transfer of Sarankye Mori's headquarters from Sankana to Buna was an event more traumatic for the Wala than his appearance there eight months earlier. His final raids on the Dagaaba undid any progress that had been made towards their pacification, and his efforts to secure the integration of the Zabarima into his army ended in failure. Malam Abu described the situation in late 1896 very succinctly: 'the Wala and the son of Samori had made an oath, and had failed'. The desertion of the Wala contingent from Sarankye Mori's army set a seal upon that failure.

The treaty with the British of 9 January 1897 was, from a Wala perspective, something of a coup. The moving force behind it was the Dzedzedeyiri faction headed by Friday Limam 'Uthman Dabila. Adama Nabiri of Dzagbeyiri defected from the pro-Samorian ranks and was among those who subscribed to it. At the time, however, 'Ali Wangara still resided in Dondoli as representative of Samori Turay. The Dondoli faction, it seems, continued to recognize the Almami's authority, and accordingly refused to subscribe to the treaty. The Wala could have been in no doubt that their situation had changed radically. The treaty, whatever its long-term consequences were to be, had the immediate effect of creating insecurity. Events in Buna had demonstrated the severity with which Sarankye Mori punished those considered guilty of treachery and betrayal. Predictably, Wa was abandoned by its people in April 1897 when Sarankye Mori once again approached it.

There was perhaps an element of panic in the Wala reaction to Sarankye Mori's return. There were certainly some who thought so. Al-Hajj Muhammad Shifa recollected that Wala refugees, approaching Busa,

> asked themselves why they were escaping since Samory [that is, Sarankye Mori] had not fought them. They sent back five men with five horses to find out if Samory did intend to fight them. When these men met Samory, he and his men became so wild, that the five men turned in panic to inform the other Walas that he did intend to fight them. In turning, one of the horses hit an anthill and fell, and Samory's men caught the rider.[104]

The time for a rapprochement between Sarankye Mori and the Wala had clearly passed. Those who mistakenly thought otherwise could only have been those who had not themselves betrayed him: that is, the adherents of the Dondoli faction. Discretion had, nevertheless, led them to join the general exodus from the town. One of them was Sarankye Mori's esteemed collaborator, Muhammad b. 'Uthman Dun. He became, according to his son, 'very worried', and left Wa for Nandaw (where he helped build a mosque).[105]

Nandaw was only about ten miles from Dasima, where Wa Na Saidu Takora took refuge. In the middle of April 1897 a message reached Sarankye Mori in Buna, asking that 'Ali Wangara be posted back to Wa.[106] It was believed to have come from the Wa Na. If it did, he must surely have been acting under the influence of the Dondoli faction and perhaps specifically of Muhammad b. 'Uthman Dun. Whatever the case, it was the last known communication between any section of the Wala and the Samorian commander. Apparently it met with no response, and the last of the *sofas* were withdrawn from Wa shortly after. The Samorian factor in Wala politics no longer existed.

To judge from the extant record, the Dzedzedeyiri faction re-emerged as a force in Wa affairs only in late 1896. On 27 December Ishaq b. 'Uthman Dabila persuaded Wa Na Saidu, as we have seen, to appear before Sarankye Mori when the latter was about to leave the town, thereby helping to avert trouble in a situation of much tension. Only thirteen days later Friday Limam 'Uthman Dabila himself signed the treaty with the British. The pro-British stance of the Dzedzedeyiri was unambiguous from this point in time onwards. In the Hausa text, AZWS, Ishaq b. 'Uthman Dabila gave an account of a meeting held on the occasion of the return of Wa Na Saidu Takora from Busa to Wa in the middle of June 1897, under French escort:

Sarkin Wa sunansa Saidu shi ya yi shiru. Ya ce, ina bin Faranshi. Ni Malam Ishaqa na tara Musulmi duka, da sarakuna duka, da arna duka. Mu duka mu ce, mu bamu	The Wa Na Saidu kept silent. He said, 'I follow the French.' I, Malam Ishaq, assembled all the Muslims, and all the Nabihi, and all the unbelievers. We all said,

bin Faranshi, mu bamu san Far-	'We do not follow the French, we
anshi ba. Mun san Ingilizi fari.	do not know the French. We
Muna bin Ingilizi bamu bin Far-	knew the English first. We are
anshi. Amma Ingilizi basu samu	following the English, not the
gari. Haba wurin ga duka ina tafi	French. But the English do not
muna bisu.	have the town. However, wher-
	ever [they] go, we shall follow
	them.'

The English version of this text has much the same sense:[107]

> The French people returned and occupied Wa by entering into a bond with the then Chief whose name was Seidu. Both Abudulai and I Mallam Isaka gathered all the Mohammedans, all the Chiefs and townspeople and said we would not follow the French. We preferred English to French, because Ferguson and one whiteman had been here before and we knew the English fashion. We again said if English could not get Wa we would follow them to where ever they would go.

In the middle of 1897, then, there were Wala leaders who could threaten to move their followers into British protected territory, should the French consolidate their position in Wa. Ishaq b. 'Uthman Dabila of Dzedzedeyiri was clearly the moving force; there will be occasion to refer to his associate Abdulai, that is, 'Abdallah b. Idris of Pontomporeyiri, later. The episode is probably to be taken as a reflection of the weakness rather than strength of the Dzedzedeyiri faction at the time.

The pro-French stance of Wa Na Saidu Takora had been formulated while he was still in exile. It was the work of those described, we have seen, as 'the Almamys of the country of Wa', who wrote to Leo in early May 1897 asking for French protection. One of their number must also have penned the Wa Na's letter of 30 May to the same effect. The 'Almamys' clearly had authority with the Wa Na, and there can be very little doubt that their senior was the Wa Limam, probably by this time Ibrahim, brother of 'Uthman Dun. Indeed, it may be suspected that Hugot's phrase, 'les Almamys du pays de Oua', was culled from the appearance in the letter of the description of its author as *al-imam al-balad Wa*, that is, Wa Limam. Whatever the case, it seems that the Dondoli faction, no longer able to hope for a restoration of the Samorian *status quo ante* and with its options restricted by Dzedzedeyiri partiality for the British, had turned to the French for support. If this reconstruction is correct, then in the middle of 1897 the position of the Dzedzedeyiri faction was indeed weak. The Wa Na had returned from exile committed to a pro-French policy, the French had established a modest presence in Wa, and the British were still smarting from their ignominious evacuation of the town. Dzedzedeyiri leaders contemplated the drastic option of resettlement elsewhere.

In the event the British did reoccupy Wa, though the French were not immediately to abandon it. The Dzedzedeyiri were quick to take advantage

Table 6.1 *Wala factions, second half*
of the nineteenth century

	Factions	
Factors	Dondoli	Dzedzedeyiri
Zabarima	anti	pro
Samorian	pro	anti
British	anti	pro
French	pro	anti

of the changed situation. Towards the end of 1897, Friday Limam 'Uthman Dabila was instrumental in providing Northcott with a clearer title to Wa than had hitherto been available to the British: he was witness to Wa Na Saidu's useful though highly tendentious declaration that he had not treated with Hugot. Again, the Wa Limam took no part in the proceedings. Finally, France relinquished any claims to Wa in the middle of 1898. Although the commissioners who drew up the international agreement would not have known it, they had thereby ordained the ascendancy of the Dzedzedeyiri faction, and the eclipse of the Dondoli, in Wa politics.

The quality rather than the quantity of the data makes any very sophisticated reconstruction of factionalism in Wa in the second half of the nineteenth century quite inappropriate. Analysis can be no more refined than the data that supports it. At best a number of hypotheses – and no more than that – can be offered. Table 6.1 does not presuppose the existence of Muslim factions in Wa politics in the later nineteenth century. It is intended, rather, to suggest their presence from the sytematically opposed responses to four 'factors'. The utility of the approach will become increasingly apparent as Wala affairs in the twentieth century are reviewed in chapter 7.

The concerns central to 'traditional' politics in Wala were land (that is, arable and pasture) and women (that is, wives), both essential to the reproduction of the community. Which community was the issue. It has been argued that the non-reciprocated recruitment of Tendaanba wives by the Nabihi and *'ulama'* facilitated the transfer of land from the Tendaanba to the Nabihi and *'ulama'*. It has also been argued that the conflict between Tendaanba and Nabihi, at one level, was manifested at another level within the princely class itself; that is, between the Na Kpasa gate to the Nam on the one hand, which claimed that its *nalun* derived from Widana and the Tendaanba, and the Busa, Pirisi and Sing gates on the other, which claimed that their *nalun* was derived from that of Mampurugu. 'Traditional' political ideologies were deeply rooted, it should by now be apparent, in the historic social formation of Wala. Fikry has compiled many pertinent texts.[108] The relationship between *tendaanlun* and *nalun* is central to the matter; in terms familiar in a late-twentieth-century global context, it is the relationship between feeding the community and defending it. And, also familiar in the late twentieth century, religion played a powerful role in nineteenth-century Wala affairs but a role that is most resistant to satisfactory analysis; it impinged upon those who fed the community and upon those who defended it. It was hegemonic in its influence.

In the second half of the nineteenth century a new politics emerged. The concerns fundamental to the new politics were market ones: most importantly, of realizing profits through buying and selling captives and provisioning armies. The Karantaw *jihad* in the middle of the nineteenth century was catalytic; the intrusion of the Zabarima was decisive. Reproduction of the community ceased to be primarily a matter of land and women, and became increasingly one of managing the market. The community in question was unambiguously the Muslim one. It did not, however, function homogeneously in the circumstances of the times. The new politics bred factionalism. In particular, the matter of the status of unbelievers set apart those who adhered to an older and conservative Suwarian tradition, the Dondoli faction, from those who were influenced by militant reformist doctrines, the Dzedzedeyiri faction. At one level the authority of the Friday Limam *vis-à-vis* that of the Wa Limam was at stake, at another level the relationship of the Wala *umma* to the wider Wala community. Yet there was an element of futility, almost of farce, in the situation. Both factions had to recognize that the old Wala 'world' had irretrievably vanished; that the future lay in some manner of association with a protecting power, be it the Zabarima, the British, the French or the Samorians. The options exercised the ingenuity of the leaders of the factional interests, but their decisions had to be made in circumstances over which they had virtually no control and about which they had singularly little information.

Dondoli support for Almami Samori Turay and Dzedzedeyiri support for the British were not, and could not have been, based upon judicious calculations as to which power was likely to emerge supreme in the region. More to the point, the support of either was unlikely in the long run to effect the outcome of events. That it turned out that the Dondoli had supported the losers, and the Dzedzedeyiri the winners, was little more than a matter of chance in the Wala context. Both had necessarily had to gamble. Yet it was precisely the emergence of faction that enabled the Wala to respond flexibly to the rapid succession of changes in the wider regional environment. Faction, however, did not wither away with the imposition of British colonial administration. It was rooted too deeply in the structures of Wala society. In the twentieth century it was to assume new and unexpected forms. No one in the late nineteenth century, notwithstanding the penchant for prediction, could have foreseen that a century later the division between Dondoli and Dzedzedeyiri factions would have become that between orthodox and Ahmadiyya Muslims.

7

'Direct rule': Wala in the
early twentieth century

Introduction

Wala came definitively within the British sphere of influence as a result of the Anglo-French Convention of 14 June 1898. The Wala probably had no sense of the portents of this event until, three months later, the British removed Wa Na Saidu Takora from office and presided over the installation of Momori Tangile in his place. Almost three decades later, the son of Momori Tangile, Wa Na Pelpuo III, addressed a letter in Arabic to George V of England. 'The Christians', he wrote, 'came into the [Wa] tribe peacefully. We entered into an association with them. We did not enter as slaves, as we had submitted to Babatu and Samori. Then good fortune came to us.'[1] It is unlikely that any section of Wala opinion in 1898 would have viewed what was happening in quite those terms. Even to their Dzedzedeyiri collaborators the British must have appeared just the most recent in a line of intruders that extended through Babatu, Sarankye Mori and the French. Not since Saliya and his warband had established themselves in Wala some two centuries earlier had any intruder entered Wa – and stayed.

The British saw things otherwise. They had drawn up treaties of protection with a plethora of societies in the Asante hinterland, ranging from relatively powerful states, such as Dagomba, on the one hand to little more than clusters of villages on the other. They had done so primarily to prevent other rival powers from consolidating positions on the trade routes radiating northwards from the Asante capital. By 1898 Asante had been under British military occupation for two years. Its wealth made it a highly desirable addition to empire. Neither the Colonial Office in London nor the Government of the Gold Coast, however, had any clear policy for administering the vast hinterland of Asante, which had conveniently been labelled the 'Northern Territories'. The whole area was virtually unmapped and its ethnography virtually unknown. It was left to the military officers in the field to devise a system of authority that would convert a region under a *de facto* occupation into a *de jure* appendage of the Gold Coast Colony.

H. P. Northcott was appointed Commissioner and Commandant of the Northern Territories in October 1897.[2] His programme for consolidating

British rule in the region had three distinct but related aspects: pacification of the countryside, the imposition of tribute, and the regulation of long-distance trade. These had been the aims of the Samorians and no doubt of the French. The Wala could scarcely have viewed them as representing any radical change in their circumstances.

The imposition of the *Pax Britannica*

The British inherited from their predecessors in Wala, the Zabarima and Samorian commanders, the problem of the Dagaaba. Its history was known to them in broad outline. The Dagaaba had rejected Wala authority, probably some time in the 1870s. Two attempts had been made by Wa Nas to recover that authority, the first with the assistance of Babatu and the second with that of Sarankye Mori. Neither succeeded and relations between the Dagaaba towns and Wa deteriorated further.[3] The essentials of the story as the British understood it are correct, but did not reveal the extent to which the matter of Dagaaba had come to dominate the internal politics of Wa in the period. We have seen, for example, that Wa Na Saidu Takora relied upon Dagaaba support in obtaining the *nam*. We have also suggested that the correct attitude towards unbelievers, and therefore towards the Dagaaba, was one that much exercised and divided the *'ulama'* of Wa.

Commissioner Northcott produced Treaties of Protection with Kaleo on 10 December 1897 and with Issa, Busie, Wogu and Nadawli between 9 and 11 January 1898.[4] Dougah has some account of the circumstances in which the treaty with Kaleo (including Charia, Jan and Sankana) was obtained. Assistant-Inspector Leland sent a certain Kunchuri to the Kaleo district. Kunchuri had a reputation as a warrior. He was also known as Mama Dagarti. He is likely to have been a Dagaaba who had fought in the ranks of the Zabarima or Samorian *sofas* and who had perhaps converted to Islam. Kunchuri informed the Kaleo of the British wish for a treaty. Basse of Kaleo led the opposition to any such idea, and prepared to fight. He mustered 7,000 men. Leland averted hostilities by 'buying' the treaty; he offered each elder prepared to subscribe to it a lavish gift of 30s, a sheep, a silk cloth and a bag of salt.[5] Taking a lesson from this episode, and from what he knew of Sarankye Mori's difficulties in campaigning in the Dagaaba country, Northcott probably obtained the treaties with the other Dagaaba villages in a similar fashion the following month. There is no doubt whatsoever that these treaties were hastily drawn up, with the immediate intention of forestalling any French initiative in the region. The pacification of the Dagaaba was to prove a much longer process, and extended through the first decade of the twentieth century.[6] It was one in which the British relied heavily on the cooperation of Wa *'ulama'*.

Al-Hajj Abu Maidoku, who was born in 1887, gave an interesting account of what he referred to as 'taming the Dagartis':[7]

Sankana, Kaleo, Chere [Charia], Jan, Nadawli, and other places, the people from these places used to come into Wa town at night with bows and arrows. They would drive out sheep and goats from the compounds. If you tried to stop them, they would shoot you. Malam Ishaq and my father, 'Abdallah, were organized by the District Commissioner to try to calm these Dagartis and make the district quiet. When the Dagartis saw a white man, they used to flee into the bush. Then Malam Ishaq and 'Abdallah went to Kaleo and told the chief that he should come to Wa and greet the District Commissioner. They gave the Kaleo chief sugar and salt, and this made him very happy. He had never tasted sugar, and for salt they had used the ash of a burnt tree. So the Kaleo chief told his people that the white men were good. Then 'Abdallah went to Jan and convinced the people there. And so Malam Ishaq and 'Abdallah slowly conquered all the Dagartis. Then the District Commissioner started calling the Dagartis in for the local dances, and each time he gave them presents. Then, when they were tame, the District Commissioner told my father to tell the Dagartis to bring children to Wa for education. My father sent a son to school, and so did Malam Ishaq. My father would leave Wa for a month or so, going from village to village and taming the Dagartis.

Whether Friday Limam 'Uthman Dabila was alive at this time is unknown. Clearly, however, his son Ishaq ('Malam Ishaq') had become a leading figure in Dzedzedeyiri affairs by 1898. His associate was 'Abdallah b. Idris, father of the informant, who belonged to Pontomporeyiri in Wa Limamyiri.[8]

Al-Hajj Abu's recollections of the activities of Ishaq and 'Abdallah in the Dagaaba country were seemingly not exaggerated by filial piety. Three decades later their role was still well remembered; they helped the Government a lot after the occupation, the Chief Commissioner of the Northern Territories noted in 1929, and had once averted a Dagarti uprising.[9] The picture of a slow but peaceful pacification of the Dagaaba, accomplished through the good offices of Wa Muslims, is nevertheless a partial one. Force was readily used whenever necessary. In the middle of 1899 three freebooters were operating out of the Dagaaba village of Ulu, forty-five miles north of Wa. Two were Grunshi and one Dagaaba. All were Muslims. They were doubtless former recruits to the Zabarima ranks. A punitive expedition of some sixty-five men was sent out from Wa. It was equipped with a maxim gun and a seven-pounder. Twenty of the people of Ulu were killed and twelve wounded. The booty brought back to Wa comprised 128 loads of grain, 61 sheep, 16 goats, 13 horses, 9 donkeys, 9 cows, 3 calves, 7 loads of cowries, a load of cotton thread, 7 saddles, 20 guns, 2 kegs of gunpowder and 2 swords. 'The moral effect of this expedition on the various towns of Dagata', its commander was able to report, 'has been excellent, all those near by have sent in messengers and runners, and tender their submission, and promise not to interfere with traders passing through their country any more.'[10] Subsequent expeditions were not reported so openly, but as late as 1907 the Governor of the Gold Coast could note that 'the pacification and development of the Lobi-Dagarti country, formerly the scene of numerous punitive expeditions, are very satisfactory'.[11]

In February 1899, Northcott toured the Black Volta District, which had been drawn up to include the Wa, Dagarti, Grunshi and Bole Sub-Districts, with district headquarters at Wa. He explained to the people, as he put it, 'the advantages flowing from our rule' and then announced that an annual tribute would be levied towards the costs of that rule. He recognized that the taxable capacity of the region was low. This he attributed to the 'rapacity' of Babatu, Samori and the French, and to the failure of the crops in 1898. The first collection was to be made on 1 January 1900, when the Grunshi Sub-District was to pay £200, and the Dagarti, Wa and Bole Sub-Districts £100 each. These sums would later be increased.[12]

Such relatively paltry amounts could not significantly have contributed to the costs of the military administration, and fiscal matters were not in fact Northcott's principal consideration in initiating the tribute. In the middle of 1899 he made lucidly clear his view of the crucial connection between authority and tribute:[13]

> The essence of easy rule over natives of West Africa is the existence of some convincing proof of paramountcy. This is displayed by the native rulers in various forms, but the only one of these that does not conflict with public opinion as known in Great Britain is the exaction of tribute. It was accordingly decided to levy a direct tax on the inhabitants of the whole country.

The attempt to impose a tribute in fact proved unsuccessful. Northcott saw no alternative to making local chiefs responsible for its collection. It would, however, be explained to the people that the tribute was 'the substitution of a regular tax for the heavy and casual requisitions of their former lords'.[14] Northcott did not live to see even the first collection. Major A. H. Morris succeeded him in late 1899. His immediate reaction was to regard the collection of tribute – soon more euphemistically labelled a 'Maintenance Tax' – as impracticable and as already giving rise to local unrest.[15] By the middle of 1901 Morris had changed his mind about the matter. He had, it seems, come to share his predecessor's view of the relationship of tribute to authority. 'I was rather premature in coming to the conclusion that it should be done away with', he informed the Governor of the Gold Coast; 'It has been the custom of the country for a great many years to pay taxes, either in kind or money, to their head Chief, which appointment we are now filling, so that, consequently this tax should be paid to us.'[16]

The Governor was unconvinced, and required further information.[17] In reply Morris agreed that only in the larger kingdoms had regular tributes earlier been paid, but that such peoples as the Dagarti and Grunshi, having 'no central form of Government', did not know 'the custom of paying a regular recurring impost'. He acknowledged also that 'the raising of this tax does afford the Chiefs a pretext for, and means of, extorting money from their people, on the grounds that it is required by His Majesty's Government'. He recommended abolition of the tribute but that more 'free labour' should be required from the people.[18] The tax was levied only at the

Table 7.1 *Livestock taxed, Wa and Bole Stations, 1902–5*

Commodity	Rate of tax	1902	1903	1904	1905
Horses	5s	38	29	57	24
Cattle	3s	4,284	3,838	4,913	3,219
Calves	1s 6d	46	32	28	12
Donkeys	2s	2,871	1,354	2,919	1,605
Sheep/goats	6d	21,703	19,981	27,686	24,110
Lambs/kids	3d	231	344	100	169
Ostrich	?	—	9	—	—
Tax raised (ostriches omitted)		£1,488 2s 3d	£1,224 11s 6d	£1,738 12s 0d	£1,255 2s 3d

beginning of 1900 and 1901. From the whole of the Northern Territories it yielded less than £1,000 on each occasion, and seemed incapable of further significant increase, granted the level of agricultural production.

Much more successful was the imposition of a caravan tax. In purely fiscal rather than political terms, Northcott himself had recognized that commerce rather than production was the realistic basis for raising revenue, and that in earlier times it was the trader rather than the peasant farmer who had the surplus that could be appropriated. In late 1897 the Wala authorities had agreed, we have seen, 'to try as soon as possible to restore Wa to its former position of a great central market for traders from the 4 points of the compass'.[19] Throughout the Northern Territories, Northcott took over the right to levy tolls on traders from whomsoever might previously have exercised it. He then offered military escorts to the larger caravans.

At his headquarters in Mampurugu Northcott consulted the 'High Priest' of Gambaga – 'the accepted representative of the traders' – about the matter of tariffs. Tax, it was decided, should be levied on all livestock and other commodities intended for sale or barter at the rate of 5s per horse, 3s per head of cattle, 2s per donkey, 6d per sheep or goat, 2s per carrier load of merchandise and 4s per donkey-load of merchandise. The taxes were to be collected at stations set up on the roads and receipts given, so that no caravan should be taxed twice while it was within British territory.[20] The Governor of the Gold Coast, F. M. Hodgson, transformed Northcott's measures into a policy directive:[21]

> I would not at present spend upon the Northern Territories – upon in fact the hinterland of the Colony – a single penny more than is absolutely necessary for their suitable administration and the encouragement of the transit trade.

The main channel of trade in the Black Volta District remained the route that ran from Kintampo northwards through Bole to Wa and beyond. Stations for the collection of tax were set up in all three towns. The lucrative commerce in slaves and firearms had been suppressed by the British. Otherwise the content of trade probably differed little from that of the period

Table 7.2 *Merchandise taxed, Kintampo, Wa and Bole Stations, 1902–5*

Merchandise	Loads: 1902		Loads: 1903		Loads: 1904		Loads: 1905	
	Kintampo	Wa/Bole	Kintampo	Wa/Bole	Kintampo	Wa/Bole	Kintampo	Wa/Bole
Kola nuts	12,939	666	15,821	262	12,199	82	13,951	79
Cloth	1,417	191	1,255	299	1,380	233	989	374
Beads	371	8	281	15	259	6	119	3
Salt	389	354	404	612	443	293	574	375
Shea butter	—	—	263	81	277	57	790	291
Dawadawa	—	—	104	1,193	197	1,395	231	1,917
Miscellaneous	4,318	597	227	514	369	565	408	597
Total Loads	19,434	1,816	18,355	2,976	15,124	2,631	17,062	3,636

before the occupation. The major commodity moving southwards was livestock destined for the markets of Asante and the Gold Coast. Table 7.1 shows the number of animals on which tax was levied at Wa and Bole.[22] There are unfortunately no separate returns extant for the two stations. The amount of livestock passing through Bole from Buna in French-occupied territory, and not therefore already taxed in Wa, was probably quite low.[23] Indeed, the Bole station was only intermittently staffed. When closed, the tax on any livestock driven through Bole from Buna was levied at Kintampo. There is, then, good reason to believe that the greater part of the livestock shown as taxed in Wa or Bole was in fact taxed at the former.

Table 7.2 shows tax raised on other forms of merchandise. The principal commodity moving northwards was kola. That passing through Kintampo was taxed there and it is impossible to estimate what proportion of it was then moved through Bole and Wa. Merchandise actually taxed in Bole and Wa had presumably not arrived there through Kintampo but through other lesser markets. Kola was taxed at 3s the carrier-load, donkeys being regarded as carrying two loads. Other merchandise was taxed at 2s a load. The movement of cloth and beads was predominantly into the north. The salt taxed in Kintampo originated from the lagoons at the mouth of the Volta or was imported through the Gold Coast ports; that taxed in Wa and Bole may have been in part of Saharan or local Daboya origin. Shea butter and *dawadawa* (included in the 'miscellaneous' category in the statistics for 1902) were northern products destined for Asante and Gold Coast markets. The miscellaneous category includes a variety of merchandise. Some commodities, like brass rods, were clearly moving northwards. Most, however, appear to have been destined for southern markets: for example, small quantities of onions, 'native' hoes, and ivory.

Table 7.3 shows the total caravan tax raised in the Northern Territories as a whole, and at the Kintampo and Black Volta (that is, Wa and Bole) Stations. The colonial administrators took the view that the caravan tax was a light imposition, and contrasted their experience with that of the French

Table 7.3 *Caravan tax, 1902–5 (to nearest £)*

	Northern Territories	Kintampo	Wa/Bole
1902	£ 6,279	£2,907	£1,703
1903	£ 8,903	£3,231	£1,565
1904	£10,084	£3,137	£2,055
1905	£11,136	£3,459	£1,906

who had persisted in levying a tribute, or maintenance tax, on the peoples west of the Black Volta:

> The French collect revenue from villages by a maintenance tax, but most of the people from whom it is collected, living away from any daily contact with the advantages of European rule, fail to distinguish between the present methods of removing their wealth (the tax has usually to be collected in cattle) and those of Samory and Barbatu, and force continually has to be resorted to.[24]

There can be little doubt that the British were wise to let the burden of taxation fall upon the relatively wealthy trader rather than the impoverished peasant. Their view of the matter was outlined by the Chief Commissioner of the Northern Territories in 1905:

> The heavy tolls they [the traders] were called on to pay in the old days to every chief through whose country they passed, added to the occasional loss of all stock by raiding parties, makes one wonder how trade ever flourished. Constant enquiries whilst on a recent tour elicited nothing but approval of this tax, and contentment at the present arrangement, and the increasing trade returns are the best answer to those who advocate its removal.[25]

The Chief Commissioner's view was apparently not shared by the merchants on the Gold Coast. They found their efforts to move British manufactured products into the interior increasingly hampered by competition from their German and French counterparts in Togo and Côte d'Ivoire respectively. They attributed the problem to the caravan tax, arguing that it predisposed the inland traders towards doing business at the hinterland markets of those two colonies rather than of the Gold Coast. They constituted a powerful lobby. In September 1908 the caravan tax was abolished.[26]

Table 7.3 does not indicate that there was any very significant growth of trade in the Black Volta region in the period 1902 to 1905. Once the business in captives and weapons had been suppressed, the British exercised little continuing control over production and consumption. The caravans were financed and organized by Muslim entrepreneurs. The towns at which they halted, did business and rested were those in which their co-religionists could provide them with protection and the facilities they required. To such matters the British presence was of little relevance. The officer commanding the Black Volta District made the point very succinctly in 1901. 'Wa', he reported, 'owing to its mosque etc. – attracts traders.'[27]

Ruling the Wala: the 'alim as collaborator

Momori Tangile of Busa became Wa Na on 28 September 1898. Al-Hajj Abu Maidoki recollected the occasion.[28] 'When the French left', he said,

> the English called Malam Ishaq and my father, 'Abdallah, and said that they did not like Wa Na Sa'id. We said that we didn't like him either. So Malam Ishaq and 'Abdallah went to a village, Busa-bihe, and brought an old man named Tangile to be Na. Tangile prayed. He was installed as Na. Everyone was happy, and Na Sa'id was sent to a village. Then the white men called Malam Ishaq and 'Abdallah and said, 'You are the leaders in the district. Always come and tell us when there is trouble. Tell people that there is no slave-raiding now, and that they must not seize people.' So Malam Ishaq and 'Abdallah went together in this work, and Wa became quiet. I could write, and I used to travel with my father.

Momori Tangile was, then, specifically the choice of the Dzedzedeyiri faction. There were apparently no other candidates. That Momori Tangile was a Muslim perhaps made him acceptable to the wider Muslim community. That he was a son of the much-respected Wa Na Pelpuo II, whose *floruit* we have assigned to the early 1840s, perhaps made him acceptable to the Wala generally. He was, however, also in his mid seventies, and unlikely to provide strong and vigorous leadership.[29] This may have been a key factor in his selection, the Dzedzedeyiri 'ulama' wanting a compliant Wa Na who would not challenge their ascendancy in Wala affairs. During his ten years in office Momori Tangile proved to be just that.

Muhammad b. Ya'qub succeeded his brother, 'Uthman Dabila, in the Friday limamate. He was an elderly man who appears to have played little part in secular affairs but to have carried out his spiritual duties until age obliged him to hand them over to Muhammad Zayd of Tamaramuni (page 110).[30] Throughout the first decade of the century it was Ishaq b. 'Uthman Dabila who collaborated closely with the colonial administrators and who, more than Wa Na and the limams, constantly advised and assisted them. As late as 1912, Ishaq was the only Muslim authority in Wa officially recognized by the British; he was gazetted in the Gold Coast civil service lists as its 'Mohamedan Chief'.[31] His close associate, 'Abdallah b. Idris, was appointed first Court Interpreter by the British.[32] The role that the two played in the pacification of the Dagaaba has been described. They 'worked closely with the British', I was told in 1969; 'they were the link between the British and the natives because they had the most education and were the most literate.'[33]

Literacy, albeit in Arabic, obliged the British to depend heavily on the Wa 'ulama' in the early period of the occupation, before a supply of clerks educated in English was available from the Gold Coast. The caravan tax, from its very conception, was recognized to require Muslim collectors.

Northcott envisaged appointing those he called 'Chief Traders', and mis-described as 'usually Hausa High Priests', to notify the administration of the arrival of a caravan, to ascertain its composition, and to explain and levy the tax, taking a commission of 2% of the amount collected.[34] It seems appropriate that *'ulama'* should be used in this capacity. It seems less appropriate that they should be used to collect the tribute or maintenance tax, but the fact of the matter was that they alone were able – in the capacity of 'holymen' – to travel unmolested in the turbulent rural areas. Indeed, in 1901 it was literate Muslims from Wa who were sent out to the Dagaaba and Sisala villages to conduct the first census of population in the region.[35]

The *de facto* occupation of the northern hinterland of Asante was fully legitimized by the Northern Territories Order in Council of 26 September 1901, executed by Edward VII at the Court of St James. The Governor of the Gold Coast, on behalf of the Crown, was to exercise 'all powers' in the Northern Territories through a Chief Commissioner and, in the districts, subordinate commissioners and other officers. The Governor, however, was required to

> respect any native laws by which the civil relations of any native chiefs, tribes, populations under His Majesty's protection are now regulated, except so far as the same may be incompatible with the due exercise of His Majesty's power and jurisdiction, or clearly injurious to the welfare of the said natives.

The Order in Council was given more specific content by the Northern Territories Administrative Ordinance No. 1 of 1902. It addressed, *inter alia*, the matter of older local jurisdictions. 'Native Tribunals', it decreed, 'shall exercise the jurisdiction heretofore exercised by them in the same manner as such jurisdiction has been heretofore exercised.' There were, however, important qualifications. One was that 'no Native Tribunal shall enforce any judgement or order by any barbarous or inhuman method, or in any way repugnant to natural justice'. The second was that the Chief Commissioner might remove specific matters from the jurisdiction of the Native Tribunal, either generally throughout the Northern Territories or locally with respect to particular tribunals. The Ordinance defined a number of these. Included, for example, were prisons, roads, ferries, markets and slaughter houses, the regulation and taxing of the caravans, and regulation of the celebration of 'Native Customs'.[36]

In the matter of the Native Tribunals, neither the Order in Council nor the Ordinance took much account of the real situation in the Protectorate. Lieutenant-Colonel A. E. Watherston presided over its affairs from 1905 to 1909. In 1907 he commented, 'The administration of the country under what is undoubtedly the only sound method, viz., by the natives themselves, is rendered particularly difficult for many reasons.' He remarked on the 'absence of any really big chiefs'. The only 'organised tribes' were the Mamprusi, Gonja, Wala and Dagomba, each having 'kings'. Otherwise, he continued,

> The remainder of the country, Lobis, Dagartis, Grunshis, Kussasis, were broken up in 1896 to 1898 by Samory and Barbatu; and each compound more or less is a law unto themselves. They obey no man really, though they have nominal chiefs, selected as a rule for their incapacity to make anyone obey them. Partial blindness, paralysis, and often idiocy appear to have been the qualifications in many parts of the country, the only *sine qua non* being that the chief should have plenty of cattle, for on him falls the privilege of paying any fines that the commissioner might impose on the town.[37]

It was the same Watherston who considered Islam a civilizing force, 'eminently suited to the native', generating 'a much more decent life', and conducive to trade.[38]

There was a paradox. The British might employ *'ulama'* in administrative capacities, but they could not envisage ruling through other than chiefs. The pluralistic nature of authority in Wa – with its Wa Na, Yeri Na, Widana, Limam and Friday Limam – was a phenomenon that they were unable to understand and preferred to ignore. They were particularly uneasy about the old Wala Muslim towns that had no chiefs. Early in 1901 the officer commanding the Black Volta District busied himself with the problem. the Nasa people, he reported, said that 'they were under the High Priest of Wa and that they had no proper Chief for their village. After consulting the Chiefs and people I made one "Sedu" the chief of Nasa.' Guropisi suffered a similar fate: 'I also made after consulting with the Chiefs and people of Guropisi one "Mahama" to be the chief of that town.'[39] The 'Chiefs' consulted about making a chief were presumably the existing Muslim authorities in these places.

Dzedzedeyiri support for the British was signalled by Friday Limam 'Uthman Dabila's subscription to the treaty of 9 January 1897. It was reaffirmed in the middle of that year, when his son Ishaq threatened migration into British territory should Wa fall under French dominion. 'Uthman Dabila was clearly instrumental in having Wa Na Saidu Takora removed from office. His son Ishaq was instrumental in the selection of Momori Tangile as successor. There is no reason to believe that the Dzedzedeyiri faction felt that there was any sort of religious barrier to collaboration with the British. It sought sway in Wala affairs, and used the British connection in pursuit of this goal as the Dondoli faction had earlier used the Samorian connection. By the turn of the century Ishaq b. 'Uthman Dabila was the power behind not only the Friday Limam but the Wa Na also. It may well be that he aspired to see Wala transformed into a more manifestly Islamic polity, regulated by the *'ulama'* under the Friday Limam. Whatever the case, British policy worked against any such change. The pluralist nature of authority in the old polity was indeed disturbed, but in a way that worked to the advantage of the Wa Nabihi rather than of the *'ulama'*. In the eyes of the colonial administrators the Wa Na was 'king' and the Nabihi were 'princes'; they and not the *'ulama'* were the natural rulers of the Wala.

There were practical aspects to these matters. Traditionally, the Wa Na and the Nabihi exercised the right to mobilize labour for purposes of war. They were also, we have seen, entitled to claim five days' labour on their farms from all adult males within their various jurisdictions.[40] The British decision in 1901 to abandon the tribute, or maintenance tax, was linked with the decision to require more 'free', that is, compulsory, labour from the populace.[41] Whereas the *'ulama'* had been used for the collection of tribute, the task of providing labour was thought appropriate to the chiefs. Financial considerations were involved. A chief, for example, was paid 1*d* per day for each carrier he supplied to the administration.[42] The labour market, moreover, was expanding as the goldmining industry in Asante and the Gold Coast Colony expanded. In 1905, Chief Commissioner Watherston argued that:

> The peaceful state of the country, which renders it no longer necessary for the natives to keep up large armed forces to preserve their own existence, should liberate a large number of young men, who at present lead an idle life for at least six months in the year. With the enormous population that exists in parts of this country I have great hopes of these young men forming in the near future a new source of labour for the mines at Tarkwa and Ashanti. This would bring money into the country, which is badly needed, and the chiefs recently interviewed on this matter have taken much interest in the question, and expressed themselves as very desirous of sending their young men to work.[43]

By 1907 there were about 400 men from the Northern Territories working in the mines. Most of them were from the northwest.[44] Chiefs became in time virtually labour contractors for the companies, and were to be paid 5*s* for each man on recruitment and 7*s* 6*d* on his completion of a nine-months' contract.[45] Meanwhile, with the abolition of the caravan tax in 1908, the Muslims found their usefulness to the administration still further diminished. Their role in the pacification of the rural areas was, moreover, at an end. The Dagaaba and Grunshi had come to accept not only the fact of colonial overrule but, the upheavals of the later nineteenth century fresh in memory, had been induced to accept the paramountcy of the Wa Na. In 1907 Watherston outlined the changed situation as he saw it:

> Much trouble has been taken to divide these people up into their original divisions, and to come under the paramount chiefs whom they were in the habit of obeying before Samory and Barbatu overran the country. It has been attended with great success in the North Western District, where every town has been allotted to some paramount chief with their own consent, and they now take their native disputes to the chiefs, which has considerably reduced the work that previously fell to the Commissioners' Courts.[46]

The colonial administrators were, we shall see, in time to rue the confidence they placed in chiefs. Conversely, the *'ulama'* were perhaps to doubt the wisdom of having collaborated so readily with the colonial administrators. Certainly, however, Islam remained a force to be reckoned with in Wala politics, and from the standpoint of the administrators, it was soon to prove an unpredictable one.

Mahdi Musa in Wala: the Muslims in turmoil

In his annual report for 1905, Chief Commissioner Watherston noted that 'the general sanitary condition of the towns in the Protectorate is improving, the revival and spread of Mohammedanism having much to do with this'. The following year he remarked that 'with the spread of Mahommedanism there is a growing demand for white baft, green fezzes, purple and green cloth, brass kettles, and Mahommedan prayer beads'. By 1908 he could observe:

> From reports generally it would appear that the recent spread of Mahommedanism has not been continued. In places it has remained dormant and in others a retrograde motion to the former paganism has taken place. They keep the praying places, however, in case any more missions should come, but during the year the country has been free from the Marabouts and foreign Malams.[47]

These cryptic comments were apparently all that the colonial administration wished to have known publicly of the vigorous movement, led by Malam Musa, which swept over the Northern Territories and the northern parts of Asante in 1905 and 1906.

Malam Musa was an Adamawa Fulani.[48] In 1904, with a large following, he moved westwards across the hinterlands of Dahomey and Togo, and in the dry season of 1904–5 entered the Northern Territories of the Gold Coast. By one report, his ultimate destination was Timbuktu.[49] He belonged to that central Sudanese mahdist tradition associated with the names of Rabih b. Fadl Allah, Hayatu b. Sa'id and Jibrila who, under the influence and authority of the eastern Sudanese Mahdi Muhammad Ahmad b. 'Abdallah, established their sway in Borno, Adamawa and Gombe in the late nineteenth century. The British occupation of Sokoto on 15 March 1903 set in motion an eastwards migration – hijra – of many thousands of central Sudanese Muslims. The attack on Sultan al-Tahir of Sokoto at Bormi on 27 July was intended, but failed, to stem the tide. By 1906, settlements of those referred to as 'western Mahdists' were springing up along the Blue Nile.[50] For reasons that are not clear, Malam Musa led a lesser though none the less significant movement of 'western Mahdists' in the reverse direction.[51]

Mahdi Musa appears to have travelled along the old trade road that connected Kano with the Asante capital, Kumase. He preached in the Konkomba and Bassari country; passed through Zabzugu and Yendi, and proceeded thence to Salaga.[52] In 1331 AH, AD 1912/13, Al-Hajj 'Umar b. Abi Bakr of Salaga and Krakye wrote a polemical poem accusing Musa and his followers of chicanery and fraud, and chronicling the hostility they met on their progress from town to town.[53] He named three of Mahdi Musa's subalterns, Al-Husayn, Abu Bakr and Al-Hasan, who preached in

Nanumba, in Kintampo and Nkoransa, and in Kete Krakye respectively. There were, however, others. Muhammad b. 'Uthman from Bagirmi arrived in Bonduku in May 1905, was arrested by the French, sent to Dakar and deported to Lagos in December 1905.[54] 'Umar Farako from Sokolo arrived in Buna in August 1905. He too was arrested and sent to Bingerville.[55] Goody has discussed the biases of Al-Hajj 'Umar and has used colonial records to give a more objective account of the mahdist impact in the region between Salaga and Yeji.[56]

A contemporary and graphic account of the ferment was penned by Captain L. E. O. Charlton of the West Africa Frontier Force:

> In 1905 there occurred in West Africa, and especially in Ashanti and the Gold Coast Hinterland, what may best be described as a religious revival. Emissaries, giving themselves out as from the holy cities, appeared with their disciples in many places at about the same time and commenced an active propaganda, while letters from important Mohammedans in Mecca were circulated from hand to hand. For a time the tendency of this movement seemed to be one of simple conversion of the heathen, and great success attended the efforts of its missionaries. Before long, however, what was nothing less than an anti-European agitation showed itself. Great local excitement prevailed, and the matter was brought actively before the eyes of the authorities. In some cases, notably in the Eastern districts, the Ashantis overturned their idols, and – obeying the behests of one group of emissaries, given no doubt with the object of playing on their superstitions – destroyed all their 'black' objects such as cattle, fowls, cloths, etc., and would perhaps have beggared themselves had not the authorities interfered.[57]

In a similar vein, Marty wrote of Muhammad b. 'Uthman, at the command of the Mahdi, reforming the Muslims and converting the pagans:

> A Bondoukou, la parole de cet envoyé du mahdi est puissante sur l'esprit des indigènes. Il fait des quêtes, ordonne la destruction des tam-tam, s'absorbe en de longues prières extatiques dans les mosquées, conseille la mort de tous les animaux de couleur noire, prescrit de ne se vêtir que d'étoffes blanches, et un beau jour, dépassant la mesure, invite tous les musulmans à faire aiguiser leurs sabres, car l'heure du Mahdi est proche et les Blancs vont être chassés.[58]

Marty maintained that Mahdi Musa's proselytization was particularly brutal, the whip being used to give force to the spoken work. Arnaud reported that ten marabouts were executed by him after they had found fault with the sermon he delivered at the 'Id al-kabir, 1323 (5 February 1906).[59] Surprisingly, those who still remembered Mahdi Musa in the 1960s and 1970s described his progress across the country as peaceful. He preached, converted people, and in each village either presided over the construction of a mosque or laid out stones to mark a place for prayer (Dagbane, *dzengle kuga*). His followers, the nonagenarian Friday Limam of Yendi told me in 1968, 'were not like soldiers. They did not use force. They were not Tijani.'[60] Haight's informants in the Bole area gave much the same account of the matter.[61] Whatever the truth, Mahdi Musa was clearly a preacher rather than a warrior, a revivalist rather than a conqueror.

Mahdi Musa entered Wa in June 1905. The event was reported by the administrator of the Black Volta District, B. M. Read, who apparently saw no reason for alarm:

> Towards the end of the month [June] a Mohammedan missionary arrived and asked for permission to order the King of Wa to collect his chiefs and people so that he could read them the orders of the prophet. This was granted and the result has been the conversion, at least the temporary conversion, of all the people to the Mohammedan faith, all the outlying villages having made fenced-in places of prayers that they are now using daily. Peto [grain beer] is now unobtainable in Wa and this commodity had been almost a necessity to the Dagarti in the past. The change in the town is altogether so remarkable that I consider it of sufficient interest to mention in my report.[62]

Chief Commissioner Watherston was impressed. 'A cleanliness and sobriety came over the country in two weeks', he commented, 'that years of our administration have failed to produce.'[63] Forty years later the appearance of Mahdi Musa was still vividly remembered in the Wala villages. 'Is there a mosque in Ducie?', I asked. 'Once there was', I was told; 'after the time of Babatu the Mahdi came here with many people. He came in peace. He converted everyone. We built a mosque. But then after the Mahdi left everyone stopped praying.'[64] At Nakori I was told, 'The Mahdi came ... and made everyone Muslim.'[65] The Mahdi came and stayed a year, I was informed at Chesa; 'he sent people everywhere'.[66]

By July 1905 the commandant of the Black Volta District was beginning to show concern. 'I brought in Mallam who was said to be preaching against the Government', he minuted, 'but no evidence.'[67] By May of 1906 Watherston was fully alerted to the political (rather than the sanitary) aspects of the situation. 'During my recent tour', he wrote,

> I met and had conversation with all the leading Mohammedans in the Country. I found that for the last two years a constant succession of missionaries had been arriving in the country, visiting the big centres and then taking districts when they had called together the people, expounded their doctrines, in nearly every case reported the future coming of a Mahdi who would punish all non-believers, white or black and have generally conveyed the idea that the Whiteman would be exterminated in the country.[68]

Mahdi Musa and his followers were subsequently eased out of the Wa region in particular and the Northern Territories generally. In his annual report for 1908 Watherston could comment that: 'the movement reported some three years ago appears to have died out, and very little remains of it amongst the Pagan tribes in the north'.[69] Musa's deputy, Al-Hasan, may have been the 'Alassan Moumeni' (Al-Hasan b. 'Abd al-Mu'min) who was active in the Kipirsi country, lying betwen the upper reaches of the Black Volta and Wagadugu, at the beginning of 1908.[70]

It seems not to have been the practice of Mahdi Musa and his followers to commit their sermons to writing; certainly none is known to be extant. One document that has survived from the period is an Hausa translation of a *wathiqa* purportedly brought from Mecca by a certain Al-Hajj Dawud. It is addressed to *mutanen yamma*, 'the people of the west.'[71] It has no apparant mahdist content, but seems to have been penned by a Qadiri with strong Sokoto connections. It is very traditional admonition: *ku mutanen yamma ku bi ubangiji Allah: ku tuba ku bi Allah shi ne maigirma* and so forth, 'people of the west, follow the Lord God: repent, follow God who is all-great'. The *'ulama'* of Wa could scarcely have objected to its contents. Those still strongly attached to the old Suwarian tradition, however, may be assumed to have been cynical about Mahdi Musa's drive to convert the unbelievers. If so, they were proved right; the evidence shows beyond doubt that most of the converts apostasized once the mahdists had departed.

The Wa *'ulama'* who had readily collaborated with the British may also be assumed to have viewed with concern the anti-Christian (or anti-European) aspects of the mahdist propaganda. Chief Commissioner Watherston certainly believed this to be the case. His tour of the Northern Territories in early 1906 convinced him that Salaga, with its immigrant Muslim population, might prove a centre of trouble. 'On the other hand', he remarked,

> at Wa which is a great Mohammadon centre, Walwale, and Gambaga I was told by the leading Lemam [Limam] and Malams in public that they had no use of whatsoever for these Marabouts, that they had told them when they began their seditious talk, that they had no complaints against the English ... and if the whiteman were removed it would mean the rising up of more Samorys and more Babatus and the country would run with blood.[72]

Watherson's 'leading Leman and Malams' must, in the Wa context, have been Friday Limam Muhammad b. Ya'qub and his nephew, Ishaq b. 'Uthman Dabila, who could only have seen the mahdist propaganda as a threat to the comfortable position that the Dzedzedeyiri faction enjoyed in Wala politics. Watherston thought that the *'ulama'* in such old Muslim centres as Wa were unlikely to be seduced by the mahdists, since they were all involved in trade and, in his view, 'their desire to make money is on very near top level with their religious devotion'.[73] *Prima facie*, it might be anticipated that the Dzedzedeyiri and Dondoli factions in Wa would take opposed positions with respect to Mahdi Musa as they had done with earlier intruders, Zabarima, Samorians, French and British (table 6.1). There is no more than a hint that this was so.

Ibrahim b. Muhammad of Dondoli, brother of 'Uthman Dun, still held the Wa limamate. He was a very old man and his nephew, Muhammad b. 'Uthman Dun, was effective leader of the Dondoli faction. It may be significant, then, that at the time of the mahdist intrusion Muhammad b. 'Uthman Dun chose to make a pilgrimage to Mecca. It was perhaps not his first and certainly not his last. It took him away from Wa for a decade and deprived the Dondoli faction, in eclipse under the British, of its only leader whose stature exceeded that of Ishaq b. 'Uthman Dabila of Dzedzedeyiri. In that sense Muhammad's decision to make the pilgrimage was a decision to withdraw from Wala affairs; to renew his identity as a member of the wider, at the expense of the local, *umma*. It may be that his decision had been affected by the revivalism of Mahdi Musa. Significantly, Ishaq b. 'Uthman Dabila never did make the pilgrimage.

The principals in the group that left Wa probably in 1905 were Muhammad b. 'Uthman Dun (who was accompanied by his nine-year-old son, Tamimu),[74] Abu and Ya'qub of Dzangbeyiri, and 'Uthman b. Dawud of Tagarayiri.[75] They were not to arrive back in Wa until March 1916, when they thanked the administration for a letter supplied to them on their departure (which had been very helpful on the road), and received the Provincial Commissioner's congratulations on the completion of a 'long and arduous journey'.[76] They were not the first Wala to make that journey. We have seen that Muhammad himself had probably earlier done so in the company of his elder brother, Ibrahim b. 'Uthman Dun, who died in Mecca in the early 1890s. There were doubtless others. It is worthy of note, however, that no *'hajji'* held either the Wa or the Friday limamate until Muhammad b. 'Uthman Dun took the former office in 1926.

The departure of Muhammad b. 'Uthman Dun from Wa left Ishaq b. 'Uthman Dabila with unrivalled power over the affairs of the Muslim community. The British consistently described him as 'Chief Malam', 'Mohammedan Chief', and the like. In 1908 he apparently represented himself to them as '19th Mallam in direct descent from Imoru', that is, from the first Wa Limam Ya'muru.[77] The choice of '19th' is highly significant. The aged Wa Limam Ibrahim died during the later part of the reign of Wa Na Momori Tangile. Generation V of the limamate was, however, still not exhausted. By the Rule of Seniority Ishaq b. 'Uthman Dabila, who belonged to the descendant generation, should not claim it. It went to Salih b. Yahya b. 'Abd al-Qadir, a member of none of the four major Houses of Limayiri. Salih was the twenty-first Wa Limam. Reference to table 4.1 will show, however, that on most lists of the limams, including ones recorded by Ishaq b. 'Uthman Dabila himself, Salih was reckoned nineteenth. In 1908, then, Ishaq b. 'Uthman Dabila may have been claiming to be the nineteenth Wa Limam. Perhaps he attempted, with the support of the Dzedzedeyiri faction, to seize the Wa limamate on the death of Ibrahim. All that is sure is that if he did, he was unsuccessful.

We shall see that the Dondoli came to place much emphasis upon the pilgrimage, the fifth of the pillars of Islam. Mahdi Musa may have been the catalyst, inspiring the Dondoli to view the *haj* as at least a gesture towards *hijra*, migration to the east. The Dondoli, aware that Dzedzedeyiri power was predicated on collaboration with the British, were perhaps not unaffected by the anti-European aspects of Mahdi Musa's message. They may also have had in mind another of Limam 'Uthman Dun's predictions, as it was told to me on numerous occasions in the 1960s, that the rule of 'blacks' (Babatu and Samori) would be followed by the rule of 'whites' (the British), and that this would be followed once again by the rule of the 'blacks' (Kwame Nkrumah).[78] These matters are speculative. It will become apparent, however, that the strategy (if a concern with pilgrimage may be described as such) was in time to do much to restore the hegemony of the Dondoli in Wala Muslim affairs.

A crisis averted: the Muslims under Na Dangana

The Wala Native Tribunal was recognized under the Northern Territories Administrative Ordinance No. 1 of 1902. In 1908, Provincial Commissioner B. M. Read reported that it comprised the Wa Na, his 'headmen' and a 'priest', the latter presumably a *tendaana*. The Wa Na's 'linguist', that is, the Foroko, received plaintiffs, questioned the defendants, and decided whether a case should go to the Tribunal. If so, he conducted the proceedings. Cases could also be heard by the Wa Limam, who might then choose to take them to the Foroko or to the Wa Na. The British criminal code had, of course, superseded older Wala custom. Read thought that the latter had been greatly affected by Muslim law. Deterrence by punishment was its thrust, rather than levying fines to provide revenue for the Wa Na. Penalties were increased for repeated offences, and the habitual thief might be put to death. The Muslims considered rape impossible on grown women, but treated the abuse of children as a crime. Murderers were executed by strangulation with a white cloth; rape and sacrilege were punished by flogging, and so forth.[79]

Prima facie, the Wa Native Tribunal system was accepted by the Muslims so long as the Wa Na, who presided over it, was himself a Muslim. Na Momori Tangile met this condition. He died in 1908, however, at the age of eighty-five or thereabouts.[80] He was succeeded by Sing Na Dangana, also known as Tahuna, a son of Wa Na Balannoya. Dangana was not a Muslim.[81] Surprisingly, there is no record of the Muslims objecting to his selection. It may be that they were not averse to having a Na who, although 'king' to the British, was 'kafir' to the believers, in whose eyes his authority was therefore not likely to command respect. In 1914, however, the Commissioner of the North-Western Province noted that Dangana,

> although he is getting somewhat infirm ... is a most loyal adherent to the Administration and is ready and able to assert his authority when necessary. In this he is backed up by the somewhat strong and influential Mohammedan part of the community who, though they have their own Chief, recognise the King of Wa as Paramount in spite of his being a Pagan.[82]

The apogee of Dangana's reign was indeed in 1914, when the Na's jurisdiction was enlarged to embrace the Lawra and Tumu districts, historically never part of the Wala polity. 'The Grunshi Chiefs at Tumu', it was reported, 'agreed to accept the paramountcy of the King of Wa, who now becomes the Paramount Chief over all others in the [North-Western] Province.'[83] The Dagaaba and others of the Lawra area were less compliant, and the new arrangement was in fact to prove unworkable.[84] Nevertheless, it was a signal of the colonial administration's firm commitment to 'kingship'. The Commissioner's belief that the Muslims recognized the Na's paramountcy was, however, soon to be shown in need of qualification.

War in Europe, and particularly the entry of the Ottomans on the German side in November 1914, gave Britain and her allies some cause for concern about the reliability of their Muslim subjects. The French in West Africa moved rapidly to obtain declarations of loyalty from the 'ulama'. Limam Kunadi Timitay of Bonduku, for example, obligingly condemned the Turks in a pastoral letter of 18 June 1915.[85] The British were slower to respond. Perhaps it was the return from Mecca of Al-Hajj Muhammad b. 'Uthman Dun and his companions in March 1916 that finally induced them to act. In June 1916 the District Commissioner of Wa was busily distributing literature in the town and in those of its villages that had Muslim populations. It was in Arabic, and was intended to show that most of the Muslims of the world were supporting the Allies and not the Germans.[86] Then, at the end of the month, a certain strange event in Dondoli came to the attention of the District Commissioner. It had no apparent connection with the war, but revealed stirrings in the Muslim community.

> New charms are everywhere seen now – Small bits of paper bound round with cotton thread and tied round the neck. Everyone wears them pagan and Mohammedan. It appears that a hyaena was found dead outside Dondoli (a section of Wa). It was cut up and opened and inside was found an injunction, that unless the people wore this charm with certain words written inside a great sickness would break out. They are sold for 50 cowries in the market and practically everyone wears one now.[87]

It may be thought that the Dondoli penchant for predicting events, but failing to avert them, was perhaps apparent once again; the influenza epidemic of 1918 was to take a heavy toll of the Wala.[88]

At the beginning of August 1916 there was friction between the Muslims and the Wa Na. Al-Hajj Abu Maidoki recollected the occasion. The rains had failed and there was little water even for drinking. Yeri Na 'Umar Kulendi, Ishaq b. 'Uthman Dabila, and his old associate 'Abdallah b. Idris, approached Wa Na Dangana to have prayers made officially. Dangana became annoyed and drove them away.[89] Ishaq took the matter to the District Commissioner.

The District Commissioner's report on the episode is fortunately on record. Though it betrays an ignorance of Wa Muslim attitudes towards conversion, it is none the less revealing. 'Mallam Izaka', it reads,

> complains that the chief of Wa treats him and his people with contempt and that at the late festival of Ramadham [sic] the Chief told Mohammedans to go away when they prayed for him and his crops ... It is peculiar what little progress the religion of the Prophet is making among the mass of the people, and this may be the cause of Mallam Izaka's irritation. Although tradition says that Mohammedanism has been preached here for at least 300 years it seems

worth remarking that, as the people have so persistently and independently rejected its seductions, they are not at all likely to be converted now, even though it is so much assisted by the peaceful conditions existing everywhere.[90]

The problem was investigated and found to involve much more than a mere matter of offended pride. 'So strong are they [the Muslims]', Commissioner Berkeley reported, 'that only recently they made a claim which amounted to an effort to either wrest the Paramount Chiefship from the Chief of Wa or to establish an equally strong Chief in Wa for the Mohammedans.' Berkeley reaffirmed the paramountcy of the Wa Na.[91]

It is clear that the Dzedzedeyiri rather than the Dondoli were principals in the dispute with Wa Na Dangana in 1916. Malam Ishaq's 'irritation', however, was less likely to have had anything to do with the lack of conversion than with an awareness that his authority within the Muslim community was being eroded. He had undoubtedly aspired to have a seal placed on that authority by securing for himself one of the two senior limamates. Success was eluding him.

The Wa limamate had become vacant again with the death of Salih b. Yahya, during the reign of Na Dangana and some time before 1917. Having failed in what may have been an earlier bid for the office, Ishaq b. 'Uthman Dabila appears to have recognized the futility of contesting the succession on this occasion. There was a further candidate available from Limam Salih's generation. This was Ya'qub b. Limam Ya'muru of Dapuyipala, a younger brother of the former Wa Limam Musa, who was installed. There was also, however, the Friday limamate. This became vacant with the death of Muhammad b. Ya'qub of Dzedzedeyiri, again during the reign of Na Dangana. Muhammad Zayd b. 'Uthman Kunduri of Tamarimuni and not Ishaq b. 'Uthman Dabila succeeded (page 110). The two were of the same generation. It is unclear why the former was preferred, but it may be that the Rule of Oscillation observed in the selection of Wa Limams was applied to that of Friday Limams; in other words, that it was regarded as undesirable to take a Friday Limam from the House of Ya'qub b. 'Abd al-Qadir – that is, Dzedzedeyiri proper – for the third time in succession.

Ishaq b. 'Uthman Dabila failed, then, to obtain either of the limamates during the reign of Na Dangana. The precise dates of the deaths of Wa Limam Salih b. Yahya and Friday Limam Muhammad b. Ya'qub are unknown. It is unclear, therefore, whether Muhammad b. 'Uthman Dun had yet returned from the pilgrimage and was perhaps active in excluding Ishaq b. 'Uthman Dabila from office. Whatever the case, his reappearance in Wa must have been viewed by Ishaq as a further threat to his authority. The colonial administrators soon recognized that there was a new factor in the scene. By 1918 their reports begin frequently to refer to 'the Hadjis of Dondoli'. In July, for example, it was the 'Mohammedans headed by Malam Izaka and the Hadjis of Dondoli' who treated with the District Commissioner.[92]

In 1916 Ya'qub b. Ya'muru probably continued to show the customary loyalty which a Wa Limam owed to a Wa Na. There is nothing to suggest that the Dondoli faction found this anything but proper. It was the Dzedzedeyiri faction which sought, if we follow Commissioner Berkeley, to challenge the very concept of the Wa Na's paramountcy. There was, however, shortly to be something of rapprochement, albeit temporary, between the two factions. In early 1919 Yakugor, a grandson of Na Dangana, took a Muslim woman from Dondoli and married her by force. The 'ulama' protested to Na Dangana. He attempted to play off the Dondoli (who it will be remembered had moved out of Limamyiri proper) against the Dzedzedeyiri (who remained resident in the old ward).

The episode was vividly recollected by Al-Hajj Abu Maidoki:

> Then the big men of the Muslim community said to the Wa Na, 'What is going to happen now?' And the Wa Na said, 'Why? The Dondoli people are not from Limamyiri.' Getting to night, the whole of Limamyiri and Tagarayiri people gathered around the Limamyiri mosque, the main gathering place for Wa. They said, 'Twice the Wa Na has wronged us. When there was no rain he sent us away. Now his grandson has married our wife, and he has sent us away again. What shall we do?' They agreed that Dangana should no longer be Na. All then said that Pelpuo should be the Na. Then 'Abdallah, my father, said, 'Be patient until after Ramadan. Then we will all pray and make Pelpuo our Na.' At the end of Ramadan all the Muslims moved to Pelpuo's gate and told him that they were prepared to make prayers for him and make him the Na. When they were gathered together, Dangana sent his son Balanuya to them to say that what they were doing was wrong. They drove Balanuya away.[93]

Pelpuo, known also as Yamusa, belonged to the Busa gate. He was a son of Wa Na Momori Tangile and grandson of Wa Na Pelpuo II (page 83). As a devout Muslim, he had declined to take any gate skin in the Busa division.[94] He was a farmer and a trader in, *inter alia*, salt. He had gained the approval of the 'ulama' by sending them food every farming season.[95] He was already in fact carrying out many of the duties of the aged Na Dangana.

Ramadan 1337 corresponded to June 1919. The meeting between the Muslims and Pelpuo probably occurred in July. Just after, Al-Hajj Abu Maidoki said,

> 'Abdallah went to District Commissioner Berkeley and told him that they had made Pelpuo the Na and that they did not want Dangana any longer. My father told the District Commissioner that Dangana was very bad, that he abused the Muslims, allowed our wives to be taken, and so forth. Berkeley said, 'Yes, he once gave me cheek. I asked him for carriers to Gambaga, and he asked me how many boys I brought with me when I came from London.' So Berkeley agreed that Dangana should be removed.[96]

The administrators' reports show that a delegation of Muslims, including Yeri Na ('Sariki'), Wa Limam and Ishaq b. 'Uthman Dabila met the Provincial Commissioner early in August, and asked him to replace Na Dangana by Pelpuo – 'who does all the work'.[97] The District Commissioner apparently put Pelpuo to the test, by taking him on a ten-day tour of the district.[98] Pelpuo met with his approval. Na Dangana, it was minuted in December, 'has very little real power, he is supported by Perepo – who should be the next king, and Malam Izaka who is virtually head of the Mahomedan element which exercises considerable power even in Dagati'.[99]

Na Dangana's son, Balannoya, quarrelled with Pelpuo. In anger, Na Dangana sent certain of the paraphernalia of the Nam to Pelpuo, reputedly saying 'that those were things he inherited from Yamusa's father, Tangile, and that he should take them back and stop worrying his children'. Pelpuo, feeling assured of both British and Muslim support, brought the breach of custom to the attention of the elders of the gates and of the Tendaanba.[100] Wa Na Dangana abdicated from office on 2 January 1920 and the next day Pelpuo was made Na.[101] To the present day, no non-Muslim has ever again held the Nam.[102]

Conflict unresolved: the Muslims under Na Pelpuo III

By report, Pelpuo III came to office with the unanimous support of the 'Chiefs and Mahommedans'.[103] Within a few days he commenced building a new palace. The colonial officers thought it 'most imposing'.[104] It was constructed in the western-Sudanese style of the Central Mosque (plates 1 and 2), signalling both the enhanced status of the Nam under the British and Na Pelpuo's personal attachment to Islam. Friday Limam Al-Hajj Siddiq remarked on this in 1969:

> Formerly chieftaincy meant nothing in Wa. The chief was just a big man in the town. Then he began to get more respect, so it was decided to make him a palace to distinguish his house from the houses of ordinary people. So a stranger coming to town will see these big buildings like the palace and the mosque, and give respect to the Na and limam. It was Wa Na Pelpuo who built the palace.[105]

P. C. Whittall was appointed District Commissioner for Wa on 25 October 1922.[106] He established a close relationship with Ishaq b. 'Uthman Dabila, of whom he later wrote, 'he was an old friend of Gvt and when I was at Wa he wrote all their history, and Babetu's in hausa script for me'.[107] It was Whittall who, shortly after his arrival in Wa, gave Ishaq the bound volume (to which reference has earlier been made) 'on condition that he writes the history of the Walas in it in Hausa.'[108] Ishaq used it, we have seen, to compile a series of documents in Arabic and Hausa pertaining to Wa. He did, however, go on to write a history of the Wala, though not in the book given to him. His *Ta'rikh Ahl Wala* and *Ta'rikh al-Muslimin* have been discussed in chapter 3. In the latter work he introduced an idea that was probably quite new: that the Yeri Nas, secular heads of the Muslim community, were *wazirs* to the Wa Nas. The Arabic conveys the sense of 'ministers', those who administered to, supported and aided the Nas. Ishaq was acknowledging, it seems, the change that had occurred in Wala society. Since the British had transformed the Wa Na, seemingly irreversibly, into a 'king', the most appropriate transformation of the Yeri Na, albeit retrospectively, was into a *wazir*.

Ishaq's forays into historiography leave the later student of Wala indebted to whatever stimulation Whittall gave him in that direction. The aging *'alim*, however, undoubtedly saw writing not as a retreat from, but as a new thrust in, politics. If the Dondoli were obtaining recognition from the British by virtue of being 'hadjis', he would counteract this by becoming their authority on the Wala past. He would not be the first, and certainly not the last, waning politician to wax as a historian, and there is no doubt that his influence over Wala affairs was waning.

Limam Ya'qub b. Ya'muru died early in the reign of Na Pelpuo.[109] No further candidate was available in his generation. In the descendant generation Muhammad b. 'Uthman Dun and Ishaq b. 'Uthman Dabila towered over their contemporaries in terms of sheer achievement and the charisma that accrued from it. The former had steered the Wala through the Samorian period, the latter through the British. Ishaq put himself forward as a candidate. At issue was Dondoli control of the Wa limamate. The Muslims argued the matter out between themselves. The momentous nature of the confrontation between Dondoli and Dzedzedeyiri factions apparently escaped the attention of the colonial administrators. It is, however, well remembered by the Wa, though they show some reluctance to speak of it. One informant recollected the situation at the time:

> The imam was Ya'qub ... The Friday Imam at that time was Malam Mahama Tamarimuni [that is, Muhammad Zayd] ... The Yeri Na was Imoru Kunandi ['Umar Kulendi]. When Imam Ya'qub, the imam al-balad, died, some people wanted to make Malam Isaka the new imam, but there was strong opposition to that. Malam Isaka was appointed to lead prayers, name children, and so forth, but he was not made imam.[110]

There was a period of some three or four years in which the limamate was left unfilled.[111] A succession of *khatibs*, 'preachers', including Friday Limam Muhammad Zayd and Malam Ishaq, deputized for the limam.[112] The fact of the matter was that Al-Hajj Muhammad b. 'Uthman Dun was preferred over Ishaq, but chose the occasion to make his second, if not third, pilgrimage to Mecca. The clearest account of the matter was obtained for me in 1986 by Al-Hajj B. K. Adama. The gap in the Wa limamate, he learned,

> was after Limam Yakubu died, and before Alhajji Mahama became limam. Yakubu died and Malam Isaka wanted to be limam. Mahama said that he should have it. Then people came to Mahama and persuaded him to change his mind. There was a quarrel. Mahama went to Mecca. While he was away his people would not let Malam Isaka have the imamate. They said that they would keep it open until Mahama returned from Mecca. So there was a gap. Malam Isaka had helped Pelpuo to become Wa Na in 1920. In fact Malam Isaka had virtually appointed him. So he expected Wa Na Pelpuo to help him

get the imamate. Pelpuo did not do so. So then Malam Isaka quarrelled with the Wa Na. But until Alhaji Mahama returned from Mecca, no limam was made.[113]

Al-Hajj Muhammad returned to Wa probably in the middle of 1926. There was some delay in installing him in the limamate. In October 1926 Wa Na Pelpuo complained that the rains were poor, and that the election of a Wa Limam might help.[114] The next day the 'ulama' agreed to act within eight days.[115] Muhammad b. 'Uthman Dun took office on 5 November 1926.[116] By that time, however, Friday Limam Muhammad Zayd had apparently died. Ishaq b. 'Uthman Dabila was chosen as his successor, and so brought back to Dzedzedeyiri the office that his father and grandfather had previously held. The confrontation between Dondoli and Dzedzedeyiri had thus assumed its classic form once again, the former holding the Wa limamate and the latter the Friday limamate.

In 1924, District Commissioner Whittall had still felt able to note that 'today the Chief Malam' – clearly meaning Ishaq b. 'Uthman Dabila – 'is a power in the land under the Chief of Wa'. He added that 'pilgrims often start from Wa to Mecca'.[117] In fact the pilgrimage of c. 1905–16 had inaugurated something of a tradition in Dondoli. A second group had left Wa in or before 1911, and it was not until 1931 that reports reached Wa that the pilgrims were nearing home.[118] Unfortunately no record of the composition of the party has been found. Another group left Wa in or about 1924. It was led by Ibrahim b. 'Ali b. Idris Mana of Dondoli (see page 110). On their return, the pilgrims were guided from Khartoum to Kano by Alfa Nuhu of Timbuktu. They reached Kano in the middle of 1934. They were destitute and applied to the colonial administration for assistance in completing their journey. The party comprised thirty-three people. This included two seven-year-old girls, obviously born on the journey, but omitted younger children. Remarkably, twenty-seven of the pilgrims were from Dondoli, three from Dzedzedeyiri and three from Tagarayiri.[119] They finally arrived in Wa in May 1936, but Ibrahim b. 'Ali had died on the road.[120] Al-Hajj Muhammad b. 'Uthman Dun, twice if not thrice a pilgrim, appears to have been largely instrumental in fostering a Dondoli commitment to pilgrimage.

The Dondoli and Dzedzedeyiri were soon to become embroiled in a new dispute that centred on the Nam. Friday Limam Ishaq and his old associate, 'Abdallah b. Idris, once again offered a challenge to the Wa Na. When Pelpuo was made Na, according to Al-Hajj Abu Maidoki,

Malam Ishaq said to him, 'Be very careful, and look after your people and their prosperity well.' Pelpuo III agreed. But then Pelpuo started marrying one wife after another. Malam Ishaq called 'Abdallah and said, 'Let us tell the Na that what he is doing is spoiling the district. The Na has a hundred wives and he is not able to control them all. Then our young men will jump on them, and the Na will punish them.' So they said this to the Na. But the Na continued to go on marrying wives.[121]

163

The informant admitted that he was one of the young men in question. They dressed up very nicely, he said, and went out to dance, and Na Pelpuo claimed that those they danced with included his wives. The Na ordered them to be beaten. 'Abdallah went to Pelpuo and said, 'This is what we told you would happen when you have so many wives.' He then took the case to the District Commissioner.

Wa Na Pelpuo was angered by these proceedings. He ordered his drummers to summon the warriors of Wa to arms. 'One hundred gunners were coming into Wa on the eastern road, fifty on the Pirisi road, and so forth', Al-Hajj Abu remembered. He feared for his life and rushed to the District Commissioner's house. This was, in fact, on 17 September 1929. The Commissioner was J. E. Miller, newly posted to Wa from stations in the southwest of the Gold Coast, and his report of being thus awakened is on record. He immediately ordered Na Pelpuo to disband his men. On inquiry, Miller found for the Na. He made Friday Limam Ishaq sign a bond of £150 to keep the peace and, among others, fined 'Abdallah and his son Abu Maidoki £25 each.[122] In the light of the excellent record of collaboration with the British of both Ishaq and 'Abdallah, however, on review the Chief Commissioner advised Miller to investigate the matter further. 'All Mohammedans are more or less immoral', he minuted, 'and I doubt if the Chief of Wa is a plaster Saint.' Miller apparently cancelled the fines, only to have to report in late November that 'the long standing dispute' between the protagonists had revived. Limam Ishaq was again bound over to keep the peace and 'Abdallah was fined £12 10s; both were required to present a cow to Na Pelpuo and to greet him publicly in 'a friendly way.' Abu Maidoki was fined £25 on this occasion, and instructed to make a public apology to the Wa Na and the Wa Limam.[123] He said that he was also ordered to report to the Na every morning, afternoon and evening 'in order to keep Wa peaceful'.[124]

Whittall, then Commissioner for the Northern Province, revisited Wa in December 1931. He found Pelpuo in the early stages of that paralysis which was to kill him four years later.[125] He was surrounded by 'the Mohammedan Headmen, the Limam, Alhajis, etc.', Whittall wrote, adding, 'but I missed old Mallam Issaka'.[126] Friday Limam Ishaq had in fact died the previous month, on 7 Rajab 1350 (18 November 1931).[127] He had exercised a dominant influence over Wala affairs for more than three decades. He was spared the turmoil of the 1930s, when the British introduced indirect rule into the Northern Territories and the Wala Muslim community was to be ravaged by schism.

8

Wala under 'indirect rule': power to the Na and schism in the *umma*

Introduction

Those who drafted Northern Territories Administrative Ordinance No. 1 of 1902 envisaged that a considerable part of the burden of local administration would be carried by the Native Tribunals. These, in fact, soon fell into virtual disuse. In 1929, Acting Commissioner A. W. Cardinall of the Northern Province, which then included Wa, described the situation after three decades of 'direct rule':

> The extent of the jurisdiction of the native courts is trivial. It covers matrimonial suits and all those little matters to which the maxim *de minimis lex non curat* would apply. They have no jurisdiction whatsoever in criminal matters. As to the constitution of the native courts or tribunals, nothing is on record. The system of direct rule has been so intense that how a court is formed, of whom it consists, what officers are attached to it, the nature of its procedure, have never been recorded or even considered.[1]

Ignorance of customary procedures acknowledged by colonial officers at the local level was more than matched by the considerable confusion about policy at the highest level. In 1921, Governor of the Gold Coast F. G. Guggisberg had committed himself to the introduction of indirect rule into the Protectorate:

> Our policy must be to maintain any paramount Chiefs that exist and gradually absorb under these any small communities scattered about. What we should aim at is that some day the Dagombas, Gonjas and Mamprusis should become strong native states. Each will have its own little Public Works Department and carry on its own business with the Political Officer as Resident and adviser ... I would like the Chief Commissioner to draw up and submit to me in due course a policy for the Northern Territories showing a definite scheme for fostering the formation of these big states without compulsion.[2]

Seven years later, however, in the middle of 1928, T. S. Thomas, Acting Governor of the Gold Coast, could observe:

> So far as I can ascertain, this Government is completely in the dark as regards the native administration of the Northern Territories: there seems to be no

clear-cut statement of policy: we do not know what is being done and what our administration is intended to bring forth.[3]

Thomas signalled his intention of proceeding with the introduction of indirect rule. 'Definite lines', he wrote in 1928, 'should be laid down without delay on which administrative officers can work; so that, when the time is ripe, a system of indirect rule can be introduced and the natives themselves given a share in the government of the country ... A system of taxation will be necessary.'[4] He recognized that the transformation would take time. 'It will require much thought and investigation on the part of political officers', he minuted: 'much accurate knowledge on their part of the organisations of the native tribes in the districts in which the system will be introduced.'[5] The following year, in a confidential memorandum of 16 December 1929, Governor of the Gold Coast A. Ransford Slater confirmed the new policy.[6]

The reaction of the officers of the Protectorate Administration was generally one of hostility. The Chief Commissioner, A. H. C. Walker Leigh, put the matter pithily: 'personally I have only one idea on the subject, that it is premature'. He spoke of inexperienced officials in Accra expecting indirect rule to be turned on as 'royalty turns on the electric power of a distant city', and he believed that the peoples of the Northern Territories were being exploited.[7] Not surprisingly, he retired or was retired on 4 March 1930. His successor, F. W. F. Jackson, was instructed to prepare the necessary legislation by October. 'Before an Ordinance is drafted', he commented, 'I have assumed it is necessary to ascertain from the chiefs their inherent rights of jurisdiction, this information as you can imagine is a slow and tedious work, however, all Commissioners are now engaged with such enquiries.'[8]

Chief Commissioner Jackson had to work through two subordinate officers, the Commissioners for the Southern and Northern Provinces between which the older districts had been distributed in 1927. A. C. Duncan-Johnstone held the former position, P. F. Whittall the latter. Jackson thought the Southern Province 'the most promising field' and the Northern Province to offer 'the more difficult political problems and less likely soil for the experiment'.[9] Duncan-Johnstone was enthusiastic in his support. In May and November 1930 he convened conferences of the Gonja and Dagomba chiefs to investigate the traditional structures and codify the customary practices of the two kingdoms.[10] He also announced that it was his intention to use 'what culture and education already exists in the country, i.e. the Mallamai ... The Mallams are local men and we shan't have to depend on foreign clerks.'[11] Muslims were employed to prepare nominal rolls in the villages for taxation purposes, and a training course was arranged for them.[12] They were also attached as scribes to local courts.[13] An Arabic printing machine or typewriter was requested for Southern Province headquarters.[14] It was, furthermore, insisted that all District Commissioners learn Hausa, widely spoken in the Southern Province, and also the *ajami* script, that is, Arabic as modified for the writing of Hausa. In 1932, Duncan-Johnstone enthusiastically reported of his subordinates, that 'Blair has started, Syme knows it, Amherst and Miller have a nodding acquaintance with Persian and Hindustani, Burns is an adept, Guiness is going to start, and Ardron will too I expect. It is not hard to learn the alphabet.'[15]

Whittall was an older man than Duncan-Johnstone and was far less enthusiastic about the introduction of indirect rule. He was, moreover, often taken away from his station by sickness and leave.[16] As District Commissioner in Wa in the early to middle 1920s he had worked closely with Ishaq b. 'Uthman Dabila, later to become Friday Limam. Nevertheless, he appears to have been less inclined than Duncan-Johnstone to co-opt the *'ulama'* into his administration. Perhaps he was deterred from any such course of action by what he knew of factional rivalries among the Muslims of Wa.[17] Whatever the reason for Whittall's relative inactivity, however, the result was quite apparent. Little progress towards an understanding of traditional jurisdictions had been made in the Northern Province generally when indirect rule was legislated into existence in 1932.[18] The Wala Native Authority and its Subordinate Native Authorities, Native Courts and Native Treasuries were created by Ordinance before any clear conception existed in the Northern Province of how these bodies should be constituted.

The Wala Constitution of 1933: perpetrating a fraud

H. G. Ardron, on transfer from the Southern Province, assumed duty as District Commissioner in Wa on 28 December 1931. Not until his arrival, it seems, were serious preparations made for the introduction of indirect rule there. A long, undated report on the Wa District, filed with papers for 1932, was probably produced by him. It included a confused review of Wala history, an account of the current state of affairs in Wa, and recommendations for the introduction of a system of direct taxation.[19] In April 1933 Ardron convened a 'Preliminary Conference for recording the Wa Constitution'. He found the Wala chiefs quite unhelpful, and speculated that this was because 'so much of their traditional law and custom has been discarded or broken, that they are shy of exposing the fact'. The Conference was suspended, purportedly for further study.[20] This did not in fact take the form of further investigation of Wala institutions. The Dagomba constitution, as codified by Duncan-Johnstone in 1930, was simply adapted, *mutatis mutandis*, for the Wala.

On 15 July 1933 it fell to Ardron's temporary replacement, H. P. Dixon, to present the new constitution to the Wala. He chose the occasion of the Damba festival. Donning his white uniform to impress the assembled dignitaries, he duly had them place their thumbprints on eight 'appendices' to the constitution. In the afternoon a cricket match was played to celebrate the happy occasion.[21] A few months later, Dixon was posted elsewhere. He was, he wrote, 'very sorry indeed to be leaving', but took consolation from the fact that 'the first decisive step has been taken and perhaps the modern history of Wala will date from Damba (July) 1933'.[22] It was a very optimistic view of affairs. Comparison of the Wa constitution of 1933 with the Dagomba constitution of 1930 reveals the nature of the fraud that had been perpetrated. Three sections of the documents will suffice to make the point:

We, the undersigned Divisional Chiefs of the Dagbamba, do hereby acknowledge that we are the subjects of Ya-Na, and agree to serve him as Na of all Dagbon from henceforth.

We, the undersigned Divisional chiefs of Wala, do hereby acknowledge that we are the subjects the Wa-Na, and agree to serve him as Na of all Wala from henceforth.

I, Ya-Na do hereby state that the following Chiefs and Counsellors form the full Dagbamba State Council, empowered to settle State affairs, as at the present Conference.

I, Peripo III Wa-Na do hereby declare that the following Chiefs and Counsellors form the full Wala State Council empowered to settle State affairs, as at the present Conference.

We, the undersigned Kpamba of Ya-Na do hereby state that we form the Judicial Council under Ya-Na, as the Supreme Dagamba Court of Appeal from the Divisions and that our order of precedence is as follows ...

We, the undersigned Judicial Councillors of Wala, do hereby state that we form, under the Wa-Na, the Wala Judicial Council and Court of Appeal from the Divisions and that our order of precedence is as follows ...[23]

On the basis of the new Constitution various orders and instructions were drawn up defining the Wala Native Authority. These were read out to Wa Na Pelpuo and his councillors on 7 May 1934. The Na was, so the District Commissioner noted, 'practically asleep and had no comments whatsoever to make regarding this *milestone in Wala history*. He is a superb stoic.'[24] Na Pelpuo is unlikely to have been indifferent to changes that conferred a clearer title to paramountcy on the Nam than it had ever before had. He was, in fact, an extremely sick man and was to die on 15 September 1935.[25]

The 1933 constitution represented Wala as, structurally, a replica of Dagomba, ignoring the fact that the two had evolved historically in quite different ways. In particular, the pluralistic nature of authority in Wala was largely discounted. Appendix A to the Constitution established the paramountcy of the Wa Na over thirteen Divisional chiefs. These were Busa Na, Pirisi Na and Sing Na, and, in order of precedence laid down in Appendix F, Dorimon Na and Wechiau Na; the heads of the Sisala towns of Kojopere, Funsi and Kundungu (Duasi); and those of the Dagaaba towns of Kaleo, Issa, Daffiama, Busie and Nadawli. Appendix B created a Wala State Council of fixed membership. It consisted of the thirteen Divisional Chiefs and eight Judicial Councillors. The latter comprised, in order of precedence listed in Appendix H, Widana, Foroko, Salanga, Kabuidana, Yijihidana,

Yeri Na, Tandaga Na and Sambadana. Appendix C recognized Busa, Pirisi and Sing as the three gates to the Wa Nam, for which they should provide incumbents in turn. Appendix D conferred upon the Wa Na the right to veto the selection of any candidate for a Nabihi skin. It also defined the skins of Dorimon, Wechiau and the eight Dagaaba and Sisala towns as terminal: 'holders of these chiefships', it read, 'may never aspire to a higher chiefship than those they hold'. Appendix E ruled that chiefs might only lose office by death or voluntary resignation. Finally, Appendix G mandated that on the death of a chief his eldest son should temporarily assume authority ('except in cases of mental incapacity'), but that a chief temporarily unable to discharge his responsibilities through, for example, sickness or absence, might appoint any elder – presumably meaning a judicial councillor – to act in his stead.

The structure of the Wala Native Authority was to be reproduced in each of the thirteen Divisions; that is, each was to have its Subordinate Native Authority, its Subordinate Native Court and its Subordinate Native Authority Treasury. From the treasuries, salaries were to be paid to chiefs and councillors, ranging from £84 a year for Wa Na to £6 a year for lesser chiefs and councillors.[26] It was, however, not until 1934 that a new revenue system was improvised. The Native Authorities Ordinance of 1932 was amended by Regulation 5 of 1934 to create a tribute tax, replacing all older forms of impositions on individuals, whether payments in money or kind, or service. In Wala, the tax was initially set at 3s per adult male. In addition such other items as Native Court fines and market fees accrued to the Native Authority.

In theory the Native Authority system seemed to promise the restoration to the Wala of a degree of autonomy they had not enjoyed since the late nineteenth century. In Wa itself various of the Na's Kpanbihi or councillors were assigned specific 'ministerial' functions which in some cases had a relationship to those exercised by their predecessors in pre-colonial times, in some cases not. The Yeri Na, traditionally responsible for the affairs of the Muslim community as such, became 'School Elder' and served as liaison officer between the District Commissioner, the Native Authority, and the schoolteachers. The Widana, head of the Tendaanba, assumed responsibility for public works, including road maintenance. The Sambadana, who presided over the old Hausa settlers of Dzangbeyiri, was in charge of animal husbandry, and the Tandaga Na, custodian of the graves of the Wa Na, had to look to matters of drainage and sanitation. The Na's spokesman, the Foroko, issued gun licences.[27]

In practice, the Native Authority system worked indifferently. A part of the problem was that, in the Dagaaba and Sisala parts of Wala, the traditional structures of authority were not such as to lend themselves to the new system of chiefs and councillors. In the Nadawli Division, for example, the highest local authority was a *tendaana*. The administration appointed an ex-soldier, not even a Nadawli man, as Nadawli Na, and attempted to conjure up three gates to the so-called *nam*.[28] Even in Wala proper, however,

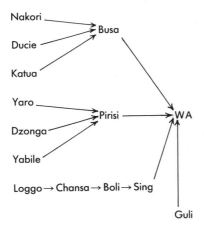

Figure 7 The gate system, early twentieth century

the 1933 Constitution was a recipe for disaster. The limams were afforded no recognition under it, and the ranking head of the Old Muslims, Yeri Na, was relegated in status to sixth of the Wa Na's Judicial Councillors. The customary liberty to remove an unsatisfactory Wa Na or other chief from office was abolished. The claims of the Na Kpasa gate to the Wa Nam were treated as extinct.

Clearly the colonial administration aspired to rid the Wala of ambiguities and contradictions inherent in the traditional body politic by decreeing, unambiguously and without contradiction, the paramountcy of the Wa Na. It failed to do this, and significantly raised rather than lowered the potential for conflict and violence. In no sphere was this more apparent than in the attempt to regulate succession to the skins of Wa and its gates.

The gate system to the Wa Nam evolved, we have seen, in the course of the eighteenth century. Guli, Gbetore and Yaro were the original gates. Gbetore in time developed into the Busa and Sing gates. Yaro became Pirisi. There may briefly have been a fifth gate, Chegli. There were also gates to the gates. These, too, changed over time with the creation of new skins and no doubt the disappearance of others; we have seen that Katua was created a gate skin to Busa only in the early 1920s. The configuration of the system in the early twentieth century is shown in figure 7.

By custom, each of the gates, Guli, Busa, Sing and Pirisi, had the right to put forward candidates for the Wa Nam. It seems that all the gates frequently did so; even unsuccessfully to compete for the Nam was successfully to assert claims to it. Hence the Guli (Na Kpasa) gate often produced candidates, though none has become Wa Na since the eighteenth century. A gate intent not merely on asserting its rights to the Nam, but also on gaining it, had to put forward a candidate able to secure the support not only of other gates but

170

Table 8.1 *Distribution of Wa Nas by gate and Divisional population*

Division	Population		Wa Nas	% population		%Nas
	1931	1948		1931	1948	
Busa	4,497	4,629	15	52	46	50
Pirisi	2,351	3,139	10	26	31	33
Sing	1,818	2,363	5	22	23	17

also of the so-called 'kingmakers', most importantly, the Widana representing the interests of the Tendaanba and the Yeri Na those of the Muslims.
Constituencies had to be wooed and won over. On being enskinned, the
successful candidate was ceremonially informed that he was henceforth
answerable to all the Wala and not only the Nabihi.[29]

Reference to table 4.6 will shows that the Wa Nam oscillated but did not
rotate between the gates. Table 8.1 shows the distribution of Nas by gate
(omitting Guli) from Pelpuo I in the early eighteenth century to Sidiki Bomi,
who was enskinned in 1961. If the proportional distribution of population
over the three Divisions, though not of course the gross figures, has been
reasonably constant over time, then the implication of the table may be that
population resources and political power are linked variables in the Wala
context. The larger the Division, the greater its chances of advancing
candidates to the Wa Nam. Conversely, it may be that the Division most
successful in advancing candidates to the Nam was the Division most likely
to achieve population growth.

The colonial administrators were not unaware of the complex nature of the
process leading to the selection of a Wa Na. In the mid-1920s Whittall knew
that it was necessary for a candidate 'to secure a strong following'; in case of
dispute 'the Tindanas and the Chief Mallam act as the judges, awarding the
Chieftainship probably to a branch other than that of the previous holder,
providing always that there is sufficient support to justify their decision'.[30]
Whittall was in error only in thinking it was the 'Chief Mallam' (he had the
powerful Ishaq b. 'Uthman Dabila in mind) who represented the Muslims in
such proceedings; it was, of course, technically the Yeri Na. At the end of the
1920s, R. S. Rattray investigated the matter. 'The Chieftainship is, in theory',
he wrote, 'supposed to be held alternately by members of four family groups
... but in practice, the claimant who was strongest would seize the *Na*-ship.'[31]
Whittall, then, seems to have thought that, other things being equal, there
was a disinclination to have the Nam held by one gate successively. Rattray,
in contrast, thought that there was a rotational system but that it did not
work. In 1933 a rotational principle was enshrined in the new constitution.

The matter of rotation is the only one on which the Wala Constitution of
1933 differed significantly from its Dagomba model:

We, the undersigned Chiefs and Councillors of the Dagbamba State Council, do hereby state that only from the following three Chieftainships may selection be made for the Nam of Yendi, viz: Karaga-Nam, Mion-Nam, Save-lugu-Nam.

We, the undersigned Chiefs and Councillors of the Wala State Council do hereby agree that at present there are three gates in Wala, i.e. Na-bisi chiefships viz: Busa, Pirisi and Sing and that these three have no seniority between themselves but all are equal and succeed in turn to the Nalumship of Wala.

The rotational system was, then, an innovation in the Wa context, and the Wala still think of it as such. In 1986, Al-Hajj B. K. Adama, son of the late Busa Na Bukari, commented, 'the British brought that idea in about 1931 or 1932. They thought it would minimize disputes.'[32] The British, however, did not dream up the idea. They seem, in fact, to have been misled into thinking it was traditional practice, by no less an authority than Friday Limam Ishaq b. 'Uthman Dabila.

The work *Al-habari Sarauta Wa* (HSW) has been discussed in chapter 2. It exists in two major variants, HSW(a) transmitted through Al-Hajj Siddiq b. Saʿid of Tamarimuni, and HSW(b) which Ishaq b. 'Uthman Dabila entered, in both Arabic and Hausa versions, in the book given to him by Whittall in December 1922. HSW(a) refers to the four gates (*abwab*) to the Nam, but merely remarks, 'when one among them sits in the sultanate and dies, his people sit and decide on one among the four'. HSW(b), however, refers to five gates (Chegli being the fifth) and has it that when the sultan dies the successor is chosen from the remaining four gates, that when he dies the successor is chosen from the remaining three gates, and so on until each gate has provided a sultan.

It is highly likely that it was Ishaq b. 'Uthman Dabila himself who inserted this description of a rotational system into the text of HSW (though it is quite unclear why he included Chegli as a gate). Since Ishaq had lists in his possession which showed that the Nam had *not* in fact rotated between the gates in any such systematic fashion, it must be presumed that he was aware he was making a recommendation rather than describing an existing state of affairs. Whatever the case, the text was among those that came into the hands of Commissioner Whittall. He duly had them trans-lated,[33] and rotational succession found its way into the Wala Constitution of 1933.

Whether or not Ishaq b. 'Uthman Dabila conjured up the idea of rotation between the gates, he set his seal of approval on it. Why he did so is not clear. The principle of rotation is not one prescribed in Muslim law. Perhaps he had a vision of Wala under a *wazir*, the Yeri Na, regulating the affairs of the *mulk*, the Wa Nam, in accordance with regulations (concerning, for example, succession) established by a consensus of the *'ulama'*. Such speculations

Table 8.2 *Succession of Wa Nas Pelpuo III, Sumaila and Saidu II from Busa gate*

Nakori	Ducie	Katua	Busa	Wa
Ya'qub (1910–20)	Mumuni (?1915–26)	Idris (?–1922)	Saliya (1912–22)	
				Pelpuo III (1920–35)
Harun (1924–34)	Jangeri (1926–32) Idris (1933–7)	Bogsuo (1922–50)	Bukari (1922–42)	
Sumaila (1934–42)			Sumaila (1942–3)	Sumaila (1943–9)
Kasimu (1943–?)	Darimani (1938–44)		Darimanu (1944–65)	
	Muhammad (1944–?)	Saidu (1950–3)		Saidu II (1953–61)

Table 8.3 *Succession of Wa Na Hamidu Bomi from Pirisi gate*

Yabile	Yaro	Dzonga	Pirisi	Wa
Chausaria (?–1933) Ya'qub (1934–?)	Saidu (1910–32)	Saka (?–1937)	Yahya (1912–23) Boyon (1924–5) Bansibo (1925–6) Hamidu (1926–36)	
				Hamidu Bomi (1936–1943)
	Balawu (1934–6)		Balawu (1936–54)	

aside, however, events were to show that the rotational principle could not and would not work.

Rotation between the gates: an exercise in futility

Tables 8.2 to 8.4 show the position of the five Nas, Pelpuo III, Hamidu Bomi, Sumaila, Mumuni Koray and Saidu II, with respect to the gates from which they came.[34] Pelpuo III of the Busa gate did not hold any skin prior to securing the Wa Nam in 1920. He was, we have seen, a wealthy trader and farmer who enjoyed the strong support of the Wa Muslim community. Retrospectively, in the light of the 1933 Constitution, District Commissioner

Table 8.4 *Succession of Wa Na Mumuni Koray from Sing gate*

Loggo	Chansa	Boli	Sing	Wa
		Bukari (1917–34)	Bukari (1934–5)	
	Mumuni (?–1934)	Mumuni (1934–5)	Mumuni (1935–44)	
Idris (1930–5)	Idris (1935–6)	Idris (1936–?48)		
Saliya (1935–6)	Saliya (1936–44)		Saliya (1944–8)	
			Mumuni Koray (1948–9)	Mumuni Koray (1949–53)
			Saliya (reinstated 1949–?)	
'Abdallah (1936–44)	'Abdallah (1944–?8)	'Abdallah (?1948–?)		

Ardron had to disapprove of the way he had come to office. 'I have', he wrote in 1934,

> consistently gently chided the Walas on breaking their tribal laws of succession. A habit of obtaining direct appointment has developed – normally aspirants to chiefdom must pass through certain recognized 'gates' (i.e. sub-chiefships) and thus acquired a most desirable training in control of people and knowledge of administrative work vis-à-vis the Nalum and the Government. The Na himself secured the Nalum in this irregular manner (he was a trader in Wa before he got appointed).[35]

Wa Na Pelpuo died in 1935. It was an occasion when both old customs and new departures were put to the test. It was somehow fitting that the Muslims and Nabihi quarrelled over the corpse. The former said that the late Na was a Muslim and that his body must be washed before burial. The latter said that the late Na was from the Nabihi and that his body must not be touched. In the event the Nabihi had their way.[36] The Nabihi, however, had other matters to exercise them. A new Na had to be chosen, for the first time under the Wala Constitution of 1933.

In accordance with the 1933 Constitution the 'correct' successor to Pelpuo III was Pirisi Na Hamidu. There was, however, a problem. Hamidu had been senile for some years, and as early as 1931 the then District Commissioner had noted that in the event of Pelpuo's death 'no-one would have him at any price.'[37] Busa Na Bukari, grandson of Wa Na Fijolina, advanced his candidacy. Katua Na Bogsuo, presumably with an eye on the Busa skin, managed the campaign. 'Headman of Katua away at Wa hoping to see his Chief Busa-Na grab the Nalum', District Commissioner Ardron noted in January 1936:

whether he has any thought that if such a thing happened it would be a shameful example of the Wala 'royal' families breaking their own native law and custom, and whether he realises the troubles and complications that would arise on the death of the next Na it is hard to say.[38]

Complicating matters further for Ardron, Guli Na Adama from the Na Kpasa gate entered the contest. Members of the gate had constantly pressed the administrators to acknowledge that the 1933 Constitution had unjustly disregarded their rights to the Nam. In February 1934 a concession was made. Guli Na was to be recognized as equal in status to Dorimon Na and Wechiau Na; that is, as holding a *namburi* skin from which there was no promotion to the Wa Nam.[39] Clearly the compromise was not acceptable, and the contest following the death of Pelpuo III was the occasion to demonstrate that it was not.

Ardron was not a little exasperated. He noted, as the struggle for the Nam entered its sixth month, that 'there is absolutely nothing to hinder the appointment except wilful procrastination on the part of the Na-bisi Chiefs and the Nalum Councillors, all of whom seem quite incapable of sinking petty ambitions for the good of Wala'.[40] He felt that the problem originated in the way Pelpuo III had achieved the Nam in 1920, passing through none of the Busa gates. 'The trouble', he wrote, 'is that Busa-Na having allowed Peripo [Pelpuo] to snatch the rightful succession to the Nalum from him, now asserts that he should have a second chance, when he knows perfectly well, as does all Wala, that it is the turn of the Najare (Pirisi) family to succeed'.[41] This account was in error. Bukari, like Pelpuo, was a man of some wealth. He took the Nam of Busa in 1922 (table 8.2) without himself having held any earlier skin. His claims to the Wa Nam in 1935 were based on seniority. The incumbent Sing Na Mumuni had attained office only the month after Pelpuo's death, and Hamidu had become Pirisi Na in 1926. Bukari, said his son, 'was senior of the royals. He felt cheated. Many people would have supported him.'[42]

Ardron was adamant that the procedures laid down in the 1933 Constitution be followed. He had made known his decision not to accept the Busa Na. Bukari thereupon announced his support for the Na Kpasa candidate, further confusing the situation.[43] The District Commissioner nevertheless congratulated himself on the rightness of his cause. 'There is', he noted, 'no question about the interest and satisfaction my insistence on and support for native law and custom being observed with regard to succession through the traditional "gate" system has created throughout Wala.'[44] On 21 March 1936 he announced his choice of Pirisi Na Hamidu Bomi as Wa Na. Na only by administrative fiat, a new nickname was given to Hamidu Bomi. He became Kabasagiya, meaning 'whether they agree or not'.[45]

It remained for Ardron to persuade the Wala formally to enskin the new Na. This was not to be accomplished until 20 September. By custom a Na-designate was supposed to enter Wa and remain 'hidden' in the Yijihi section of the town until the ceremony commenced. Ardron decided that this part of the ritual should be omitted, since it was feared that Hamidu Bomi would be poisoned.[46] The first Wa Na to be selected in accordance with procedures laid down in the 1933 Constitution obviously enjoyed little support beyond the District Commissioner's office.

Busa Na Bukari refused to be reconciled to Na Hamidu Bomi, and declined to have any dealings with the Wala Native Authority. In early 1938, referring to Bukari's 'passive resistance', the District Commissioner sought a way of removing him from office. Bukari had not passed through any gates to Busa so he was not 'the real customary Chief', it was argued; he might therefore be forced into 'compulsory retirement'.[47] The plan was, however, seen on reflection to be ruled out by the provisions of the 1933 Constitution.

In his annual report on Wala for 1938–9, the District Commissioner decided to put a brave face on what was in truth a sorry situation. Blithely, he commented on 'the stability making for increased efficiency in the general administration of the people'; urged that 'tribal discipline in Wala may fairly be termed excellent', and added for good measure:

> It does not seem out of place to remark that today the Administrative Officer keeps in touch with the whole division by working through, and in cooperation with, a Native Authority which, though not indigenous, is endowed with a long tradition of rule. Orders and advice can be effectively communicated to some 75,000 fairly primitive people through a system of decentralised control based on tribal areas. It is a good example of the resurgence of the social and political organisation of a native division after a long period of disintegration.

He did admit, however, 'to Na Hamidu's proneness to listen to the blandishments of syncophants rather than the more prosaic talk of his Elders'.[48]

The fact of the matter was that in so far as the Wala Native Authority was working at all, it was despite rather than because of Na Hamidu Bomi. Late in 1939, Busa Na Bukari brought a complaint against Na Hamidu to the District Commissioner, who allowed its validity. 'I did not pay much attention to this sudden flare up', he noted, 'which is occasioned by the Na's usual disregard of constitutional procedures in dealing with his subordinate chiefs, and his incorrigible love of intrigue with village headmen.'[49] Early in 1942 matters were worsening. 'The Wala ruling families are', thought the District Commissioner, 'a supine lot, and all are riddled with jealousy and intrigue.'[50] The death of Busa Na Bukari on 12 November 1942 did nothing to settle matters. All the gates, including Hamidu Bomi's own, petitioned for the Na's deskinment.[51] On 29 October 1943, District Commissioner L. J. Mothersill made a telling observation in his diary. 'Poor Wala during the last eight years', he wrote; 'how they have done as well as they have under the circumstances is a mystery. Not much indirect rule about it, I think, for this was impossible.'[52] On 4 November 1943, Wa Na Hamidu Bomi was removed from office, notwithstanding the provisions of the 1933 Constitution. He did not go gently. He pulled out the doors and windows of the palace and filled the wells with horse manure.[53]

It was, by the 1933 Constitution, the turn of Sing Na to take the Nam. The affairs of the Sing gate, however, were already in a state of disarray as a result of administrative interference. Sing Na Najre had died in 1934. The Sing electors chose a certain 'Abdallah to succeed, a man who had held no previous skins within the gate but who commanded strong support. The District Commissioner refused to accept the decision since 'Abdallah had not gone through the 'constitutional stages to chiefdom' and therefore lacked 'service ... in the traditional manner'.[54] 'Abdallah was obliged to accept the Loggo skin when it became vacant in 1936 and was to advance to Chansa only after another eight years (table 8.4). Instead, the elderly Boli Na Bukari was created Sing Na in 1934. He died a year later. The Boli Na Mumuni, also elderly, succeeded to Sing. In 1943 he was senile, deaf and almost blind.[55]

Not surprisingly, Sing Na Mumuni did not command strong support when it became his turn, by the Constitution, to take the Wa Nam in 1943. A delegation, comprising representatives of the gates, the Wa Limam, the Yeri Na and the Widana, informed the District Commissioner that they wanted to pass over him and to elect Busa Na Sumaila, who had succeeded Bukari in 1942. Fighting a rearguard action on behalf of the 1933 Constitution, the administrator noted: 'as it is the Sing-Na's turn, I want to make quite certain that it is the wish of all the people.'[56]

Another candidate appeared. This was Mumuni Koray of Sing, a grandson of Wa Na Dangana. He had attended primary school in Wa. He then joined the Public Works Department, the Gold Coast Constabulary and the Marine Police successively. In 1943 he was Superintendent in the Customs Preventative Service at Denu, on the Togo border.[57] He had also joined the Ahmadiyya Movement in 1929. In his bid for the Wa Nam he was supported by the Sing gate and by the Wala Ahmadis.[58] The orthodox 'ulama' opposed him, and the fact that he had previously held no skin made him quite unacceptable to the administration. On 20 November 1943, Busa Na Sumaila was installed as Wa Na. In pique, Mumuni Koray apparently threatened to pull down the mosque and destroy the Qur'ans of the 'ulama' who had opposed him.[59]

The Sing electors drew the obvious implication from the accession of Sumaila to the Nam, that the system of rotational succession could not be enforced by the colonial administration. They manipulated, in careful fashion and in the long-term interests of Mumuni Koray, the passage of individuals through their gates. Sing Na Mumuni died in 1944. Boli Na Idris, who was both aged and sick, was persuaded to relinquish his claims on the vacant skin in favour of Chansa Na Saliya. It was in the nature of a holding operation. Wa Na Sumaila's popularity was declining as his reign lengthened. He was also, apparently, epileptic.[60] In 1948 the Sing electors made a critical move. Sing Na Saliya abdicated on the grounds of ill-health, and Mumuni Koray was elected to the skin. Wa Na Sumaila, seeing the writing on the wall, refused to confirm the change. The western-educated Wala went on strike and Na Sumaila was obliged to retract his opposition.[61]

Plate 15 Wa Na Mumuni Koray, 1949–53

The timing was perfect. Wa Na Sumaila died in 1949. Four candidates advanced claims on the Nam, but there was no serious contest. Mumuni Koray was made Wa Na (plate 15). One of his first acts was to reinstate Saliya as Sing Na.[62] The system of rotational succession embodied in the 1933 Constitution was truly a dead letter. If the election of Wa Na Sumaila had violated the rotational principle, that of Wa Na Mumuni Koray defied the whole concept of advancement through gates.

Turmoil in the Muslim community: the Ahmadiyya Movement

Mirza Ghulam Ahmad was born probably in 1835 in the Punjab village of Qadian. By the early 1880s he was claiming to be a *mujaddid*, a renewer of Islam. A decade later he declared himself both Messiah (*masih ma'wud*) and Mahdi, and formally inaugurated the Ahmadiyya Movement. Much emphasis was placed on *tabligh*, missionary activity, and on *jihad*: but *jihad* 'with the help of the Qur'an' and not *jihad* by the sword.[63] Ghulam Ahmad died in 1908. He was succeeded by Maulvi Nur-ud-Din and, on his death in 1914, by Bashir-ud-Din Mahmud Ahmad.[64] One of Ghulam Ahmad's disciples, Al-

Hajj 'Abd al-Rahim Nayyar, arrived on the Gold Coast in 1921. He was responding to a request for assistance addressed to Bashir-ud-Din Mahmud Ahmad by a small group of Fante Muslims. He took the opportunity to visit Accra and Kumase. As a result of his tour he recommended the creation of a mission in the Gold Coast. In 1922 Al-Hajj Maulvi Fadl-ur-Rahman Hakeem was posted there.

Establishing local headquarters of the Ahmadiyya Movement at Saltpond, Maulvi Hakeem began to open stations in the Colony and Asante.[65] In 1929 Mumuni Koray, then in the Customs Preventative Service, became an Ahmadi after corresponding with Maulvi Hakeem. He was the first Wala to do so. At the time, however, he was apparently not well known in Wa, which he visited infrequently.[66] Maulvi Hakeem returned to Qadian late in 1929, and was replaced by Maulvi Nazir Ahmad Ali.

By the late 1920s, several missions were located in the Adanse district of southern Asante. One was at Brofoyedru on the main road from Cape Coast to Kumase. A number of young men from Wa were settled, with their wives and children, at Amumoso, some nine miles away. They traded, and worked seasonally on the cocoa farms. Their leader was Salih b. al-Hasan who combined his business activities with teaching.[67] He was from Dzedzedeyiri. Born in or about 1896, he was a grandson of Wa Friday Limam Muhammad b. Ya'qub and a close relative therefore of Friday Limam Ishaq b. 'Uthman Dabila (page 110).[68] He had shown an early aptitude for learning, and (factional rivalries notwithstanding) had apparently studied under Muhammad b. 'Uthman Dun at the Dondoli school.[69] In Adanse, Salih b. al-Hasan made his first contacts with Ahmadis. Initially sceptical, he debated with them. In 1932 he heard Maulvi Ahmad Ali preach at Broyfoyedru. A few weeks later he went to Saltpond and joined the Ahmadiyya Movement.[70]

On his return to Amumoso, Salih induced others of the Wala there to follow his lead.[71] Among those that did so were his brother 'Abd al-Mu'min; Yahya, also of Dzedzedeyiri; and Khalid, a Kantonsi domiciled in Dzedzedeyiri.[72] In 1933 Salih sent the three to preach in Wa.[73] On 1 June they were received by Wa Na Pelpuo and Wa Limam Muhammad b. 'Uthman Dun, who clearly became alarmed at what they heard. Within a few days the Ahmadis were expelled from their family dwellings and obliged to stay outside the town. On 9 June the Nalum Council asked that their activities be stopped. Five days later the District Commissioner met the Wa Na, the Wa Limam and the 'ulama'. Allowing that the Ahmadis did not give proper respect to the Wa Limam, he found himself in a quandary. On the one hand there were precedents for excluding missionaries from Wa. Chief Commissioner Watherston had refused the White Fathers permission to work there in 1906, on the grounds that it was an important Muslim settlement, and six years later his successor, Armitage, had banned the Wesleyan Mission for the same reason.[74] On the other hand the Ahmadi preachers were both Wala and Muslim. Moreover, their Movement had a long history of loyalty to the

British Raj in India and enjoyed the tacit support of the Gold Coast Government. The District Commissioner temporized. He thought to address a request for the withdrawal of the preachers through Ahmadiyya head-quarters in Saltpond but the need for such action vanished when, in the face of intense hostility in Wa, the Ahmadis returned to Adanse.[75]

In February 1934, Salih b. al-Hasan arrived in Wa in person.[76] Three days later he was summoned before Wa Limam Muhammad. He defended his beliefs, that the Qur'an prophesied the coming of the Messiah (who had appeared in the person of Ghulam Ahmad); that prayers should be made with arms folded; that there should be no ceremonial observances at the burial of the dead; and that amulets and talismans were the work of the devil. He was then called before Wa Na Pelpuo, who was not unreceptive, at least to Ahmadi claims to have a right to preach in Wa.[77] The orthodox 'ulama' daily protested Salih's presence in Wa to the District Commissioner, who after a month bowed to pressure. He issued written instructions that Salih should leave the town.[78]

Salih's brother, 'Abd al-Mu'min, and some eight or nine other Ahmadis remained in Wa. They had to stay in disused huts in the Zongo. After three days they were required to appear before Wa Na Pelpuo. 'Abd al-Mumin was attacked while he was addressing the Na. Their lives in danger, and their own families refusing to accommodate them, they too left Wa.[79] At much the same time, in March 1934, some twenty young Wala men who had been working on the cocoa farms in the Colony arrived home. All had become Ahmadi. Again, their families refused them accommodation. The major purpose of labouring in the south was to save enough money to procure a wife. Even more to the point, then, no one would allow his daughter to marry an Ahmadi.[80] There is no doubt that these policies towards the Ahmadis were mandated by Wa Limam Al-Hajj Muhammad.

On 9 May 1934 Salih b. al-Hasan, with the backing of Maulvi Hakeem (who had returned to the Gold Coast in April 1930), brought his grievances to the attention of W. J. A. Jones, Chief Commissioner of the Northern Territories, who ruled that the Ahmadis could not be excluded from Wa.[81] Salih re-entered the town on 8 August 1934.[82] Five days later Wa Limam Muhammad led a deputation to the District Commissioner to request yet again the expulsion of the Ahmadis. In the meantime the limam had issued orders to the effect that

1 Mallam Salih's wives and children should not go to the ponds for water.

2 Mallam Salih's family should go neither to the farms nor the market for food.

3 Mallam Salih should not go out of his house.[83]

The Ahmadis had no choice but to disregard the orders. They sent two men to bring food from the Dzedzedeyiri farms. The Wa Limam had them beaten, bound and brought before him. He sent them to the Wa Na Pelpuo, who in turn sent them to the District Commissioner. The latter, not unexpectedly, had their assailants arrested and committed to prison. On 15 August there was extensive rioting. After evening prayers the Dondoli attacked Dzedzedeyiri, despoiling the houses and beating the occupants, whether or not they were Ahmadi. They were, according to Ahmadi informants, intent on killing Salih but, as if by a miracle, they failed to find him. In the fighting many were wounded though none died on the spot. The District Commissioner armed the police, read the riot act and ordered the streets cleared.[84] Among the Ahmadis arrested and imprisoned was Salih's close associate, Khalid. Among the orthodox imprisoned was Muhammad Kankanya of Limampalayiri. The former was to become Ahmadiyya Limam in 1961, and the latter Wa Limam in 1971.[85]

Despite the Chief Commissioner's ruling, the District Commissioner in Wa saw no alternative to expelling Salih b. al-Hasan from Wa for a second time. Once again communications passed between Salih, Ahmadiyya headquarters in Saltpond, and the Chief Commissioner in Tamale, and once again it was ruled that the Ahmadis could not be excluded from Wa. The District Commissioner was given twenty days' notice to prepare for Salih's return. He called in police from the surrounding areas. Donning his uniform as Captain in the Reserve of Officers, and with a decade of experience in the Northern Territories by then behind him, Ardron summoned the Wa Na and the notables and told them that *he* was ready for battle if necessary.[86] At the end of 1935 or beginning of 1936 Salih al-Hasan returned to a Wa that was virtually an armed camp. The town, moreover, was locked in secular as well as religious crisis: Wa Na Pelpuo had died in September 1935 and the dispute over his successor was still unresolved.

In such inauspicious circumstances the Ahmadis confronted Wa Limam Muhammad b. 'Uthman Dun, a man by that time of formidable authority and reputation. Salih b. al-Hasan was of a junior generation, born at the very time when Al-Hajj Muhammad was already consorting with Sarankye Mori, son of Almami Samori. By 1934, moreover, the influence of the Dzedzedeyiri faction in Wala affairs had weakened; it had, *inter alia*, lost control of the Friday limamate. The office had become vacant with the death of Ishaq b. 'Uthman Dabila in late 1931, and had been taken by Al-Hajj Sa'id Soribo. Al-Hajj Sa'id was not from one of the four major houses of Wa Limamyiri. Neither his father, Siddiq, nor his grandfather, Adam, a son of Wa Limam 'Abd al-Qadir, had held the Wa limamate. He was, however, strongly aligned with Wa Limam Al-Hajj Muhammad. The two had indeed made the pilgrimage together, arriving back in Wa in 1926, and in Mecca Sa'id Soribo had received the Tijani *wird* from a highly prestigious source.[87] The details are lacking, but Wa Limam Al-Hajj Muhammad had undoubtedly been instrumental in obtaining the Friday limamate for his *haj*-companion in 1931.

It was against such seemingly overwhelming opposition that Salih b. al-

Hasan pitted himself in 1936. His natural constituency was Dzedzedeyiri, effectively leaderless since the death of Friday Limam Ishaq. Fikry reports a prediction putatively long current in Dzedzedeyiri, that one day there would emerge in that quarter 'a new prophet in the religion in Wa here'.[88] The arrival of Ahmadiyya was seen to fulfil the prediction. There were, moreover, many aspects of the Ahmadiyya Movement that seemed to echo old themes in Dzedzedeyiri history. Ahmadi emphasis on conversion and (albeit peaceful) *jihad* perhaps stimulated the remembrance of Wa Limam Ya'qub's espousal of the Karantaw cause almost a century before. Ahmadi concern for the autonomy of the Muslim community could be construed as based on the very premises that had led earlier to the creation of the Friday limamate in Wa. Loyalty to authority, specifically to the British, had been Ahmadiyya policy in India since the nineteenth century as it had been Dzedzedeyiri policy in Wala. In such respects Ahmadi beliefs could be seen to articulate in a new guise many of the elements that had set the *'ulama'* of Dzedzedeyiri apart from their peers, who had remained more firmly committed to the older Suwarian tradition. There was, however, a further aspect of the situation.

In the 1930s the Wala Ahmadis were young men, and young men who had for the most part traded and laboured in Asante and the Gold Coast Colony. They saw Ahmadiyya as a liberating movement. It had the potential to free them from the constraints of the conservative *'ulama'*. It also had the potential to free them from the constraints of the Wa Na and the whole apparatus of the traditional polity which the British, under indirect rule, were so sedulously nurturing. This matter had not escaped the attention of the colonial officers. A. C. Duncan-Johnstone, Commissioner of the Southern Province of the Northern Territories, had been in close contact with Ahmadis in Asante. 'There are', he wrote in 1931,

> one or two [Ahmadiyya] rules which innocent as they may look at present may possibly lead to trouble in the future. The first is that each village must have a Chief, and each Chief a Secretary and a Committee consisting of three or five persons. Each Chief must appoint an Emir to rule the community with a council of elders from twelve to forty and a general secretary. This may possibly lead to abuse in the future and the setting up of a separate authority to that of the local Chief. Indeed in some of the Ashanti Akim villages this has actually happened, the Ahmadis refusing to do road work with the other villagers and trying to go in a body under their own elected chief. They have also objected to taking cases to the village tribunal contending that their own head should try them according to Moslem Law. So far these are only isolated cases, but they have occurred and may continue to not only occur but to increase.[89]

In Wala, uniquely among the territories administered by the Governor of the Gold Coast, the challenge was to go far beyond anything envisaged by Duncan-Johnstone. The Ahmadis were to succeed for a time in taking control of the Wa Nam and dominating the Wala Native Authority.

Changing fortunes: Ahmadiyya gains the Nam

Wa Limam Al-Hajj Muhammad b. 'Uthman Dun died in September 1936, less than a year after the exile of Salih b. al-Hasan had ended.[90] Malik b. 'Uthman of Tamarimuni (page 110), who had returned from Mecca in 1936 after an absence of some twelve years, assumed the limamate on 8 March 1937.[91] For the Ahmadis it was a providential change. It is highly unlikely that, under the regime of the former limam, they would have consolidated their position in Wa to the extent that they did.

The Ahmadis, under Wa Na Hamidu Bomi, Wa Limam Al-Hajj Malik and Friday Limam Al-Hajj Sa'id Soribo, continued to be subjected to constant harassment. They converted a dwelling in Dzedzedeyiri into a mosque. They ran their own school. About such matters Limam Malik and the orthodox 'ulama' complained constantly to the District Commissioner. The Ahmadis collected dues from their followers. The Wa Na pointed out to the District Commissioner that the right to tax belonged to the Wala Native Authority.[92] By 1939 there were about a hundred members of the Ahmadiyya Movement in Wa, excluding children.[93] Most were in Dzedzedeyiri. Those who joined were still often cast out of their homes by their own families and often deprived of their wives and children by their wives' families. They were obliged to begin practising, within their own ranks, patrilateral cross-cousin marriage of a kind religiously permitted but traditionally avoided in Wala.[94]

In 1939 to 1940, Salih b. al-Hasan made an extended preaching tour of the Northern Territories and succeeded in establishing a number of new Ahmadiyya centres.[95] His return to Wa in October 1940 was the cause of renewed agitation. The orthodox, the Ahmadi Khalid recollected, 'used to come out in battle order and say that they'll come and kill them'.[96] Police protection had to be extended to Salih's house.[97] Early in 1941 the District Commissioner entered into negotiations with the Missionary-in-Charge at Saltpond, Al-Hajj Maulvi Nazir Ahmad Mubashir (who had arrived in Ghana from Qadian in 1936). In the interests of peace it was suggested that the Wala Ahmadis should be resettled elsewhere. Maulvi Mubashir was not opposed to the scheme provided the colonial authorities arranged and financed it. The Chief Commissioner of the Northern Territories also approved, but only subject to the agreement of the Wala Ahmadis. Salih b. al-Hasan firmly rejected the idea.[98]

There was rioting in Wa in October 1941, at the end of Ramadan.[99] A year later, again at the end of Ramadan, more trouble was anticipated; the District Commissioner summoned the Wa Limam, the Yeri Na and representatives of the Ahmadiyya before him and warned them against violence.[100] The following year, a few weeks after the end of Ramadan, Wa Na Hamidu Bomi was forced out of office. The secular struggles that surrounded the choice of his successor took on a religious character when, as we have seen, Superintendent Mumuni Koray of the Customs Preventative Service arrived on the scene.[101] The election of Sumaila of Busa on 20 November 1943 was the signal for trouble. Mumuni Koray's threat to pull down the mosque of the orthodox was doubtless rhetorical; that of the orthodox to pull down the Ahmadi mosque was quite real.[102] It was apparently in this disturbed period that Wa Limam Al-Hajj Malik fell ill ('he would cry out so loudly that people heard him from far') and died.[103] The exact date has not been established. Dondoli, however, secured the limamate once again. Muhammad, son of Wa Limam Ibrahim, succeeded (page 110). He was generally known as Muhammad Saghir, 'junior', to distinguish him from his first cousin, the late Wa Limam Muhammad b. 'Uthman Dun.

With a new Wa Na and Wa Limam in office, the occasion was a propitious one for the Ahmadis to attempt to regularize their position in Wa. Maulvi Mubashir hired counsel and on 23 March 1944 petitioned Governor of the Gold Coast Sir Alan Burns for redress of the wrongs done to the Wala Ahmadis. The matter was carefully investigated and six months later the Ahmadi right to freedom of worship was endorsed at the highest level.[104] Henceforth, at the local level, it became incumbent on the District Commissioner and the Wala Native Authority to guarantee that freedom.

It was apparently at this juncture in time that Salih b. al-Hasan decided to undertake the pilgrimage to Mecca.[105] He availed himself of modern forms of transportation – boat, rail and lorry – and was away from Wa probably little over a year. The orthodox 'ulama' were highly incensed and, the Ahmadis claim, sent a letter to the Meccan authorities urging them to put Salih to death.[106]

On Al-Hajj Salih's return to Wa tension built up rapidly. The orthodox announced that the Ahmadis should thenceforth only use certain roads in the town and approach the market only by one entrance. They are said to have taken oaths to 'come boldly out' and kill the Ahmadis. They invited the Ahmadis to a meeting purportedly to debate matters. Al-Hajj Salih agreed to attend and then, fearing trickery, changed his mind. The orthodox brought the matter, as an instance of the intransigence of the Ahmadis, to the attention of the District Commissioner. Yet again they urged that the Ahmadis be banished from Wa. The administrator declined to be persuaded by their arguments. So, apparently, did Wa Na Sumaila. The orthodox then announced that they could no longer recognize the Na's authority. Sumaila reported this to the District Commissioner, who told him to go about his business as usual.[107] According to Al-Hajj Salih's close associate, Yahya, the attitude of the Wa Na changed. 'When we went to the Wa Na, and we raised our hands like that', he told Fikry,

> then he put his hand on the ground, meaning that he didn't like our prayers. Just because he simply feared the other Muslims. Then at that time, Na Ismaila [Sumaila] said that he didn't like them (the Orthodox) and that they are not to say prayers to him and that he now likes the Ahmadi, who will come and say prayers to him. At the time of his death he was more friendly with the Ahmadis.[108]

184

Such are the Ahmadi accounts of the situation prior to Wa Na Sumaila's death in October 1949. In a period of extended crisis, one event in particular caused something of a stir. In April 1945, there had been a rather singular sort of explosion at the Wa incinerator. A bomb, apparently consisting of gunpowder placed between sheets of the Qur'an, enclosed between two flat stones and wrapped in a piece of hyena skin, was placed where the hot ashes would detonate it. It was, the District Commissioner noted, believed to be 'bad medicine' for the Wa Na.[109] From its description, the bomb bears the imprint of the orthodox rather than of the Ahmadis; Limam 'Uthman Dun's preparation of charmed gunpowder for use against the Zabarima in 1887 will be recollected.

By the end of Na Sumaila's reign the Wala Ahmadis numbered some six hundred, counting children.[110] This figure presumably included the converts they had made in the Wala villages, for example, in the old Muslim centre of Guropise, where the first Ahmadiyya mosque outside Wa was built in 1944.[111] The great majority of the Wala Ahmadis were still to be found among the descendants of Wa Limam Ya'qub b. 'Abd al-Qadir, and the sect has to be seen, first and foremost, as a redefinition of the factional interests of the Dzedzedeyiri. Al-Hajj Salih b. al-Hasan was, in this respect, effective successor of Friday Limam Ishaq b. 'Uthman Dabila in the leadership of the faction. There was, however, more to it than that.

The Ahmadis under the leadership of Al-Hajj Salih obviously drew strength from their sense of being a persecuted minority. There was an element of fanaticism in the situation. They were young men (and women) with a cause. They were a radical element in Wala society in so far as they were, we have said, challenging the authority of the conservative *'ulama'* in particular and of the apparatus of the traditional polity in general. The orthodox lacked any comparable cause. They responded defensively to the Ahmadis; they were not looking for change, but resisting it. In the event, the zeal of the Ahmadis was to do much to compensate for their lack of numbers. The orthodox were to find themselves overtaken by events when Mumuni Koray became Wa Na in November 1949. The new Na made no effort to reconcile the orthodox to his election. Al-Hajj Salih, as Ahmadi Limam, presided over his formal installation. Mumuni Koray then had his skin and the other paraphernalia of the Nam placed in the Ahmadiyya mosque.[112]

New directions and old conflicts: Wala under Mumuni Koray

The Wala Native Authority system was probably capable of working well enough provided the key figures in it, the Wa Na and his subordinates in the gates, were able men. We have argued, however, that in attempting to introduce a system of automatic succession to office the British discarded the very procedures that had traditionally worked to bring the more able into positions of authority. Mumuni Koray became Wa Na despite rather than because of the Wala Constitution of 1933. The situation in Wala epitomized,

Table 8.5 *Composition of the Wala District Council*

Council	Elected members	Traditional members
Wa Urban	3	—
Wa Tianbilli Local	2	—
Kaleo Local	3	1
Nadawli Local	2	1
Busie-Daffiama Local	2	2
Issa-Kojopere Local	2	2
Funsi-Kundungu Local	2	2
Dorimon Local	2	1
Wechiau Local	2	1
Busa–Pirisi–Sing–Guli Local	3	4
Total	23	14

in a particularly acute form, one of the more general problems facing the Gold Coast Government: that of evolving a structure of local administration that would be at one and the same time nation-wide in its applicability yet responsive to the peculiarities of place.

In October 1949, a Gold Coast Government Committee on Constitutional Reform, headed by Justice Sir Henry Coussey, recommended *inter alia* the abolition of the Native Authorities and their replacement by a dual system of State Councils concerned only with traditional affairs, and Local Councils which would assume all other functions of local government.[113] The writing was on the wall. The Local Government Ordinance of 29 of 1951 gave legislative effect to the recommendations. An Instrument of 25 February 1952 established the Wala District Council and provided that its first meeting be held on 20 June 1952. It was to consist of ten new Local Councils based upon, but not corresponding exactly to, the divisions of the older Wala Native Authority. Two-thirds of the local councillors were to be elected by secret popular ballot, and one-third nominated by the relevant traditional authorities. Each Local Council was to send members – in the approximate ratio of two elected to one nominated – to the District Council. The composition of the Wala District Council is shown in table 8.5.[114] The Wa Na was to be its *ex officio* President and the Dorimon Na its Chairman.

The Wala State Council was reconstituted under the State Councils (Northern Territories) Ordinance 5 of 1952 with very restricted powers, namely, the determination of traditional constitutional matters and the declaration of customary law in Wala. It was the old Native Authority as defined by the Constitution of 1933 and consisted of the thirteen Divisional chiefs and eight judicial councillors with one addition in the first category: the Guli Na. The order of seniority laid down in 1933 was closely followed, though the salaries paid to the members reflected a more realistic appreciation of their *de facto* importance. Wa Na received £420 per annum, with entertainment, car and driver allowances of £40, £144 and £84. Kaleo Na received £240 per annum, Dorimon and Wechiau Nas each £108, and the eleven other divisional chiefs each £84. Of the councillors, Widana's salary was £81 per annum, and that of Yeri Na and the other six, £60 each.[115]

Under the Local Government Ordinance, Wa Na Mumuni Koray became President of the Wala District Council, the Wa Urban Council and the Wa Tianbilli Local Council, and Paramount Chief of the Wala State Council. He also made his entry into regional and national government. The Coussey Committee had not confined its recommendations to matters of local government. It urged the progressive integration of the Protectorate of the Northern Territories into the Gold Coast. A Committee of the Legislative Council of the Gold Coast under Kenneth Ewart gave practical effect to this goal. Its report, debated in the Legislative Council in July 1950, envisaged the addition to its numbers of nineteen members from the Northern Territories. They were to be chosen by an electoral college in Tamale, the members of which would be nominated by the (then still existing) Native Authorities.[116]

The electoral college met on 8 February 1951. Of the nineteen successful candidates from a slate of thirty-four, three were from Wala: Wa Na Mumuni Koray was fourth in the poll, Dorimon Na Abudu Mumuni eleventh, and Katua Na Saidu nineteenth.[117] One immediate effect of the changes was not only to bring the Northern Territories in general and Wala in particular into the structure of national (Gold Coast) government for the first time, but also to involve them in national (Gold Coast) party politics.

The United Gold Coast Convention (UGCC) had opened its first branch in the Northern Territories in 1948, at Tamale. Early in 1949 several of its senior officers had visited, *inter alia*, Wa.[118] They advocated a programme to achieve the gradual transition of the Gold Coast from colonial to self-governing status. Kwame Nkrumah's more radical Convention Peoples Party (CPP), founded in the middle of 1949, demanded immediate self-government. After their election to the Legislative Assembly in 1951, Mumuni Koray and the other Wala members tended to embrace the politics of the UGCC.[119] Reacting against Mumuni Koray, the orthodox '*ulama*' of Wa came out in support of the CPP. They were led by Mumuni Adama of Dondoli. He had himself served the colonial administration as interpreter, and his father was the Adama Bile, son of Wa Limam 'Uthman Dun, said to have been passed over for the Wa limamate because at the time of the Zabarima wars he showed himself to be more of a warrior than a scholar.[120]

The Wala Ahmadis claim that they too were initially well disposed towards the CPP, and Nkrumah's policies may well have been attractive to them. When they tried to join the CPP, however, the orthodox told them, 'We have enlisted because of you people. If we allow you to come, then we have defeated our aim.'[121] True or not, there is no doubt that by 1951 the conservative orthodox Muslims were firmly aligned with the radical CPP and the radical Ahmadiyya, if only by default, with the conservative UGCC. The paradox reflects the pre-eminence of local over national politics in the period.

The report of the Coussey Committee which ushered in these changes in local and national government had only just been published when Mumuni Koray became Wa Na in November 1949. Purely local issues still dominated his election. It was predictable that the main opposition would come from the Pirisi gate, which had not held the Nam since the incumbency of Hamidu Bomi, and from Wa Limam Muhammad Saghir and the orthodox 'ulama'.[122] In view of Mumuni Koray's uncompromising demonstration that the Nam had passed under Ahmadi control, it was not predictable that his installation could occur without renewed violence. It did, but the reaction was in fact only a delayed one.

In June 1951 Mumuni Koray was attending his duties in the Legislative Assembly in Accra when Wa Limam Muhammad Saghir died.[123] The orthodox 'ulama' moved rapidly to fill the vacancy. Al-Hajj Sa'id Soribo, Friday Limam and Tijani muqaddam, was made Wa Limam, and Siddiq b. 'Abd al-Mu'min of Tamarimuni became Friday Limam.[124] Mumuni Koray returned to Wa. He refused to recognize the choice of Al-Hajj Sa'id as Wa Limam and appointed Al-Hajj Salih b. al-Hasan to the office. The orthodox announced that if there were to be two Wa Limams there should be two Wa Nas. They began to organize the candidacy of Ducie Na Muhammad of the Busa gate.[125] Traditional politics were polarized as never before. Secular rivalries between the gates to the Nam had become inextricably bound up with sectarian religious conflict. Members of Na Mumumi Koray's gate, Sing and its town ward Gumbilimuni, began to swell the ranks of the Ahmadiyya.

On 11 December 1951 the CPP held a rally in Wa. J. B. Jinsun, an Ahmadi and a relative and personal advisor of Wa Na Mumuni Koray, challenged the speakers on several occasions. His actions precipitated the violence that had been barely contained since Mumuni Koray had become Na. Two days of sporadic rioting followed. The District Commissioner and the police intervened when the casualty list was sixteen wounded (but only four of them seriously). On the evening of the second day, Wa Na Mumuni Koray summoned his warriors from the Divisions, using traditional war drums and, more prosaically, messengers on bicycles. Thousands of armed men – some reports, implausibly, say 10,000 – converged upon Wa. The District Commissioner implored the Wa Na to cancel the mobilization, and at the same time swore in special constables under (for such was the desperate nature of the situation) the Reclamation Officer in the Tsetse Control Department. More to the point, he called in police reinforcements from the Lawra and Bole districts. There was more fighting and more casualties. Only with the arrival of further armed reinforcements from Tamale was order finally restored.[126]

The rioting in Wa was an embarrassment to the CPP as much as to the colonial administration. R. S. Iddrusu, Northern Territories Regional Chairman of the CPP, was sent by the party to investigate affairs in Wa. He was, as it happened, himself an Ahmadi. He proclaimed that membership of the CPP was open to all, regardless of religion, and withdrew recognition from the Wa branch. In the interests of peace he ruled that no meetings should be held in the town other than when outside speakers visited it. As a gesture of goodwill, however, he announced that party headquarters had agreed to pay the fines imposed on branch members for their parts in the riot. The sum involved was £118. Wa Na Mumuni Koray gave Iddrusu assurances that he was not opposed to the CPP as such, but only to those of its members who were trying to undermine his authority. Nevertheless, at the beginning of 1952 there were said to be 800 members of the technically suspended Wa branch of the CPP, of whom only eight were Ahmadis, the remainder being principally orthodox Muslims.[127]

The situation remained tense. Indeed, the level of agitation rose further when a Dagarti Youth Association was formed in 1952 to protest at the neglect of Dagaaba interests. Its sponsors were angered particularly by the fact that no one from the Dagaaba local council areas was among those chosen to represent the Wala District in the Northern Territories Electoral College. They began to talk of seceding from the Wala District and forming – echoes of the past – a separate Dagarti Confederacy.[128]

Anderson has given some account of the Muslim community in Wa during the incumbency of Na Mumuni Koray. Unfortunately, he appears to have relied heavily upon information supplied by Salih b. al-Hasan, whose knowledge of the law books was probably inferior to that of many of the orthodox *'ulama'*. Anderson maintained that in matters of marriage, divorce and inheritance, Islamic law was still quite apparently a superimposition on 'local custom'. He noted, however, that British law as such was a constraint upon the stricter application of *sharia'*; thus, for example, Mumuni Koray had imposed the maximum penalty available to him on an Ahmadi found guilty of adultery on the grounds that, were it not for the British, the culprit would have been stoned to death.[129] Under the regime of Mumuni Koray, in fact, Wa probably approximated more closely to the model of an Islamic community than ever before.

There had been a succession of Nas before Mumuni Koray who were Muslim, but never one for whom the obligations of the faith – albeit Ahmadiyya – so clearly took precedence over the traditional mores of the *nam*. No earlier Na, we may be sure, had thought of keeping the regalia of office in a mosque. Mumuni Koray's approach to purely secular affairs turned out to be bold and decisive. In 1951, for example, he attempted to resolve the matter of Guli. Cutting through ancient controversies about the rights of the descendants of Na Kpasa to the *nam*, he decreed that henceforth Guli should be unambiguously acknowledged a fourth gate.[130] He also addressed problems within the Busa gate that had been created by the 1933 Constitution. We digress, to spell these out.

Busa Na Bukari, enskinned in 1922, died in 1942. Since a member of his immediate lineage currently held the Katua skin, the District Commissioner had arbitrarily decided that the order of succession to Busa should be

Nakori, Ducie, Katua (Table 8.2). Nakori Na Sumaila was thus promoted to Busa. In 1943 he became Wa Na. Ducie Na Darimani was then automatically moved to Busa.[131] However, a son of the late Busa Na Bukari, Sumani, contested the succession. He had, it seems, strong popular support. The gate was still in a state of turmoil when Mumuni Koray became Wa Na. He revived the old title of Gbetore Na which had been virtually extinct since Saliya, founder of the dynasty, and one of his sons, Pelpuo, had held it over two hundred years earlier. He awarded it to Sumani as a gesture of reconciliation. Mumuni Koray, an informant observed, 'had book know-ledge, so he didn't fear these things. But the princes in general fear to make a Gbetore Na. They don't like to fill these posts and revive old claims.'[132]

In late 1952 Wa Na Mumuni Koray was seriously ill and confined to his bed. Still only in his early fifties, he died on 23 March 1953. Wala braced itself for yet another crisis. The Pirisi gate claimed the Nam by the terms of the 1933 Constitution. Pirisi Na Balawu was, however, aged and infirm. The candidacy of Malam Dodi, a Pirisi prince and (as his name indicates) a Muslim, was accordingly advanced. The 1933 Constitution was, however, generally and understandably regarded as a dead letter by the other gates, and Malam Dodi had limited support. The District Commissioner therefore decided that the matter should be settled by a vote of the newly constituted Wala State Council.

There were seven candidates, including one from the Guli gate. The Pirisi Na refused to take part in the proceedings which he rightly said were an innovation and not in accordance with custom. Malam Dodi occupied the palace and proclaimed himself Wa Na. On 20 August 1953 however, by twelve out of twenty votes in the State Council, Katua Na Saidu was elected to the Nam. Born in 1913, he had been a pupil at the Tamale Middle Boarding School, had become Registrar of the Wala Native Authority in 1937, and Member of the Legislative Assembly in 1951. The Pirisi Na brought the matter on appeal to the Governor of the Gold Coast, who confirmed the decision of the State Council. Rioting was only averted by once again moving police reinforcements into Wa from Bole and Lawra. Five of the principals in the dispute were each required to sign a bond of £100 to keep the peace. Malam Dodi went into exile in Accra, where he continued to call himself Wa Na.

Wa Na Saidu II was finally installed in office on 9 November 1953.[133] He was an orthodox Muslim. Salih b. al-Hasan, claiming to be legitimate Wa Limam, refused to surrender the paraphernalia of the Nam still kept in the Ahmadiyya mosque.

The durability of faction: Wala under Na Saidu and Na Sidiki Bomi

Wa Na Saidu II held office from 1953 to 1961. They were years of rapid change. The Wala had enjoyed a fair measure of local autonomy while the British experimented with indirect rule. This was to be progressively eroded by the rising new regime, that of Kwame Nkrumah's CPP, committed to a vision of a modern, democratic, socialist and unitary Ghanaian nation-state. The process through which the Wala, and the peoples of the Northern Territories in general, became enmeshed in a flurry of legislation designed fully to incorporate them into that nation-state has been well described by Ladouceur.[134] In 1954, however, the Northern Peoples Party (NPP) was formed to represent northern interests in opposition to the perceived southern biases of the CPP; there was, it was claimed, no advantage in replacing 'white' by 'black' imperialism.[135] In the 1954 popular election to the Legislative Assembly, the two Wala seats were won by the NPP candidates, B. K. Adama and Jato Kaleo. They retained them in the 1956 election which was the preliminary to Gold Coast, or Ghana, Independence on 6 March 1957.[136] Throughtout these momentous events the Wala continued to grapple with their own problems. That Ghana had taken its place in the United Nations was of little relevance to the conflict between orthodox and Ahmadis in Wala, or to that between rival gates to the Nam.

Wa Limam Sa'id Soribo died in 1954. Salih b. al-Hasan continued to regard himself as legitimate Wa Limam and to be recognized as such by the Ahmadis. The orthodox *'ulama'* elected Yusuf b. Adam as the new Limam. The choice was an unusual one. It violated the Rule of Seniority, since there was at least one candidate available in the senior generation (who was in fact to hold the limamate next), namely, Idris of Dapuyipala, a son of Wa Limam Musa. Yusuf b. Adam, moreover, was from Manzuyiri, from which no limam had been selected for a century. He must be regarded as a compromise candidate, orthodox, to be sure, but only distantly related to the descendants of Limam 'Abd al-Qadir, who had come virtually to monopolize the office. Wa Na Saidu signalled his approval of the election.

With the accession of Yusuf b. Adam to the Wa limamate, Salih b. al-Hasan accepted the inevitable. He appears to have relinquished his claims to be Wa Limam in return for recognition as Wa Ahmadiyya Limam. Schism in the Muslim community was thereby formally acknowledged. The Ahmadis had their own limamate, their own ward of the town founded on the outskirts of Dondoli where they had their mosque, and their own pattern of inter-marriage. In 1955 the District Commissioner of Wa was able optimistically to report:

> Both the Orthodox and the Ahmadiyya movements flourish in Wa. Occasion-ally friction may occur, (and when it does it is normally over a state matter), but on the whole there is little trouble. The Orthodox mosque was built originally in the local traditional style, but it has recently been surrounded by a screen of ambitious architectural design. The Ahmadyyias are also building a new mosque of generous proportions, but it is taking some time to complete. Both movements run a primary day School, but only that of the Ahmadiyyas is assisted by government.[137]

The progressive withdrawal of the Ahmadis from their parent Limamyiri community undoubtedly did alleviate tension. There were, however, many issues around which conflict could still materialize. Thus in 1958–9 Ahmadi Limam Salih, having been accused by the orthodox of being 'a political agitator, a pessimist, and a danger to the progress of the Government's party in Wa', was obliged to defend himself before officials of the CPP and Nkrumah himself.[138] The roots of conflict ran deep. The refusal of the orthodox to allow their daughters to marry Ahmadis remained a factor of fundamental importance. An informant in 1969 lucidly drew attention to this aspect of the matter. Orthodox and Ahmadis, he said,

> will walk together and if it is prayer time, they will pray together, one making their arms the one way, the other making them the other way. It is marriage that still keeps us apart ... We don't marry each other easily. When the Ahmadiyya bury a man, they consign him to Allah and that is the end of it. There is no funeral. The wives are free to remarry after forty days, when it is clear that they are not pregnant. But the orthodox Muslims make a funeral; when a man dies, for example, his sons-in-law will come along and make gifts, even a cow if they can afford it. But ... if I marry an Ahmadiyya girl not even my wife will come to my funeral, and my family will receive no help when I die. So, you see, we don't marry easily.[139]

The authority of Wa Na Saidu II became increasingly eroded by circumstances beyond his control. His stature nationally was diminished when, in 1954, it was made impossible for him, as a chief, to continue to represent his people in the National Assembly. His stature locally was diminished by the Local Courts Act 23 of 1958 and the Local Government (Amendment) Act 14 of 1959, which together virtually removed the traditional authorities from all participation in local government. The Chiefs (Recognition) Act 11 of 1959, moreover, required an order of the Governor General to effect the election or deposition of a chief, and the Chieftaincy Act of 1961 gave the Minister of Local Government power to appoint Judicial Commissioners to determine all matters concerning chieftaincy.

To compound Wa Na Saidu's difficulties, his personal stature was much affected in 1956 when, driving his car, he had an accident which resulted in the death of one of his passengers, the Wechiau Na, and serious injury to others. He was arrested on charges of careless driving and manslaughter, tried, and imprisoned in Tamale. The Wala State Council met in emergency session. Numerous charges were made against him, and one Ahmadi councillor, Tendaga Na Ibrahim, did not neglect to accuse the Na of having illegally removed Salih b. al-Hasan from the Wa limamate. There were reports, too, that he was drunk at the time of the accident; others that immediately prior to the accident he had driven past the place where Na Gura had vanished, a site that it was forbidden for any Wa Na to set eyes on.[140] Na Saidu was subsequently acquitted of all charges on appeal, and he was able to survive the attempts to remove him from office.[141]

On 2 January 1961 Ahmadiyya Limam Salih b. al-Hasan died.[142] At that time there were 2,508 Ahmadis in Wala.[143] The Movement had extended its membership into the Dapuyipala and Limampalayiri sections of Wa

Plate 16 Graves of Wa Nas Saidu II (right) and Mumuni Koray, 1966

Limamyiri, into the Kantonsi section known as Sembeleyiri, and beyond Sing into other of the gate divisions. Despite their growing strength, however, the Ahmadis continued to disengage themselves from traditional Wala politics. By this time, their loyalty seems to have been more engaged by the Ahmadiyya Amirate in Saltpond than by the Nam in Wa. Limam Salih had been officially designated an 'African Missionary' by the Ahmadiyya Movement.[144] So, too, had his old associate, Khalid, who succeeded him.

An epidemic of cerebro-spinal meningitis swept through Wa in 1961. Among those who succumbed to it was Wa Na Saidu. He died on 14 March of that year.[145] Representatives of the four gates met. The Guli Na put forward his candidacy. The heads of the gates unilaterally announced their choice of Pirisi Na Sidiki. When the decision became known, the CPP Commissioner for the Upper Region intervened and cancelled the decision. 'The action of the four Gates', he quite rightly observed, 'is neither constitutional nor democratic because the chief purported to have been installed does not belong to the four Gates alone but to the whole of the Wala State. The installation made by the four Gates is therefore not recognized by Government.'[146]

Following the precedent established in the election of Wa Na Saidu II, the Regional Commissioner instructed the Wala State Council to decide the matter by secret ballot. Of the three candidates, Perisi Na Sidiki was elected with an overwhelming majority and was installed, as Wa Na Sidiki Bomi II, on 2 June 1961. He was a grandson of Saidu Takora, who had been Wa Na in the Samorian period and had been forced out of office in 1897 by the British, in collusion with the Dzedzedeyiri faction.[147] Through his mother he had close ties with Wa Tagarayiri, and at the time of his election he was engaged in the study of the Qur'an.[148] In April 1963 I spoke with Wa Na Sidiki Bomi. 'Wa', he said, 'had been troubled in the past, but everyone wanted him to become Na and bring peace to the town. Some other candidates had tried for the position like Guli Na, but they had no support.'[149]

A few weeks earlier I had talked with one of the leading *'ulama'* of Wa, Al-Hajj Tamimu, whose father, Al-Hajj Muhammad b. 'Uthman Dun, had been limam to Wa Na Saidu Takora. Al-Hajj Tamimu gave an authoritative account of the structure of Muslim authority in Wa, though one from Dondoli rather than Dzedzedeyiri perspectives. Of the head of the Muslims, he said,

> this is the man we call the Shehu Wangara or the Sarkin Wangara, or in Arabic the *amir al-Muslimin* or *amir al-mu'minin*. He is not an *'alim*; he does not have to be learned. He is chosen by all the town, by the princes from Dagomba and the Muslims from Wangara. But not all the people join in choosing him. The Fulani, for example, have no say, because they are strangers – they are Zongo people. The position of the Shehu Wangara is that before anything is done for Wa, we have to go to him. He is the leader to the Na. As *amir*, questions of *sharia'* have to be referred to him. He is the chief *qadi* for Wa. But then he will call together all the *'ulama'* to decide the case. He himself cannot give a *fatwa* or ruling without calling all the learned men together. It is the *ijma' 'l-'ulama'*, the consensus of the faithful, which gives a *fatwa*. We never send to Kong or anywhere else for a *fatwa*. The Qur'an is one, and we cannot change it. We believe in *ijtihad* [independent evaluation of the law] and not in *taqlid* [imitation]. The *'ulama'* of Wa are the *sunni* [orthodox], but this does not include the Ahmadiyya Muslims. We war with the Ahmadiyya.[150]

There was clearly an incompatibility between Wa Na Sidiki's desire to 'bring peace to the town' and Al-Hajj Tamimu's concept of 'war' between orthodox and Ahmadiyya. Wala had not seen the end of violence. Skirmishing broke out between orthodox and Ahmadis at the Friday prayer in 1978, and in 1980 the struggle for the Nam left vacant by the death of Sidiki Bomi erupted into pitched street battles.

In the late twentieth century the Wala are in no way unusual in remaining locked into concerns with their own tangible interests. Matters of national politics, of ideological currents to do with the future of Ghana, have to be translated in order to affect them. They have to be translated into the language of the Wala factions, whether religious or secular. Factionalism articulates aspects of change in the material base of Wala society. Issues of the ownership and use of land are fundamental, for land remains crucial to the reproduction of the Wala communities. Rights to land, and to the authority that underscores those rights, are still validated by reference to history. To know the past is to be secure in the future. Al-Hajj Abu Maidoki (whose recollections we have several times drawn upon) put the point well to Fikry, when talking of the importance of teaching his own children history:

as they're here ... and now they quarrel with someone and then he'd want to undermine you and know how you come about, your history, and so they must teach them to know so as to defend themselves ... And if you're not able to face your origin, then they don't regard you as one of them.[151]

9

Review: the peculiarities of Wala

Introduction

The level of conflict in Wala seems not to have diminished, and may well have risen, over the sixty years of British colonial overrule and the subsequent thirty or so years of Ghanaian independence. It has been a premise of this study that conflict – major conflict – is generated within structures of society too deep easily to be affected by changes in the form of local government mandated from Accra. Many references have been made in this study to the ambiguities and contradictions which become evident when the attempt is made to describe these deep structures. The ambiguities and contradictions are not the products of ignorance. They are neither puzzles capable of solution nor confusions capable of resolution. They are expressed in statements about society, but statements that cannot in practice and perhaps in principle be decided true or false. They articulate the diverse and divergent aspirations, beliefs, conceptions, expectations, ideals (and the like) that the Wala have. The ambiguities and contradictions, in other words, reflect equally valid but none the less incompatible views of the nature of Wala society. They are anomalous and antinomic in character, and they serve to define the peculiarities of Wala.

Not all conflict in Wala arises in its deep structures. The struggles of the Dagaaba against Wala domination, for example, were unambiguously cases of resistance to aggrandizement, small-scale anti-imperial struggles, as it were. It is the pluralistic nature of Wala society as such, and the correspondingly pluralistic nature of authority in Wala, that generates the anomalies and antinomies. They have to do with the triadic relationship of Tendaanba (Landowners), Yerihi (Old Muslims) and Nabihi (Princes) and with their exercise of *tendaanlun* or *nalun*. But they also have to do with the position, with respect to Tendaanba, Yerihi and Nabihi, of the *'ulama'*, who emerged as an hegemonic force in Wala society and exercised a third sort of authority, based upon the precepts of Islam.

In explication of the origins of their polity, the Wala traditionalists – those who engage in *lasiri* – begin with the triad of the three warlords. The earliest was Sidi 'Umar, founder of the Old Muslim settlement of Nasa. The next was

196

Suri, who became head of the Tendaanba in the Wa area. The latest was Saliya, ancestor of the Nabihi, who established himself at Gbetore. So much is received opinion in Wala, though there are differences of detail in the tellings. The story of the creation of the Wala polity does not command the same consensus. It involves the descendants of Sidi 'Umar, Suri and Saliya who became Yeri Nas, Widanas and Wa Nas respectively. It also involves Ya'muru, who was first Wa Limam, and his descendants, who are the *'ulama'*. In one tradition (if we have interpreted it correctly) the first Wa Na was Pelpuo, and his Yeri Na was Bunsalibile. In a second tradition the first Wa Na was Kpasa, and his Yeri Na was Konjekuri.

Suri gave his daughter in marriage to Saliya. This item appears to be generally accepted. It is a key element in the binding together – *lasiri* – of Tendaanba and Nabihi. It is, however, also the point at which tradition bifurcates. Na Kpasa founded the Guli gate to the Nam, but none of his descendants has ever become Wa Na. This is the Antinomy of the Impassable Gate. The natural constituents of Na Kpasa's descendants, the Tendaanba, were unable to acquire wives. This gives rise to the Antinomy of the Landless Landowners. The descendants of Limam Ya'muru came to exercise their office on behalf of the Wala polity as such, its unbelievers as well as believers. This produces the Antinomy of a Limam for Pagans.

The Antinomy of the Impassable Gate

The Nabihi, we have noted, frequently say that their 'grandmothers' came from the Tendaanba. The paradigmatic case of the Tendaanba 'grandmother' is that of Ashaytu, daughter of Widana Suri. She married Saliya (page 42). Their descendants comprise the Guli gate to the Wa Na. The other original gates, Gbetore and Yaro, were created by the descendants of Saliya by different (non-Tendaanba) wives. The Guli claim that Ashaytu's son, Na Kpasa, was the first Wa Na. The other gates – now Busa, Pirisi and Sing – claim this position for Na Pelpuo, son of Saliya's second wife. The Guli claim that the authority, *nalun*, exercised by Na Kpasa was derived not from his father Saliya, but from his maternal grandfather Suri. The other gates claim that the authority exercised by Na Pelpuo was derived from his father, Saliya, and ultimately from the Mampurugu skin. Busa, Pirisi and Sing acknowledge that Guli has the status of a gate to the Nam, in that the Guli Nabihi are descendants of Saliya. They obstruct passage through the Guli gate to the Nam, however, precisely because the Guli assert their claim to it by reference to Suri and not to Saliya. As a result, Guli has not held the Nam since the time of Na Kpasa, a period of about a quarter of a millennium. They continue, however, to contest it. They did so most recently in the dispute following the death of Wa Na Sidiki Bomi in 1978.

The Widana, we have seen, represents Tendaanba interests in the Kpanbihi, the council of Wala elders. As such he is greatly involved, with the Yeri Na and the Foroko, in the enskinment of a Wa Na of whatever gate. On 8

January 1979 however, in his capacity as representative of the Tendaanba and the *tendaanas*, the Widana claimed that he was the only 'kingmaker' and announced the election of Yakubu Seidu as Wa Na.[1] In this he was supported, among others, by a section of Tagarayiri headed by the acting Yeri Na, Al-Hajj Aseku.[2] Five judges of the Supreme Court of Ghana subsequently and wisely invalidated the action, but it is doubtful whether they fully appreciated its rationale. The representative of the Tendaanba saw fit to announce the election of a Na from the Guli gate precisely because the rights that gate claimed to the Nam were derived ultimately from the Tendaanba. Not surprisingly, other 'kingmakers' and representatives of Busa, Pirisi and Sing moved to declare J. N. Momori from Sing gate the new Na. There were thus two Nas-designate. In the event the Guli candidate was once again, after some forty people had died in the fighting, to be excluded from office, thus instancing most recently the Antinomy of the Impassable Gate.

The Antinomy of the Landless Landowners

Virtually all land in Wala is held by forms of customary tenure. The exceptions are those few tracts acquired, for special purposes, by the colonial or post-colonial administrations under statute. Two major principles apply to customary tenures. *Ownership* of land rests upon allodial rights, and these are most commonly viewed as vested in the descendants of the first settlers, that is, the first to bring the land into cultivation. *Use* of the land, however, may pass to others, whose undisputed access to it confers security of tenure after a period of time that does not seem to be clearly defined by custom. It follows, then, that landowners may be unable to use the land they own. This is the Antinomy of the Landless Landowners.

Those who are the descendants of first settlers are the Tendaanba. As the owners of the land, they remain answerable for its well-being to the Earth-god. Others to whom the use of the land may have passed will, we have seen, customarily make supplications to the Earth-god through the Tendaanba and specifically through the relevant local *tendaana*, the custodian of the local Earth shrine. In a few areas, such as Nasa, allodial rights belong to Old Muslims, and there the Yeri Na has the status of *tendaana* and the Earth-god is Allah.

Throughout Wala proper – that is, Wa and the divisions of Busa, Guli, Pirisi and Sing – Tendaanba retain the use of relatively little of the land they own. Rights of undisputed access are exercised for the most part by Nabihi and Muslims. There is no suggestion in the traditions that the Nabihi or Muslims forcibly expropriated the lands of the Tendaanba. They did, we have argued, expropriate their daughters. In Wala this is referred to as 'marriage by capture'. Abduction and kidnapping are not necessary connotations of the expression. Daughters were acquired from the Tendaanba in marriage but no daughters were offered to them in return. The Tendaanba apparently acquiesced in the process; their daughters were making marriages viewed as prestigious ones.[3] The corollary was that the Tendaanba had too few sons to work their farms, which they therefore transferred to their sons-in-law. They retained the ownership but increasingly lost the use of their lands.

In the 1960s, I often heard Tendaanba men gloomily remark that their communities were doomed, and specifically to associate this with their difficulty in obtaining wives and therefore in producing enough children. In the same period I often heard both Nabihi and Muslim men cheerfully remark that their 'grandmothers' came from the Tendaanba. At the time I failed to appreciate the inverse relationship between these two seemingly disconnected sentiments.

The Antinomy of the Landless Landowners will, *a priori*, generate increasingly higher levels of conflict as land comes into shorter supply and land values rise correspondingly higher. This situation currently obtains in Wala. Fikry has sensitively documented 'the undertones of social hatred' that now characterize relations between poor (Tendaanba) and rich (Nabihi and Muslims) in Wala society. 'Chief's son', one song goes, 'don't shout. All children are the same. Allow me to eat a little.'[4]

The Anomalies of Chieftaincy

Antinomies such as those of the Impassable Gate and the Landless Land-owners are quite obviously correlated with faction and therefore with factional conflict in Wala. In the sphere of the traditional politics of the Wa Nam, conflict manifests itself most visibly in succession disputes. The actual pattern of incumbency in the Nam shows that long-term oppositions underlie the short-term coalitions and alliances which materialize when the Nam becomes vacant. Thus Busa, Pirisi and Sing have consistently succeeded in excluding Guli from the Nam, while Pirisi and Sing have had to restrain Busa aspirations to a monopoly of it.

In 1969, Friday Limam Al-Hajj Siddiq remarked, 'formerly chieftaincy meant nothing in Wa. The chief was just a big man in the town'.[5] The comment had reference to the trappings of royalty with which the colonial administration had invested the Wa Nam. To become a 'big man', however, was not a matter of assuming an aura of royalty. It was a matter of demonstrating achievement. The concept of *nalun* is closely bound up with that of wealth, but in the old sense of commonwealth: not of accumulated riches but of benefits to be distributed. Good management was the issue. The capabilities of a Na constituted his claims to office. In the election of a Na these had to be put to the test. A candidate was required to demonstrate that he could muster support, and he did this by wheeling and dealing for it, on occasion virtually buying it, and on other occasions having resort to arms. We have seen, for example, that Wa Na Fijolina opened the way to power by having his predecessor, Na Danduni, assassinated; that Na Saidu Takora attained office only with military assistance from the Dagaaba of Kaleo; that Na Pelpuo III sedulously wooed the '*ulama*' with produce from his farms; and that the gates to Sing were skilfully manipulated to bring Na Mumuni Koray through to office. Contest was built into the very system of ensuring that a man was 'big' enough to qualify for the Nam; that he was likely effectively to exercise those functions of management – especially defence and the preservation of internal order – that were required of a Na.

Succession disputes were in such respects clearly functional. In other respects they were equally clearly disfunctional. They were often disruptive of social order and sometimes destructive of life and property. Therein lie the Anomalies of Chieftaincy. The British colonial administration attempted to legislate such disputes out of existence, but their efforts to regulate and routinize chiefly office throughout Wala proved self-negating and disastrous in their consequences. They spelled the doom of the experiment in indirect rule by permitting, indeed virtually guaranteeing, the accession to office of men incapable of effectively discharging their responsibilities. In attempting to avert conflict, the colonial administrators thereby discounted leadership. The various post-colonial governments of Ghana have remained trapped in the dilemma.

The position of chiefs in Ghana has been much affected by local government legislation introduced since 1957. As Arhin has remarked, 'the Governments of Ghana have taken away the authority of traditional rulers by passing laws, called *acts*, if they are discussed and approved by the Assembly in Accra, and *decrees*, if they are made by a military government and published in the Government information paper known as the *Gazette*'.[6] The Houses of Chiefs Act of 1958 created a House of Chiefs in each region of Ghana with powers to settle disputes about chieftaincy, and in 1969 a National House of Chiefs was established to which cases might go on appeal. The Chieftaincy Act of 1971 required chiefs, chosen locally according to customary procedures, to be registered with the National House of Chiefs and approved by the Minister of Local Government. It gave the Houses of Chiefs powers to determine customary laws of marriage, divorce and inheritance, and to advise the government and courts of Ghana accordingly. 'The manner in which the Governments of Ghana have applied some of these laws', Arhin writes, 'has greatly weakened the position of traditional rulers and made it clear even to those who had no idea of the new laws that traditional rulers can act only if the central Government wishes them to do so.'[7] In such circumstances, the potential for conflict in the sphere of chieftaincy should, *prima facie*, have diminished. This has not been the case in Ghana in general and in its northern regions in particular. It has most certainly not been the case in Wa.

We have referred several times to the period of conflict, unprecedented in intensity, at least in the twentieth century, that was ushered in by the death of Wa Na Sidiki Bomi in 1978. Detail may be added in a recapitulation of the episode. It seemed that the succession would easily be resolved. There was a general feeling that it was the turn of the Sing gate. Sing Na Iddi Bukpali stood aside in favour of Chansa Na J. N. Momori. Momori had been Clerk of Council in Wa. Elected Member of Parliament for Wa East in 1969, he was placed in detention after the military coup of 13 January 1972 led by Colonel I. K. Acheampong. Another candidate, however, had entered the contest. This was Yakubu Seidu of the Guli gate, a very wealthy cattle trader who had previously held no skin. Matters of personality were at issue and so too were different images of an acceptable Na. Underlying such concerns were the ancient problems of *tendaanlun* and *nalun*, of the plight of the Tendaanba and of the gate that, in a sense, best expressed their interests.

Early in January 1979 we have seen that Widana, as representative of the Tendaanba, announced the election of Yakubu Seidi as Wa Na. The election of J. N. Momori was then announced by his supporters. There were two Wa Nas. Yakubu Seidu took the case to the Upper Region House of Chiefs in Bolgatanga, and won it. J. N. Momori prepared an appeal to the National House of Chiefs in Kumase.[8] Tensions rose. In March 1980 those describing themselves as the 'Wa Kingmakers' petitioned President Hilla Limann. Arguing that it was unheard of for the Tendaanba alone to make a Wa Na, they contended that J. N. Momori had been properly elected as Na Momori Bondiri II and asked for the President's intervention to avert possible violence.[9] Time had run out, however. Late in March an attempt was made formally to enskin Yakubu Seidu. Three days of fighting followed. Yakubu Seidu was in Fongo, the Guli section of Wa town. It was besieged. The defenders, having been allowed to send out their women and children, converted a large building into a stronghold, fortifying the walls with sacks of grain. Only when their ammunition ran out were they finally forced to make their escape.[10]

The press reported twenty-seven slain in the fighting and forty-two seriously wounded, but the number of dead seems likely to have exceeded forty. Property damage was estimated at three million cedis; three houses including that of Yakuku Seidu, a drug store, two trucks, a tractor, a car and two mills were destroyed by fire.[11] The Inspector General of Police arrived in Wa to oversee the restoration of law and order. On 10 April 1981 the National House of Chiefs rejected J. N. Momori's appeal. Violence threatened again. The police and soldiers barely restrained it. Flight-Lieutenant Rawlings seized power from Limann on 31 December 1981. Six months later he banished both putative Nas from Wa.

It was not until July 1985 that the Supreme Court of Ghana finally took the case. Five judges of appeal found that the Guli, or Na Kpasa gate, had legitimate claims to the Nam; expressed their inclination to favour a rotational process of election as 'a just and convenient way of resolving problems of succession to the Wa skin'; set aside the elections of both Yakubu Seidu and J. N. Momori; and named as 'kingmakers' or electors: '(a) the head of the Tindaobas [Tendaanba]; (b) the Princes (Nabisis) of the 4 gates: Perisi, Busa, Sing and Nakpaha [Na Kpasa]; (c) the Yeri Na; (d) the

Foriko [Foroko]'.[12] On 29 August 1985 the 'kingmakers' met in Wa. Yakubu Seidu boycotted the proceedings. 'If a contestant of the Wa Skins does not approach we the Kingmakers and establish and justify his candidature, thus paying us the established customary rites, how can we give the chieftaincy to him', the Busa Na asked? J. N. Momori was unanimously elected Wa Na.[13]

Those who petitioned President Limann in 1980 observed: 'it is the view of the kingmakers that the Wa skin is one of the oldest and recognised traditional institutions in the country and we, as custodians of it, are striving to preserve this noble institution'. An uncomfortable paradox has to be faced, that it is precisely the conflict and violence of 1980 that attests most unmistakably to the enduring strength of the institution of the Nam.

The Anomalies of Islam

In the last half-century, Muslim factionalism in Wa has taken the form of confrontation between orthodox and Ahmadiyya. It has, however, a longer ancestry. It can be traced back, in the developing opposition between Dondoli and Dzedzedeyiri, at least to the middle of the nineteenth century. Segmentation in the Limamyiri community, that is, the division of the descendants of Limam Ya'muru into Houses, was the framework within which struggles for leadership and direction emerged. There was, however, an ideological dimension to those struggles.

Ambiguity and contradiction were inherent in situations in which Muslims lived in predominantly pagan lands. The rigidity of the distinction in Islam between Muslim and Kafir, believer and unbeliever, enlightened and benighted, gave rise to major problems of praxis. It was these problems that Suwarian doctrines, embraced by the traditional *'ulama'* of Wala, addressed. The Suwarian *'ulama'* emphasized the importance of learning in maintaining the correctness of the *sunna* of the believers. But they also construed *kufr*, unbelief, as ignorance rather than wickedness, and viewed enlightenment as an inexorable process in which intervention – by active proselytization – was inappropriate. Conversion would occur in its due time, though the presence of the *'ulama* was not irrelevant to it. In sustaining their *sunna*, their way of life visible in the mosques and schools, the *'ulama'* saw themselves as presenting the unbelievers with an example, *qudwa*, and as making possible emulation, *iqtida'*. Perhaps, indeed, the adoption of Muslim names by unbelievers, and the assimilation of old agricultural and other festivals to Muslim celebrations, were seen as early signs of emulation.[14]

The Suwarian tradition was, then, an ideology which facilitated a distinctive kind of accommodation between the interests of believers and those of unbelievers. In its theoretical aspects it enabled the *'ulama'* religiously to justify their position within pagan lands by defining them as domains of ignorance rather than of warfare (*harb*). In its practical aspects it allowed for the coexistence of believers and unbelievers within an overarching social and political order. The Suwarian synthesis could, however, become strained.

The authority of a Wa Na was essentially secular, based upon *nalun*. In the past an incumbent of the skin might or might not have been a Muslim. If he was, he deferred in matters of religion to the *'ulama'*. Whether he was or was not, however, his role was to see to the defence of the polity and the maintenance of public order. Matters relating to the affairs of the Muslims as such were not within his purview, but within that of the Wa Yeri Na. There was nothing anomalous in the position of a Muslim Wa Na with respect to his non-Muslim subjects nor in that of a non-Muslim Wa Na with respect to his Muslim subjects. When, for example, Sidiki Bomi was elected Wa Na he was engaged in Qur'anic studies. He had not completed them. 'Now he is too busy', I was told; 'he has to look to the pagans as well as the Muslims.'[15] His studies undoubtedly helped to make his candidacy the more acceptable to the Muslims, but they had no relevance to his exercise of *nalun*.

The authority of the Wa Limam was essentially spiritual, and rested upon the Qur'an. Yet from the time of the first incumbent Ya'muru, the Wa Limam was responsible for the well-being of the Wala polity as such. He was required to exercise his offices on behalf of the *'ulama'* and the Old Muslims, but also on behalf of the Nabihi and Tendaanba, whether believers or not. He was, by the definition of his office, Limam for the Muslims, but there was a sense in which he also had to be Limam for the Pagans. His relationship to the Wa Na was structurally the same whether the incumbent of that office was a believer or unbeliever. In this respect, the Wa Limam's position exemplifies the Antinomy of a Limam for Pagans. It was a position that the Suwarian tradition, for all its flexibility, could scarcely endorse without crossing the line from orthodoxy to heterodoxy. The contradictions in the situation were well exemplified in 1887 when Wa Limam 'Uthman Dun, educated it seems in the prestigious schools of Buna, nevertheless felt it proper to prepare charmed gunpowder for use by a largely pagan Wala army against the Muslim troops under Babatu. There was danger as well as contradiction in the situation. Babatu, in turn, saw no impropriety in carrying out a massacre of Wala Muslims.

In the nineteenth century, the anomalous position of Wa Limam *vis-à-vis* the unbelievers provoked a response that may be loosely characterized as reformist. The matter of correct Muslim attitudes towards participation in the affairs of a non-Muslim polity was particularly at issue. The reformists espoused policies of separation. These might assume the more extreme form of physical relocation. Old Muslims left Wala to join the Karantaw *jihad* in the middle of the nineteenth century, and there is reason to think that at least sections of the *'ulama'* supported them. In particular, no less than Ya'qub b. 'Abd al-Qadir of Dzedzedeyiri seems to have relinquished the Wa limamate, preferring that of Shukr li-'llahi offered him by Mahmud Karantaw. Fifty years later Limam Ya'qub's grandson, Ishaq b. 'Uthman Dabila, threatened to lead his followers out of Wala when the Wa Na and Wa Limam opted for the French rather than the British. Separation, however, did not necessarily entail emigration. The creation of the Friday limamate was an assertion of

Muslim autonomy within Wala society, of disengagement from the affairs of the Nam.

Dondoli leadership of the conservative 'ulama' seems never to have been challenged. It rested in part on the fact that its founder, Muhammad, was the most senior of the sons of Limam 'Abd al-Qadir to hold the Wa limamate. Dzedzedeyiri was equally secure in its leadership of the reforming 'ulama'. Its founder, Ya'qub, was the third of 'Abd al-Qadir's sons to hold the limamate, and it may be that his defection to the Karantaw cause gave rise to a tradition of dissent among his descendants in Wa. Whatever the case, the polar opposition between Dondoli and Dzedzedeyiri defined Muslim factionalism in Wala. In the late nineteenth century the Dzedzedeyiri faction shared neither the pro-Samorian nor pro-French stance of the Dondoli, but pursued a pro-British policy of its own. In the 1930s and 1940s Dzedzedeyiri provided the bulk of the early recruits to the Ahmadiyya Movement, and the 'ulama' of the Dondoli faction anathematized them as heterodox. Factionalism finally became schism with the creation of the Ahmadiyya limamate.

Predictably, Muslim factionalism has been little affected by the succession of changes in local government since Ghana became independent. Between 1949 and 1953, however, Muslim and chiefly affairs became locked together as never before. The Ahmadi Wa Na Mumuni Koray appointed the Ahmadi spiritual leader Salih b. Al-Hasan to the Wa limamate, and the paraphernalia of the Wa Nam was deposited in the Ahmadiyya mosque. The situation occasioned serious rioting in 1951 and the prognostications were ominous. The death of Mumuni Koray eased the tension. Thereafter the Ahmadis appear to have redefined their priorities. Reverting to older Dzedzedeyiri factional policy, they appear to have distanced themselves from the affairs of the Wa Nam and, we have said, looked to the Ahmadiyya Amir in Saltpond for leadership. Anything like total disengagement was, however, impossible short of physical relocation. The Ahmadiyya number many Nabihi among their converts, and not a few Tendaanba.

Violence, we have seen, flared up once more in 1978. Police permits had to be obtained to attend the Friday prayer and all those doing so were searched for weapons. At issue on this occasion was whether or not the Ahmadis were entitled to use the central mosque. In asserting their right to do so the Ahmadis were at the same time affirming a basic article of their beliefs, that the Ahmadiyya Movement is in no way heterodox: 'Ahmadis are Muslims and their religion is Islam.'[16] Conversely, the attempt to exclude them from the central mosque was at the same time a denial of their orthodoxy.

Whither Wala?

In April 1983 the ruling Provisional National Defence Council of Ghana, the PNDC, made public its plans for the decentralization of authority as a way of creating 'a new democracy which will bring about greater efficiency and productivity in the state machinery through the involvement and effective participation by the people at all levels in administration'.[17] At the time of writing (early 1988), 110 districts have been delimited on the basis of population, economic viability and administrative convenience. Each will have its District Assembly. Voter registration is in progress, and the elections are projected for late 1988. Two-thirds of the members of an assembly will be elected by popular vote and one-third will be appointed as representatives of the traditional authorities and other local organizations involved in the 'productive life' of the district. Each District Assembly will be responsible for setting up a hierarchy of lower level town, area, zonal and unit committees. There will be five District Assemblies in the Upper West Region of which Wa will, apparently, remain capital.[18]

Spokesmen for the PNDC have consistently recognized the loyalties which the traditional authorities continue to command locally, and have stressed the advantages to be gained from fully involving them in the decentralization process. The PNDC, so Head of State J. J. Rawlings observed in April 1987, 'recognises the institution of chieftaincy as a positive focal point for local development'. It must, he added, 'rid itself of the accumulated negative aspects which have clouded its real value ... these disputes [which] tend to dissipate energies which could better be channelled into the provision of infrastructure to bring about socio-economic progress'.[19] On tour of the Upper West Region six months later, Rawlings returned to the theme. He urged that the traditional authorities 'should be seen to play the role of promoters of peace and fosterers of unity and communal understanding'.[20] This was an accurate enough description of the perceived customary respon- sibilities of those who held the Nam. Chieftaincy disputes, he added, were 'one of the surest ways of creating disunity'. This closely reproduced the views of the colonial administrators, but failed to address the Antinomies of Chieftaincy, specifically, the intimate connection between conflict and quality of leadership.

Early in 1988 the Ghana Chieftaincy Secretariat required the Traditional Councils to make returns detailing the status of all chiefly offices, the composition of the 'kingmakers', the correct installation procedures, and so forth. The Secretary for Chieftaincy Affairs announced that the returns were intended to identify rightful successors to office, thereby to 'assist administra- tors and judges to carry out researches and administer justice in chieftaincy disputes' and to reduce 'protracted, factional litigations at the law courts'.[21]

The implications of this study is that, in Wala at least, it will prove impossible (and may not in any case be wise) to eradicate conflict and dispute. Factionalism, we have said, is rooted in the past. It is generated within the deep structures of society. It has to do with fundamental matters of landownership and land use, and it has to do with basic matters of religion. Only revolutionary change could, in totally breaking with the past, deprive the factions of any continuing relevance in Wala affairs. A radical socialist (or perhaps Muslim)[22] regime committed to the nationalization and redistribution of land might accomplish such a social transformation. The appearance of either in Ghana seems scarcely imminent.

Decentralization (like indirect rule earlier) is an experiment full of promise, but is unlikely in itself to effect far-reaching changes in society. The Wala District Assembly will in all probability remain as factionalized as any of its predecessors, and it is perhaps not entirely unhealthy that it should. Faction is one way in which community is expressed, though the violence which it generates from time to time has obviously to be constrained. In the twentieth century the level of that violence has tended to be compounded by ill-advised decisions made and executed by colonial administrators and those who succeeded them. To be effective, we repeat, the administrator and policy maker require a sound, even profound, understanding of the peculiarities of locality.

Wala is in a very real sense its peculiarities: its ambiguities, contradictions, anomalies and antinomies. It is, in other words, its past. Marx, in his *Eighteenth Brumaire*, knew that men make their own history and he knew that they make it 'under circumstances directly encountered, given and transmitted from the past'. But, he added, 'the tradition of all the dead generations weighs like a nightmare on the brain of the living'. The Wala might well regard this as a fair comment on their predicament.

Notes

Preamble

1 Robertson, 1819, p. 180 and map, followed by Hutton, 1821, map.
2 Barth, 1859.
3 *Neue Preussische (Kreuz) Zeitung,* 1, vi, 1892.
4 Freeman, 1892, p. 136.
5 CO.879/38, African (West) no. 448, p. 70.
6 CO.879/52, African (West) no. 549, pp. 354–6: Report on Wa and Daboya by Captain Mackworth, dd. 6 June 1898.
7 Wilks, FN/61, 8 March 1963.
8 Wilks, FN/267, 8 February 1987.
9 S. Moore, *Biography of Mahommah G. Baquaqua, a Native of Zoogoo, in the Interior of Africa,* Detroit, 1854, see Austin, 1984, pp. 609 and 614.
10. *Daily Graphic,* 11 March 1980.
11 Government of Ghana, PNDC Law 16, Wa Skin Property (Preservation), and Law 21, Wa Chieftaincy Affairs (Prohibition). See Wilks, FN/235, 10 January 1986.
12 Supreme Court of Ghana, Asanni Zei and J. N. Momori v. Yakubu Seidu, 3, 5, 9, 17 and 29 July 1985. See Wilks, FN/233, 9 January 1896.
13 Proceedings of Meeting of Kingmakers of the Wa Skins held at Yijisi on Thursday, 29 August 1985, see Wilks, FN/233, 9 January 1986.
14 Harvey, 1966, p. 80.
15 Ferguson and Wilks, 1970; Ladouceur, 1972; Staniland, 1975; and for recent developments, *West Africa,* 4 May 1987, p. 889; 11 May 1987, p. 939; 18 May 1987, p. 984; 1 June 1987, p. 1079; 8 June 1987, p. 1131; 22 June 1987, p. 1220; 29 June 1987, p. 1267; and 10 August 1987, p. 1548.
16. Meek, Macmillan and Hussey, 1940, p. 84. I am indebted to Kojo S. Amanor for drawing my attention to Macmillan's comment.
17 *West Africa,* 13 July 1987, pp. 1343–5; 27 July 1987, p. 1462; 3 August 1987, pp. 1477–8. The programme was first publicized in a pamphlet, *Decentralization in Ghana,* published under the auspices of the Provisional National Defence Council and dated April 1983.

1 Wa and the Wala

1 See further, Agricultural Department Office, Wa: J. H. Hinds, Report on Agriculture in the Lawra District and the Wa District, 1943, condensed in Hinds, 1957, pp. 192–5. Dougah, 1966, pp. 1–11.
2 See Arhin, 1974, p. 137.

3 *Journal Le Temps*, 28 August 1895.

4 Henderson, 1898, p. 492.

5 CO.879/41, African (West) no. 479, pp. 8–9.

6 Treaty of 3 May 1895, see PRO, CO.879/52, African (West) no. 549, p. 224: M. Gosselin and W. Everett to Sir Edmund Monson, dd. Paris, 29 March 1898.

7 CO.879/113, African (West) no. 1010, pp. 94–6.

8 *Bulletin du Comité de l'Afrique Française*, October 1901, p. 342: Hugot's Journal.

9 Kanya-Forstner, 1969, pp. 245, 248.

10 Arhin, 1974, pp. 137–8.

11 Henderson, 1898, p. 489.

12 CO.879/52, African (West) no. 549, p. 43: telegram dd. Wa, 13 January 1898. See also Northcott, 1899, p. 16.

13 Northcott, 1899, p. 16. CO.879/52, African (West) no. 549, pp. 155–6: Northcott to Acting Governor dd. 2 January 1898.

14 CO.879/52, African (West) no. 549, p. 354: Director of Military Intelligence to Colonial Office, dd. 7 June 1898, enclosing Report on Wa by D. Mackworth, dd. 6 June 1898.

15 Map by the Intelligence Division of the War Office, October 1899, in Northcott, 1899.

16 NAG Tamale, ADM.1/7, Northern Territories Order 8 of 1925.

17 NAG Tamale, ADM.1/257, Wa District Native Affairs: District Commissioner to Acting Chief Commissioner, Northern Territories, 3 September 1933. Guli was originally included in Pirisi, but was afforded distinct status in 1934, see NAG Tamale, ADM.1/241, Informal Diaries: entries for 22 January and 16 February 1934.

18 *The Gold Coast, 1931. Appendices Containing Comparative Returns and General Statistics of the 1931 Census*, 1932, pp. 198–202. *The Gold Coast. Census of Population 1948*, 1950, pp. 354–9.

19 NAG Accra, ADM.56/1/96: Census of Wa District, Provincial Commissioner, Northern Province, to Deputy Chief Commissioner, Tamale, dd. 21 August 1921.

20 *1960 Population Census of Ghana*, vol. I, Census Office, Accra, p. xxiii; *1970 Population Census of Ghana. Special Report 'D'*, Northern and Upper Regions, Census Office, Accra, 1971, p. xx; *1984 Population Census of Ghana. Preliminary Report*, Central Bureau of Statistics, Accra, 1984, p. 82.

21 See, for example, Fikry, 1970, vol. I, pp. 270–3.

22 Mid 1880s ('about 6,000 inhabitants, at least'), PRO, CO.879/52, African (West) no. 549, p. 355: Report on Wa by D. Mackworth, dd. 6 June 1898. 1902 ('about 2,000 inhabitants'): Delafosse, 1908, p. 172. Population Censuses of the Gold Coast and Ghana, 1921 (2,810), 1931 (5,223), 1948 (5,156), 1960 (14,342), 1970 (21,374), and 1984 (36,000).

23 *The Gold Coast. Census of Population 1948*, table 23, pp. 367–9, and p. 407.

24 *1960 Population Census of Ghana, Special Report 'E', Tribes in Ghana*, p. ix.

25 Ibid. App. B, App. D, table S1, and see also pp. xi–xv. The Special Report is based upon a 10% sample and is therefore subject to standard errors, see pp. xci–xcvi.

26 Goody, 1954, pp. 26–31; 1956, pp. 16–26.

27 *Colonial Reports – Annual*, nos. 722 and 1011, Northern Territories of the Gold Coast, Report for 1911, p. 18; Report for 1918, p. 21. See also Goody, 1954, p. 8.

28 Goody, 1954, p. 8; 1956, p. 16.

29 NAG Tamale, ADM.1/573: A Gazetteer of the Wa District 1955.

30 Westermann and Bryan, 1952, p. 63. See further, Goody, 1954, p. 4.

31 Goody, 1954, p. 9.

32 Rattray, 1932, vol. II, p. 452.

33 Binger, 1892, vol. II, p. 36.

34 Armitage, 1924, p. 20.

35 St J. Eyre-Smith first suggested the analogy. His sensitive though generalized description of

the organization of society around the Earth-god still bears reading, Eyre-Smith, 1933, pp. 15–25. For more recent studies of relevance, see for example Fortes, 1945, 1949; Pogucki, 1955; Goody, 1956; Tait, 1961.

36 See, for example, Sawyer, 1976; Hooke, 1985.

37 Compare Goody, 1956, especially pp. 27–37; Yelpaala, 1982, pp. 35–47; Pogucki, 1955, pp. 8–12.

38 Pogucki, 1955, especially chapter 3.

39 NAG Tamale, ADM/1/573: A Gazetteer of the Wa District 1955.

40 The distinction was the subject of a heated exchange recorded by Fikry, 1970, vol. I, pp. 265–8. The three parties to the exchange belonged to different sections of Wa, though all as it happened were Muslims by faith.

41 See, e.g., NAG Tamale, ADM.1/257, Wa District Native Affairs: District Commissioner to Chief Commissioner, Northern Territories dd. 7 October 1933, Composition of Divisional Tribunal Courts in Wala State.

42 NAG Tamale, ADM.1/437, Essay on the People of the Northwestern Province, B. M. Read, 22 November 1908.

43 See, for example, Fikry, 1970, vol. I, pp. 102–10, 263–8.

44 Wilks, FN/136, 16 April 1964.

45 The analysis of Western European feudal society in terms of those who fight, those who pray, and those who work is an analogue perhaps worthy of pursuit, see for example Duby, 1975.

46 Goody, 1967, pp. 186–8.

47 Wilks, FN/169, 4 January 1969.

48 A Lebanese trader newly arrived in Wa shot a crocodile from Dzandzan Pool. He was obliged to provide a goat for sacrifice, and a fine in cloth and other commodities in pacification, see Wilks, FN/167, 3 January 1969.

49 Fikry, 1970, vol. I, pp. 233–5. Dancers wearing the masks appear by custom only at night, for funerals, rainmaking and the like. Colonial administrators forced the reluctant dancers to make public appearances from time to time, for purposes of entertainment. The visit of Princess Marie Louise to Wa in 1925 was one such occasion. That they were obliged to appear in daylight at least enabled them to be photographed, probably for the first time ever, Marie Louise, 1926, facing p. 120.

50 NAG Tamale, ADM.1/608: Appointments, Deaths, etc., Wa District, 27 January 1944. Hamidu Bomi became Pirisi Na in 1926 and succeeded Pelpuo as Wa Na ten years later.

51 Northcott, 1899, p. 16. CO.879/52, African (West) No. 549, pp. 155–6.

52 NAG Tamale, ADM.1/257, Wa District Native Affairs: District Commissioner to Acting Chief Commissioner, Northern Territories, 3 September 1933. Document entitled 'Wala State. Composition of Divisional Tribunals (Court) in the Wala State', Appendix H.

53 CO.879/113, African (West) no. 1010, pp. 94–6.

54 Wilks, FN/24, 8 August 1964.

55 Wilks, FN/24, 8 August 1964.

56 Descriptions of the procedure will be found in Marie Louise, 1926, p. 112, and Dougah, 1966, pp. 109–12.

57 NAG Tamale, ADM.1/316: Informal Diary, 9 August 1938.

58 NAG Tamale, ADM.1/257, Wa District Native Affairs: undated report, signed 'District Commissioner'. The report is filed with one by St J. Eyre-Smith, Assistant Secretary for Native Affairs, dd. 7 March 1932, and is presumably of much the same date.

59 Fikry, 1970, vol. I, pp. 369–70; vol. II, pp. 182–94.

60 NAG Accra, ADM.56/1/96: Census of the Wa District, Provincial Commissioner, Northern Province, to Deputy Chief Commissioner, Tamale, dd. 21 August 1921.

61 See, for example, NAG Accra, ADM.56/1/416, Monthly Report, Black Volta District, February 1901; ADM.66/5/5, Wa District Letter Book, 1916.

62 *1960 Population census of Ghana*, Special Report 'E', 1964, pp. 83–98.

63 Wilks, 1984. see also Wilks, 1968, pp. 177–80.

64 *The Gold Coast Gazette*, no. 33, 28 March 1952, pp. 543–6. Dougah, 1966, p. 81.

2 Wala origins: *lasiri* and *kubaru*

1 Wilks, Levtzion and Haight, 1986, pp. 99, 100.

2 Very few tobacco pipes of local manufacture, useful indicators of date, occur in the occupational debris that litters the town of Wa. Of several fragments I have found, none appears earlier than the late seventeenth century.

3 Fikry, 1970, vol. I, p. 26.

4 The story is a well-known one in Wa, though surprisingly it is not among those recorded in Fikry, 1970. The pupils of the Wala Native Authority school enacted it for the Annual Conference of Chiefs in 1938, and I have followed that version closely since it is, as far as I know, the earliest on record, see NAG Tamale, ADM.1/319.

5 See, for example, Fikry, 1970, vol. II, pp. 6, 10, 12, 26, 37.

6 For the appearance of the *khabar* form in the region, see Wilks, Levtzion and Haight, 1986, p. 19.

7 Wilks, FN/112, 3 August 1964. The work is entitled, *Ta'rikh Ahl Tarawiri min Mandi*, 'History of the Tarawiri from Mande'.

8 Fikry, 1970, vol. I, p. 28.

9 Wilks, Levtzion and Haight, 1986.

10 Wilks, FN/149, 4 May 1966.

11 The vowelization differs in the two manuscripts. A very tentative reading might be Dubutuga, Yabutuga, Kpiyili, Bamuni and Kunturu.

12 S. Pilaszewicz, 'The Story of Wala, Our Country', in *Africana Bulletin* (Warsaw), no. 11, 1970, pp. 59–78.

13 Sulayman b. Ibrahim, Imam of the Hausa mosque in Wa and son of the redactor of AWK, maintained that 'Niyirtiwu' referred to a place in Lobi country; 'I mean Lobi', he said, 'not Dagarti.' Wilks, FN/149, 4 May 1966.

14 See, e.g., Wilks, FN/154, 6 May 1966.

15 Wilks, FN/130, 18 April 1964. The interview was with the extremely aged Ishaq Dodu of Tagarayiri, Chief Butcher of Wa who, having named Konjekuri as third Yeri Na, then hesitated and said that he may have been a Wa Na. In the course of 1929–30 R. S. Rattray talked with the then Yeri Na ('an old man': it must have been 'Uthman Daleri), and was told that 'our ancestor was called Kagyekpegu', Royal Anthropological Institute, London, Rattray Papers, MS Bundle 109, Notebook 8. The memory of Kajikpara (Konjekuri, Kagyekpegu), unlike that of Sandamu or Sanda Muru, appears now to be receding.

16 Wilks, FN/52–3, 30 June and 1 July 1964.

17 Ibid.

18 The identity of the Kanbali is unclear, though a village of that name is now part of the western outskirts of Wa.

19 Wilks, FN/112, 3 August 1964.

20 NAG Accra, Acc. no. 1427 of 1959. Also IASAR/22. Whittall was appointed District Commissioner, Wa, on 25 October 1922.

21 Wilks, FN/145, 8 March 1963.

22 I have never heard Chegli referred to as a gate to the Nam. But see Royal Anthropological Institute, London, Papers of R. S. Rattray, MS Bundle 109, Notebook 8, 1929–30, p. 166. Rattray refers to Na Kunlugi as being from 'Kyeguru', presumably Chegli, and comments that he was the only chief from the village ever to take the Nam.

23 NAG Accra, ADM.66/5/1, Wa District General Information Book, 1924–5: 'Notes on the

History of the Wa District'.

24 This story was told to me in the course of a session of story-telling in a *pito* bar. 'How can a father succeed his son in office?' I was asked. 'I give up', I said... For obvious reasons the conversation was not adequately documented.

25 In 1929 or 1930 Rattray, whose notes on Wa are highly slipshod, nevertheless was aware of the problem of Gura and Saliya. His comment on the matter was that Saliya ('Sorlya') had a younger brother, Na Gura, who died before him and so never became Na; see Royal Anthropological Institute, London, Papers of R. S. Rattray, MS Bundle 109, Notebook 8, 1929–30, p. 166.

26 Other strands of tradition support this view, see e.g., Wilks, FN/129, 17 April 1964.

27 Fikry, 1970, vol. I, p. 126.

28 Dougah, 1966, pp. 14–15. Wilks, FN/267, 8 February 1987.

29 The very location of Gbetore is now in doubt. Dougah, 1966, p. 14, places it a few miles from Busa. In Wilks, FN/267, 8 February 1987, it is described as near Guli.

30 Wilks, FN/165, 4 January 1969.

31 Ibid. Wilks, FN/234, 10 January 1986.

32 The story of the creation of the gate from Djonyusi sources is given in Fikry, 1970, vol. I, pp. 126–33.

33 Wilks, FN/267, 8 February 1987.

34 For another version, see Fikry, 1970, vol. I, pp. 129–31.

3 Wala origins: the *'alim* as local historian

1 Wilks, FN/112, 3 August 1964.

2 N. Levtzion, IASAR (tr.)/152, 1963. Pilaszewicz, 1969, pp. 53–76.

3 CO.879/52, African (West) no. 549, pp. 354–6: Report on Wa by D. Mackworth, dd. 6 June 1898.

4 CO.879/58, African (West) no. 585, p. 18: Director of Military Intelligence, dd. London, 21 January 1899.

5 Armitage, 1924, p. 20.

6 It appears, misspelled as 'Bunghu', between Denkerepe ('Dankiri') and Busa ('Bu'asa') on a route book which Dupuis copied in Kumase in 1820, see Dupuis, 1824, App., p. cxxxi.

7 Wilks, FN/127, 14 April 1964.

8 'Gonja Traditional and Customary Practice and Procedure in Chieftaincy Matters – Since 1923', compiled by Osafroadu Amankwatia, Counsel to the Northern Regional House of Chiefs, Tamale, 1973, pp. 9–10.

9 Goody, 1954, p. 3 and map facing p. 2.

10 Armitage, 1924, p. 20.

11 Dougah, 1966, p. 14, shows a knowledge of the story, though he sets it in the time of Saliya.

12 NAG Tamale, ADM.1/437: Essay on the People of the Northwestern Province, 22 November 1908.

13 R. S. Rattray recorded his name as Gbungburo, 'Hyena', see Royal Anthropological Institute, London, Rattray Papers, MS Bundle 109, Notebook 8, 1929–30, p. 153.

14 Labouret, 1931, pp. 21–2.

15 Eyre-Smith, 1933, p. 12.

16 Goody, 1956, pp. 4–5.

17 Goody, 1956, pp. 11 and note 4; 16–26.

18 Arhin, 1974, pp. 137–9. See also 'Le Gourounsi', in *Bulletin du Comité de l'Afrique Française*, 1 January 1898, p. 50 and map.

19 Robertson, 1819, p. 180.

20 The text, entitled 'Wala Lasiri', was kindly made available to me by J. D. Fage. It was

recorded by David Tait in the 1950s but its provenance is otherwise unknown. J. C. Dougah shows a knowledge of it (Dougah, 1966, pp. 14–15) and may perhaps have been its source.

21 Wilks, FN/112, 3 August 1964; FN/50, 6 August 1964. See also NAG Accra, ADM.66/5/4, General Information Book, 23 February 1926. My attempt to visit the site in 1964 was unsuccessful; the road was impassable even for a Landrover.

22 Arhin, 1974, p. 138.

23 Wilks, FN/50, 6 August 1964.

24 The form of the name 'Kantonsi' could only have evolved within one of the Voltaic vernaculars. The root, however, may be the Malinke *ton*, 'locusts', a word also applied to the Akan; see Wilks, Levtzion and Haight, 1986, p. 119. The analogy between a warband and a plague of locusts is obvious enough.

25 Wilks, FN/112, 3 August 1964.

26 Wilks, FN/50, 6 August 1964. The *kubaru* was said to be in the possession of Limam 'Abd al-Qadir of Aboso, near Tarkwa in southwestern Ghana. Its contents were repeated from memory by the limam's brother, 'Abdallah Samuni of Wa Sembeleyiri.

27 Wilks, FN/193, 14 May 1966. Al-Hajj 'Abd al-Rahman Sienu said that he had copied the work from an older manuscript, now lost. He was unwilling for his copy to be photographed, but it was possible to verify the accuracy of the translation he made into Juula. The first Limam of Koho, also known as Shukr li-'llahi, in the middle of the nineteenth century, was Ya'qub Tarawiri from Wa Limamyiri. The present limam, Al-Hasan Kunatay, aged about 100, who was present at the interview, is a descendant of Limam Ya'qub's daughter. It is thus possible that the *kubaru* was brought to Koho from Wa.

28 Wilks, FN/53, 1 July 1964; FN/112, 3 August 1964; FN/107, 7 August 1964. I was shown its supposed site in 1964. The area was highly eroded, marked only on the surface by the scatter of occupational debris.

29 Wilks, FN/50, 6 August 1964; FN/107, 7 August 1964.

30 Wilks, FN/48, 7 August 1964.

31 See, e.g., Wilks, FN/112, 3 August 1964; FN/50, 6 August 1964.

32 For the Kantonsi dispersion see Levtzion, 1968, pp. 143–57; Holden, 1980, pp. 18–24; Davis, 1984, pp. 150–5.

33 Wilks, FN/65, 11 April 1966; FN/205, 18 May 1966.

34 Wilks, FN/129, 17 April 1964.

35 Holden, 1965. Wilks, FN/117, 14 April 1964; FN/136, 16 April 1964; FN/111, 16–18 April 1964.

36 Wilks, FN/136, 16 April 1964; FN/175, 5 January 1969.

37 Wilks, FN/198, 14 January 1963; FN/126, 15 April 1963; FN/52, 30 June 1964; FN/25, 9 August 1964; FN/3, 2 February 1965; FN/154, 6 May 1966; FN/172, 5 January 1969. For what it is worth, Sidi 'Umar appears in the fifth ascendant generation to nonagenarians and centenarians in the 1960s, and in the seventh or eighth to those then in their forties or fifties. The pedigrees are clearly incomplete, the name of Sidi 'Umar being conventionally added to each as apical ancestor. The Old Muslim Tarawiri of Nasa presumably had highly restricted access to literacy until the arrival of the Nasa Limamyiri people, from which time onwards genealogies may have been preserved in writing.

38 Dougah, 1966, p. 16.

39 Wilks, FN/126, 15 April 1963; FN/25, 9 August 1964.

40 Wilks, FN/130, 18 April 1964; FN/25, 9 August 1964.

41 Wilks, FN/25, 9 August 1964; FN/129, 17 April 1964; FN/51, 29 June 1964; FN/119, 5 August 1964; FN/144, 19 August 1966; FN/168, 3 January 1969; FN/170, 4 January 1969; FN/172, 5 January 1969.

42 Wilks, FN/234, 10 January 1986.

43 Wilks, FN/25, 9 August 1964; FN/154, 6 May 1966. See also Rattray, 1932, II, p. 472;

Goody, 1954, p. 32.

44 NAG Accra, ADM.66/5/5, Wa District Letter Book, 26 June 1916. NAG Tamale, ADM.1/ 228, Wa District Informal Diary, 24 November and 13 December 1931.

45 Wilks, FN/112, 3 August 1964.

46 See e.g. Cissé and Diabeté, 1970, *passim*, in which the dispersion of the Tarawiri, among others, is treated.

47 Dieterlen, 1955, pp. 61–75; 1959, pp. 121–4.

48 See *A Map of Part of West Africa*, London: Edward Stanford, 1899.

49 Dupuis, 1824, Appendix, p. cxxxi. Barth heard of Lanfiera ('Langafera') in the middle of the nineteenth century, 1859, vol. III, p. 648.

50 Wilks, FN/112, 3 August 1964.

51 Wilks, FN/198, 14 January 1963.

52 Wilks, FN/145, 8 March 1963.

53 Dieterlen, 1959, pp. 124–32.

54 Levtzion and Hopkins, 1981, p. 287. Saad, 1983, pp. 8, 18, 31, 59–60. Hunwick, 1985, p. 18.

55 Wilks, FN/52, 30 June 1964; FN/53, 1 July 1964.

56 Wilks, FN/172, 5 January 1969. I am confident that 'Zakiyu' was my mishearing of 'Zatiyu', that is, Jata.

57 Wilks, FN/265, 22 December 1962.

58 Marty, 1922, pp. 130, 146.

59 Wilks, FN/79, 11 December 1963.

60 Al-Sa'di, 1898–1900, Arabic text p. 20, French translation p. 34.

61 For these two figures, see Hunwick, 1964, 1966.

62 Wilks, FN/46, 3 May 1966; FN/151, 5 May 1966. The pedigrees given by Adamu, 1978, p. 151, appear to have been extracted from these interviews and cannot, therefore, be regarded as independent testimony.

63 In or about 1930 Rattray interviewed Ibrahim, son of 'Murshedu', that is, 'Umar Sa'id. His notes are, unfortunately, virtually unusable. Royal Anthropological Institute, London. Papers of R. S. Rattray, MS Bundle 109, Notebook 8, 1929–30, p. 168.

64 Wilks, FN/147, 3 May 1966.

4 Wa chronology: an exercise in date-guessing

1 I have borrowed the term 'date-guessing' from Miller, 1975–6, pp. 96–109. For a discussion of geneametry and regno-chronology, see Wilks, 'Quantitative methods in Historical Research: Applications to African History', paper presented to the Faculty Colloquium, Program of African Studies, Northwestern University, January 1968. Many of the themes in this paper were worked out in lengthy discussions with P. C. Gibbons, see Gibbons, 1966, p. 25. Here they will be applied in use, rather than expounded in the abstract.

2 Fikry, 1970, vol. I, p. 68. The list in Dougah, 1966, pp. 54–5, has not been used, since its source is unknown. The sequence of limams is, however, identical with those in table 4.1, lists I, J, K and L.

3 The watermark resembles a toadstool.

4 IASAR/343 consists of notes made by N. Levtzion in 1964 from a MS closely related to list K. Without access to the original, however, it is impossible to be sure of the variant readings.

5 Wilks, FN/52, 30 June 1964, and IASAR/296; FN/112, 3 August 1964.

6 Wilks, FN/175, 5 January 1969.

7 Wilks, FN/3, 2 February 1965; FN/112, 3 August 1964.

8 Wilks, FN/52, 30 June 1964, and IASAR/296; FN/172, 5 January 1969.

9 Wilks, FN/112, 3 August 1964.

10 Wilks, FN/3, 2 February 1965.

11 Compare Fikry, 1970, vol. I, p. 247.
12 Wilks, FN/148, 3 May 1966.
13 Wilks, FN-144, 19 August 1966.
14 Wilks, FN/172, 5 January 1969.
15 Wilks, FN/144, 19 August 1966.
16 Wilks, FN/148, 3 May 1966.
17 Wilks, FN/28, 4 May 1966.
18 Wilks, FN/119, 5 August 1964.
19 Wilks, FN/28, 4 May 1966.
20 Wilks, FN/232, 7 January 1986.
21 Wilks, FN/28, 4 May 1966.
22 Wilks, FN/148, 3 May 1966; FN/35, 5 May 1966.
23 Friday Limam Siddiq b. 'Abd al-Mu'min b. Friday Limam Muhammad Bile b. 'Uthman Kunduri b. Limam Sa'id b. 'Abd al-Qadir, see Wilks, FN/3, 2 February 1965.
24 IASAR/18. See Wilks, FN/124, 6 March 1963.
25 Wilks, FN/144, 19 August 1966; FN/172, 5 January 1969.
26 Wilks, FN/148, 3 May 1966; FN/28, 4 May 1966; FN/70, 5 May 1966. Yusuf may have been limam of the Limamyiri mosque rather than Wa Limam.
27 Wilks, FN/28, 4 May 1966; FN/144, 19 August 1966.
28 Wilks, FN/148, 3 May 1966; FN/172, 5 January 1969.
29 Wilks, FN/234, 10 January 1986.
30 Wilks, FN/162, 2 January 1969.
31 Wilks, FN/35, 5 May 1966; FN/169, 4 January 1969; FN/170, 4 January 1969.
32 Dougah, 1966, p. 34.
33 Wilks, FN/111, 16 April 1964. Ferguson, in Arhin, 1974, p. 137. Krause, *Neue Preussische (Kreuz) Zeitung*, 1, vi, 1892. Henderson, 1898, p. 491. PRO, CO.879/52, Africa (West) no. 549, pp. 354–6: Report on Wa by D. Mackworth, dd. 6 June 1898.
34 CO.879/54, African (West) no. 564, p. 339: Northcott to Colonial Secretary, dd. Gambaga, 21 September 1898.
35 *Gold Coast Civil Service Lists*, 1917, 1918, 1922.
36 Wilks, FN/144, 19 August 1966; FN/234, 10 January 1986.
37 NAG, Tamale, ADM/1/22, 5 November 1926.
38 *Al-Akhbar Zabarima*, 'The Story of the Zabarima'. A copy of an apparently older work was made by Friday Limam Ishaq in 1922 or 1923 at the request of District Commissioner Whittall, see NAG Accra, Acc. No. 1427 of 1959; IASAR/22, p. 6.
39 Holden, 1965, pp. 60, n. 1, 66. Levtzion, 1968, pp. 152–3. Neither notes, in support of the date, the comment of Henderson, 1898, p. 490.
40 NAG Accra, ADM.56/1/201: Acting Provincial Commissioner, Northern Province, to Chief Commissioner, Northern Territories, dd. 25 July 1930.
41 See Wilks, 1975, pp. 275–9. Chapman's diary is being prepared for publication by T. C. McCaskie, and I am grateful to him for making a text available to me.
42 Wilks, FN/124, 6 March 1963. IASAR/18.
43 Wilks, FN/53, 1 July 1964.
44 Wilks, 1968, pp. 174, 181; 1984, *passim*.
45 Wilks, FN/179, 31 July 1965; IASAR/246, p. 4.
46 Wilks, FN/180, 8 May 1966. Limam 'Abbas died on Tuesday, 8 Dhu 'l-hijjat 1215, after afternoon prayer, according to an obituary note by his son, 'Umar, penned on the cover of a work on syntax in the library of Al-Hajj Muhammad Marhaba Saghanughu.
47 Wilks, FN/69 and 70, 4 and 5 May 1966. In Wa there is a reluctance to refer to the revered by name, and honorifics are frequently used. 'We do not like to call the names of our holy men', the informant remarked.

48 Wilks, FN/172, 5 January 1969. Friday Limam Siddiq attributed the building of the mosque to his own grandfather, Friday Limam Muhammad Zayd, 'after the white man came to Wa', Wilks, FN/169, 4 January 1969. This almost certainly refers to one of several reconstructions of the mosque intended, by the utilization of new building techniques, to increase its capacity. It was reconstructed again in 1337 AH, AD 1918/19, and yet again apparently in the mid 1950s, Wilks, FN/169 and FN/172, 4 and 5 January 1969.

49 Wilks, FN/179, 31 July 1965; IASAR/246, p. 11.

50 NAG Accra, ADM.66/5/3, Wa District General Information Book, 1923. See also NAG Accra, ADM.66/5/1, Wa District General Information Book, 1924–5.

51 CO.879/58, African (West) No. 585, pp. 3–4: Northcott to Colonial Secretary, dd. Gambaga, 13 October 1898.

52 Dougah, 1966, p. 24.

53 NAG Accra, No. 1427 of 1959; IASAR/22.

54 NAG Accra, ADM.56/1/201: Acting Provincial Commissioner, Northern Province, to Chief Commissioner, Northern Territories, dd. 25 July 1930.

55 In 1964 Acting Yeri Na Asheku claimed that his father, 'Uthman Daleri, was about a hundred at his death, see Wilks FN/25, 9 August 1964. This must have involved a modest exaggeration.

56 See, e.g., Dougah, 1966, pp. 29–30.

57 The principal sources for table 4.8 are Wilks, FN/234, 10 January 1986, and Dougah, 1966, pp. 19–20, 29–30.

58 Wilks, FN/234, 10 January 1986; compare Dougah, 1966, p. 19.

59 NAG Accra, ADM.66/5/4: entries for 21 and 25 March 1936.

60 Dougah, 1966, p. 18; Fikry, 1970, vol. I, pp. 49–50, 126–33.

61 Wilks, Levtzion and Haight, 1986, pp. 100, 129.

62 Ibid. p. 99.

63 Wilks, FN/267, 8 February 1987.

64 Wilks, FN/165, 4 January 1969.

65 See, e.g., Levtzion, 1973, pp. 80–91. Hunwick, 1985, pp. 21–2.

66 Wilks, 1982, pp. 333, 472.

67 Wilks, Levtzion and Haight, 1986, pp. 13–15, 36–51.

68 Anquandah and Van Ham, 1985. Anquandah, 1986. Anquandah, 1987. For the rapid and deplorable dispersion of this material into the international art market, see as witness *Galerie Walu. Archaologische Funde aus Komaland*, Zurich, 1987. 'Komaland' represents, of course, the invention of yet another mythical society.

69 Wilks, FN/50, 6 August 1964. The tradition was recited by memory from 'an Arabic book which tells us about it'.

70 Wilks, 1982, p. 349.

71 Labouret, 1931, p. 22. Person, 1964, pp. 329–30.

72 Wilks, Levtzion and Haight, 1986, pp. 36–51.

73 Wilks, 1967, pp. 157–63.

74 Barth, 1859, vol. III, p. 496. For mysterious and not-so-mysterious connections between Buna and Asante, see Wilks, 1975, pp. 315–16.

75 Tamakloe, 1931, pp. 19–20.

76 Institute of African Studies, University of Ghana: Tait MSS, Text A. See also Fage, 1956.

77 John M. Chernoff and Alhaji Ibrahim M'ba Lunga, *A Drummer's Testament: The Culture of the Dagbamba of Northern Ghana*, forthcoming. I am indebted to Chernoff for allowing me access to a text of this extraordinarily interesting work.

78 Wilks, Levtzion and Haight, 1986, pp. 98, 122.

79 Ferguson, 1972, pp. 3–17.

80 Again, I follow Chernoff and Alhaji Ibrahim. Na Dariziogu was killed in war with the

Gonja. The succession passed to his father's junior brother, Na Luro, and then to Na Luro's sons, Na Tutugri, Na Zagli, Na Zokuli and Na Gungobli.

81 'Wala Lasiri.' I must again record my debt to J. D. Fage for making this text, in Walii and English translation, available to me.

82 A. A. Iliasu, 'Mamprugu. The Oral Traditions of Its People', Northern History Scheme, Department of History, Legon, vol, I, pp. 19–21, 60–1, no date.

83 NAG Accra, Acc. no. 1521: G. F. Mackay, 'A Short Essay on the History and Customs of the Mamprusi Tribe', 1931, p. 3. Rattray, 1932, vol. II, p. 547.

84 Withers-Gill, 1924.

85 Goody and Wilks, 1968, p. 243. Wilks, Levtzion and Haight, 1968, pp. 28, 150.

86 Davis, 1984, chapter 2.

87 Wilks, Levtzion and Haight, 1986, pp. 101, 129–30.

88 Supreme Court of Ghana, Asanni Zei and J. N. Momori v. Yakubu Seidu, 3, 5, 9, 17 and 29 July 1985.

5 *Tajdid* and *jihad*: the Muslim community in change

1 Freeman, 1892, p. 136.

2 CO.879/38, African (West) no. 448, p. 35: Ferguson to Governor, dd. 29 August 1892.

3 CO.879/52, African (West) no. 549, p. 356: Report on Wa by D. Mackworth, dd. 6 June, 1898.

4 NAG Tamale, ADM.1/437, Essay on the People of the Northwestern Province, B. M. Read, 22 November 1908.

5 Wilks, FN/168, 3 January 1969.

6 Wilks, FN/144, 19 August 1966; FN/170, 4 January 1969. The Nayiri Yeri Na was appointed from the Sungumi section of Wa Tagarayiri, whose members are described as 'sons' of the Yeri Nas but have no claims to the Yeri Nam. It is unclear when the position was created. Dodi Bawku held it in 1969, having succeeded Ya'qub only some three years earlier. Ya'qub succeeded Idris Dogu, who held the position so long that I found no one who remembered his precedessor.

7 See Wilks, 1968, especially pp. 165, 192–3.

8 Hunwick, 1966, pp. 24–5; 1985, pp. 19, 115–17.

9 Wilks, FN/124, 6 March 1963.

10 Wilks, FN/53, 1 July 1964; FN/207, 8 March 1967; FN/208, 17 July 1967; FN/165, 4 January 1969; FN/172, 5 January 1969.

11 Wilks, FN/61, 8 March 1963; FN/27, 3 May 1966; FN/28, 4 May 1966; FN/70, 5 May 1966. The number of Qur'anic pupils appears to have declined by almost half by 1969, perhaps as a result of the popularity of the Fongo Arabic school, Wilks, FN/161, 2 January 1969.

12 Wilks, 1968, p. 172; 1984, *passim.*

13 Wilks, FN/53, 1 July 1964.

14 Wilks, FN/70, 5 May 1966.

15 See e.g. Wilks, FN/190, 14 April 1966. For the Bonduku limamate, though the account is in need of considerable revision, see Tauxier, 1921, pp. 126–7.

16 See e.g. Wilks, FN/190, 14 April 1966. In this chain Muhammad b. Ibrahim Watara is shown as the student of Abu Bakr al-Siddiq b. Ibrahim Saghanughu but as teacher of Limam Ibrahim Timitay of Bonduku, who succeeded his brother Limam Sa'id b. Muhammad in office.

17 Renouard, 1836, p. 102. Madden, 1837, II, p. 184. The source is the brief autobiography of Abu Bakr al-Siddiq of Timbuktu and Jenne, but apparently from the Watara of Kong by origin. My attempts to locate the Arabic original of this text have been without success. My earlier inference, that Abu Bakr referred to 'Abdallah b. Al-Hajj Muhammad Watara

rather than to 'Abdallah b. Al-Hajj *and* Muhammad Watara, was erroneous, see Wilks, 1967, pp. 153, 157 n. 12.

18 Wilks, FN/180, 8 May 1966; FN/181, 9 May 1966; FN/189, 13 May 1966. See also the *isnad* in Wilks, FN/36, 12 April 1966.

19 Wilks, FN/157, 10 April 1966.

20 Wilks, 1968, p. 196.

21 Hunter, 1977. Sanneh, 1979.

22 Sanneh, 1979, p. 19.

23 Wilks, 1982, pp. 348–9.

24 Wilks, Levtzion and Haight, 1986, pp. 91–3.

25 Ferguson, 1972, pp. 48–73.

26 Wilks, 1968, pp. 173–4; 1984, *passim*.

27 Sanneh, 1979, p. 21.

28 Wilks, 1984.

29 An account of the origins of the dispute is contained in a short work in Hausa, *Al-Akhbar Sarkin Safu Buli*, 'The Story of Bolewura Safo', which Friday Limam Ishaq of Wa included in his compilation of texts made in 1922 or 1923; see NAG Accra, Acc. No. 1427 of 1959; IASAR/22.

30 NAG Accra, ADM.56/1/201: Acting Provincial Commissioner to Chief Commissioner, Northern Territories, dd. 25 July 1930. The fighting in Daboya may be that referred to in Samuel Moore, *Biography of Mahommah G. Baquaqua, A Native of Zoogoo, in the Interior of Africa*, Detroit, 1854, see Austin, 1984, pp. 613–15.

31 For Asante and other sources for these events, see Wilks, 1975, pp. 275–8; the account, however, confuses Yagbonwura Saidu with a later occupant of that office, Nyantakyi.

32 NAG Accra, ADM.56/1/201, dd. 25 July 1930.

33 Basic sources for the Karantaw are Binger, 1892, vol. I, pp. 416–18; Tauxier, 1912, pp. 410–11; and Tauxier, 1924, pp. 147–8. Tauxier drew his material principally from a 'Monographie de la Residence de Boromo' which he says he had in his hands in 1910. Recent accounts are to be found in Levtzion, 1968, pp. 147–51; Duperray, 1984, pp. 56–60.

34 Wilks, FN/154, 6 May 1966; FN/266, 22 June 1966 (IASAR/232; 438). Muhammad Karantaw's teacher appears as Sharif Muhammad al-Abyad b. Abi Bakr on these chains. Al-Hajj Muhammad Marhaba Saghanughu maintained that Abu Bakr was a son of Muhammad al-Mustafa Saghanughu; if so, he was brother of his own teacher, Sa'id b. Muhammad al-Mustafa, see Wilks, FN/189, 13 May 1966. Some reservation is necessary on this point. I have seen one *isnad* that refers to Sharif Muhammad al-Abyad simply as Sharif Tarawiri, see Wilks, FN/197, 15 May 1966.

35 Wilks, FN/143, 16 April 1963; IASAR/66. The Arabic is poor, and I am grateful to Salah Ibrahim (then of the Institute of African Studies, University of Ghana) for having assisted me in understanding it.

36 Wilks, FN/268, 1 August 1965; IASAR/77. For translations from this work, see Martin, 1965, pp. 81–2; Al-Naqar, 1972, pp. 121–2. Attention is also drawn to the poetry in praise of Al-Hajj Mahmud, see Wilks, FN/146, 17 April 1963, and IASAR/65, 70 and 83.

37 Shaykh Al-Hajj Taslima Saghanughu belonged to the Dafin as opposed to the Kong branch of the Saghanughu, see Wilks, FN/180, 8 May 1966; FN/189, 13 May 1966; FN/191, 14 May 1966.

38 Wilks, FN/194, 15 May 1966; FN/200, 16 May 1966.

39 Wilks, FN/192, 14 May 1966. Al-Hajj Sa'id claimed that 'Ali Tarawiri was a man of much learning, but that he left Wa because he did not wish to be involved in affairs of the limamate. As a Tagarayiri man 'Ali Tarawiri could not, of course, have made claims to the office.

40 Tauxier, 1912, p. 410.

41 I have followed the translations by Martin, 1966, p. 82, and Al-Naqar, 1972, p. 122.

42 Wilks, FN/192, 14 May 1966.

43 Binger, 1892, vol. I, p. 416, and pp. 369, 380 for the suggestion that many Dafin may have preferred to resettle elsewhere rather than be coerced into support for the *jihad*.

44 Wilks, FN/193, 14 May 1966. The two informants consulted together at length to get the genealogical details correct.

45 Binger, 1892, vol. I, p. 416. Levtzion, 1968, pp. 148–9. Duperray, 1984, p. 56.

46 For an early but still useful attempt to define it, see Binger, 1892, vol. II, pp. 34–5.

47 There is a considerable body of recent scholarly literature on the Zabarima intrusion, see especially Holden, 1965, 1980 (the latter, of major importance, unfortunately as yet unpublished); Levtzion, 1968, pp. 151–60; Duperray, 1984, pp. 61–70.

48 NAG Accra, Acc. No. 1427 of 1959. IASAR/22. I am grateful to Hamidu Bobboyi for his help in translating this text.

49 Binger, 1892, vol. II, p. 39.

50 See Fikry, 1970, vol. II, pp. 565–7. The account of Malam Idris was given by Al-Hajj Muhammad Shifa of Wa Banwarayiri, who was born in or about 1864.

51 Binger, 1892, vol. I, p. 504.

52 Wilks, FN/75, 18 June 1966, and compare Holden, 1965, p. 66.

53 NAG Accra, ADM.56/1/201, dd. 25 July 1930. For a more detailed account of these events, see Dougah, 1966, pp. 20–2, and, from the Gonja point of view, Braimah, 1970, pp. 11–33.

54 CO.879/52, African (West) no. 549, p. 66: Major C. Jenkinson, dd. 2 December 1897. Captain D. Mackworth placed the event thirty years earlier, ibid., p. 25, undated but late 1897, though subsequently revised this to fifteen years, ibid., p. 356, Report on Wa, dd. 6 June 1898.

55 Library of the School of Oriental and African Studies, London, Acc. no. Hausa 98017. A notation shows that the work was written by Malam Abu at the request of Dr J. F. Corson, then of the Northern Territories of the Gold Coast.

56 Wilks, FN/64, 12 April 1962; FN/2, 14 April 1964.

57 J. D. Fage kindly made this text available to me. It was apparently written in the mid 1950s in circumstances that are otherwise unknown. A closely related account, however, is offered by Dougah, 1966, pp. 22–3.

58 Tamakloe, 1931, pp. 52–3. A clerk in Tumu in 1912, Tamakloe collected information on the Zabarima for the then Acting District Commissioner, P. C. Whittall, who entered it in the Tumu District Record Book, see NAG Tamale, ADM.1/228, Informal Diary, Provincial Commissioner, Northern Province, entry dd. 2 December 1931.

59 CO.879/52, African (West) no. 549, p. 356: Report on Wa by D. Mackworth, dd. 6 June 1898.

60 Tamakloe, 1931, p. 53.

61 Dougah, 1966, p. 23.

62 Fikry, 1970, vol. I, pp. 58–9. Wilks, FN/61, 8 March 1963.

63 Fikry, 1970, vol. II, pp. 567–9, citing the centenarian Al-Hajj Muhammad Shifa.

64 This account follows Dougah, 1966, p. 23. Dougah lists 'Abd al-Rahman, Kafrimanten and Adam Kpon of Dondoli, and Mukhtar of Vuori, among the eight 'prominent Muslims' slain.

65 Tamakloe, 1931, p. 53. Dougah, 1966, pp. 23–4.

66 Fikry, 1970, vol. II, pp. 568–9.

67 Wilks, FN/136, 16 April 1964; FN/175, 5 January 1969.

68 CO.879/52, African (West) no. 549, p. 356: report dd. 6 June 1898.

69 Wilks, FN/74, 6 March 1963; FN/168, 3 January 1969. The informant was the centenarian Ishaq Dodu of Tagarayiri, who was taken captive at Nasa and made cook to Babatu.

70 Wilks, FN/111, 16–18 April 1964. The informant, Al-Hajj Muhammad Ashifa, claimed on

another occasion that Mahama Fua died immediately before the fighting, see Fikry, 1970, vol. II, p. 570. Dougah, 1966, p. 24, says that Mahama Fua took poison.

71 Wilks, FN/111, 16–18 April 1964.
72 See Arhin, 1974, p. 137.
73 CO.879/52, African (West) no. 549, p. 355: report dd. 6 June 1898. Henderson, 1898, p. 491.
74 G. A. Krause, *Neue Preussische (Kreuz) Zeitung*, I, vi, 1892.
75 Holden, 1965, pp. 60–1.
76 See, e.g., Wilks, FN/214, 23 May 1966; FN/56, 24 May 1966.
77 Levtzion, 1968, pp. 149, 154. Duperray, 1984, p. 60.
78 See e.g., Hunwick, 1985, pp. 47, 129–30.
79 CO.879/52, African (West) no. 549, p. 356: report dd. 6 June 1898.
80 Wilks, FN/112, 3 August 1964. Dougah, 1966, p. 48 says that they went in the reign of Wa Na Mahama Fua.
81 Wilks, FN/169, 4 January 1969.
82 Wilks, FN/112, 3 August 1964. Dougah, 1966, p. 48.
83 Wilks, FN/168, 3 January 1969, according to which he was accompanied by thirty of his students.
84 Mackworth saw the mosque, after its destruction by Babatu, and commented: 'it was built of swish, and its walls were about 20 feet high, and 20 yards by 40 yards in area', CO.879/52, African (West) no. 549, p. 355: report dd. 6 June 1898. It was reconstructed within a few years, and is the building of plate 2. It survived into the early 1950s, when Dougah, 1966, p. 48, described it as about 100 feet by 70 feet, and 30 feet in height, capable of holding 500 to 600 people. It was rebuilt in 1954, and this larger and architecturally undistinguished building, which I first saw in 1956, was also structurally unsound. It collapsed in a storm. It was replaced by a concrete building in a not unpleasing but totally foreign Middle Eastern idiom.
85 Dougah, 1966, p. 48.
86 Wilks, FN/168, 3 January 1969.
87 Wilks, FN/61, 8 March 1963.
88 Wilks, FN/161, 2 January 1969 and see also FN/61, 8 March 1963.
89 Dougah, 1966, p. 48.
90 Wilks, FN/168, 3 January 1969.
91 Levtzion, 1965, p. 313 and n. 21.
92 Wilks, FN/61, 8 March 1963.
93 Berberich, 1974, pp. 14–27.
94 Robertson, 1819, pp. 179–80 and map.
95 Dupuis, 1824, Appendix, pp. cxxiv–cxxxv. Compare Bowdich, 1819, pp. 171–2; 483. Bowdich knew of no town on the Black Volta beyond Gbuipe.
96 Barth, 1859, vol. III, pp. 643–8.
97 Sanneh, 1979, p. 19.
98 Binger, 1892, vol. II, p. 140, and compare vol. I, p. 448. In 1892 Ferguson fell in with two caravan leaders making their way to Kintampo for kola; 'we know the routes from Wa to Sati', they told him, CO.879/38, African (West) no. 448, p. 61.
99 Binger, 1892, vol. I, p. 440.
100 CO.879/38, African (West) no. 448, p. 82: Director of Military Intelligence to Colonial Office, dd. 28 February 1893.
101 Binger, 1892, vol. II, p. 101.
102 Ibid, vol. II, p. 102.
103 Wilks, FN/75, 18 June 1966.
104 Fikry, 1970, vol. I, p. 275.
105 The root of the word is probably the Malinke *dyo*, 'slave', but compare the Fulani *dimajo*,

having the same meaning.

106 Holden, 1970, pp. 102–4.

107 CO.879/52, African (West) no. 549, p. 355: report on Wa, dd. 6 June 1898.

108 Levtzion, 1968, pp. 142, 159. Compare Wilks, FN/132, 14 April 1964; FN/133, 15 April 1964; FN/138, 15 April 1964.

109 Binger, 1892, vol, I, p. 325.

110 'Le Gourounsi', *Bulletin du Comité de l'Afrique Française*, No. 2, February 1898, p. 48.

6 Colonial intrusions: Wala in disarray

1 Holden, 1965, p. 75.

2 Fikry, 1970, vol. II, p. 570. Although founded by the early Wa Limam Ishaq, with the failure of his line Vuori was absorbed into Dzedzedeyiri, Wilks, FN/165, 4 January 1969.

3 Wilks, FN/168, 3 January 1969.

4 Wilks, FN/74, 6 March 1963.

5 Wilks, FN/252, 19 April 1964.

6 Library of the School of Oriental and African Studies, London, Acc. No. Hausa 98017.

7 Wilks, FN/168, 3 January 1969, and compare Holden, 1965, p. 77.

8 Wilks, FN/168, 3 January 1968.

9 Wilks, FN/74, 6 March 1963.

10 Wilks, FN/158, 1 January 1969. One of the informants remarked: 'I would never go to Dondoli. I would get an arrow in my back if they knew I was from Kaleo.' The remark was not made, I am sure, entirely in jest.

11 CO.879/38, African (West) no. 448, p. 53: Ferguson to Governor, dd. 9 December 1892.

12 Holden, 1965, pp. 78–80. Person, 1975, vol. III, p. 1709.

13 Fikry, 1970, vol. II, p. 571. Al-Hajj Muhammad claimed to have been 'old enough to carry a gun' when Babatu sacked Nasa. He fled to Buna, returning to Wa after three years, Wilks, FN/111, 16–18 April 1964.

14 CO.879/38, African (West) no. 448, pp. 35–9, Ferguson to Governor, dd. 19 November 1892; pp. 45–8, report by Director of Military Intelligence, dd. 4 January 1893; pp. 62–3, memorandum of interview at Bole, 9 June 1892; p. 84, Ferguson to Governor, dd. 28 February 1893.

15 Ibid, p. 63.

16 Wilks, FN/168, 3 January 1969. The informant referred to him as Friday Limam Ya'qub, clearly meaning 'Uthman Dabila b. Ya'qub.

17 Ferguson, Memorandum of Political Proceedings 1894, see Arhin, 1974, p. 137.

18 Al-Hajj Muhammad Shifa maintained that Saidu Takora 'was on the skin five years before Samori came', which was in mid 1896; Wilks, FN/111, 16–18 April 1964.

19 Wilks, FN/158, 1 January 1969. Dougah, 1966, p. 24.

20 CO.879/41, African (West) no. 479, pp. 8–9.

21 CO.96/270, Report on the Mission of Decoeur and Baud, dd. 21 December 1895, enclosed in Maxwell to Chamberlain, dd. 15 February 1896.

22 CO.96/277, Final Report on the Second Mission to the Interior, dd. 31 August 1896, enclosed in Hodgson to Chamberlain, dd. 5 October 1896.

23 *Bulletin du Comité de l'Afrique Française*, no. 12, December 1895, p. 350.

24 CO.879/52, African (West) no. 549, p. 224: Niger Commissioners Gosselin and Everett to Ambassador Monson, dd. Paris 29 March 1898.

25 Henderson, 1898, p. 488, has a useful comment on the usage. 'The term Sofa is not used to designate any particular tribe, race, or sect, but means literally "Master of the horse", and is applied to any marauders, followers of Samory or otherwise, who are supposed to possess horses.'

26 The career of Samori Turay is reconstructed in monumental detail in Y. Person, 1975, vols. I–III. It will become apparent, however, that my treatment of the Samorian intrusion into Wala affairs differs considerably from his.

27 Person, 1975, vol, III, p. 1725, is in error in identifying Fanyinama (or Fangamade) with Sarankye Mori. He and his brother, Samgala, were warriors from the Korhogo area and both joined Samori's forces. Fanyinama's son, of the same name, was Sarkin Zongo of Kintampo when I talked with him, see Wilks, FN/221, 27 May 1966.

28 Braimah, 1970, pp. 37–44.

29 NAG Accra, Acc. no. 261 of 1961. A copy is accessioned as IASAR/20.

30 Wilks, FN/149, 4 May 1966.

31 NAG Accra, Acc. no. 1427 of 1959. IASAR/22. An English version of AZWS, perhaps translated from the dictation of Friday Limam Ishaq, is extant, see Wilks, FN/248, 3 January 1969.

32 This text was kindly made available to me by J. D. Fage. Dougah, 1966, pp. 24–5, seems to have made use of it, and may possibly have recorded it.

33 Dougah, 1966, pp. 24–5.

34 Wilks, FN/158, 1 January 1969. There is more to the story. Years earlier Wa Na Mahama Fua is said to have used Kaleo as a base for an attack on Sankana. A child was born in Kaleo while he was there, who was accordingly named Fua. The kidnapped wife of Adama Bile was given to him. She had left ('orphaned') children in Dondoli. One was Mumuni, that is, 'Abd al-Mu'min, who in time became Interpreter for the British and avenged his mother in 1945 when he contrived the removal of the then Kaleo Na from office.

35 An informant in 1986 remarked that Adama Bile 'was a proper Limamyiri man. They could have made him limam but they passed him by. He was very active in the Babatu wars. He was like a warrior in some ways. So they did not take him for limam, but now they have taken his son', that is, Wa Limam Al-Hajj Nuhu, who died in 1984. Wilks, FN/232, 7 January 1986.

36 Wilks, FN/74, 6 March 1963.

37 NAG Accra, ADM.56/1/101: Provincial Commissioner, Wa, to Chief Commissioner, Northern Territories, dd. 25 February 1916. Muhammad's son, Al-Hajj Tamimu, accompanied his father to Mecca. He remembered that he was born three days before Samori came to Wa, that is, in 1896; that he was seven or eight when he was taken to Mecca; and that he was around fourteen when he was in Mecca. Wilks, FN/61, 8 March 1963; FN/27, 3 May 1966.

38 Wilks, FN/61, 8 March 1963.

39 Wilks, FN/111, 16–18 April 1964.

40 These quantities have become exaggerated in the telling. Al-Hajj Muhammad Shifa, for example, spoke of 110 horses and 500 sheep, Wilks, FN/111, 16–18 April 1964.

41 Wilks, FN/111, 16–18 April 1964.

42 The text AS has: *wata bawa bubban salla kwana ashirin da biyar*. I have taken this to mean 25 Dhu 'l-Qa'da (Hausa, *watan bawa*), but other interpretations are possible.

43 Wilks, FN/221, 27 May 1966. Fanyinama subsequently placed his services at the disposal of the British, and fought in their ranks against the Asante in 1900. He died in or about 1953.

44 CO.879/52, African (West) no. 549, p. 199: undated letter from Samori Turay to the Governor of the Gold Coast. Unfortunately the Arabic original of this letter has not been found, and it is not known what Arabic word 'slave' translates.

45 Wilks, FN/74, 6 March 1963.

46 Holden, 1970, pp. 103–7.

47 Henderson, 1898, pp. 496, 617.

48 Holden, 1965, pp. 78–80.

49 The sequence of events is reviewed by Holden, 1965, p. 80.

50 *Bulletin du Comité de l'Afrique Française*, no. 2, February 1898, p. 49: report on 'Le Gourounsi' by Lieutenant Chanoine. Chanoine suggests that Babatu went to Sankana freely, eager to secure the support of Sarankye Mori. Malam Abu and the author of AS are likely to have been better informed.

51 Ibid, no. 8, August 1897, pp. 256–7 and map: 'La Mission Voulet-Chanoine au Mossi'.

52 Ibid, no. 8, p. 257.

53 Holden, 1970, p. 75, notes Henderson's report that Sarankye Mori sent an advance party to Buna to prepare his accommodation there, but that its members were slain on 6 December 1896.

54 Henderson, 1898, p. 496.

55 See, e.g., CO.96/280, Maxwell to Chamberlain, dd. 28 December 1896, citing the evidence of a Hausa trading at Krakye.

56 In AZWS Ishaq b. 'Uthman Dabila makes no reference to this event. He says that seventy Wala gunmen went to Bole and then returned to Wa. ST reports that Sarankye Mori demanded 500 Wa gunmen for the invasion of Buna but that all deserted with the exception of their leader, Adama Nabiri.

57 CO.96/288, enclosures in Maxwell to Chamberlain dd. 29 January 1897.

58 Henderson, 1898, p. 490.

59 Ibid, p. 491.

60 CO.879/113, African (West) no. 1010, pp. 94–5.

61 Wilks, FN/168, 3 January 1969. Saidu Mogona was from Terinmu, 'Umar Kulendi from Konukumba.

62 CO.879/54, African (West) no. 564, p. 339: Northcott to Colonial Secretary, dd. Gambaga, 21 September 1898.

63 The one possible candidate is the Mahama mysteriously described as 'Aladimam'. My guess is that this is the Hausa and Borno title, *galadima*, and that Mahama was head of the Zabarima strangers in Wa. The title is known to have been used among Babatu's followers, see Holden, 1965, p. 62.

64 Henderson, 1898, pp. 491–4.

65 Holden, 1970, p. 96, citing CO.96/291, 7 April 1897.

66 CO.879/50, African (West) no. 538: Henderson to Colonial Office, dd. Bramford, Suffolk, 1 October 1897, and see Arhin, 1974, p. 166. Henderson's informant was his *sofa* interpreter and guard, Siraku.

67 For a review of the reasons for Sarankye Mori's actions, see Holden, 1970, pp. 97–103.

68 See also Wilks, FN/74, 6 March 1963.

69 Henderson, 1898, pp. 494–6.

70 Holden, 1970, p. 96, citing CO.96/291, 7 April 1897.

71 CO.879/52, African (West) no. 549, p. 199: Samori to Governor of the Gold Coast, n.d. but probably 1897, enclosed in Foreign Office to Colonial Office, dd. 26 March 1898. The original has not been found. The translation was made for the Colonial Office by Charles Wells.

72 Holden, 1970, pp. 94–6.

73 Henderson, 1898, pp. 607–8. Person, 1975, vol. III, pp. 1814–15.

74 Henderson, 1898, pp. 608–13.

75 CO.879/52, African (West) no. 549, p. 118: statement of Wa Na, dd. 31 December 1897.

76 Henderson, 1898, p. 614.

77 CO.879/52, African (West) no. 549, p. 356: report on Wa by Captain D. Mackworth, 6 June 1898. On 12 April Cramer and Haslewood, with 57 'miliciens' and a number of carriers presented themselves at Leo and asked the French garrison there for asylum, *Bulletin du Comité de l'Afrique Française*, no. 8, August 1897, p. 262: 'La Mission Chanoine au Gourounsi'.

78 Holden, 1970, p. 96.

79 CO.879/52, African (West) no. 549, p. 117: Northcott to Acting Governor, dd. 31 December 1897.

80 *Bulletin du Comité de l'Afrique Française*, October 1901, p. 340: journal of Captain Hugot, entry dd. Boromo, 13 May 1897.

81 CO.879/52, African (West) no. 549, p. 199: Samori Turay to Governor of the Gold Coast, n.d. but probably late 1897.

82 Henderson, 1898, pp. 615–18. There is additional detail in CO.879/50, African (West) no. 538: Henderson to Colonial Office, dd. Bramford, Suffolk, 1 October 1897, and see Arhin, 1974, pp. 155–66.

83 Henderson, 1898, p. 491.

84 *Bulletin du Comité de l'Afrique Française*, no. 8, August 1897, pp. 260–1: 'La Mission Chanoine au Gourounsi'.

85 Ibid. Also *Bulletin du Comité*, no. 2, February 1898, pp. 48–50: 'Le Gourounsi'. For the jurisdiction claimed by Sibu Napona, see CO.879/54, African (West) no. 564, p. 74: Northcott to Colonial Secretary, dd. Gambaga, 9 June 1898, and pp. 131–3: Middlemast to Staff Officer, dd. Gambaga, 11 June 1898. According to these sources the chiefs of the easternmost parts of Wala, including Funsi and Kundungu, claimed to serve Mampurugu. This is probably a fabrication of the British, enabling them to consider the areas within the British ambit.

86 *Bulletin du Comité*, No. 8, August 1897, p. 262: 'La Mission Chanoine'. CO.879/50, African (West) no. 538: Salisbury to Monson, dd. 2 October 1897.

87 CO.879/52, African (West) no. 549, p. 355: report by Mackworth, dd. 6 June 1898.

88 CO.879/50, African (West) no. 538: estimated damages of Babatu's raids. Among the captives was Mahama Chakalle Watara. 'I was taken captive by Babatu', he said; 'I was sold at Savelugu in Dagomba, and it was there that I converted. After that I spent a long time trading in Bonduku, and I assumed the name Watara in Bonduku', Wilks, FN/134, 15 April 1964.

89 Section Outre-Mer des Archives Nationales, Paris, Fonds Missions, Hugot: Hugot to Battalion Commandant, Niger-Volta Region, dd. Funsi, 3 June 1897, enclosing Hugot 'aux Almamys de Oua', dd. Leo, 22 May 1897, and 'Emir Saidou' to Hugot, dd. 28 Dhu 'l-Hijja.

90 CO.879/52, African (West) no. 549, pp. 118–9: sworn statement by Wa Na, dd. 31 December 1897.

91 *Bulletin du Comité de l'Afrique Française*, October 1901, p. 342: 'Un Soudanais. Le Journal du capitaine Hugot'.

92 CO.879/50, African (West) no. 538: Salisbury to Monson, dd. 2 October 1897, referring to Hugot's letters of 4 and 12 June 1897.

93 CO.879/52, African (West) no. 549, pp. 118–19: statement by Wa Na, dd. 31 December 1897.

94 CO.879/52, African (West) no. 549, pp. 5–6: Mackworth to Governor, dd. Wa, 20 October, 1897.

95 CO.879/52, African (West) 549, p. 66: Jenkinson to Colonial Secretary, dd. Wa, 2 December 1897.

96 CO.879/52, African (West) no. 549, pp. 116–17: Millot to Leland, dd. Leo, 7 December, 1897.

97 CO.879/52, African (West) no. 549, pp. 74–5: Northcott, telegram, dd. Wa, 4 February 1898; pp. 345–6: Northcott to Mercier, dd. Gambaga, 26 March 1898. Kanya-Forstner, 1969, pp. 245, 252.

98 CO.879/52, African (West) no. 549, pp. 117–18: Northcott to Acting Governor, dd. Wa, 31 December 1897.

99 Ibid, pp. 118–19: Northcott to Colonial Secretary dd. Wa, 31 December 1897.

100 Ibid, p. 356: report by Mackworth, dd. 6 June 1898.
101 Northcott, 1899, pp. 59–77. The situation in Wa had become very tense. On 15 April 1898 the headman of the Sisala village of Samoa had arrived in Wa and placed himself under British protection. Lieutenant Mercier of the French garrison seized and then executed him. CO.879/54, African (West) no. 564, pp. 35–6: Northcott to French commander, Leo, dd. Gambaga, 21 April 1898. In early June Northcott was insisting on Mercier's expulsion from Wa, ibid., pp. 136–7: Northcott to Millot, dd. Gambaga, 3 June 1898.
102 CO.879/58, African (West) no. 585, pp. 3–4: Northcott to Colonial Secretary, dd. Gambaga, 13 October 1898.
103 Marty, 1922, p. 235 and Appendix XIII. See further, Holden, 1970, p. 97.
104 Fikry, 1970, vol. II, p. 571.
105 Wilks, FN/61, 8 March 1963. It should be noted that the informant, Al-Hajj Tamimu, was only an infant at the time.
106 CO.879/50, African (West) no. 538: Henderson to Colonial Office, dd. Bramford, Suffolk, 1 October 1897, and see Arhin, 1974, p. 166.
107 Wilks, FN/248, 3 January 1969.
108 Fikry, 1970, vol. I, Part IV, and vol. II, *passim.*

7 'Direct rule': Wala in the early twentieth century

1 NAG Accra, Acc. no. 1427 of 1959; IASAR/22. The letter was clearly drafted with care. Four variant texts, in Arabic and Hausa, are preserved in this corpus of manuscripts.
2 CO.879/50, African (West) no. 538, p. 130: Chamberlain to Maxwell, dd. 15 October 1897.
3 CO.879/52, African (West) no. 549, pp. 66–7: Jenkinson to Colonial Secretary, dd. Wa, 2 December 1897.
4 CO.879/52, African (West) no. 549, p. 43: Northcott, telegram, dd. Wa, 13 January 1898. Texts of these treaties are compiled in African (West), No. 1010.
5 Dougah, 1966, pp. 29, 61–2. According to Dougah, the Kaleo chiefs finally came into Wa to make the treaty.
6 See, e.g. *Government of the Gold Coast. Annual Report on the Northern Territories for the Year 1903*, London, 1904, p. 3. Colonial Reports – Annual, *Northern Territories of the Gold Coast*, 1908, p. 5.
7 Wilks, FN/164, 3 January 1969.
8 The people of Pontomporeyiri, exceptionally in Limamyiri, do not claim descent from Limam Ya'muru. A later Tarawiri immigrant appears to have been ancestral to the group. Presumably his lineage affiliations were such as associate him with the Tarawiri of Wa Limamyiri rather than of Wa Tagarayiri.
9 NAG, Accra, ADM.56/1/200: endorsement by H. W[alker] L[eigh], dd. 5 November 1929, in Informal Diary, Wa District.
10 CO.879/58, African (West) no. 585, pp. 246–8: report by Captain E. N. B. Boyd, Black Volta District, dd. 15 June 1899.
11 Colonial Reports – Annual. no. 530. *Northern Territories of the Gold Coast. Report for 1906*, p. 5.
12 CO.879/58, African (West) no. 585, pp. 141–4: Northcott to Colonial Secretary, dd. Gambaga, 4 March 1899.
13 CO.879/58, African (West) no. 585, pp. 178–88: Northcott to Colonial Secretary dd. Ealing, 9 July 1899, enclosing Report on the Administration of the Northern Territories 1898–9.
14 Ibid.
15 Kimble, 1963, p. 326 and especially note 6.
16 CO.879/67, African (West) no. 649: Morris to Governor, dd. 12 July 1901.
17 Ibid. Governor to Morris, dd. 19 August 1901.

18 Ibid. Morris to Governor, dd. 30 September 1901.

19 CO.879/52, African (West) no. 549, pp. 66–7: Jenkinson to Colonial Secretary, dd. Wa, 2 December 1897.

20 CO.879/58, African (West) no. 585, pp. 178–88: Northcott to Colonial Secretary, dd. 9 July 1899.

21 CO.96/346: confidential despatch, Hodgson to Chamberlain, dd. 20 December 1899.

22 The sources for the tables are *Government of the Gold Coast. Annual Report on the Northern Territories for the Year 1903*, London, 1904, pp. 12, 14. Colonial Reports – Annual. *Northern Territories of the Gold Coast*, 1904, pp. 16–17; 1905, pp. 18–19.

23 In 1903 the disturbed state of the 'Lobi country' west of the Black Volta was such that traders from further north could only reach Buna by crossing the river at Manoa, some 60 miles NNW of Wa, proceeding through Wa, and then re-crossing the river at Tantama some 45 miles SSW of Wa, see Foreign Office Confidential Print, 8267, 1903, Further Correspondence Respecting West Africa, pt. V, p. 66: Des Voeux to Watherston, dd. 8 May 1903.

24 Colonial Reports – Annual. *Northern Territories of the Gold Coast*, 1905, p. 10.

25 Ibid.

26 Colonial Reports – Annual. *Northern Territories of the Gold Coast*, 1908, p. 3.

27 NAG Accra, ADM.56/1/416, Monthly Reports, Black Volta District: Lieutenant T. J. Reynolds, January 1901.

28 Wilks, FN/164, 3 January 1969.

29 Dougah, 1966, p. 29.

30 Ibid, pp. 48–9.

31 *The Gold Coast Civil Service List*, 1910–11, 1912. The descendants of Ishaq b. 'Uthman Dabila claim that he held the Friday limamate for 30 years, that is, from 1311 AH, AD 1893/4. This is incorrect but, perhaps significantly, it was on the occasion of Sarankye Mori's departure from Wa in 1896 that he first emerges as a force in Wala politics.

32 NAG Tamale, ADM.1/257, Wa District Native Affairs: report on Wa District, undated but perhaps *c.* 1932.

33 Wilks, FN/158, 1 January 1969.

34 CO.879/58, African (West) no. 585, p. 151: Northcott to Acting Colonial Secretary, dd. Gambaga, 10 March 1899.

35 NAG Accra, ADM.66/1/2: Memorandum Book, Wa.

36 CO.879/67, African (West) no. 649, p. 40: Draft Northern Territories Proclamation.

37 Colonial Reports – Annual. *Northern Territories of the Gold Coast*, 1907, pp. 7–8.

38 Watherston to Colonial Secretary dd. 18 May 1906, cited in Kimble, 1963, pp. 79–80.

39 NAG Accra, ADM.56/1/416, Monthly Reports, Black Volta District, Lieutenant T. J. Reynolds, February 1901.

40 NAG Tamale, ADM.1/257, Wa District Native Affairs: report on Wa District, undated but perhaps *c.* 1932.

41 CO.879/67, African (West) no. 649: Morris to Governor, dd. 30 September 1901.

42 *Government of the Gold Coast. Annual Report on the Northern Territories for the Year 1903*, 1904, p. 9.

43 Colonial Reports – Annual. *Northern Territories of the Gold Coast*, 1905, pp. 9–10.

44 Colonial Reports – Annual. *Northern Territories of the Gold Coast*, 1907, pp. 11–12.

45 Kimble, 1963, pp. 41–2, and see more generally, Thomas, 1973.

46 Colonial Reports – Annual. *Northern Territories of the Gold Coast*, 1907, pp. 8–9.

47 Colonial Reports – Annual. *Northern Territories of the Gold Coast*, 1905, p. 11; 1906, p. 7; 1908, p. 14.

48 Wilks, FN/55, 9 September 1968. Arnaud, 1912, p. 9.

49 Marty, 1922, p. 70.

50 A major source for mahdism in the central Sudan is the confidential report of G. J. F. Tomlinson and G. J. Lethem, submitted by H. R. Palmer to the Governor of Nigeria in 1927, and printed in London under the title, *History of Islamic Political Propaganda in Nigeria*, Waterlow and Sons, London, Dunstable and Watford, n.d.

51 For an earlier strain of mahdism in the Western Sudan, see Martin, 1963.

52 Wilks, FN/55, 9 September 1968.

53 IASAR/109(ii), IASAR/135.

54 Marty, 1922, p. 69.

55 Ibid. p. 70. 'Umar Farako is to be identified with the 'Umar al-Faraqu Jabaghatay whose son, 'Abdallah, was a well-known teacher in the region of Dya and Jenne, see Wilks, FN/152, 5 May 1966; FN/153, 6 May 1966.

56 Goody, 1970, pp. 143–56.

57 Charlton, 1908, p. 52.

58 Marty, 1922, p. 69. Compare Arnaud, 1912, p. 8.

59 Arnaud, 1912, p. 9.

60 Wilks, FN/55, 9 September 1968.

61 Haight, 1981, vol. I, pp. 112–28.

62 NAG Accra, ADM.56/1/411: monthly report, Black Volta District, June 1905, see Goody, 1970, pp. 151–2.

63 NAG Accra, Watherston to Colonial Secretary dd. 18 May 1906, cited in Kimble, 1963, p. 80.

64 Wilks, FN/134, 15 April 1964.

65 Wilks, FN/135, 18 April 1964.

66 Wilks, FN/139, 18 April 1964.

67 NAG Accra, ADM.1/56/411: monthly report, Black Volta District, July 1905, see Goody, 1970, p. 152. This may be the episode reported by Arnaud, 1912, p. 6, that in the third quarter of 1905 'un marabout quêteur' was brought before the Native Tribunal in Wa, found guilty of a few misdeeds, and convicted for fraud.

68 NAG Accra, ADM.56/1/3, Letter Book: Watherston to Acting Colonial Secretary, dd. 1 May 1906.

69 Colonial Reports – Annual. *Northern Territories of the Gold Coast*, 1908, p. 10.

70 Arnaud, 1912, p. 7.

71 Charlton, 1908, pp. 52–60.

72 NAG Accra, ADM.56/1/3, Letter Book: Watherston to Acting Colonial Secretary, dd. 1 May 1906.

73 Ibid.

74 Wilks, FN/61, 8 March 1963; FN/27, 3 May 1966.

75 Wilks, FN/144, 19 August 1966.

76 NAG Accra, ADM.56/1/101: Acting Provincial Commissioner, N.W. Province, to Major Read, Tamale, dd. 21 March 1916.

77 NAG Tamale, ADM.1/437, Essay on the Peoples of the North West Province, by B. M. Read, dd. Wa, 22 November 1908, and see also ADM.1/222, Informal Diary, Commissioner, Southern Province, entry for 3 January 1932.

78 I am unable to give chapter and verse for the prediction. It was contextualized, however, in terms of the politics of the late 1950s. It was frequently cited, pessimistically, by Walas opposed to Nkrumah who saw it as nevertheless indicating the inevitability of his rise to power.

79 NAG Tamale, ADM.1/437, Essay on the Peoples of the North West Province, by B. M. Read, dd. 22 November 1908.

80 Dougah, 1966, p. 29.

81 Wilks, FN/144, 19 August 1966.

82 Colonial Reports – Annual. *Northern Territories of the Gold Coast*, 1914, p. 23.

83 Ibid.

84 NAG Tamale, ADM.1/148: report on native administration, Northern Territories, dd. 13 August 1928.

85 Marty, 1922, pp. 488–9. See more generally, L'Opinion Musulmane au Soudan Française et les événements de Turquie, in *L'Afrique Française*, April 1915.

86 NAG Accra, ADM.66/5/5, Letter Book, Wa, entries for 4, 8, 12, 13 and 14 June 1916.

87 Ibid., entry for 30 June 1916.

88 Patterson, 1983, p. 498, puts the deaths in the Wa District at 2,613, or 6.1% of the population.

89 Wilks, FN/165, 4 January 1969.

90 NAG Accra, ADM.66/5/5, Letter Book, Wa, entry for 8 August 1916.

91 NAG Accra, ADM.56/1/370: P. Whittall, District Commissioner, Wa, to Chief Commissioner dd. 28 July 1924. Whittall clearly had Commissioner Berkeley's report in hand; I have been unable to locate the original in either NAG Accra or NAG Tamale.

92 NAG Accra, ADM.66/5/5, Letter Book, Wa: entry for 10 July 1918. In September the help of the '3 Wa alhajis' rather than Malam Ishaq was solicited to deal with Ahmadu Madani, a 'wild unbalanced man' who arrived in Wa on his way back from Mecca to his home in Senegal; ibid, entry for 19 September 1918.

93 Wilks, FN/165, 4 January 1969.

94 NAG Tamale, ADM.1/241, Informal Diary, Wa District: entry for 5 June 1934.

95 Wilks, FN/165, 4 January 1969.

96 Ibid.

97 NAG Accra, ADM.56/1/200, Wa District Native Affairs: Provincial Commissioner to Acting Chief Commissioner dd. 5 August 1919.

98 Wilks, FN/165, 4 January 1969.

99 NAG Accra, ADM.66/5/2, Wa District General Information Book: entry for December 1919.

100 Dougah, 1966, p. 30.

101 NAG Accra, ADM.56/1/200, Wa District Native Affairs: entry for 3 January 1920.

102 Wilks, FN/169, 4 January 1969.

103 NAG Accra, ADM.66/5/2, Wa District General Information Book: entry for 2 January 1920.

104 NAG Accra, ADM.66/5/5, Letter Book, Wa: entries for 12 January and 17 February 1920; ADM.56/1/485: Provincial Commissioner to Chief Commissioner, dd. 31 March 1920.

105 Wilks, FN/169, 4 January 1969.

106 *Gold Coast Colony. Civil Service List*, 1930, p. 24.

107 NAG Tamale, ADM.1/228, Provincial Diary, Northern Province: entry for 2 December 1931.

108 NAG Accra, Acc. no. 1427 of 1959.

109 Ya'qub b. Ya'muru was still gazetted as limam in 1922, but this may have been already a year out of date. A report that he died in 1347 AH, AD 1928/9, has to be rejected as in error, see Wilks, FN/208, 17 July 1967.

110 Wilks, FN/144, 19 August 1966.

111 Tamarimuni informants said that the limamate was vacant for about a decade, but this is in error. Friday Limam Al-Hajj Siddiq remarked that 'there was some quarrelling about it but it is too long ago now to know about it'. See Wilks, FN/53, 1 July 1964; FN/208, 17 July 1967.

112 IASAR/46. See also IASAR/343.

113 Wilks, FN/234, 10 January 1986.

114 NAG Tamale, ADM.1/122, Informal Diary, Wa: entry for 14 October 1926.

115 Ibid., entry for 15 October 1926.
116 NAG Tamale, ADM.1/22.
117 NAG Accra, ADM.56/1/370: Whittall to Chief Commissioner, dd. 28 July 1924.
118 NAG Tamale, ADM.1/228: Wa District Informal Diary, entries for 8 and 17 December 1931.
119 NAG Accra, ADM.56/1/101: Acting Chief Secretary Findlay, Lagos, to Colonial Secretary, Gold Coast, dd. 6 July 1934.
120 NAG Accra, ADM.56/1/101: D.C., Wa to Chief Commissioner, dd. 30 May 1936.
121 Wilks, FN/164, 3 January 1969.
122 NAG Accra, ADM.56/1/200, Informal Diary, Wa: entry for 17 September 1929.
123 NAG Accra, ADM.56/1/289: District Commissioner, Wa, to Provincial Commissioner, dd. 26 November 1929. NAG Accra, ADM.56/1/200: Provincial Commissioner to Chief Commissioner, dd. 9 December 1929.
124 Wilks, FN/164, 3 January 1969.
125 Dougah, 1966, p. 31.
126 NAG Tamale, ADM.1/228, Diary, Northern Province: entry for 2 December 1931.
127 Wilks, FN/3, 2 February 1965.

8 Wala under 'indirect rule': power to the Na and schism in the *umma*

1 NAG Tamale, ADM.1/196–202, Memorandum of Native Administration in the Northern Territories, by Acting Chief Commissioner E. A. T. Taylor, dd. 18 March, 1931, p. 9.
2 NAG Tamale, ADM.1/8, Confidential Diary, entry for 19 October 1928, referring to the Governor's Conference of 11 March 1921.
3 NAG Tamale, ADM.1/196–202, Memorandum of Native Administration, dd. 18 March 1931, p. 1.
4 Ibid. pp. 1–2.
5 Ibid. p. 5.
6 Ibid. p. 5.
7 Ibid. pp. 3–4.
8 Ibid. p. 6.
9 Ibid. pp. 13–14.
10 NAG Accra, 'Conference of Kagbanya (Gonja) Chiefs held at Yapei on the 17th to 21st days of May, 1930, to enquire into the Constitution of the Gbanya Kingdom.' A. C. Duncan-Johnstone, *Enquiry into the Constitution and Organisation of the Dagbon Kingdom*, Accra, 1932.
11 NAG Tamale, ADM.1/222, Informal Diary, Commissioner of the Southern Province, entry for 16 January 1932.
12 Ibid., entries for 11 and 16 January 1932.
13 NAG Tamale, ADM.1/202, District Commissioner, Bole, to Chief Commissioner, dd. 15 November 1933.
14 NAG Tamale, ADM.1/222, Informal Diary, Southern Province, entry for 11 January, 1932. A collection of administrative and other papers in Arabic from the Kpembe division of Gonja are accessioned as IASAR/263–91. In Yendi, I was shown Arabic originals of both Census and taxation returns, see Wilks, FN/105, 14 August 1968.
15 NAG Tamale, ADM.1/222, Informal Diary, entry for 16 January, 1932.
16 NAG Tamale, ADM.1/196–202, Memorandum of Native Administration, dd. 18 March 1931.
17 When Wa District Commissioner P. C. R. Moreton was about to proceed on leave in December 1931, he noted, 'the Mahommedans sent up a letter expressing their appreciation of my efforts here; a spontaneous testimonial, which is unusual and much appreciated'.

Whittall commented in the margin, 'A somewhat doubtful honour from these particular folk!' NAG Tamale, ADM.1/228, Wa District Informal Diary, 1 December 1931.

18 Native Courts Ordinance 1 of 1932; Native Authority (Northern Territories) Ordinance 2 of 1932; Native Treasuries Ordinance 10 of 1932. See Hailey, 1951, pp. 262–72.

19 NAG Tamale, ADM.1/257, Report on Wa District, n.d. but filed with papers of the Assistant Secretary for Native Affairs, dd. 7 March 1932.

20 NAG Tamale, ADM.1/241, Informal Diary, Wa District, April, 1933.

21 Ibid., entry for 15 July 1933.

22 Ibid., entry for 28 November 1933.

23 Duncan-Johnstone, 1932. NAG Tamale, ADM.1/257, Wa District Native Affairs: District Commissioner to Provincial Commissioner, dd. 17 July 1933, enclosing constitutional documents and appendices A to H, dd. 15 July, 1933.

24 NAG Tamale, ADM.1/241, Informal Diary, Wa District, entry for 7 May 1934.

25 Dougah, 1966, p. 31.

26 Hailey, 1951, p. 266.

27 NAG Tamale, ADM.1/502, Annual Reports, Wa, 1938–9 and 1939–40. Dougah, 1966, pp. 76–7.

28 NAG Tamale, ADM.1/257, Wa District Native Affairs: Composition of Divisional Tribunals (Court) in the Wala State, approved by Wa Na Pelpuo III and the Wala Judicial Council, 4 October 1933.

29 Marie Louise, 1926, pp. 122–3, citing Commissioner P. F. Whittall. Compare Dougah, 1966, pp. 110–11.

30 Marie Louise, 1926, p. 122, citing Whittall.

31 Rattray, 1932, vol. II, pp. 452–3. Rattray's notes of his work in Wala were consulted at the Royal Anthropological Institute, London, Papers of R. S. Rattray, MS Bundle 109, Notebook 8, 1929–30. It is sad to have to comment on the extremely poor quality of the material he recorded.

32 Wilks, FN/234, 10 January 1986.

33 NAG Tamale, ADM.1/228, Provincial Diary: entry for 2 December 1931.

34 These tables are compiled from the imperfect data in the files of the District Commissioners, especially their annual reports, and from the Gold Coast Civil Service lists from 1902 to 1922, and 1941.

35 NAG Tamale, ADM.1/241, Informal Diary, Wa: entry for 5 June 1934.

36 NAG Tamale, ADM.1/272, Informal Diary, Wa: entry for 16 September 1935.

37 NAG Tamale, ADM.1/193, Annual Report for Wa, year ending 31 March 1931; ADM.1/241, Informal Diary, Wa District: entry for 27 May 1932.

38 NAG Tamale, ADM.1/272, Informal Diary, Wa: entry for 9 January 1936.

39 NAG Accra, ADM.66/5/4, General Information Book: entry for May 1935. NAG Tamale, ADM.1/241, Informal Diary: entries for 22 January and 16 February 1934.

40 NAG Tamale, ADM.1/272, Informal Diary: entry for 25 February 1936.

41 NAG Tamale, ADM.1/272, Informal Diary: entry for 11 January 1936.

42 Wilks, FN/234, 10 January 1986.

43 NAG Accra, ADM.66/5/4, General Information Book: entry for 25 March 1936.

44 NAG Tamale, ADM.1/272, Informal Diary: entry for 4 February 1936.

45 Dougah, 1966, p. 31.

46 NAG Tamale, ADM.1/272, Informal Diary: entry for 19 September 1936.

47 NAG Tamale, ADM.1/316, Informal Diary: entry for 9 February 1938.

48 NAG Tamale, ADM.1/446, Annual Report, Wala District, 1938–9.

49 NAG Tamale, ADM.1/316, Informal Diary: entry for 4 November 1939.

50 NAG Tamale, ADM.1/350, Informal Diary: entry for 28 February 1942.

51 Dougah, 1966, pp. 31–2.

52 NAG Tamale, Informal Diary: entries for 12 July and 29 October 1943.
53 NAG Tamale, ADM.1/350, Informal Diary: entry for 22 November 1943.
54 NAG Tamale, ADM.1/272, Informal Diary: entry for 8 May 1936. NAG Accra, ADM.66/5/4, General Information Book: various entries 1934–6.
55 Dougah, 1966, p. 32.
56 NAG Tamale, ADM.1/356, Informal Diary: entry for 15 November 1943.
57 Dougah, 1966, p. 33. NAG Tamale, ADM.1/608: telegram, District Commissioner, Wa, to Chief Commissioner, n.d.
58 NAG Tamale, ADM.1/608: telegram, District Commissioner, Wa, to Chief Commissioner, n.d.
59 NAG Tamale, ADM.1/350, Informal Diary, Wa: entry for November 1943.
60 Dougah, 1966, pp. 32–3.
61 Ibid, p. 33.
62 NAG Accra, ADM.66/5/4, General Information Book, entry for 1949. Wilks, FN/211, 6 May 1966.
63 A major statement of Ahmadi doctrine, including the thesis of the death of Jesus in Kashmir, was made by Ghulum Ahmad's son and second successor, Bashir-ud-Din Mahmud Ahmad, in 1926. His *Dawat al-Amir*, originally written in Urdu, now exists in an accessible English translation, *Invitation to Ahmadiyyat*, see Ahmad, 1980.
64 For the early history of the Movement, see Lavan, 1974.
65 The history of the Ahmadiyya Movement in Ghana is treated briefly in Fisher, 1963, pp. 117–20, and in *Ahmadiyya Movement in Ghana. 1921–1961*, Ahmadiyya Movement, Saltpond, n.d. More informative in many respects is the report, 'The Ahmadiyya Movement in the Gold Coast 1921–1931', by A. C. Duncan-Johnstone, 5 November 1931, in NAG Tamale, ADM.1/222, Informal Diary, Commissioner, Southern Province of the Northern Territories.
66 *Ahmadiyya Movement in Ghana*, p. 14.
67 Of major importance for the career of Salih b. al-Hasan are the accounts given to Fikry in 1967 by two of his closest associates, Khalid and Yahya, see Fikry, 1970, vol. I, pp. 207–22. See also Dougah, 1966, pp. 49–54. I have relied heavily on these two sources. My own close association with the orthodox Muslim community in Wa in the 1960s precluded all but the occasional meeting with the Ahmadis.
68 Salih's son, al-Hasan, said that his father was aged 65 on his death in 1961, Wilks, FN/119, 5 August 1964. Dougah, 1966, pp. 50, 54, places his birth in 1886, but this seems unlikely.
69 Dougah, 1966, p. 50. Fikry, 1970, vol. I, pp. 207, 210–11, citing Ahmadiyya Limam Khalid.
70 Dougah, 1966, p. 50. Fikry, vol. I, 1970, p. 208.
71 Dougah, 1966, p. 50. Fikry, 1970, vol. I, p. 209.
72 Wilks, FN/119, 5 August 1964; FN/232, 7 January 1986. Khalid, later Ahmadiyya Limam, appears to have been adopted into Dzedzedeyiri by matrifiliation.
73 Fikry, 1970, vol. I, p. 209. Dougah, 1966, p. 51.
74 Watherston to White Fathers, dd. 1 June 1906, and Armitage to Governor, dd. 5 June 1912, cited in Kimble, 1963, pp. 80–1.
75 NAG Tamale, ADM.1/241, Informal Diary, Wa: entries for 1, 9 and 14 June 1933. Dougah, 1966, p. 51.
76 *Ahmadiyya Movement in Ghana*, p. 14.
77 Fikry, 1970, vol. I, pp. 209–11.
78 Dougah, 1966, pp. 51–2.
79 Fikry, 1970, vol. I, p. 211.
80 NAG Tamale, ADM.1/241, Informal Diary, Wa: entry for 28 March 1934.
81 *Ahmadiyya Movement in Ghana*, p. 14. Dougah, 1966, p. 52.
82 NAG Tamale, ADM.1/241, Informal Diary: entry for 8 August 1934.

83 Dougah, 1966, p. 52. Fikry, 1970, vol. I, p. 212.

84 Fikry, 1970, vol. I, pp. 212–13. Dougah, 1966, pp. 52–3. NAG Tamale, ADM.1/241, Informal Diary, entry for 15 August 1934. One informant remembered the school children being used to carry the wounded to the dispensary on what must have been this occasion, Wilks, FN/163, 2 January 1969.

85 Wilks, FN/234, 10 January 1986; FN/267, 8 February 1987.

86 Fikry, 1970, vol. I, pp. 213–14. Dougah, 1966, p. 53.

87 Stewart, 1965, p. 38 and Appendix V.

88 Fikry, 1970, vol. I, p. 187.

89 NAG Tamale, ADM.1/222, Informal Diary, Commissioner, Southern Province: 'The Ahmadiyya Movement in the Gold Coast 1921–1931', report by A. C. Duncan-Johnstone, dd. 5 November 1931.

90 NAG Accra, ADM.66/5/4, General Information Book, Wa District: entry for 8 March 1937.

91 NAG Accra, ADM.66/5/4: General Information Book: entry for 8 March 1937. NAG Tamale, ADM.1/272, Informal Diary, Wa: entry for 9 April 1937.

92 Fikry, 1970, vol. I, p. 214.

93 *Ahmadiyya Movement in Ghana*, p. 15.

94 Fikry, 1970, vol. I, pp. 196–7, 215.

95 NAG Tamale, ADM.1/231: account of Salih's preaching tour, dd. 25 June 1941. *Ahmadiyya Movement in Ghana*, p. 15.

96 Fikry, 1970, vol. I, p. 215.

97 *Ahmadiyya in Ghana*, p. 16.

98 Fikry, 1970, vol. I, p. 215. *Ahmadiyya in Ghana*, p. 16.

99 NAG Tamale, ADM.1/350, Informal Diary, Wa: entry for 25 October 1941.

100 Ibid, entry for 10 October 1942.

101 NAG Tamale, ADM.1/356, Informal Diary: entry for 15 November 1943.

102 NAG Tamale, ADM.1/350, Informal Diary: entry for November 1943. *Ahmadiyya Movement in Ghana*, p. 16.

103 Fikry, 1970, vol. I, p. 215.

104 *Ahmadiyya Movement in Ghana*, pp. 16–17.

105 This follows the recollections of Salih's close associate, Yahya, as recorded in Fikry, 1970, vol. I, p. 215. Dougah, 1966, p. 53, dates Salih's pilgrimage to 1951, but this is probably in error. Among those who accompanied Salih was his Qur'an carrier, Ya'qub b. Ishaq b. Sa'id of Dzedzedeyiri, a descendant of Limam Ya'qub b. 'Abd al-Qadir. Ya'qub b. Ishaq did not travel back with Salih, but remained in Mecca for – as the informant put it – 'more than ten years. Maybe fourteen or more'. He abandoned Ahmadiyya. On his return to Wa in the 1960s he opened a school in Sankana, and was called from there to become Wa Limam in 1984. Wilks, FN/232, 7 January 1986.

106 Fikry, 1970, vol. I, p. 215.

107 Ibid. p. 216.

108 Ibid. p. 217.

109 NAG Tamale, ADM.1/350, Informal Diary, Wa: entry for 2 April 1945.

110 *Ahmadiyya Movement in Ghana*, p. 17.

111 NAG Tamale, ADM.1/350, Informal Diary, Wa: entry for 20 February 1944. Tension was apparently much lower at the village level to judge from this report, which noted that the orthodox of Guropise assisted in the construction of the Ahmadi mosque.

112 I am indebted to J. H. Price, who gave me access in June 1956 to his draft essay on Islam in Ghana, for information on this topic.

113 *Gold Coast: Report to His Excellency the Governor by the Committee on Constitutional Reform*, Colonial Office, London, 1949, especially pp. 14–15, 22.

114 *The Gold Coast Gazette*, no. 33, 1952, part 1, pp. 543–6; part 2, pp. 2192–3. Dougah, 1966, pp. 70–81. NAG Tamale, ADM.1/573, A Gazetteer of the Wa District 1955, pp. 16–19.
115 NAG Tamale, ADM.1/573, A Gazetteer of the Wa District 1955, Appendix A.
116 Ladouceur, 1979, pp. 75–7.
117 Ibid. pp. 102–4.
118 Ibid. 1979, pp. 79–81.
119 Ibid. 1979, pp. 105–6.
120 Wilks, FN/232, 7 January 1986. The brother of Mumuni Adama, Al-Hajj Nuhu b. Adama Bile, became Wa Limam. He died in 1984.
121 Fikry, 1970, vol. I, p. 218.
122 NAG Accra, ADM.66/5/4, General Information Book: entry for 10 November 1949.
123 Dougah, 1966, p. 34.
124 Wilks, FN/169, 4 January 1969.
125 Dougah, 1966, p. 34.
126 Dougah, 1966, pp. 34–6. Fikry, 1970, vol. I, p. 218.
127 'The CPP Finds its Feet in the North', *West Africa*, no. 1822, 26 January 1952, p. 55 and No. 1823, 2 February 1952, pp. 85–6. The Correspondent in the Northern Territories who wrote these highly useful accounts was, I believe, Dennis Austin.
128 Dougah, 1966, pp. 36–7.
129 Anderson, 1954, pp. 264–6.
130 Supreme Court of Ghana, Asanni Zei and J. N. Momori vs. Yakubu Seidu, 3, 5, 9, 17 and 29 July 1985, see Wilks, FN/233, 9 January 1986; FN/235, 10 January 1986.
131 NAG Tamale, ADM.1/608, Appointments, Deaths, etc, Chiefs, Wa: entry for 27 January 1944.
132 Wilks, FN/165, 4 January 1969. See also FN/234, 10 January 1986.
133 Dougah, 1966, pp. 37–9.
134 Ladouceur, 1979, *passim*.
135 Wilks, 'Northern Territories Palaver', *West Africa*, No. 2044, 16 June 1956. As Resident Tutor for the Northern Territories (Institute of Extra-mural Studies, University College of the Gold Coast) from 1955 to 1958, I was inevitably involved in the struggle between the CPP and the NPP for power there. Classes on politics run in conjunction with the Peoples Educational Association were transformed, in many cases, into local branches of one or the other party. Over these years I visited Wa frequently. I much regret that in this period I kept no systematic notes of my conversations with Wa Na Saidu, the limams, and many others. What I learned from them, however, proved invaluable when I later decided to undertake a study of Wa.
136 It may recorded that on this auspicious occasion I was included in a party of newly fledged Ghanaians who fired a volley of musket shot from the upper floor of the hitherto almost exclusively European club in Tamale.
137 NAG Tamale, ADM.1/573, A Gazetteer of the Wa District 1955, p. 14.
138 Fisher, 1963, p. 182.
139 Wilks, FN/163, 2 January 1969.
140 Wilks, FN/267, 8 February 1987.
141 Dougah, 1966, pp. 39–45.
142 Wilks, FN/119, 5 August 1964.
143 *Ahmadiyya Movement in Ghana*, p. 17.
144 Ibid, p. 22.
145 Dougah, 1966, p. 45.
146 Secretary to the Regional Commissioner, Bolgatanga, to District Commissioner, Wa, dd. 13 April 1961. See Dougah, 1966, p. 45.
147 Wilks, FN/171, 4 January 1969.

148 Wilks, FN/168, 3 January 1969; FN/169, 4 January 1969.
149 Wilks, FN/255, 15 April 1963.
150 Wilks, FN/61, 8 March 1963.
151 Fikry, 1970, vol. I, p. 29.

9 Review: the peculiarities of Wala

1 Supreme Court of Ghana, Asanni Zei and J. N. Momori v. Yakubu Seidu, 3, 5, 9, 17 and 29 July 1985. Wilks, FN/233, 9 January 1986.
2 Wilks, FN/232, 7 January 1986.
3 See the story, 'Why Daughters who don't Marry are Given to the Chiefs as Wives', in Fikry, 1970, vol. II, pp. 247–50. The moral of the story is: 'this is the reason why when a parent continues not to allow his daughter to marry to the point that she gets tired of it all, then she is brought to the Chief to be married to him'.
4 Fikry, 1970, vol. I, pp. 102–10, 263–70.
5 Wilks, FN/169, 4 January 1969.
6 Arhin, 1985, pp. 108–9.
7 Ibid, p. 113.
8 Wilks, FN/232, 7 January 1986; FN/233, 9 January 1986; FN/234, 10 January 1986.
9 Daily Graphic, 11 March 1980.
10 Wilks, FN/267, 8 February 1987.
11 Daily Graphic, 1 and 2 April 1980.
12 Supreme Court of Ghana, Asanni Zei and J. N. Momori v. Yakubu Seidu, 3, 5, 9, 17 and 29 July 1985.
13 Wilks, FN/233, 9 January 1986.
14 Dougah, 1966, pp. 98–104; Fikry, 1970, vol. I, pp. 306–16.
15 Wilks, FN/169, 4 January 1969.
16 Haji Mirza Bashir-ud-din Mahmud Ahmad, Invitation to Ahmadiyyat, 1980, p. 3.
17 Decentralization in Ghana, Information Services Department, Accra.
18 West Africa, 13 July 1987, pp. 1343–4; 27 July 1987, p. 1462; 3 August 1987, pp. 1477–8.
19 West Africa, 20 April 1987, pp. 787–8.
20 West Africa, 19 October 1987, p. 2092.
21 West Africa, 8 February 1988, p. 232.
22 Hodgkin, 1980.

Bibliography

Sources cited

Books, articles and dissertations

Adamu, Mahdi. 1978. *The Hausa Factor in West African History*, Zaria and Ibadan

Ahmad, Hazrat Haji Mirza Bashir-ud-Din Mahmud. 1980. *Invitation to Ahmadiyyat*, London, Boston and Henley

Ahmadiyya Movement in Ghana. 1921–1961 [n.d.], Saltpond

Anderson, J. N. D. 1954. *Islamic Law in Africa*, London

Anquandah, J. R. 1986. Investigating the Stone Circle Mound Sites and Art Works of Komaland, N. Ghana, *Nyame Akuma*, 27, 10–13

1987. L'Art du Komaland. Une découverte récente au Ghana septentrional, *Art Afrique Noire*, 62, 11–18

Anquandah, J. R. and L. Van Ham. 1985. *Discovering the Forgotten 'Civilization' of Komaland, Northern Ghana*, Rotterdam

Arhin, Kwame, ed. 1974. *The Papers of George Ekem Ferguson. A Fanti Official of the Government of the Gold Coast, 1890–1897*, Leiden and Cambridge

1985. *Traditional Rule in Ghana*, Accra

Armitage, C. H. 1924. *The Tribal Markings and Marks of Adornment of the Natives of the Northern Territories of the Gold Coast Colony*, London

Arnaud, Robert. 1912. L'Islam et la politique Musulmane Française en Afrique Occidentale Française, *Renseignements Coloniaux*, no. 1, supplement to *L'Afrique Française*, pp. 3–154

Austin, Allan D. 1984. *African Muslims in Antebellum America. A Sourcebook*, New York and London

Barth, Henry, 1859. *Travels and Discoveries in North and Central Africa*, 3 vols., New York

Berberich, C. 1974. A Locational Analysis of Trade Routes of the Northeast Asante Frontier Network in the Nineteenth Century, unpublished PhD dissertation, Northwestern University

Binger, L. G. 1892. *Du Niger au Golfe de Guinée par les Pays de Kong et le Mossi*, 2 vols., Paris

Bowdich, T. E. 1819. *Mission from Cape Coast Castle to Ashantee*, London

Braimah, J. A. 1970. *The Ashanti and Gonja at War*, Accra

Case, Glenna L. 1979. Wasipe under the Ngbanya: Polity, Economy and Society in Northern Ghana, unpublished PhD dissertation, Northwestern University

Charlton, L. E. O. 1908. *A Hausa Reading Book*, Oxford

Cissé, Diango and Diabété, Massa Makan. 1970. *La Dispersion des Mandeka*, Bamako

Davis, David C. 1984. Continuity and Change in Mampurugu: A Study of Tradition as Ideology, unpublished PhD dissertation, Northwestern University

234

Delafosse, M. 1908. *Les Frontières de la Côte d'Ivoire, de la Côte de l'Or et du Soudan*, Paris

Dieterlen, G. 1955. Mythe et organisation sociale au Soudan Français, *Journal de la Société des Africanistes*, 25, 1/2, 39–76

1959. Mythe et organisation sociale en Afrique Occidentale, *Journal de la Société des Africanistes*, 29, 1, 119–38

Dougah, J. C. 1966. *Wa and Its People*, Institute of African Studies, Legon

Duby, G. 1975. *The Early Growth of the European Economy: Warriors and Peasants*, London

Duncan-Johnstone, A. C. 1932. *Enquiry into the Constitution and Organisation of the Dagbon Kingdom*, Accra

Duperray, Anne-Marie. 1984. *Les Gourounsi de Haute-Volta: conquête et colonisation 1896–1933*, Stuttgart

Dupuis, Joseph. 1824. *Journal of a Residence in Ashantee*, London

Eyre-Smith, St J. 1933. *A Brief Review of the History and Social Organisation of the Peoples of the Northern Territories of the Gold Coast*, Accra

Fage, J. D. 1956. The Investigation of Oral Tradition in the Northern Territories of the Gold Coast, *Journal of the Historical Society of Nigeria*, 1, 1, 15–19

Ferguson, Phyllis. 1972. Islamization in Dagbon. A Study of the Alfanema of Yendi, unpublished PhD dissertation, University of Cambridge

Ferguson, Phyllis and Wilks, Ivor. 1970. Chiefs, Constitutions and the British in Northern Ghana, in Michael Crowder and Obaro Ikime, eds., *West African Chiefs. Their Changing Status under Colonial Rule and Independence*, pp. 326–69, Ile-Ife

Fikry, Mona. 1970. Wa: A Case Study of Social Values and Social Tensions as Reflected in the Oral Traditions of the Wala of Northern Ghana, unpublished PhD dissertation, Indiana University, 1969 (two volumes, University Microfilms, Ann Arbor, Michigan)

Fikry-Atallah, Mona. 1972. Wala Oral History and Wa's Social Realities, in Richard M. Dorson, ed., *African Folklore*, pp. 327–53, New York

Fisher, Humphrey J. 1963. *Ahmadiyyah. A Study in Contemporary Islam on the West African Coast*, London

Fortes, Meyer. 1945. *The Dynamics of Clanship among the Tallensi*, London

1949. *The Web of Kinship among the Tallensi*, London

Freeman, R. Austin. 1892. A Journey to Bontuku in the Interior of West Africa, *Royal Geographical Society*, 3, 2, Supplementary Papers

Gibbons, P. C. 1966. King-Lists and Chronology: A Note on Work in Progress, *Ghana Notes and Queries*, 8, p. 25

Goody, J. 1954. *The Ethnography of the Northern Territories of the Gold Coast West of the White Volta*, London

1956. *The Social Organisation of the LoWiili*, London

1967. The Over-Kingdom of Gonja, in Daryll Forde and P. M. Kaberry, eds., *West African Kingdoms in the Nineteenth Century*, pp. 179–205, London

1970. Reform, Renewal and Resistance: A Mahdi in Northern Ghana, in Christopher Allen and R. W. Johnson, eds., *African Perspectives*, pp. 143–56, Cambridge.

Goody, J. and Ivor Wilks. 1968. Writings in Gonja, in J. Goody, ed., *Literacy in Traditional Society*, pp. 241–61, Cambridge

Haight, Bruce Marvin. 1981. Bole and Gonja. Contributions to the History of Northern Ghana, unpublished PhD dissertation, Northwestern University, 3 vols

Hailey, Lord. 1951. *Native Administration in the British African Territories*. Pt III: *West Africa: Nigeria, Gold Coast, Sierra Leone, Gambia*, London

Harvey, William Burnett. 1966. *Law and Social Change in Ghana*, New Jersey

Henderson, F. B. 1898. West Africa and the Empire: Being a Narrative of a Recent Journey of Exploration Through the Gold Coast Hinterland, *The Idler*, April, 407–16; May, 487–97; June, 607–18

235

Bibliography

Hinds, J. H. 1957. The People of the Lawra and Wa Area, Northern Region, *The Gold Coast Farmer*, 1, 5, 192–5

Hodgkin, Thomas. 1980. The Revolutionary Tradition in Islam, *Race and Class*, 21, 3, 221–237

Holden, J. 1965. The Zabarima Conquest of North-West Ghana, Part I, *Transactions of the Historical Society of Ghana*, 8, 60–86

1970. The Samorian Impact on Buna: an Essay in Methodology, in Christopher Allen and R. W. Johnson, eds., *African Perspectives*, pp. 83–108, Cambridge

1980. Zabarimas and 'Grunshis' in Northern Ghana, 1860–1900. Unpublished typescript

Hooke, Della. 1985. *The Anglo-Saxon Landscape. The Kingdom of the Hwicce*, Manchester

Hunter, T. C. 1977. The Development of an Islamic Tradition of Learning among the Jakhanka of West Africa, unpublished PhD dissertation, University of Chicago

Hunwick, J. O. 1964. A New Source for the Life of Ahmad Baba al-Tinbukti (1556–1627), *Bulletin of the School of Oriental and African Studies*, 27, 568–93

1966. Further Light on Ahmad Baba al-Tinbukti, *Research Bulletin of the Centre of Arabic Documentation*, 2, ii, 19–31

1985. *Shari'a in Songhay: the Replies of Al-Maghili to the Questions of Askia Al-Hajj Muhammad*, Oxford

Hutton, W. 1821. *Voyage to Africa*, London

Kanya-Forstner, A. S. 1969. *The Conquest of the Western Sudan. A Study in French Military Imperialism*, Cambridge

Kimble, David 1963. *A Political History of Ghana. The Rise of Gold Coast Nationalism 1850–1928*, Oxford

Labouret, Henri. 1931. *Les Tribus du Rameau Lobi*, Paris

Ladouceur, P. A. 1972. The Yendi Chieftaincy Dispute and Ghanaian Politics, *Canadian Journal of African Studies*, 6, 1, 97–115

1979. *Chiefs and Politicians: The Politics of Regionalism in Northern Ghana*, London and New York

Lavan, Spencer. 1974. *The Ahmadiyah Movement: A History and Perspective*, Delhi

Levtzion, Nehemia. 1965. The Spread and Development of Islam in the Middle Volta Basin in the Pre-Colonial Period, unpublished PhD dissertation, University of London

1968. *Muslims and Chiefs in West Africa*, Oxford

1973. *Ancient Ghana and Mali*, London

Levtzion, Nehemia and J. F. P. Hopkins, eds., 1981. *Corpus of Early Arabic Sources for West African History*, Cambridge

Madden, R. R. 1837. *Twelve Months Residence in the West Indies*, 2 vols., London

Maier, D. J. E. 1983. *Priests and Power. The Case of the Dente Shrine in Nineteenth-Century Ghana*, Bloomington, Indiana

Marie Louise, H. H. Princess. 1926. *Letters from the Gold Coast*, London

Martin, B. G. 1963. A Mahdist Document from Futa Jallon, *Bulletin de l'I.F.A.N.*, 25, series B, nos. 1–2, pp. 47–65

1965. Arabic Materials for Ghanaian History, *Research Review*, Institute of African Studies, University of Ghana, II, 1, pp. 74–83

Marty, Paul. 1922. *Etudes sur l'Islam en Côte d'Ivoire*, Paris

Meek, C. K., W. M. Macmillan and E. R. J. Hussey. 1940. *Europe and West Africa. Some Problems and Adjustments*, Oxford

Miller, M. 1975–6. Date-guessing and Pedigrees. *Studia Celtica*, 10–11, 96–109

Al-Naqar, 'Umar. 1972. *The Pilgrimage Tradition in West Africa*, Khartoum

Northcott, H. P. 1899. *Report on the Northern Territories of the Gold Coast*, London

Patterson, K. D. 1983. The Influenza Epidemic 1918–19 in the Gold Coast, *Journal of African History*, 24, 4, 485–502

Person, Y. 1964. En Quête d'une chronologie Ivoirienne, in J. Vansina, R. Mauny and L. V. Thomas, eds., *The Historian in Tropical Africa*, London

1975. *Samori. Une Revolution Dyula*, Mémoires de l'Institut Fondamental D'Afrique Noire no. 89, 3 vols., IFAN–Dakar

Pilaszewicz, S. 1969. The Story of the Wala Peple, *Africana Bulletin*, Warsaw, no. 10, 53–76

1970. The Story of Wala, Our Country, *Africana Bulletin*, Warsaw, no. 11, 59–78

Pogucki, R. J. H. 1955. *Gold Coast Land Tenure*, vol. I: *A Survey of Land Tenure in Customary Law of the Protectorate of the Northern Territories*, Accra

Rattray, R. S. 1932. *The Tribes of the Ashanti Hinterland*, 2 vols., Oxford

Renouard, G. C. 1836. Routes in North Africa by Abu Bekr es siddik, *Journal of the Royal Geographical Society*, 6, 100–13

Robertson, G. A. 1819. *Notes on Africa*, London

Saad, Elias N. 1983. *Social History of Timbuktu: The Role of Muslim Scholars and Notables 1400–1900*, Cambridge

al-Saʿdi, ʿAbd al-Rahman. 1898–1900. *Taʾrikh al-Sudan*, ed. and trans. O. Houdas, Paris

Sanneh, L. O. 1979. *The Jakhanke*, London

Sawyer, P. H., ed. 1976. *Medieval Settlement, Continuity and Change*, London

Staniland, Martin. 1975. *The Lions of Dagbon: Political Change in Northern Ghana*, Cambridge

Stewart, Charles C. 1965. The Tijaniya in Ghana; an Historical Study, unpublished MA dissertation, University of Ghana

Tait, David. 1961. *The Konkomba of Northern Ghana*, London

Tamakloe, E. F. 1931. *A Brief History of the Dagbamba People*, Accra

Tauxier, L. 1912. *Le Noir du Soudan. Pays Mossi et Gourounsi*, Paris

1921. *Le Noir de Bondoukou*, Paris

1924. *Nouvelles Notes sur le Mossi et le Gourounsi*, Paris

Thomas, Roger. 1973. Forced Labour in British West Africa: The Case of the Northern Territories of the Gold Coast 1906–1927, *Journal of African History*, 14, 1, 79–103

Westermann, D. and M. A. Bryan. 1952. *Handbook of African Languages. Part II. West Africa.* Oxford

Wilks, Ivor. 1967. Abu Bakr al-Siddiq of Timbuktu, in P. Curtin, ed., *Africa Remembered*, pp. 152–69, Madison

1968. The Transmission of Islamic Learning in the Western Sudan, in J. Goody, ed., *Literacy in Traditional Society*, pp. 161–97, Cambridge

1975. *Asante in the Nineteenth Century: The Structure and Evolution of a Political Order*, Cambridge

1982. Wangara, Akan and Portuguese in the Fifteenth and Sixteenth Centuries. I. The Matter of Bitu. II. The Struggle for Trade, *Journal of African History*, 23, 3, 333–49 and 23, 4, 463–72

1984. The Suwarians. Laissez-faire, laissez-nous faire? Paper presented to the Conference on Islam in Africa, Northwestern University, 28–31 March 1984

Wilks, Ivor, Nehemia Levtzion and Bruce M. Haight. 1986. *Chronicles from Gonja. A Tradition of West African Muslim Historiography*, Cambridge

Withers-Gill, J. 1924. *The Moshi Tribe. A Short History*, Accra

Yelpaala, K. 1982. The Theory of State and Fundamental Legal Concepts in a Non-Centralized Political System – The Case of the Dagaaba in Transition. Unpublished typescript

1983. Circular Arguments and Self-Fulfilling Definitions: 'Statelessness' and the Dagaaba, in *History in Africa*, 10, 349–85

Bibliography

Field notes [cited as Wilks FN]

Copies of these notes are deposited in the archives of the Africana Library, Northwestern University, Evanston, Illinois.

FN/2   14 April 1964:   Karamo Shaybu Sissay, Walembele
FN/3   2 February 1965:   Field diary
FN/24   8 August 1964:   Malam Abu, Wa
FN/25   9 August 1964:   Acting Yeri Na Al-Hajj Aseku, Wa
FN/27   3 May 1966:   Al-Hajj Tamimu b. Muhammad, Wa
FN/28   4 May 1966:   Al-Hajj Tamimu b. Muhammad et al., Wa
FN/35   5 May 1966:   Wa Limam Al-Hajj Muhammad Bakuri, Wa
FN/36   12 April 1966:   Malam Saliya Bamba et al., Kumase
FN/46   3 May 1966:   Malam Mahama Turay, Wa
FN/48   7 August 1964:   Al-Hajj Salifu Imoru, Bamanu
FN/50   6 August 1964:   Abdallahi Samuni, Wa
FN/51   29 June 1964:   Siddiq b. Sa'id, Legon
FN/52   30 June 1964:   Siddiq b. Sa'id, Legon
FN/53   1 July 1964:   Siddiq b. Sa'id, Legon
FN/55   9 September 1968:   Limam Al-Hajj 'Abdallah b. Al-Hajj al-Hasan, Yendi
FN/56   24 May 1966:   Al-Qasim al-Bayhati et al, Say (Niger)
FN/61   8 March 1963:   Al-Hajj Tamimu b. Muhammad, Wa
FN/64   12 April 1962:   Limam Yusuf b. 'Uthman, Walembele
FN/65   11 April 1966:   'Abd al-Mu'min b. Sa'id Kunatay, Kumase
FN/69   4 May 1966:   Al-Hajj Mu'min b. 'Issa Tarawiri, Wa
FN/70   5 May 1966:   Al-Hajj Mu'min b. 'Issa Tarawiri, Wa
FN/74   6 March 1963:   Ishaq Dodu, Wa
FN/75   18 June 1966:   Limam 'Abbas, Accra
FN/79   11 December 1963:   Ya'qub b. 'Uthman Kamaghatay, Namasa
FN/105   14 August 1968:   Al-Hajj Muhammad b. Limam Khalid, Yendi
FN/107   7 August 1964:   Al-Hajj Sulayman et al., Wa
FN/111   16–18 April 1964:   Al-Hajj Muhammad Ashifa, Wa
FN/112   3 August 1964:   Al-Hajj Malik b. Ishaq, Wa
FN/117   14 April 1964:   Limam Al-Hajj Sa'id Tarawiri et al., Guropise
FN/119   5 August 1964:   Al-Hajj al-Hasan b. Mu'min, Wa
FN/124   6 March 1963:   Friday Limam Siddiq b. 'Abd al-Mu'min, Wa
FN/126   15 April 1963:   Acting Yeri Na Aseku, Wa
FN/127   14 April 1964:   Bulenga Na Ya'qub et al., Bulenga
FN/129   17 April 1964:   Ishaq Dodu, Wa
FN/130   18 April 1964:   Ishaq Dodu, Wa
FN/134   15 April 1964:   Ducie Na Hasan Jato et al., Ducie
FN/135   18 April 1964:   Limam Karamoko Idris, Nakori
FN/136   16 April 1964:   Limam Sa'id Kunatay et al., Nasa
FN/139   18 April 1964:   Field diary
FN/143   16 April 1963:   Limam 'Umar, Diebougou (Burkina Faso)
FN/144   19 August 1966:   Sa'id b. 'Uthman Tiaro, Legon
FN/145   8 March 1963:   Wa Limam Sa'id b. Hamid, Wa
FN/146   17 April 1963:   Abu Bakr Kunatay, Boromo (Burkina Faso)
FN/147   3 May 1966:   Al-Hajj Sulayman Karamoko Sako, Wa
FN/148   3 May 1966:   Wa Limam Al-Hajj Muhammad Bakuri, Wa
FN/149   4 May 1966:   Sulayman b. Ibrahim, Wa
FN/151   5 May 1966:   Malam Mahama Turay, Wa

FN/152	5 May 1966:	Sarkin Dzangbeyiri Malam Mahama, Wa
FN/153	6 May 1966:	Limam Karamoko Sa'id Fufana, Wa
FN/154	6 May 1966:	Karamoko Husayn et al., Wa
FN/157	10 April 1966:	Siddiq b. Sa'id, Obuase
FN/158	1 January 1969:	D. M. Yelifari and Gabriel Turay, Wa
FN/161	2 January 1969:	Al-Hajj Yusuf b. Malam Baba, Wa
FN/162	2 January 1969:	Field diary
FN/163	2 January 1969:	Field diary
FN/164	3 January 1969:	Al-Hajj Abu b. 'Abdallah, Wa
FN/165	4 January 1969:	Al-Hajj Abu b. 'Abdallah, Wa
FN/167	3 January 1969:	Field diary
FN/168	3 January 1969:	Ishaq Dodu et al., Wa
FN/169	4 January 1969:	Friday Limam Al-Hajj Siddiq, Wa
FN/170	4 January 1969:	Malam Dodi Bawku, Wa
FN/171	4 January 1969:	Field diary
FN/172	5 January 1969:	Al-Hajj Siddiq b. Sa'id, Wa
FN/175	5 January 1969:	'Abdallah b. 'Abd al-Rahman et al., Nasa
FN/179	31 July 1965:	Al-Hajj Marhaba Saghanughu, Legon
FN/180	8 May 1966:	Al-Hajj Marhaba Saghanughu, Bobo-Dioulasso (Burkina Faso)
FN/181	9 May 1966:	Al-Hajj Marhaba Saghanughu, Bobo-Dioulasso
FN/189	13 May 1966:	Al-Hajj Marhaba Saghanughu, Bobo-Dioulasso
FN/190	14 April 1966:	Al-Hajj 'Uthman b. Ishaq Boyo, Kumase
FN/191	14 May 1966:	Limam Karamoko Ahmad Saghanughu, Wahabu (Burkina Faso)
FN/192	14 May 1966:	Al-Hajj Sa'id Tarawiri, Wahabu (Burkina Faso)
FN/193	14 May 1966:	Limam al-Hasan Kunatay et al., Shukr li-'llahi (Burkina Faso)
FN/194	15 May 1966:	Al-Hajj Khalid Saghanughu, Boromo (Burkina Faso)
FN/197	15 May 1966:	Limam Ibrahim b. Mu'min, Boromo (Burkina Faso)
FN/198	14 January 1963:	Siddiq b. Sa'id, Obuase
FN/200	16 May 1966:	Al-Hajj Mu'min Sanaf, Ozani (Burkina Faso)
FN/205	18 May 1966:	Al-Hasan b. Ya'qub, To (Burkina Faso)
FN/207	8 March 1967:	Field diary
FN/208	17 July 1967:	Field diary
FN/211	6 May 1966:	Field diary
FN/214	23 May 1966:	Maigizo b. 'Issa et al., Niamey (Niger)
FN/221	27 May 1966:	Sarkin Zongo Fanyinama, Kintampo
FN/232	7 January 1986:	Al-Hajj B. K. Adama, Accra
FN/233	9 January 1986:	Field diary
FN/234	10 January 1986:	Al-Hajj B. K. Adama, Accra
FN/235	10 January 1986:	Field diary
FN/248	3 January 1969:	Field diary
FN/252	19 April 1964:	Field diary
FN/255	15 April 1963:	Field diary
FN/265	22 December 1962:	Field diary
FN/266	22 June 1966:	Al-Hajj Ibrahim b. Al-Hajj Muhammad Sa'id, Wenchi
FN/267	8 February 1987:	Balanoe Yemme, Evanston
FN/268	1 August 1965:	Al-Hajj Marhaba Saghanughu, Accra

Index

Unless otherwise indicated, Wala villages are identified by Division and may be approximately located by reference to map 2 (page 12). For purposes of alphabetization, in Arabic names *ibn* (abbreviated to b.), 'son of', and the definite article, *al-*, are ignored.

'Abbas b. Ibrahim (Kano trader), 113–14
'Abbas b. Muhammad al-Mustafa Saghanughu (Kong Limam), 76, 95–8, 214 n. 46
'Abdallah (Wa Na), 29; identity, 84–5
'Abdallah (Boli Na), 174 table 8.4, 177
'Abdallah b. Idris (Wa court interpreter), 138, 143, 148, 158; dispute with Na Pelpuo, 163–4
'Abdallah Watara (Buna teacher), 97
'Abdallah Watara (mosque builder), 109
'Abd al-Mu'min b. Adama Bile (Wa court interpreter), 187, 221 n. 34, 232 n. 120
'Abd al-Mu'min b. al-Hasan (Wa *'alim*), 179–80
'Abd al-Mu'min b. Muhammad Zayd (Wa *'alim*), 95, 97 table 5.1, 110 figure 6
'Abd al-Qadir b. Muhammad (6th Wa Limam), 66 table 4.1; descent, 68 table 4.2, 78 figure 4; descendants, 68 table 4.2, 71–3, 79, 109, 110 figure 6; House of, 71 table 4.4; *also* 67
'Abd al-Rahim Nayyar (Ahmadi missionary), 178–9
Abu (Wa pilgrim), 126, 156
Abu (Wa *'alim*), *see under* Abu Tarawiri
Abu (writer), *see under* Malam Abu
Abu b. 'Abdallah, *see under* Abu Maidoki
Abu Bakr (revivalist), 152–3
Abu Bakr Kunatay (Kantonsi *'alim*), 55, 99

Abu Bakr al-Siddiq (of Timbuktu and Jenne), 86–7, 216 n. 17
Abu Bakr Tarawiri, *see* Bukari Biri
Abu Maidoki (Wa *'alim*), cited, 84–5, 142–3, 148, 158, 160, 163–4, 194–5
Abu Tarawiri (Wa *'alim*), 48, 123
Abudu Mumuni (Dorimon Na), 187
Abuduyiri (Busa village), 54
Adam b. 'Abd al-Qadir (Wa *'alim*), 68 table 4.2, 73, 181
Adama (Foroko), 119, 129
Adama (Guli Na), 175
Adama, B. K. (Wa politician), 83–4, 191; cited, 162–3, 172
Adame Bile b. 'Uthman Dun (Wa *'alim*), 110 figure 6, 122, 221 n. 35
Adama Nabiri (Sambadana), envoy to Sarankye Mori, 123, 136; supports Samori, 124, 128; and treaty with British, (1897) 129, 136
Adu Gyese (Asante trader), 1, 52
Ahmad Abi 'l-'Abbas b. Sa'id (Wa *'alim*), 35, 95
Ahmad Baba (Timbuktu jurist), 93
Ahmad Ghulam, Mirza (founder of Ahmadiyya), 178
Ahmad b. 'Umar (*qadi* of Jenne), 62
Admad Sansankori (Wa *'alim*), 63
Ahmadiyya Movement, origins 178; doctrines 100, 178, 230 n. 63; introduction to Gold Coast and Asante,

179; establishment in Wa, 179–82; involvement in Wa politics, 177, 183–5, 191–3, 204, *and see under* Salih b. al-Hasan; disturbances, 1–2, (1934) 180–1, (1939–41) 183, (1951) 74, 188, 204, (1978) 194, 204; *also* 25, 70, 77, 140

al-Akhbar Saltanat Bilad Wa [ASBW], manuscript of, 35

al-Akhbar Saltanat Bilad Wa [HSW], manuscript of, 36–7, 38 plate 5, 39 plate 6

al-Akhbari Wala Kasamu [AWK], manuscript of, 32

al-Akhbar Zabarima, manuscript of, 82, 103, 104 plate 11

al-Akhbaru Samuru [AS], manuscript of, 121–2

Alfa Gazare (Zabarima leader), 105–6, 108, 113

Alfa Hano (Zabarima leader), 75, 82, 103–5, 108, 113

Alfa Mahmud (Dya *'alim*), 60–1, 80

Alfa Nuhu (of Timbuktu), 163

Alhabari Samuri daga Mutanen Wa [ASMW], manuscript of, 121 plate 13, 122

Alhabari Zabarimawa, Wala da Samuru [AZWS], manuscript of, 122

'Ali b. Idris Mana (Wa *'alim*), 110 figure 6

'Ali b. Salih (Wa *'alim*), supports Mahmud Karantaw, 101–2, 217 n. 39

'Ali b. 'Umar (Zabarima envoy), 107

'Ali Wangara, Samorian functionary in Wa, 124–5, 128, 136, 137; expulsion, 130

Amariya (Grunshi leader), 126, 132

ambiguities, and contradictions in Wala society, 3–4, 40–6 *passim*, 85, 170, 196, 206; *see also under* anomalies; antinomies

al-Amin b. Muhammad al-Abyad Kulibali (Kong *'alim*), 98

Anglo-French Convention (1898), 135, 141

anomalies, of chieftaincy in Wa, 199–202, *see also under* Wa Nam; of Islam in Wa, 202–4, *see also under* Wa limamate

antinomies, of the impassable gate, 197–8, *see also under* Guli; of the landless landowners, 198–9, *see also under* Tendaanba

Ardron, H. G. (District Commissioner), 167, 173–5, 181

Armitage, C. H. (Chief Commissioner), 179

Asamoa Nkwanta (Kumase Anantahene), 100

asanid, see teaching chains

Asante (kingdom), 76, 82, 100, 102, 103, 119, 127, 141

Ashaytu (daughter of Suri), 33, 41–2, 197

Asheku (acting Yeri Na), 58, 198

Atabia (Nayiri of Mamprusi), 88–9

Baayiri (Pirisi village), 106–7

Babatu (Zabarima leader), 106; attack on Wala (1887–8), 1, 56, 106–8, and occupation of, 116; Grunshi rebellion against (1897), 118, 132–3, and French attack on, 133; relations with Samori Turay, 126–8; *also* 82, 113, 203

Babatu Daga Paalun Pigubu (text in Walii), 106

Bachigme (Wa Na), 80, 81 table 4.6

Baderi (trickster), 30

Bajuri (Busa prince), 106–7

Balannoya (Sing prince), 160

Balannoya (Wa Na), 81 table 4.6, 157

Balawu (Pirisi Na), 173 table 8.3, 190

Bansibo (Pirisi Na), 173 table 8.3

Banwarayiri (Wa Limamyiri, map 3), 68, 73

Barabara (Kantonsi immigrant), 55

Bariga (Nayiri of Mamprusi), 88

Barth, Henry (traveller), 1, 112

Basse (of Kaleo), 142

Baud, Lieutenant (French officer), treaty with Wa (1895), 6–7, 119–20

Balume, see *under* Widana

Bele, see *under* Gulunbele

Bellumi, see *under* Widana

Bighu (abandoned), 86, 99

Binger, L. G. (French administrator), 16, 102, 105, 113–14

Birifor, see *under* Lobi

Black Volta District, 10, 147–8

Bogso (Katua Na), 22, 173 table 8.2, 174

Bole (Gonja divisional capital, map 1), 10; bid for Yagbon (1830s–1840s), 75–6, 100; British treaty (1892), 118; Samorian base, 120–2, and withdrawal through, 128; and trade routes, 113, 145–7; Wa refugees at, 118; *also* 116

Boli (Sing village), 100, 170 figure 7, 174 table 8.4, 177

Bondiri (Wa Na), 81 table 4.6, 82, 100

Bomiyiri (Pirisi section of Wa, map 2), 44

Bonduku (Côte d'Ivoire), mosque, 77; Samorian occupation, 120; Timitay scholars of, 97–8; and trade routes, 112–3; *also* 116, 153

Boromo (Burkina Faso), 56, 101–2

Boron (Côte d'Ivoire), 99

Boyon (Pirisi Na), 173 table 8.3

British, first treaty with Wa (1894), 118–19; second treaty (1897), 128–9; construction of fort, 7, 130; expulsion, 130–2; reoccupation, 133–5; direct rule, 141–64; indirect rule, 165–95; *see also under* treaties

Bruma (Yeri Na), 82, 100

Bugu (Pirisi village), 55

Bukari (Busa Na), 44, 83, 172, 173 table 8.2, 174–6, 189–90

Bukari (Sing Na), 174 table 8.4, 177

Bukari (Wa prince), 123

Bukari Biri (Dya *'alim*), 60–1; possibly *qadi* of Jenne, 62, 80

Bulenga (Busa village), 17, 114

Buna (Côte d'Ivoire, map 1), 86; mosque, 77; schools, 86–7, and teachers, 97–8; and Kantonsi, 54, 86; and Sarankye Mori, 126, 128, 130–2; trade routes, 113; *also* 76, 85, 100, 105, 116, 136; *see also under* Bunkani

Bunkani (ruler of Buna), 41–2, 50–1, 87

Bunsalibile (Yeri Na), 57–8, 91, 197

Buntigsu (Wa Na), 81 table 4.6

Busa (Wala Division, map 2), 11 table 1.1; gate to Wa Nam, 22, 81 table 4.6, 168, 170–3, 197, 199; origin of gate, 38–9, 44, 53, 84; lines of descent, 83–4; Busa–Pirisi–Sing–Guli Local Council, 186 table 8.5

Busie (Dagaaba Division, map 2), 11 table 1.1, 15, 168; Zabarima attacks, 106; and Samori, 125, 127; British treaty (1898), 8, 142; Busie-Daffiama Local Council, 186 table 8.5

Busse (Burkina Faso), 59

caravan tax, *see under* taxes

Cardinall, A. W. (Provincial Commissioner), 165

Chakalle (Grusi-speaking people), 16–17, 22, 50, 85, 106

Chanoine, C. P. J., (French officer), 114–15, 126, 132

Chansa (Sing village), 170 figure 7, 174 table 8.4, 177

Charia (Wa village), 127, 142

Charingu (Pirisi village), 36

Charipon (Nadawli village), 8

Chausaria (Yabile Na), 173 table 8.3

Chegli (Pirisi village), 36, 38–40, 45, 172

Chesa (Wa village), 154

chieftaincy, Local Courts Act (1958), 192; House of Chiefs Act (1958), 200; Chieftaincy Act (1961), 192; Chieftaincy Act (1971), 200; and Provisional National Defence Council, 204–5

compulsory labour, traditional, 23–4; 151; and under British, 151

Convention Peoples Party, 187–9, 191–2, 193

Cramer, Captain (British officer), 131

Daanayiri (section of Wa, map 3), 26, 56

Dabo (Old Muslims), 53–4, 55, 85

Daboya (Gonja divisional capital, map 1), 49, 100, 112, 113

Daffiama (Dagaaba Division, map 2), 11 table 1.1, 15, 168; Busie-Daffiama Local Council, 186 table 8.5

Dagaaba (Dagari-speaking people, map 1), 8, 10, 13–7; Divisions of Wala, 11 table 1.1, 12 map 2, 15, 168–9, and assimilated groups, 16, 51–2; rebellions against Wa (late nineteenth century) 8, 106; Samorian attacks on, 122–4, 125, 127; Zabarima attacks on, 106–7, 116, 127; British pacification of, 142–3; British policy towards, 157; *also* 85

DagaaWiili, *see under* Lobi

Dagari-Juula, *see under* Kantonsi

Dagarti, *see under* Dagaaba

Dagarti Youth Association, 189

Dagomba (kingdom, map 1), 41; and origins of Wa Widana, 49–50, 85, 87–8; and Zabarima, 103; Constitution (1930), 166, 167–8, 171–2; also 3, 37, 63

Dakpana (Dagomba warlord), 41, 50–1

Dalgudamda (Ya Na of Dagomba), 87

Damba (festival), 25, 88, 168

Danduni (Wa Na), 40, 81 table 4.6, 83

Dangana (Wa Na), 81 table 4.6, 82; reign, 157–61; *also* 177

Dapuyipala (Wa Limamyiri, map 3), 73, 109, 192

Darimani (Busa Na), 173 table 8.2, 190

Dariziogu (Ya Na of Dagomba), 50–1, 88, 215 n. 80

Dasima (map 1), 8, 106, 126, 131, 133, 137

decentralization, policy of the Provisional National Defence Council, 4, 204–6, 207 n. 17

Denga, *see* Dakpana

Degu (Wa village), 44

Dia, *see* Dya

Dibayiyege (Wa Na), 80, 81 table 4.6

Dixon, H. P. (District Commissioner), 167

Djonyusi (Wa Na), 81 table 4.6; founder of Sing gate, 37–40, 44–5, 53, 84–5; dating, 84; *also* 80

Dodi Bawku (Wa Nayiri Yeri Na), 216 n. 6

Dogo b. Muhammad Saburi (Nasa *'alim*), 91

Dokita (Burkina Faso), 131

Domfe Ketewa (Kumase Nsumankwaahene), 100

Dondoli (Wa Limamyiri, map 3), 26; origins, 73, 109; school, 95–8, 179; and Wa limamate, 111–12; Kaleo attacks on, 117, 119, 122, 221 n. 34; support for Samori, 122, 125, 136; Dondoli faction, 111–12, 135–40, 150, 155–7, 162–3, 202–4, and attack on Dzedzedeyiri (1935), 181; prophecies, 107, 156, 158; *also* 158

Dorimon (Wala Division, map 2), 11 table 1.1, 15, 22, 168; origins, 41, 50–1, 53, 85; rebellion, 10, 22; Local Council, 186 table 8.5

Doumakoro (Burkina Faso), 101

Douroula (Burkina Faso), 101

Ducie (Busa village, map 1), gate to Busa, 170 figure 7, 173 table 8.2, 189–90; Chakalle population, 17; and Mahdi Musa, 154; Zabarima attack on (1897), 132–3; *also* 10, 49, 52, 54

Dumba (of Kaleo), 118

Duncan-Johnstone, A. C. (Provincial Commissioner), 166–7, 182

Dya (Mali), 60–2

Dyan, *see* Lobi

dyonso (plantations), 114, 116

Dzandzan Pool, 7, 21, 209 n. 48

Dzangbeyiri (section of Wa, map 3), origins, 26, 62–3; head of (Sambadana), 26, 119, 169

Dzedzedeyiri (Wa Limamyiri, map 3), origins, 73, 109; and Friday Limamate, 111–12; and Ahmadiyya, 181–2, 185, and Dondoli attack on (1935), 181; Dzedzedeyiri faction, 111–12, 128, 135–40 *passim*, 150, 155–7, 162–3, 181–2, 185, 202–4; prophecy, 182

Dzonga (Pirisi village), 170 figure 7, 173 table 8.3

Eyre-Smith, St J. (District Commissioner), 51, 208 n. 35

factionalism, 139–40, 187–8, 192–5, 204, 205–6; *see also under* Dondoli; Dzedzedeyiri

Fa'dat Ism al-Auliya' Allah, manuscript of, 61–2

Fadl-ur-Rahman Hakeem (Ahmadi missionary), 179–80

Fanta Sidiki, *see* Siddiq b. Sa'id

Fanyinama (Samorian commander), 121, 122, 124, 221 n. 27, n. 43

Ferguson, G. E. (agent of British), mission (1892), 1, 91, 118; mission (1894), 7, 8, 52, 54, 82, 108, 119–20; return to Wa (1897), 128, 131; grave, map 3

Fijolina (Wa Na), 81 table 4.6, 83–4, 174, 199

Fongo (section of Wa, map 3), 26, 28; origins 43; Arabic school, 95; siege of (1980), 2, 201

Foroko (Wa elder), 23, 119, 129, 157, 168–9, 197, 201–2

French, 119–20, 126, 128, 132–5, 137–40; *see also under* treaties

Friday limamate, *see under* Wa Friday limamate

Funsi (Sisala Division, map 2), 11 table 1.1, 15, 48, 52–3, 85, 89, 106, 132, 133, 168; Funsi-Kundungu Local Council, 186 table 8.5

Gangume (Wa Na), 81 table 4.6, 105; dating, 82–3; *also* 63

gate system, 38–40, 43–6, 84, 173–7; Wa Nas by gate, 81 table 4.6, 171 table 8.1; and indirect rule, 170–3; *see also under* Busa, Guli, Pirisi, Sing

Gbani (Kaleo Na), 118

Gbetore (abandoned village), early gate to Wa Nam, 54, 59, 84, 85; origin, 18, 43–4, 48, 197; title held by Saliya, 44, by

Pelpuo I, 44, 54, used by Pelpuo III, 44, and revived for Busa Na Sumani, 44, 190

Gonja (kingdom, map 1), 112; origins 86, and limamates 99; Tampolense struggles, 49; wars of succession (mid-nineteenth century), 75–6; 100–1, 106; Samorian intrusion (1895), 120–1, *see also under* Bole

Grunshi, *see under* Sisala

Guggisberg, F. G. (Governor of the Gold Coast), 165

Guli (Wala Division, map 2), 11 table 1.1; gate to Wa Nam, 22, 59, 160 table 4.6, 170, 175, 189, and impassability of, 40, 45–6, 170, 197–8; origin of gate, 18, 38–9, 43–4, 48, 53, 84, 85, 197; Tendaanba constituents of, 46, 198; Busa–Pirisi–Sing–Guli Local Council, 186 table 8.5; *also* 25, 59, 208 n. 17

Gulunbele (Busa village), 50, 52, 54

Gumbilimuni (section of Wa, map 3), 45

Gungobli (Ya Na of Dagomba), 87

Gura (putative Wa Na), 81 table 4.6; arrival in Wa, 33, 41; foundation of Guli gate, 43 *and see under* Guli; as father of Saliya, 41–2, 51; as son of Saliya, 37, 42–3, 53; death, 33; *also* 192

Guropise (Busa village), 24, 114, 150; mosque, 231 n. 111

Gwo (Dorimon village), 33, 41, 48, 50, 87

Gyaman (Abron kingdom), 76, 100; and Samorian invasion, 120

al-Habari Sarauta Wa [HSW], manuscript of, 36–7

Hamid b. 'Umar (Wa *'alim*), 68 table 4.2, 110 figure 6

Hamidu Bomi (Wa Na), 22, 81 table 4.6, 82; accession, 173 table 8.3, 174–5; and Native Authority system, 176; and Ahmadis, 183

Harun, *see* Pelpuo I

Harun (Nakori Na), 173 table 8.2

al-Hasan (revivalist), 152–3, 154

al-Hasan Kunatay (Shukr li-'llahi Limam), 102

al-Hasan b. Muhammad (Wa *'alim*), 110 figure 6

al-Hasan b. Mu'min (Wa *'alim*), 69

al-Hasan b. 'Umar (Salaga Friday Limam), 88

Haslewood, Captain (British officer), 131

Hayatu b. Sa'id (mahdist), 152

Henderson, F. B. (British officer), enters Wa, 127–8, and signs treaty, 7, 129–30; expels 'Ali Wangara, 131; occupies Dokita, 131; prisoner of Samori, 132

Hodgson, F. M. (Governor of the Gold Coast), 145

Hugot, Capt. (French officer), 8, 132–3

al-Husayn (revivalist) 152–3

Ibrahim (Borno *'alim*), 122

Ibrahim (Tendaga Na), 192

Ibrahim (Visi Na), 55

Ibrahim (Yeri Na), *see* Bruma

Ibrahim b. 'Ali (Wa *'alim*), 110 figure 6, 163

Ibrahim Banwara (Wa *'alim*), 123

Ibrahim b. Muhammad (20th Wa Limam), 66 table 4.1, 129–30, 138; dating, 75, 156; descent, 68 table 4.2, 110 figure 6

Ibrahim b. Muhammad al-Mustafa (Bobo-Dioulasso Limam), 97 table 5.1, 98

Ibrahim Timitay (Bonduku Limam), 216 n. 16

Ibrahim b. 'Umar (15th Wa Limam), 66 table 4.1, 68 table 4.2, 71, 75

Ibrahim b. 'Uthman Dun (*'alim*), descent, 110 figure 6; education, in Wa, 95, in Kong, 110–11; as *mujaddid*, 93; pilgrimage, 122, 156; teacher, 95, 110–11; death, 156

Ibtida' Din Wa fi 'Am 875 ila 'Am 1382, 73, 76, 93–4 and plate 9

Iddi Bukpali (Sing Na), 201

Iddrusu, R. S. (CPP official), 188–9

Idris (Boli Na), 174 table 8.4, 177

Idris (Ducie Na), 173 table 8.2

Idris (Kantonsi *'alim*), 105

Idris (Katua Na), 173 table 8.2

Idris (Nakori Na), 129

Idris Dogu (Wa Nayiri Yeri Na), 216 n. 6

Idris Mana (Wa *'alim*), 110

Idris b. Muhammad (5th Wa Limam), 66 table 4.1, 68 table 4.2, 71 table 4.4, 73, 78, 80

Idris b. Musa (28th Wa Limam), 66 table 4.1, 68 table 4.2, 70, 191

Idris b. Ya'qub (14th Wa Limam), 66 table 4.1, 68 table 4.2, 75, 82, 100, 109, 110 figure 6

Ikhtilaf Rijalat, 101–2
indirect rule, *see under* British
Insah, *see under* Adama Bile
Ishaq Dodu (Chief Butcher), xiv, and
   Babatu 116, 218 n. 69; and Samori,
   122; cited 56, 117, 122, 124
Ishaq b. Muhammad (8th Wa Limam), 66
   table 4.1, 68 table 4.2, 69, 71 table 4.4.
   78
Ishaq b. 'Uthman Dabila (4th Friday
   Limam), 58, 76, 100, 112, 162–3; dating, 82, 164; descent, 110 figure 6, 156;
   author and editor, 36, 48–9, 58, 59–60,
   82, 122, 161–2, 172; and Sarankye Mori
   (1896), 128, 137; threatened emigration
   (1897), 138, 150, 203; collaboration
   with British, 143, 148, 150, 156; and
   Mahdi Musa (1906), 155; bids for Wa
   limamate, 74, 156, 159; opposition to
   Na Dangana, 158–61; opposition to Na
   Pelpuo III, 163–4; and political ideas,
   150, 161–2, 172–3; *also* 167, 179, 182,
   185
Isma'il Kamaghatay (Bighu *'alim*), 99
Issa (Dagaaba Division, Map 2), 11 table
   1.1, 15, 52, 100, 106, 168; British treaty
   (1898), 8, 142; and Samori, 125; Issa-
   Kojopere Local Council, 186 table 8.5

Ja', *see* Dya
Jackson, F. W. F. (Chief Commissioner),
   166
Jaligungu (Visi Kantonsi), 55
Jamani (Kongwura), 121
Jan (Kaleo village), 117, 123–4, 142
Jangeri (Ducie Na), 173 table 8.2
al-Jawahir wa 'l-Yawaqit fi Dukhul al-Islam,
   76–7
Jayiri (Sing village), 106
Jembrugu, *see under* Jumburugu
Jenkinson, C., Major (British officer), 133–4
Jenne (Mali) 7, 50, 61–2, 112–13
Jibrila (mahdist), 152
jihad (religious struggle), 99, 101–3, 108, 178,
   see also under Mahmud Karantaw
Jimini (Côte d'Ivoire), 120, 125–6
Jinsun, J. P. (Wa Ahmadi), 188
Jinsun (Wa Na), 81 table 4.6
Jirapa (Dagaaba town, map 1), 35–6, 57–9,
   125
Jones, W. J. A. (Chief Commissioner), 180

Jumburugu (Widana), 119–20, 129
Juri, *see under* Na Djare
Juula (language), 16

Kaba (Mali), 58–9
Kabanya (section of Wa, map 3), 26, 28;
   origins, 54, 56
Kabuidana (Wa elder), 168
Kajikpara, *see* Konjekuri
Kaleo (Dagaaba Division, map 2), 11 table
   1.1, 15, 117, 118–19, 122, 168, 200;
   Samorian attacks on, 123–4, 127; Bri-
   tish treaty (1897), 8, 142–3; Local
   Council, 186 table 8.5; *and see under*
   Sankana
Kaleo, Jato (politician), 191
Kali (Yagbonwura), 100
Kanbali (unidentified), 36
Kandia (Busa village), 50, 55
Kangaba, *see* Kaba
Kani (Côte d'Ivoire), 99
Kantonsi (Old Muslims), origins, 53–6; 85–6;
   212 n. 24; dispersion, 56; and Karan-
   taw *jihad*, 102; and Zabarima; 105; *see
   also under* Dabo; Kunatay; Sienu; Zono
Karamoko Siddiq (mosque builder), 109
Karamoko Yara (Safane *'alim*), 101
Karanbileyiri (Wa Limamyiri), 73
Karni (Dagaaba village), 125
Kasimu (Nakori Na), 173 table 8.2
Kassana (Sisala village, map 1), 105, 116
Katsina (Hausa town), 63
Katua (Busa village), 22; gate to Busa, 170
   figure 7, 173 table 8.2, 189–90
Khalid (Wa Ahmadiyya Limam), 179, 181,
   183, 193
Kintampo (Asante market town), 113–14,
   116, 145–7, 153
Kitab Ghanja ('Book of Gonja'), 29, 84, 89
Kobitigi (Wa elder), 119
Koho, *see* Shukr li-'llahi
Kojopere (Wala Division, map 2), 11 table
   1.1, 16–17, 22, 168; origins, 52, 85, 89;
   and Zabarima, 106; and Samori, 125;
   Issa-Kojopere Local Council, 186 table
   8.5
Konate Clan [KC], manuscript of, 55
Kong (Côte d'Ivoire), limamate, 99; mosque,
   77; mosque builders from, 109–11; and
   Samori, 120, 135; teachers at, 76–7, 93–
   8; *also* 61, 116

Index

Kong (Gonja divisional capital), 106, 121
Konjekuri (Yeri Na), 34, 41, 53, 57–8, 91,
    197
Konkoradori (Gberi Na), 123
Konukumba (section of Tagarayiri), 58
Konukumba (Yeri Na), 63
Koro (Côte d'Ivoire), 99
Kpaguri (Wa village), 18
kpanbihi (Wa council of elders), 22–3, 28,
    197
Kpasa (Wa Na), 81 table 4.6; founder of
    Guil gate, 38–9, 43–4, 53, 84 *and see
    under* Guli; as son of Saliya and
    Ashaytu, 33, 42 figure 2, 43, 45, and as
    son of Na Djare, 38–9, 45; rights to Wa
    Nam, 33–4, 42–3, 45–6, 89–90, 197–8;
    as first Wa Na, 42, 197; and Yeri Na
    Konjekuri, 34, 57–8, 197; *also* 84
Krakye (market), 127, 152–3
Krause, G. A., (traveller), 1, 108
kubaru (written tradition), 30–2, 40–1, 47
Kulmasa (Gonja village, map 1), 8, 130
Kumase (Asante capital), 7, 50, 112
Kumblunaa (Wa elder), 119
Kunadi Timitay, *see* Sa'id b. Muhammad
    Timitay
Kunatay (Old Muslims), found Visi, 53, 55–
    6; and Kabanya section of Wa, 54, 56;
    support for Mahmud Karantaw, 102–3
Kunchuri (Dagaaba envoy), 142
Kundungu (Sisala Division, map 2), 11
    Table 1.1, 15, 50, 53, 86, 168; Funsi-
    Kundungu Local Council, 186 Table
    8.5
Kunjokun (Wa Na), 80, 81 table 4.6; as
    Kunlugi ('Ghuluki'), 38–40, 45, 53
Kunlugi, *see under* Kunjokun
Kwaku Dua Panin (Asantehene), 100

Lambussie (Dagaaba village), 125
landowners, *see* Tendaanba
land tenure, 18–19, 23–4, 198–9
Lanfiera (Burkina Faso), 59–60, 112
lasiri (oral tradition), 30–2, 40, 42–3, 45
Lawra (Dagaaba town, map 1), 10, 125, 157,
    188
Leigh, A. H. C. Walker (Chief Commis-
    sioner), 166
Leo (Burkina Faso, map 1), 130, 132–3
Limamates, *see under* Wa Friday limamate;
    Wa limamate

Limampalayiri (Wa Limamyiri, map 3), 73,
    192
Limamyiri (section of Wa, map 3), 26, 28;
    origins 59–62, 67; *see also under* Ban-
    warayiri; Dondoli; Dapuyipali; Dzedze-
    deyiri; Limampalayiri; Manzuyiri;
    Tamarimuni; Vuori
Lobi (Birifor, DagaaWiili, Lowilisi, etc.), 13–
    15; as autochthones of Wala, 15, 32,
    33, 51–2, 85; as migrants into Wala
    (twentieth century), 14–15; disturbances
    (1903), 225 n. 23
Lokosso (Burkina Faso), 113
Loggo (Sing village), 100; gate, 170 figure 7,
    174 table 8.4, 177
Lowilisi, *see under* Lobi

Mackworth, D. (British officer), reoccupa-
    tion of Wa (1897), 133; cited, 10, 91,
    107–8, 114
Magana Muslimi Na Daurri [TM], manus-
    cript of, 47
Magana Wala [TAW], manuscript of, 47
Mahama Chakalle Watara (Ducie convert),
    223 n. 88
Mahama Fua (Wa Na), 81 table 4.6; dating
    82; descent, 83 figure 5; suicide, 107,
    218 n. 70; *also* 117
Mahdi Musa (revivalist), 152–7
Mahmud Baghayughu (*qadi* of Jenne), 62
Mahmud Karantaw (*jihad* leader), 100–3;
    105, 113, 203–4
Mahmud b. 'Uthman, *see under* Alfa
    Mahmud
Malam Abu (writer), identity unknown, 106,
    218 n. 55; cited, 106–8, 116, 121, 122–4,
    126–8, 131, 136
Malam Dodi (Busa prince), 190
Malam Isaka, *see* Ishaq b. 'Uthman Dabila
Malam Ladan (of Katsina), 113–14
Mali (empire), 85–6; dispersion of Mandeka,
    58–9, 61–2, 98–9
Malik b. 'Ali (Kantonsi *'alim*), 102–3
Malik b. 'Uthman (24th Wa Limam), 109,
    110 figure 6, 132 table 4.1, 135 table
    4.2, 183; death, 184
Mama Dagarti, *see under* Kunchuri
Mamprusi (kingdom, Map 1), and Wa
    Nabihi origins, 35, 41, 45, 52, 88–9,
    197; *see also under* Saliya (ancestor of
    Wa Nabihi)

Mampurugu, *see under* Mamprusi
Mandeka, *see under* Mali
Manfara (Mali), 99
Mango (Wa village), 32–3, 36, 41, 44
Mangursi (Samorian commander), 124
Manzuyiri (Wa Limamyiri), 68, 73, 191
Ma'sala 'inda 'l-Rajalayn, 101
Mengwe (Busa village), 21
Miller, J. E. (District Commissioner), 164, 167
Momori, J. N., *see* Momori Bondiri II
Momori Bondiri II (Wa Na), accession, 2–3, 89, 198, 201–2
Momori Tangile (Wa Na), 81 table 4.6, 157; dating, 81–2, 135; descent, 83 figure 5; accession, 148; *also* 141, 150, 160
Morris, A. H. (Chief Commissioner), 144
mosques, Wa Ahmadiyya 183, 184, 185, 191; Dondoli, 111; Nasa, 57, 107; Qubba, 111; in villages, 24, 114, 154; Wa Central, 7, 57, 77, 107, 108, 109–11, 191, 219 n. 84; Wa Limamyiri, 77, 215 n. 48
Mothersill, L. J. (District Commissioner), 176
Mu'adh (3rd Wa Limam), 66 table 4.1, 67, 68–9, 73, 78 figure 4
Mubashir, Nazir Ahmad (Ahmadiyya missionary), 183
Muhammad (Ducie Na), 173 table 8.2, 188
Muhammad b. 'Abd al-Qadir (10th Wa Limam), 66 table 4.1; dating, 76–7, 79–80; descent, 68 table 4.2, 110 figure 6; founder of Dondoli, 73, 109, 204
Muhammad b. 'Abd al-Karim al-Maghili (North African jurist), 93
Muhammad al-Abyad b. Abi Bakr (teacher), 101, 217 n. 34
Muhammad al-Abyad b. Isma'il (Gonja Limam), 99
Muhammad al-Ahmar (4th Wa Limam), 66 table 4.1, 68 table 4.2, 78–9
Muhammad Ahmad b. 'Abdallah (Sudanese Mahdi), 152
Muhammad al-Aswad (2nd Wa Limam), 66 table 4.1, 67, 68 table 4.2, 72, 79
Muhammad Baghayughu (Jenne *'alim*), 62, 93
Muhammad Bakuri, *see* Muhammad b. Harun
Muhammad Bile, *see under* Muhammad Zayd

Muhammad Faraqu (7th Wa Limam), 66 table 4.1, 67, 68 table 4.2, 69, 71 table 4.4, 78 figure 4
Muhammad Gado Bakwakwa (of Djougou), 2
Muhammad b. Harun (30th Wa Limam) 66 table 4.2, 69, 70; dating, 65, 94; descent, 68 table 4.2; reputation, 94; cited, 69–70
Muhammad b. Ibrahim (Kano trader), 113–14
Muhammad b. Ibrahim Watara (Buna teacher), 97, 216 n. 16
Muhammad Jatiyyu, *see* Muhammad Sunsu Jara
Muhammad Kankanya b. Ibrahim (31st Wa Limam), 65, 66 table 4.1, 68 table 4.2, 181
Muhammad Karantaw (Marka scholar), 101, 217 n. 34
Muhammad Kulendi (Wa Yeri Na), 58
Muhammad Marhaba Saghanughu (mufti and writer), cited 76, 101
Muhammad Saburi (Nasa Yeri Na), 91
Muhammad Saghir b. Ibrahim (25th Wa Limam), 66 table 4.1, 184, 188; dating, 74, 188; descent, 68 table 4.2, 110 figure 6
Muhammad Shifa (Wa *'alim*), 220 n. 13; cited 118, 123, 137
Muhammad Sunsu Jara (Malian *'alim*), 60–1
Muhammad b. 'Uthman (revivalist), 153
Muhamad b. 'Uthman Dun (23rd Wa Limam), 66 table 4.1, 67; dating, 74, 80; teaching chain, 95–7; and Dondoli mosque, 111; and Dondoli school, 95; descent, 68 table 4.2, 110 figure 6; pilgrimages, 74, 122, 155–6, 162–3; reputation, 93; embassy to Sarankye Mori, 122–3; support for Samori, 124–5, 128, 135–6; move to Nandaw, 137; accession to limamate (1926), 162–3; opposition to Ahmadiyya, 179–81, 183; *also* 158, 194
Muhammad b. Ya'qub (2nd Friday Limam), 110 figure 6, 112, 148, 155, 159, 179
Muhammad Zanjina (Ya Na of Dagomba), 87
Muhammad Zayd b. 'Uthman Kunduri (3rd Friday Limam) 112, 162; descent 110 figures 6, 214 n. 23; accession, 148, 159;

and central mosque, 215 n. 48; learning, 95; teaching chain, 95, 97 table 5.1

mujaddidun (renewers of religion), concept, 93; in Wa, 93–5

Mukhtar Karantaw (successor of Mahmud Karantaw), 108, 113

Mumuni (Ducie Na), 173 table 8.2

Mumuni (Sing Na), 174 table 8.4, 177

Mumuni Adama, *see under* 'Abd al-Mu'min b. Adama Bile

Mumuni Koray (Wa Na), 44, 74, 81 table 4.6, 82, 174 table 8.4; joins Ahmadiyya, 177; early career and bid for Nam (1943), 177; accession (1949), 178, 185, 200, and riots, 188–9; local government offices, 187; Legislative Assemblyman, 187; policies, on Muslim law, 189, on gates, 189–90, on Ahmadiyya, 204; death 190

Musa b. Muhammad (9th Wa Limam), 66 table 4.1; dating, 77; descent, 68 table 4.2, 69

Musa b. Ya'muru (19th Wa Limam), 66 table 4.1, 117; dating, 75, 129–30; descent, 68 table 4.2; Grunshi envoys to (c. 1890), 118; treaty with British (1894), 74, 119; treaty with French (1895), 74, 120

Muslim law, in Wa 157, 189, 194

Mwankuri (Dagaaba village), 8, 106

Narung (Kaleo village), 106, 125

Nabihi, *see under* Wa Nabihi

Nabon (Burkina Faso), 101

Nadawli (Dagaaba Division, map 2), 11 table 1.1, 15, 168, 169; British treaty (1898), 8, 142–3; and Samori, 125; Local Council, 186 table 8.5

Na Djare (Wa Na), 81 table 4.6; founder of Pirisi gate, 37–40, 42 figure 2, 44, 53, 84; possibly 'Abdallah (died 1730/1), 84; patron of Muslims, 36, 60–1, 84–5; *also* 43, 45

Najre (Sing Na), 177

Nakori (Busa village), 154, 170 figure 7, 173 table 8.2, 189–90

Nalerigu (Mamprusi capital), 35, 41, 52, 54

nalun (chiefly authority), 18–19, 20, 21–2, 196–201, 203; origins, 40–6, 89–90, 91–2; and *tendaanlun*, 19, 33–4, 139–40; *see also under* Wa Nam

namburi (terminal skins), 22, 175

Nandaw (Dagaaba village), 8, 125, 137

Nasa (Wala town, Map 1), 24, 56–7; Old Muslim settlement, 36, 41, 53–5, 86; arrival of *'ulama'*, 36; Nasa Limam, 20, and Yeri Na, 20, 57–8, 91; Zabarima attack, 56–7, 74, 107; *also* 10, 44, 150

Native Courts, *see* Wala Native Authority

Native Treasuries, *see* Wala Native Authority

Native Tribunals, 149, 157, 165

Nayiri (section of Wa, map 3), 26, 28

Nayiri Yeri Na, 92, 216 n. 6

Niyirtiwu (unidentified), 32, 41, 50, 87

Nkoransa (Asante town), 112–13, 153

Northcott, H. P. (Chief Commissioner), 141–2; in Wa (1897), 131, 134–5, 139; Dagaaba treaties (1897–8), 8–9, 142; taxation policy, 144–5

Northern Peoples Party, 191

Northern Territories of the Gold Coast, Protectorate of, 8, 10, 141–2, 149; integration into Gold Coast Colony, 187, 190–1; *see also under* British

Nuhu (Wa pilgrim), 126

Nuhu b. Adam (32nd Wa Limam), 65, 66 table 4.1, 69, 74, 80, 221 n. 35, 232 n. 120; descent, 68 table 4.2, 110 figure 6

Numaba (mosque builder), 109

Nur-ud-Din (head of Ahmadiyya), 178

Nwandawno (Sisala village), 126

Old Muslims, *see under* Dabo; Kantonsi; Sienu; Tarawiri (Old Muslims); Zono

Palewogo (abandoned, map 1), Old Muslim settlement, 53–5, 85–6, 105, 132

Pasaala (Sisala-speaking peoples), 15, 50, 85

Pelpuo I (Wa Na), 81 table 4.6; son of Saliya, 36–40, 42 figure 2, 53, 83 figure 5, 85; as Gbetore Na, 44, 54, 59; founder of Busa gate, 39, 44, 84; acquisition of Wa Nam, 34, 42–3, 45, 89, and as first Wa Na, 42, 45, 197; and Yeri Na Bunsalibile, 57–8, 197

Pelpuo II (Wa Na), 81 table 4.6, 83 figure 5, 199; dating, 82–3, 148

Pelpuo III (Wa Na), 81 table 4.6, 82, 83 figure 5; accession 44, 160–1, 173 table 8.2, 200; new palace; 161; creation of

Katua skin, 22; dispute with Friday Limam, 162–3; Wala Constitution (1933), 168; and Ahmadiyya, 179–81; letter to George V, 141; paralysis and death, 164, 168; dispute over burial, 174

pilgrimage, as factor in Wala politics, 155–7, 159, 162–3

Pirisi (Wala Division, map 2), 11 table 1.1, gate to Wa Nam, 22, 81 table 4.6, 168, 170–3, 197, 199; origin of gate, 38–9, 44, 53, 84; Busa–Pirisi–Sing–Guli Local Council, 186 table 8.5

Pontomporeyiri (Wa Limamyiri), 143, 224 n. 8

Potuli (Sisala-speaking peoples), 16–17, 85

Provisional National Defence Council (PNDC), 204, and decentralization, 204–6, 207 n. 17

Qadiriyya, 101, 155
Qasim (head of Kabanya), 129

Rabih b. Fadl Allah (mahdist), 152
Rattray, R. S., 171
Rawlings, J. J. (Ghana Head of State), 2, 205
Read, B. M. (British officer), 91, 154, 157
rinderpest, 118

Sadja (Wa Na), 81 table 4.6
Safane (Burkina Faso), 59, 63, 101, 112
Safo (Bolewura), 100
Sa'id b. 'Abd al-Qadir (11th Wa Limam), 66 table 4.1; dating, 76–7; descent, 68 table 4.2, 110 figure 6; founder of Tamarimuni, 73, 109; learning, 76–7, 93, 95; as *mujaddid*, 93; author, 35; and Karantaw *jihad*, 102–3, 112
Sa'id b. 'Abd al-Rahman (Wa *'alim*), 94
Sa'id b. Abi Bakr (Wahabu *'alim*), 101
Sa'id b. 'Ali (Wa partisan of Mahmud Karantaw), 101
Sa'id b. Hamid (29th Wa Limam), 66 table 4.1, 68 table 4.2, 110 figure 6
Sa'id b. Muhammad (founder of Dzangbeyiri), 62–3
Sa'id b. Muhammad al-Mustafa (Bobo-Dioulasso Limam), 97 table 5.1, 98, 101
Sa'id b. Muhammad Timitay (Bonduku

Limam), 97, 158, 216 n. 16
Sa'id b. al-Siddiq (5th Friday Limam and 26th Wa Limam), 66 table 4.1, 68 table 4.2; accession to Friday limamate, 181, and to Wa limamate, 74, 188; pilgrimage, 181; Tijani, 181; and Ahmadis, 183; death 191
Sa'id Soribo, *see* Sa'id b. al-Siddiq
Sa'id b. 'Uthman Tiaro (Wa *'alim*), 69
Sa'id b. Yusuf (17th Wa Limam), 66 table 4.1, 68 table 4.2, 75
Saidu (Yagbonwura), 100
Saidu (Yaro Na), 173 table 8.3
Saidu II (Wa Na), 81 table 4.6; accession, 173 table 8.2, 190; Legislative Assemblyman, 187; erosion of authority, 192; death, 193
Saidu Mogona (Yeri Na), 117, 120, 129, 222 n. 61
Saidu Takora (Wa Na), 81 table 4.6, 82; accession (1891), 118–19, 199–200, 220 n. 18; treaty with British (1894), 7, 119; treaty with French (1895), 7, 120; and Samorians, 122, 128, 137; treaty with British (1897), 7, 22, 129; treaty with French (1897), 7–8, 133; pro-French stance, 137–8; trial by British (1897), 134–5; loss of the Nam (1898), 135, 148; *also* 141, 150, 193–4
Saka (Wa Na), 81 table 4.6; descent 53, 83
Saka (Dzonga Na), 173 table 8.3
Salaga (Gonja market town), 103, 112–13, 116, 152, 155
Salanga (Wa elder), 168
Salih b. al-Hasan (Wa Ahmadiyya Limam), 66 table 4.1; dates, 192, 230 n. 68; descent, 68 table 4.2, 110 figure 6; joins Ahmadiyya (1932), 179; introduces Ahmadiyya to Wa, 179–82, 183–5; claims to Wa limamate, 67, 70, 74, 188, 191; pilgrimage, 184, 231 n. 105; designated African missionary, 193; *also* 47, 192
Salih b. Yahya (21st Wa Limam), 66 table 4.1, 68 table 4.2, 156; dating 75, 159
Salim Suwari (of Mali, teacher), 61, 98–99; *see also under* Suwarian tradition
Saliya (ancestor of Wa Nabihi), 18, 20, 30, 81 table 4.6, 83 figure 5; dating, 88–9; Mamprusi origins, 35–6, 41, 52, 89; arrival in Wa, 35–6, 52–3, and Wanalun,

41–6, 196–7; three wives of, 36, 42–3, and sons, 37–8, 43, 53, 84

Saliya (Busa Na), 83, 173 table 8.2

Saliya (Sing Na), 174 table 8.4, 177–8

Samambaw (Issa village), 8

Sambadana, *see under* Dzangbeyiri

Samori Taahuu [ST], manuscript of, 122

Samori Turay, Almami (state-builder), background, 120–1; general policy, 124–5, 135, and retrenchment in Jimini, 126–7, 136; cited, 130, 131–2; *see also under* Sarankye Mori

Sampina (Nadawli village), 8

Samuni, *see* Kantonsi

Sanda Muru, *see* Sidi 'Umar

Sankana (Kaleo village), 116, 142; Zabarima attack, 116; Samorian attacks, 123–4, 127; Samorian headquarters, 124, 135, and withdrawal from, 127, and British 143

Sarankye Mori (Samorian commander), 120–1, 135; in Bole 122; negotiations with Wa, 122–3, 135–6; enters Wa (1896), 123; occupies Kaleo, 123–4; policy towards Dagaaba, 125; policy towards Zabarima, 126–8; Sankana headquarters, 124, 135; withdrawal to Buna (1896–7), 126–8, 136; re-enters Wa (1897), 132, 137

Sarkin Zongo (head of Wa Zongo), 26, 28

Sati (Burkina Faso), 113, 116, 118, 126

Sembeleyiri (section of Wa, map 3), 54, 56, 193

Shukr li-'llahi (Burkina Faso), 54, 102–3, 203, 212n. 27

Sibu Napona (Sisala notable), 132

Siddiq b. 'Abd al-Mu'min (6th Friday Limam), accession, 188; descent, 110 figure 6, 214 n. 23; learning, 94–5, and teaching chains, 95–7, 98; cited 20–1, 73, 93–5, 199

Siddiq b. Adam (Wa 'alim), 68 table 4.2, 181

Siddiq b. Musa (16th Wa Limam), 66 table 4.1, 68 table 4.2, 71; dating, 75, 82; and Zabarima, 75, 103–5

Siddiq b. Sa'id (Wa 'alim), xiv, 35, 60; cited, 35–6, 51–2, 60–1, 69, 77; *also* 172

Sidi 'Abbas (Tarawiri ancestor), 60–1

Sidi 'Umar (Old Muslim warlord), Mande origins, 58–9; arrival in Wala, 20, 34,

36, 41, 53, 57, 197; apical ancestor of Yeri Nas, 34, 60, 91, 212 n. 37

Sidiki Bomi II (Wa Na), 81 table 4.6, 82; accession, 193–4; study of Qur'an, 203; crisis on death of, 2, 23, 58, 89, 200–2

Sienu (Old Muslims), 53–5, 56, 85, 102

Sikasso (Mali), 61

Sing (Wala Division, map 2), 11 table 1.1; gate to Wa Nam, 22, 168–9, 170–2, 174 table 8.4, 197, 199; origin of gate, 38–9, 45, 53, 84; Tendaanba of, 21; Busa–Pirisi–Sing–Guli Local Council, 186 table 8.5

sinsola (oral tradition), 30

Sisala (Sisala-speaking peoples, map 1), Divisions of Wala, map 2, 11, 168–9, and population of, 13–15; slaves from (Grunshi), 113; and Zabarima incursions, 103–5, 118; Amariya as ruler of, 126; Babatu as ruler of, 132; and direct rule, 157

Slater, A. Ransford (Governor of the Gold Coast), 166

slaves, employment in Wala, 114–15

Sobuun (Wa Na), 81 table 4.6

Sokpariyiri (section of Wa, map 3), 26, 33, 50, 56

succession disputes, *see under* Wa Nam

Sulayman b. 'Abdallah Baghayughu (of Timbuktu), 99

Sumaila (Wa Na), 81 table 4.6; accession, 173 table 8.2, 177, 183–4, 190; and Ahmadiyya, 184–5; death, 177–8

Sumani (Busa Na), 44, 83, 190

Sungma (masks), 21, 209 n. 49

Sungumi (section of Tagarayiri), 58, 216 n. 6

Suri (Wa Widana), warlord, 20, 41–2, 197; migration from Dagomba, to Wala, 32–4, 49–51, and dating, 87–8; and Wa *nalun*, 33–4, 41–2, 197–8; *also* 81 table 4.6

Suriyiri (section of Wa, map 3), 26, 33, 42, 50

Suwarian tradition, 25, 98–100, 101, 103, 112–13, 114–15, 155, 182, 202–3

Tagarayiri (section of Wa, map 3), 26, 28, 34, 91; origin of, 54; structure, 58; and Zabarima, 107

Tahuna, *see under* Dangana

tajdid (renewal), 93–100 *passim*

Tamarimuni (Wa Limamyiri, map 3), origins, 73, 109; school, 95–8; and limamates, 110 figure 6, 111–12

Tamimu b. Muhammad (Wa *'alim*), 69–70, 221 n. 37; 110; descent, 110 figure 6; learning, 94; pilgrimage, 156; as teacher, 95, and teaching chain, 97; cited, 69–70, 122–3, 194

Tampolense (Sisala-speaking people), 49–51, 85

Tampolima Yabum (Tampolense village), 49–50

Tantama (Côte d'Ivoire, map 1), 8, 225 n. 23

Tarawiri (Old Muslims), 53–9, 84, 85; and Karantaw *jihad*, 101–2; *see also under* Nasa; Tagarayiri; Wa Yeri Nam

Tarawiri (*'ulama'*), 59–62, 84–5; *see also under* Limamyiri; Wa Friday limamate; Wa limamate

Ta'rikh Ahl Tariwari min Mandi [TATM], manuscript of, 58

Ta'rikh Ahl Wala [TAW], manuscript of, 47; as draft, 58–9

Ta'rikh al-Muslimin [TM], manuscript of, 47; as draft, 58–9

Ta'rikh Tadhkirat al-Imamiyyin fi Biladina Wa [TTI], manuscript of, 60

Taslima, *see* Nabon

Taslima Saghanughu (Dafin *'alim*), 101, 217 n. 37

Tawula Kunatay (Visi Na), 55–6

taxes, traditional 23–4, 144, 151; British head taxes, 144–5, 169; British caravan taxes, 145–7, 148–9; *see also under* compulsory labour

teaching chains, 95–8

teng ('parish'), 17–18, 23

Tendaanba (Landowners), 17–18, 20, 24; autochthonous status, 51–2; Widana as head of, 32–3, 89–90, 171, 197–8; loss of farming rights, 18–19; 139–40, 198–9; and Guli gate, 46, 139–40, 196–7

tendaana (earth priest), 17–19, 21, 23, 24, 169, 171, 198

tendaanlun (priestly authority), 17–19, 21, 31, 196; and *nalun*, 33–4, 41–2, 139–40

Tendaga Na (Wa elder), 26, 169

tengani (earth shrines), 17, 21, 23

Terinmu (section of Tagarayiri), 58

Thomas, T. S. (Acting Governor of the Gold Coast), 165–6

Tijaniyya, 101, 181

Timbuktu (Mali), 55, 86, 93, 99, 113, 152

trade, in slaves, 113–15, 127; in weapons, 113–14; early twentieth century, 145–8, and trade routes, 112–113

tradition, *see under kubaru; lasiri; sinsolo*

treaties, (British), with Bole (1892), 118; with Wa (1894), 7, 74, 119–20; with Wa (1897), 7, 129, 136; with Kaleo (1897), 8, 142; with Issa, Busie, Wogu and Nadawli (1898), 8–9, 142. (French), with Wa (1895), 7, 74, 120; with Wa (1897), 7–8, 133

tributes, *see under* taxes

Tuomuni (section of Wa, map 3), 23, 26, 119

'ulama', (scholars), 26, 33, 196; origins, 59–62; and Karantaw *jihad*, 102–3; employment by British, 142–3, 148–52; *also* 18–19; *also see under* Kunatay; Tarawiri (*'ulama'*)

Ulu (Dagaaba village), 143

'Umar b. Abi Bakr (of Salaga and Krakye), 152

'Umar Dhakidi (Wa *'alim*), 68 table 4.2

'Umar Farako (revivalist), 153, 226 n. 55

'Umar Fitini, *see* Ya'muru (1st Wa Limam)

'Umar Kulendi (Yeri Na), 129, 134, 158, 162, 222 n. 61

'Umar b. Muhammad (Wa *'alim*), 68 table 4.2, 110 figure 6

United Gold Coast Convention, 187–8

'Uthman b. Bukari Biri (of Dya), 60–2, 80

'Uthman Dabila (1st Friday Limam), 48, 109–12; descent, 110 figure 6; refugee in Bole, 118–19; and treaty with British (1897), 129, 136, 150; support for British, 134, 137, 139; *also* 123

'Uthman Daleri (Wa Yeri Na), 48, 76, 82, 100, 109, 215 n. 55

'Uthman b. Dawud (Wa *'alim*), 156

'Uthman Dun b. Muhammad (18th Wa Limam) 66 table 4.1; dating, 65, 74–5, 79–80; descent, 68 table 4.2, 110 figure 6; predictions, 107, 156; reputation, 79, 123; teaching chain, 97; and Zabarima, 74, 107–8, 203, *also* 185

'Uthman Kunduri b. Sa'id (Wa *'alim*), 95–8, 110 figure 6, 214 n. 23

Index

'Uthman b. Muhammad Saburi (Wa Yeri Na), 91
'Uthman b. Siddiq (Wa 'alim), 94–5

Visi (abandoned), location, 55; Kantonsi origins, 48–9, 53–6, 85–6; also 105, 107
Voulet, Lieutenant (French officer), 126
Vuori (Wa Limamyiri, map 3), 69, 116, 220 n. 2

Wa (capital of Wala, map 1, map 2), appearance, 5–7, 11–13; European knowledge of, 1, 112; fort, 7, 130; palace, 7, 161; population, 1, 11–13; sections of, map 3, 25–8; as Babatu's capital (1888–9), 116; as Samorian eastern capital (1896), 135
Wa (Wala Division, map 2), 11 table 1.1; local councils, 186 table 8.5
Wa Friday limamate, 26; origins and incumbents, 109–12
Wa limamate, 26; origins see under Ya'muru (1st Wa Limam); authority of, 92, 111–12, 157, 203; incumbents, 64–80; also 7
Wa Nabihi (Princes), 18, 20, 25, 26, 196–7; origins, 36–40, 51–3 and see under Saliya (ancester of Wa Nabihi); acquisition of farming rights, 19, 198–9; genealogies, 83
Wa Nam, 7, 21–4; incumbents, 80–5; under British direct rule, 140–64, and under indirect rule, 165–95; anomalies of, 199–202, and succession disputes, 200, (c. 1891) 118–19, (1935–6) 83, 174–6, (1943) 176–7, 183–4, (1949) 188, (1953) 190, (1961) 193–4, (1978–85) 2–3, 46, 58, 89–90, 194, 198, 200–2; see also under gate system; nalun
Wa Tianbilli Local Council, 186 table 8.5, 187
Wa Urban Council, 28, 186 table 8.5
Wa Yeri Nam, see under Yeri Nam
Wagadugu (Mossi capital), 7, 113, 126
Wala, extent, 5–8; Divisions of, 8–13; population, 11–13, peoples of, 13–17; rural economy 5
Wala Constitution (1933), 167–73
Wala District Council, 186
Wala local councils, 186–7
Wala Native Authority, 10–11; structure, 168–9; 176; abolition, 186

Wala State Council, 186–7, 190, 193
Walembele (Sisala town map 1), 8, 48, 52–3, 85, 89, 106, 113
Walewale (Mamprusi town), 52, 54, 119
Walii (language), 16
Walker, H. S., (British officer), 135
Wasipe (Gonja division), see under Daboya
Watherson, A. E., (Chief Commissioner), 149–50, 179
Wechiau (Wala Division, map 2), 11 table 1.1, 15, 22, 169; origins, 50, 85, 87; and Local Council, 186 table 8.5
Whittall, P. J. (District Commissioner), 36, 48, 51, 81–2, 161–2, 163, 164, 166–7, 171
Widana (Wa elder), 23, 168–9, 187; origins, 20, 32–5, 50–3; and nalun, 89–90; as kingmaker, 171, 198; see also under Suri
Wogu (Issa village), 8, 106, 125, 142
World War One, and loyalty of Muslims, 158

Yabile (Pirisi village), 170 figure 7, 173 table 8.3
Yagaba (market town, Map 1), 52, 54, 86, 112, 132
Yahya (Wa Ahmadi), 179, 184
Yahya (Pirisi Na), 173 table 8.3
Yahya b. Muhammad al-Mustafa Saghanughu (Kong 'alim), 95, 97 table 5.1
Yahya b. 'Uthman Dabila (Wa 'alim), 109–11
Yakina (of Palewogo), 55
Yakubu Seidu (contender for Wa Nam), 2–3, 46, 58, 89–90, 198, 201–2
Yakugor (Sing prince), 160
Ya'muru (1st Wa Limam), 66 table 4.1; ancestry, 60–2; arrival in Wa, 36, 59–60, 84–5; dating, 79–80, 85; descendants, 68 table 4.2, 79–80; as mujaddid, 93
Ya'muru b. 'Abd al-Qadir (13th Wa Limam), 66 table 4.1, 68 table 4.2, 76; founder of Dapuyipala, 73, 109
Yamusa (Busa Na), see Pelpuo III
Ya'qub (of Dzangbeyiri), 156
Ya'qub (Nakori Na), 173 table 8.2
Ya'qub (Wa Nayiri Yeri Na), 216 n. 6
Ya'qub (Yabile Na), 173 table 8.3
Ya'qub b. 'Abd al-Qadir (12th Wa Limam),

66 table 4.1; dating, 75–6, 82; descent, 68 table 4.2, 110 figure 6; founder of Dzedzedeyiri, 73, 109; and Karantaw *jihad*, 102–3, 112, 303; *also* 100, 185

Ya'qub b. Ishaq (33rd Wa Limam), 65, 66 table 4.1, 231 n. 105

Ya'qub b. Sa'id (Wa *'alim*), 95–7

Ya'qub b. Ya'muru (22nd Wa Limam), 66 table 4.1, 159–60; dating 74–5, 162, 227 n. 109; descent, 68 table 4.2

Yaro (Pirisi village), gate to Pirisi, 170 figure 7, 173 table 8.3; former gate to Wa Nam, 18, 43, 44, 48, 85; and arrival of *'ulama'*, 59–60, 84–85; *also* 107

Yendi (Dagomba capital), 41, 49, 112, 152

Yeri Nam, origins of, 34, 41, 53–4, 91–2; Nasa Yeri Na, 20, 57, 91; Wa Yeri Na, 20, 23, 26, 57–8, 91–2, 197–8, 201, as *wazir*, 161–2, as *qadi*, 194, as school manager, 169; and Wala State Council, 187; under indirect rule, 168–9, 170, 171

Yerihi (Old Muslims), *see under* Dabo; Kantonsi; Sienu; Tarawiri (Old Muslims);

Zono

Yijihi (section of Wa, map 3), 44, 175; and Yijihidana, 168; *see also under* Yijisi

Yijisi (name for Busa gate), 60, 83–4, 118–19, and putative Wa Na, 39, 44, 80, 81 table 4.6

Yusuf (1st Nasa Limam), 36, 59–60, 62

Yusuf b. 'Abd al-Qadir (Wa *'alim*), 68 table 4.2, 73

Yusuf b. Adam (27th Wa Limam), 66 table 4.1, 68 table 4.2, 70; accesssion, 191

Yusuf Zorozoro (Wa *'alim*), 123

Zabarima (Songhai-speaking people), background, 108; invade Sisala country, 75, 82, 103, 105; negotiations with Wa, 103–6; attack on Wa, 106–8, 116; trade, 113–15; defeat as Sankana, 116; *also* 61, 95; *see also under* Alfa Hano; Alfa Gazare; Babatu

Zarma (Tendaanba leader), 32–3

Zokuli (Ya Na of Dagomba), 87–8

Zongo (section of Wa, map 3), 26–8

Zono (Old Muslims), 53–4, 56, 85

Other books in the series

6 Labour in the South African Gold Mines, 1911–1969
Francis Wilson

11 Islam and Tribal Art in West Africa
René A. Bravmann

14 Culture, Tradition and Society in the West African Novel
Emmanuel Obiechina

18 Muslim Brotherhoods in Nineteenth-century Africa
B. G. Martin

23 West African States: Failure and Promise: A Study in Comparative Politics
edited by John Dunn

25 A Modern History of Tanganyika
John Iliffe

26 A History of African Christianity 1950–1975
Adrian Hastings

28 The Hidden Hippopotamus: Reappraisal in African History: The Early Colonial Experience in Western Zambia
Gwyn Prins

29 Families Divided: The Impact of Migrant Labour in Lesotho
Colin Murray

30 Slavery, Colonialism and Economic Growth in Dahomey, 1640–1960
Patrick Manning

31 Kings, Commoners and Concessionaires: The Evolution and Dissolution of the Nineteenth-century Swazi State
Philip Bonner

32 Oral Poetry and Somali Nationalism: The Case of Sayyid Mahammad 'Abdille Hasan
Said S. Samatar

33 The Political Economy of Pondoland 1860–1930: Production, Labour, Migrancy and Chiefs in Rural South Africa
William Beinart

34 Volkskapitalisme: Class, Capital and Ideology in the Development of Afrikaner Nationalism 1934–1948
Dan O'Meara

35 The Settler Economies: Studies in the Economic History of Kenya and Southern Rhodesia 1900–1963
Paul Mosley

36 Transformations in Slavery: A History of Slavery in Africa
Paul E. Lovejoy

254

37 Amilcar Cabral: Revolutionary Leadership and People's War
    Patrick Chabal
38 Essays on the Political Economy of Rural Africa
    Robert H. Bates
39 Ijeshas and Nigerians: The Incorporation of a Yoruba Kingdom, 1890s–1970s
    J. D. Y. Peel
40 Black People and the South African War 1899–1902
    Peter Warwick
41 A History of Niger 1850–1960
    Finn Fuglestad
42 Industrialisation and Trade Union Organisation in South Africa 1924–55
    Jon Lewis
43 The Rising of the Red Shawls: A Revolt in Madagascar 1895–1899
    Stephen Ellis
44 Slavery in Dutch South Africa
    Nigel Worden
45 Law, Custom and Social Order: The Colonial Experience in Malawi and Zambia
    Martin Chanock
46 Salt of the Desert Sun: A History of Salt Production and Trade in the Central Sudan
    Paul E. Lovejoy
47 Marrying Well: Marriage, Status and Social Change among the Educated Elite in Colonial Lagos
    Kirstin Mann
48 Language and Colonial Power: The Appropriation of Swahili in the Former Belgian Congo, 1880–1938
    Johannes Fabian
49 The Shell Money of the Slave Trade
    Jan Hogendorn and Marion Johnson
50 Political Domination in Africa: Reflections on the Limits of Power
    edited by Patrick Chabal
51 The Southern Marches of Imperial Ethiopia: Essays in History and Social Anthropology
    edited by Donald Donham and Wendy James
52 Islam and Urban Labor in Northern Nigeria: The Making of a Muslim Working Class
    Paul M. Lubeck
53 Horn and Crescent: Cultural Change and Traditional Islam on the East African Coast, 500–1900
    Randall L. Pouwels
54 Capital and Labour on the Kimberley Diamond Fields 1871–1890
    Robert Vicat Turrell
55 National and Class Conflict in the Horn of Africa
    John Markakis
56 Democracy and Prebendal Politics in Nigeria: The Rise and Fall of the Second Republic
    Richard A. Joseph
57 Entrepreneurs and Parasites: The Struggle for Indigenous Capitalism in Zaire
    Janet MacGaffey
58 The African Poor: A History
    John Iliffe
59 Palm Oil and Protest: An Economic History of the Ngwa Region, South-eastern Nigeria, 1800–1980
    Susan M. Martin

Other books in the series

60 France and Islam in West Africa, 1860–1960
   Christopher Harrison
61 Transformation and Continuity in Revolutionary Ethiopia
   Christopher Clapham
62 Prelude to the Mahdiyya: Peasants and Traders in the Shendi Region, 1821–1885
   Anders Bjørkelo